Lecture Notes in Business Information Processing   532

Series Editors

Wil van der Aalst⬩, *RWTH Aachen University, Aachen, Germany*
Sudha Ram⬩, *University of Arizona, Tucson, AZ, USA*
Michael Rosemann⬩, *Queensland University of Technology, Brisbane, QLD, Australia*
Clemens Szyperski, *Microsoft Research, Redmond, WA, USA*
Giancarlo Guizzardi⬩, *University of Twente, Enschede, The Netherlands*

LNBIP reports state-of-the-art results in areas related to business information systems and industrial application software development – timely, at a high level, and in both printed and electronic form.

The type of material published includes

- Proceedings (published in time for the respective event)
- Postproceedings (consisting of thoroughly revised and/or extended final papers)
- Other edited monographs (such as, for example, project reports or invited volumes)
- Tutorials (coherently integrated collections of lectures given at advanced courses, seminars, schools, etc.)
- Award-winning or exceptional theses

LNBIP is abstracted/indexed in DBLP, EI and Scopus. LNBIP volumes are also submitted for the inclusion in ISI Proceedings.

Glenda Carla Moura Amaral

An Ontology Network in Finance and Economics

Money, Trust, Value, Risk and Economic Exchanges

Springer

Glenda Carla Moura Amaral
University of Twente
Twente, The Netherlands

ISSN 1865-1348　　　　　　ISSN 1865-1356　(electronic)
Lecture Notes in Business Information Processing
ISBN 978-3-031-71081-0　　　ISBN 978-3-031-71082-7　(eBook)
https://doi.org/10.1007/978-3-031-71082-7

© The Editor(s) (if applicable) and The Author(s), under exclusive license
to Springer Nature Switzerland AG 2025

This work is subject to copyright. All rights are solely and exclusively licensed by the Publisher, whether the whole or part of the material is concerned, specifically the rights of translation, reprinting, reuse of illustrations, recitation, broadcasting, reproduction on microfilms or in any other physical way, and transmission or information storage and retrieval, electronic adaptation, computer software, or by similar or dissimilar methodology now known or hereafter developed.
The use of general descriptive names, registered names, trademarks, service marks, etc. in this publication does not imply, even in the absence of a specific statement, that such names are exempt from the relevant protective laws and regulations and therefore free for general use.
The publisher, the authors and the editors are safe to assume that the advice and information in this book are believed to be true and accurate at the date of publication. Neither the publisher nor the authors or the editors give a warranty, expressed or implied, with respect to the material contained herein or for any errors or omissions that may have been made. The publisher remains neutral with regard to jurisdictional claims in published maps and institutional affiliations.

This book is a revised version of the PhD dissertation written by the author at the Free University of Bozen-Bolzano, Italy. The original PhD dissertation is accessible at: https://hdl.handle.net/10863/33227.

This Springer imprint is published by the registered company Springer Nature Switzerland AG
The registered company address is: Gewerbestrasse 11, 6330 Cham, Switzerland

If disposing of this product, please recycle the paper.

Acknowledgements

I believe that doing a PhD goes beyond conducting a scientific research and producing a thesis at the end. Doing a PhD is a unique experience, an incredible journey that must be enjoyed. And I am deeply grateful to God for giving me the opportunity to do this PhD, and for putting such great people in my life during this journey.

I start by thanking my promoter, Professor Giancarlo Guizzardi, a kind person and brilliant researcher, for trusting me from the beginning, and for have been there when I needed. I am thankful for the various insightful and exciting discussions we had over these years. I feel privileged to have had the opportunity to learn from him. His passion for research, and his enthusiasm for understanding and describing the things in the world are inspiring and contagious. I also thank my daily supervisor, Professor Tiago Sales, an outstanding researcher, extremely competent and disciplined, for his valuable comments and reviews, which played an essential role in improving the quality of this thesis.

A special thanks to Professor Maria Luiza M. Campos, who has been my role model since I was her student in the bachelor of informatics databases course, at the Federal University of Rio de Janeiro. I am a great admirer of her, both as a person and as a scientist. I thank her for helping me find this PhD position. I wouldn't be in Bolzano if it was not by her.

I would also like to thank the members of the examination committee, Professor Hans Weigand, Professor Jelena Zdravkovic, Professor Luiz Olavo Bonino and Professor Enrico Franconi for the time they have dedicated to read my thesis and to participate in my defense. I am honoured to have them in my committee.

I am immensely grateful to the Central Bank of Brazil (BCB) for their trust and for granting me a paid leave to do my PhD. I thank the Head of Information Technology Department, Haroldo Jayme M. F. Cruz, and the Head of Information Governance Office at that time, Gabriela Ruberg, for their support in the approval of my leave to do the PhD. I also thank Luiz Lopes, current Head of Information Governance Office, for his support in the activities conducted in collaboration with the BCB. I also express my gratitude to

Fabio Araújo and Arnaldo Vitaliano, my colleagues at the BCB, for their contribution to the validation of great part of the research on money and trust. Additionally, I would like to acknowledge to the team of the Pix Project for sharing their experience with the Pix instant payment system, in a collaborative case study that is part of this thesis validation. I also thank the Brazilian national agency CAPES for financial support (PhD grant 88881.173022/2018-01).

This thesis wouldn't be the same without the collaboration of some bold, talented, and kind people, and I can do no other than express my gratitude to them all. In this respect, I would like to thank Dr. Nicola Guarino, Professor John Mylopoulos, Professor Daniele Porello, Professor João Paulo A. Almeida and Professor Fernanda Baião. A special recognition goes to Professor Renata Guizzardi for our fruitful discussions, teamwork, and great insights. I appreciate the work we have done together.

I thank all my colleagues and friends from the KRDB Research Centre for Knowledge and Data. I feel fortunate to have shared lots of pleasant moments with them. Special thanks to Claudenir Fonseca, the first friend I met in Bolzano, for his support in solving practical issues when my family and I arrived in Italy.

I have no words to thank my parents Carlos Alberto and Naly for their love and care, for sparing no effort to invest in my education. I am deeply grateful for everything they taught me. I am also thankful to my beloved little brother Junior. Thank you for your love and support. Thank you for taking care of our parents in these many years of distance.

Finally, I acknowledge to the three loves of my life, Jocelio, Gabriel and Daniel. Doing a PhD is challenging. Starting a new life in a different country, with two teenagers at important stages of their school life, while doing a PhD is even more challenging. And I couldn't have done it without the support of my husband Jocelio, my friend, my partner, my love. Thank you for taking such good care of our kids while I was focused on the PhD. Thank you for your love, patience, and unconditional support. Thank you for always lightening things up and making me laugh. You are awesome! Last but not least, I thank the two biggest inspirations of my life, my beloved sons Gabriel and Daniel. You make everything more colorful and fun. Thank you for making me so proud of how far you have come and how much you are going to achieve. This thesis is dedicated to these three great men, for being my partners in this and all life adventures. I love you guys endlessly.

Glenda Carla Moura Amaral
November 2022

Abstract

Finance and information technology are deeply intertwined and have been mutually reinforcing over time. Historically, finance has played a key role in innovation in the overall economy. The industrial revolution of the XVIII and XIX centuries, for example, was facilitated by the provision of capital provided by financial intermediaries. Similarly, information technology lies at the very heart of the financial sector. New technology developments can foster greater efficiency and financial inclusion, as well as to improve the quality and reduce the costs of financial products and services. However, at the same time that they open several opportunities, these advances may also pose significant challenges. In fact, much of the literature on finance history shows that several challenges faced by the financial sector over the years are interwoven with technological issues.

Over the past few decades, innovative technologies, such as blockchains, cryptocurrencies, asset tokenization, and central bank digital currencies have revolutionized the world of money, payments, and economic exchanges. They have fostered the creation of financial products and services on top of decentralized technologies, giving rise to the concept of decentralized finance — the decentralized provision of financial products and services. Although these new developments have the power to make payments and other financial services cheaper, faster and more accessible, they also pose several challenges related to the safeguarding of financial stability, the definition of law and regulation, the adjustment of current regulatory frameworks, among many others. In this new scenario, as nicely put by the Darwinian evolutionary theory, success is directly related to the ability to promptly adapt to evolution and respond adequately to the changes in the environment.

In this work, we claim that many challenges faced by the finance sector due to recent innovations, are related to a lack of conceptual clarity, which hinders the communication among the different actors in the financial industry, and consequently, the definition of laws, regulations and proper governance models. Also, without a common understanding about concepts it is difficult to integrate information and provide semantic interoperability. However, the vast majority of initiatives developed to provide an unified view of these domains share two common limitations: (1) they are not specified using an ontologically well-founded conceptual modeling language, supported by expressive logical theories, which allows the representation of the subject domain with truthfulness, clarity and expressivity and (2) they were conceived in the light of the traditional finance paradigm, and consequently, do not address issues that have arisen with the introduction of decentralized finance, like the emergence of new forms of trust, money and payment instruments, as well as new business models for economic exchanges.

In this thesis, we address these limitations by means of ontologically well-founded reference conceptual models to make the nature of the conceptualizations explicit, as well as to safely establish the correct relations between them, thereby supporting semantic interoperability. In particular, we focus on the notions of money, trust, value, risk and economic exchanges, as these are intertwined concepts, directly related to recent challenges faced by the financial industry, due to emergence of new technologies. One main contribution of this thesis is the Ontology Network in Finance and Economics (OntoFINE), a network of reference ontologies, grounded in the Unified Foundational Ontology, which provides ontological foundations on money, trust, value, risk and economic exchanges. We demonstrate the usability and relevance of OntoFINE by means of several applications in the fields of requirements engineering, enterprise modeling, decentralized finance and game theory.

Keywords. Finance, Economics, Money, Trust, Value, Risk, Economic Exchanges, Ontology Network, Business Ontology, Formal Ontology, OntoUML, Unified Foundational Ontology.

Contents

I	**INTRODUCTION**	**1**
1	**Introduction**	**3**
	1.1 Context and Motivation	3
	1.2 Scope and Objectives	9
	1.3 Methodological Aspects	11
	1.4 Thesis Structure	21
II	**THEORETICAL FRAMEWORK**	**29**
2	**Theoretical Framework**	**31**
	2.1 Ontologies and their classifications	31
	2.2 Ontology Networks	34
	2.3 The Unified Foundational Ontology	35
	2.4 Final Considerations	47
III	**ONTOLOGICAL FOUNDATIONS**	**49**
3	**The Ontology Network in Finance and Economics**	**51**
	3.1 The Ontology Network in Finance and Economics	52
	3.2 COVER: Common Ontology of Value and Risk	57
	3.3 OntoFINE Applications	59
	3.4 Related Work	65
	3.5 Final Considerations	70

4 The Reference Ontology of Trust — 71
4.1 Introduction 72
4.2 On Trust 73
4.3 ROT: Reference Ontology of Trust 75
4.4 Use Case Illustrations 91
4.5 Related Work 96
4.6 Final Considerations 99

5 The Reference Ontology of Money and Virtual Currencies — 101
5.1 Introduction 102
5.2 On Money and Virtual Currencies 103
5.3 ROME: Reference Ontology of Money and Virtual Currencies 111
5.4 Use Case Illustration 122
5.5 Related Work 126
5.6 Final Considerations 128

6 The Core Ontology for Economic Exchanges — 131
6.1 Introduction 132
6.2 The Action Theory of Economic Exchanges 133
6.3 COEX: Core Ontology for Economic Exchanges 134
6.4 Use Case Illustration 139
6.5 Related Work 141
6.6 Final Considerations 144

IV APPLICATIONS — 145

7 Ontology-based Modeling and Analysis of Trustworthiness Requirements — 147
7.1 Introduction 148
7.2 The Non-functional Requirements Ontology (NFRO) 149
7.3 Trustworthiness Requirements 150
7.4 ROTwR: Reference Ontology of Trustworthiness Requirements 152
7.5 Trustworthiness Requirements and ObRE: The Pix Case Study 157
7.6 Related Work 170
7.7 Final Considerations 170

Contents

8 Modeling Trust Dynamics: The Case of CBDC Ecosystems   **173**
    8.1   Introduction 173
    8.2   Research Method 175
    8.3   Research Context: CBDC Ecosystems 176
    8.4   Modeling Citizen's Trust in CBDC Ecosystems 177
    8.5   Discussion 186
    8.6   Final Considerations 188

9 Modeling Payments and Linked Obligation Settlements   **189**
    9.1   Introduction 190
    9.2   Linked Obligation Settlements 192
    9.3   Ontology-based Modeling of Payments and Linked Obligation Settlements 193
    9.4   Application Example 206
    9.5   Related Work 207
    9.6   Final Considerations 208

10 Modeling Trust in Enterprise Architecture: A Pattern Language for ArchiMate   **209**
    10.1   Introduction 210
    10.2   A Pattern Language for Trust Modeling in ArchiMate 211
    10.3   Case Study 232
    10.4   Final Considerations 237

11 Modeling the Emergence of Value and Risk in Game Theoretical Approaches **239**
    11.1   Introduction 240
    11.2   On Game Theory 242
    11.3   Modeling the Emergence of Value and Risk from Outcomes in UFO . . 247
    11.4   Use Case Illustration: Bank Run 250
    11.5   Modeling Game Outcomes in Enterprise Architecture 252
    11.6   Final Considerations 256

12 Capability Agreements and Risk   **259**
    12.1   Introduction 259
    12.2   Ontological Analysis 260
    12.3   Capability and Capability Agreement 261

| | 12.4 Capability Incorporation and Risk . . . . 263 |
| | 12.5 Final Considerations . . . . 264 |

V CONCLUSIONS 267

13 Conclusions 269
13.1 Research Contributions 258
13.2 Relevance for the Application Domain 276
13.3 Limitations 278
13.4 Future Work 279

Bibliography 283

List of Tables

3.1	OntoFINE applications by type.	64
5.1	Design choices by money type.	110
7.1	Questions related to key ontology concepts.	162
7.2	Requirements table of Pix focusing on security.	166
8.1	Questions related to key ontology concepts.	176
8.2	Citizens' trust in the CBDC Ecosystem - Intentions.	180
8.3	Representation of ROT concepts in i* Goal Model.	187
10.1	Overview of the relevant ArchiMate concepts for the TPL.	211
10.2	Representation of trust and risk-related concepts in ArchiMate.	229
11.1	Payoff matrix example	243
11.2	Bank Run example	245

List of Figures

1.1	Recent innovations in the financial industry.	7
1.2	Research scope.	11
1.3	Design science research cycles proposed by (Hevner and Chatterjee, 2010).	12
1.4	Research methodology (adapted from (Hevner and Chatterjee, 2010)).	14
1.5	Adapted version of SABiO (Almeida Falbo, 2014) proposed by (Sales, 2019).	17
1.6	Overview of the ontology network development method (adapted from (Suárez-Figueroa et al., 2012) and (Sales, 2019)).	21
1.7	Overview of the thesis structure and related objectives.	27
2.1	Ontology generality levels as a continuum.	34
2.2	Quality Space example (color).	37
2.3	Fragment of UFO (Guizzardi, Botti Benevides, et al., 2021).	42
2.4	Fragment of UFO-B (Almeida, Falbo, et al., 2019).	43
2.5	Fragment of UFO-C (Guizzardi, Falbo, et al., 2008b).	44
2.6	Example of classes specializing Endurant in UFO.	46
3.1	OntoFINE: the network view.	57
3.2	COVER fragment on value experiences (Sales, Baião, et al., 2018).	59
3.3	COVER fragment on risk experiences (Sales, Baião, et al., 2018).	59
3.4	OntoFINE applications.	62
4.1	Trust	76
4.2	Aspectual Belief	77
4.3	Social Trust	80
4.4	Institution-based Trust	81
4.5	Quantitative Perspective of Trust	83

4.6	Mental Moment.	85
4.7	Trust Calibration Signal.	87
4.8	Trustworthiness Evidence.	88
4.9	Influences.	89
4.10	Trust and Risk.	90
4.11	Social Trust: Mother trusts a babysitter.	92
4.12	Social Trust: Risk emerging from the trust relation.	93
4.13	Institution-based Trust: Person trusts the monetary system.	94
4.14	Institution-based Trust: Risk emerging from the trust relation.	94
5.1	Money and Status Function.	117
5.2	Currency Quality Space.	117
5.3	Monetary Objects and Monetary Credit/Debt.	118
5.4	Money, Exchange Power and Purchasing Power.	119
5.5	Money and Trust.	120
5.6	Virtual Currency.	121
5.7	Virtual Currency and Trust.	121
5.8	Virtual Currency and Exchange Power.	122
5.9	Money and Status Function Instantiation.	124
5.10	Monetary Objects and Monetary Credit/Debt.	124
5.11	Exchange Power and Purchasing Power Instantiation.	125
5.12	Virtual Currency Instantiation.	126
5.13	Virtual Currency and Exchange Instantiation.	126
5.14	The money flower proposed by (Bech and Garratt, 2017).	127
6.1	OntoUML model of preference relations.	137
6.2	OntoUML diagram depicting economic offerings.	138
6.3	OntoUML diagram depicting economic exchanges.	139
6.4	Economic Offering instantiation.	140
6.5	Economic Exchange instantiation.	141
7.1	A fragment of the Non-functional Requirements Ontology (adapted from (Guizzardi, R. et al., 2014)).	149
7.2	Trustworthiness Quality Space.	151
7.3	Modeling trustworthiness requirements in OntoUML.	156
7.4	Modeling the emergence of trustworthiness-related risks.	157

7.5	Ontology-based Requirements Engineering Method.	159
7.6	Ontology instantiation focusing on usability.	164
7.7	Ontology instantiation focusing on availability.	165
7.8	Ontology instantiation focusing on security (end users' perspective).	165
7.9	Ontology instantiation focusing on security (participants' perspective).	166
7.10	Goal Model of the Pix Ecosystem.	168
8.1	Ontology instantiation - Privacy (INT1).	180
8.2	Ontology instantiation - Security (INT2).	181
8.3	Ontology instantiation - Usability (INT3).	181
8.4	Ontology instantiation - Cost (INT4).	182
8.5	Ontology instantiation - Location (INT5).	182
8.6	Ontology instantiation - Availability (INT6).	183
8.7	Ontology instantiation - Currency acceptance (INT7).	183
8.8	Ontology instantiation - Currency stability (INT8).	184
8.9	Ontology instantiation - Product and service offering (INT9).	184
8.10	A fragment of the goal model of the CBDC ecosystem.	186
9.1	Overview of the ontology-based modeling approach inspired in the NeOn methodology (adapted from (Suárez-Figueroa et al., 2012)).	194
9.2	A fragment of COEX (chapter 6) depicting economic exchanges.	196
9.3	The Digital Transfer Pattern.	197
9.4	The Digital Exchange Pattern.	197
9.5	Digital asset transfer in OntoUML.	198
9.6	Instantiation example of digital asset transfer.	198
9.7	Payment model in OntoUML.	199
9.8	Instantiation example of payment.	199
9.9	Monetary amount in OntoUML.	200
9.10	Instantiation example of monetary amount.	201
9.11	Delivery versus Payment in OntoUML.	202
9.12	Instantiation example of Delivery versus Payment.	202
9.13	Payment versus Payment in OntoUML.	204
9.14	Instantiation example of Payment versus Payment.	204
9.15	Delivery versus Delivery in OntoUML.	206
9.16	Instantiation example of Delivery versus Delivery.	205
9.17	Regulatory data analytics example.	206

10.1 The Trust Assessment Pattern - Object Trustee. 214
10.2 The Trust Assessment Pattern - Agent Trustee. 214
10.3 The Capability Belief Pattern. 215
10.4 The Vulnerability Belief Pattern. 216
10.5 The Intention Belief Pattern. 216
10.6 The Trust Composition Pattern - Object Trustee. 218
10.7 The Trust Composition Pattern - Agent Trustee. 219
10.8 The Risk Experience Pattern (adapted from (Sales, Almeida, et al., 2018)).221
10.9 The Risk Assessment Pattern (adapted from (Sales, Almeida, et al., 2018)).222
10.10 Trustworthiness Evidence Pattern - Resource. 222
10.11 Trustworthiness Evidence Pattern - Representation. 223
10.12 Trustworthiness Evidence Pattern - Requirement. 223
10.13 Trust-warranting Signal. 224
10.14 Uncertainty Signal. 224
10.15 Trustworthiness Evidence Influence. 225
10.16 Trust Calibration Signal Influence. 226
10.17 Mental Moment Influence. 226
10.18 Trust Influencing Trust. 227
10.19 Trust Influencing Trust (trust by delegation). 228
10.20 Combining the patterns. 231
10.21 Application of the Trust Assessment Pattern. 233
10.22 Capability and Vulnerability Beliefs. 234
10.23 Composition. 235
10.24 Risk Experience. 236
10.25 Risk Assessment. 236
10.26 Trust Influencing Trust. 237
10.27 Trust Influencing Trust (trust delegation). 237

11.1 Modeling the emergence of value and risk from outcomes in OntoUML. 248
11.2 Value and risk events. 249
11.3 The emergence of value from outcomes. 251
11.4 The emergence of risk from outcomes. 252
11.5 The Value Experience Pattern. 253
11.6 The Experience Valuation Pattern. 254
11.7 The Risk Experience Pattern. 254

11.8 Application of the Value Experience and Experience Valuation Patterns. 255
11.9 Application of the Risk Experience Pattern. 256

12.1 Capability Agreement. 262
12.2 Capability Agreement execution. 262
12.3 Shared capability and risk. 264

13.1 Envisioned integration between OntoFINE and FIBO 280

List of Acronyms

AI Artificial Intelligence.

ATE Action Theory of Economic Exchanges.

ATM Automated Teller Machine.

B2B Business-to-Business.

B2G Business-to-Government.

BCB Central Bank of Brazil.

BFO Basic Formal Ontology.

BIS Bank for International Settlements.

CBDC Central Bank Digital Currency.

CIDO Coronavirus Infectious Disease Ontology.

COEX Core Ontology for Economic Exchanges.

COFRIS Core Ontology for Financial Reporting Information Systems.

COVER Common Ontology of ValuE and Risk.

DARPA Defense Advanced Research Projects Agency.

DeFi Decentralized Finance.

DLT Distributed Ledger Technology.

DOLCE Descriptive Ontology for Linguistic and Cognitive Engineering.

DvD Delivery versus Deliver.

DvP Delivery versus Payment.

EA Enterprise Architecture.

ECB European Central Bank.

EDMC Enterprise Data Management Council.

EER Extended-ER.

ER Entity-Relationship.

FAIR Findable, Accessible, Interoperable and Reusable.

FIB-CM FIBO Conceptual Map.

FIB-DM FIBO Data Model.

FIBO Financial Industry Business Ontology.

FIRO Financial Industry Regulatory Ontology.

FOAF Friend of a Friend.

FR Functional Requirement.

FRO Financial Regulation Ontology.

GFO General Formal Ontology.

GORE Goal-Oriented Requirements Engineering.

gUFO Gentle Unfied Foundational Ontology.

HSV Hue Saturation Value.

ISO International Organization for Standardization.

NFR Non-functional Requirement.

NFRO Non-functional Requirements Ontology.

List of Acronyms

ObRE Ontology-based Requirements Engineering.

ODP Ontology Design Pattern.

OWL Web Ontology Language.

OWL-DL Description Logic-based Web Ontology Language.

P2B Person-to-Business.

P2G Person-to-Government.

P2P Person-to-Person.

PML-T Proof Markup Language Trust Ontology.

PvP Payment versus Payment.

RDF Resource Description Framework.

RE Requirements Engineering.

REA Resource Event Agent.

RGB Red Green Blue.

ROME Reference Ontology of Money and Virtual CurrEncies.

ROT Reference Ontology of Trust.

ROTwR Reference Ontology of Trustworthines Requirements.

SABiO Systematic Approach for Building Ontologies.

SPARQL SPARQL Protocol and RDF Query Language.

SUMO Suggested Upper Merged Ontology.

SWIFT Society for Worldwide Interbank Financial Telecommunications.

TOEFL Test of English as a Foreign Language.

TOGAF The Open Group Architecture Framework.

TPL Trust Pattern Language.

UFO Unified Foundational Ontology.

UML Unified Modeling Language.

WHO World Health Organization.

Part I

INTRODUCTION

Chapter 1

Introduction

This thesis contributes to the definition of ontological foundations for economics and finance, with focus on the domains of money, trust, value, risk and economic exchanges. This chapter discusses the motivations behind this work (section1.1) and presents the scope and main objectives of our research (section 1.2). It also presents the methodological aspects that have guided this research work (section 1.3). The chapter concludes by presenting an overview of the thesis structure (section 1.4).

1.1 Context and Motivation

Finance and technology have a long and symbiotic relationship. At the same time that finance has always shaped technological developments, technology plays a key role in the evolution of the financial industry[1]. Evidence of financial transactions can be found in some samples of ancient Mesopotamia written records, one of the earliest applications of information technology in finance (Battilossi et al., 2020). Similarly, early technologies for calculation such as the abacus have been used to keep track of finance in the past (Baxter, 1989). The double entry accounting, a technology fundamental to modern economics, emerged in the late Middle Ages, from the intertwined evolution of finance and trade (Arner, Barberis, et al., 2015). In the XIX century, technology, such as the telegraph, railroads, canals and the laying of the first transatlantic cable, allowed rapid transmission of financial information, transactions and payments around the world. At

---

[1] Michael Atkin, the Managing Director for the Enterprise Data Management Council, which is an international business forum for financial institutions, in a recent keynote at the 14th International Semantic Web Conference (ISWC) explicitly defended that Banks are basically IT companies and that Financial Risk Management is basically Data Management.

the same time, the financial sector provided the necessary resources to develop these technologies (Arner, Barberis, et al., 2015). Starting in 1967 to the late 1980s, financial services moved from an analogue to a digital industry, thanks to key developments, such as the creation of the handheld financial calculator, the advent of the automated teller machine (ATM), the establishment of the Society for Worldwide Interbank Financial Telecommunications[2] (SWIFT) and the introduction of online banking (Arner, Barberis, et al., 2015). Finally, the emergence of the internet and the introduction of smartphones set the stage for a new era of increasing technological pervasiveness in finance, coupled with the emergence of new actors and channels for finance services provision.

The close relation between finance and technology creates new opportunities and growth to the financial industry, but also poses some challenges. For example, the financial crisis of 2007-2008 exposed a significant lack of timely and accurate information, and data gaps that hindered the ability of policy makers and market participants to develop effective responses. According to the Basel Committee (2013) "one of the most significant lessons learned from the global financial crisis of 2007-2008 was that banks' information technology and data architectures were inadequate to support the broad management of financial risks". Many banks lacked the ability to aggregate risk exposures and concentrations quickly and accurately, at the bank group level, across business lines and between legal entities. Some banks were unable to manage their risks properly because of weak risk data aggregation capabilities and risk reporting practices. This had severe consequences to the banks themselves and to the stability of the financial system as a whole (Basel Committee, 2013).

More recently, technology-driven innovations have revolutionized the world of money, payments, and economic exchanges (see figure 1.1). These innovations, which include blockchains and distributed ledger technologies[3] (Zheng et al., 2017), cryptocurrencies[4]

---

[2]SWIFT is a messaging network that financial institutions use to securely transmit information and instructions through a standardized system of codes (Khadjimamedov and Kizi, 2021).

[3]A distributed ledger is a decentralized database managed by multiple participants, across multiple nodes, which eliminates the need for a central authority or intermediary to process, validate or authenticate transactions. Blockchain is a type of distributed ledger technology, in which data is stored in a continuous flow of blocks chained together using a cryptographic hash function, thus maintaining a continuously growing list of verifiable records.

[4]Cryptographic tokens issued and registered on a blockchain / distributed ledger infrastructure, where it can be stored, traded or transferred electronically, and which can function as (1) a medium of exchange; and/or (2) a unit of account; and/or (3) a store of value.

1.1. Context and Motivation

(Berentsen and Schär, 2018), assets tokenization[5] (Sazandrishvili, 2020), smart contracts[6] (Schär, 2021), programmable money[7] (Weber and Staples, 2022), stablecoins[8] (Arner, Auer, et al., 2020), and central bank digital currencies[9] (Bank for International Settlements et al., 2020) have challenged regulatory frameworks and business models in the financial industry. They have fostered the creation of financial products and services on top of decentralized technologies, giving rise to the concept of decentralized finance (DeFi) (Schär, 2021; Zetzsche et al., 2020) — the decentralized provision of financial products and services. DeFi provides financial services without the need of centralised intermediaries, by operating through automated protocols on decentralized peer-to-peer networks. It creates a new form of trust that is distributed through the participants, rather than centered on a single trusted party (Lemieux and Feng, 2021; Sadhya et al., 2018). In this scenario, this new form of trust coexists with existing ones, such as trust in the currency used to make economic transactions, and trust in the institutions that ensure currency stability and guarantee the safety and integrity of the financial system (e.g., central banks). In addition, the decentralized paradigm introduces novel protocols for economic transactions, with support for both centralized and decentralized exchanges, and new forms of digital money and payment instruments.

The advent of cryptocurrencies, based on blockchain technologies, is an example of technology-related challenge that lies ahead of the financial sector. At the same time that they have the potential to make payments and other financial services cheaper, faster and more accessible, they pose significant challenges regarding the safeguarding of financial stability, the definition of laws and regulations, anti-money laundering and counter-terrorist financing measures, among others.

The growing attention received by cryptocurrencies, the debate on stablecoins and the entry of large technology firms (big techs) into payment services and financial services have led central banks around the world to step up efforts to prepare the ground

---

[5] Broadly speaking, to *digitize* means to turn non-digital into digital. Tokenization is a special form of digitization that supports fractional investment and ownership. In the context of asset tokenization, physical assets are turned into digital assets, which can be subdivided, and the subunits can be represented by a digital token.

[6] Code scripts designed to execute certain tasks when predefined conditions are met; these scripts generally (but not necessarily) run on blockchains and distributed ledger networks (Zou et al., 2019).

[7] Programmable money concerns the ability to endow digital money with an inherent logic that allows it to be programmed to act in a certain way, based on predefined rules.

[8] Cryptocurrencies with values tied to fiat currencies or other assets. Fiat currency is a currency designated and issued by a central authority (Searle, 2017), which cannot be redeemed for a commodity. Its value is based on the trust that the issuer will keep its value relatively stable (Zelmanovitz, 2015).

[9] A digital form of central bank money, denominated in the national unit of account, which is a direct liability of the central bank, such as physical cash and central bank settlement accounts.

for a new form digital money termed central bank digital currency (CBDC). A CBDC is a form of digital money, denominated in the national unit of account, which is a direct liability of the central bank, such as physical cash and central bank settlement accounts (Bank for International Settlements et al., 2020). The development of a digital money backed by the central bank, which is fast, reliable, interoperable, secure, privacy preserving, and that implements proper mechanisms anti-money laundering and counter-terrorist financing, boosts the development of DeFi products and services on top of decentralized technologies. However, understanding the implications of CBDC issuance for financial stability, as well as their potential effect on market structures, is still an open issue, which has been the subject of intense debate and discussion among central banks worldwide.

In the same direction, the introduction of smart contracts — code scripts that run on blockchains (or distributed ledgers) and are designed to execute certain tasks when predefined conditions are met — fostered the implementation of programmable money, which allows digital money to be programmed to act in a certain way, based on predetermined criteria. The development of new means of payment and settlement, alongside the tokenization of assets — a method that converts rights to an asset into digital tokens that can be bought, sold, and traded on blockchains — paved the way for innovative forms of economic exchanges such as the decentralized trading of digital assets, which have the potential to disrupt a variety of industries, including financial, real estate, art, music and green investments (Sazandrishvili, 2020).

Eventually, all these new developments enable the improvement of DeFi products and services and contributes to the open finance initiative, by serving as a common platform around new payments ecosystems. Open finance can be defined as the sharing of data, products and services between regulated entities — financial institutions, payment institutions and other entities licensed by central banks — at the customers' discretion, as far as their own data is concerned (individuals or legal entities). It aims at empowering customers to have control over their data, so they can leverage it to have access to a wider range of financial products and services in a more open and competitive market (Bank for International Settlements, 2020). The open finance initiative relies on standards, data sharing principles, and on a common understanding of key financial concepts to provide interoperability at different levels of DeFi ecosystems. Nevertheless, having an integrated view that shares a common conceptualization regarding the domain to ensure semantic interoperability in this new decentralized finance paradigm is still a challenge.

1.1. Context and Motivation

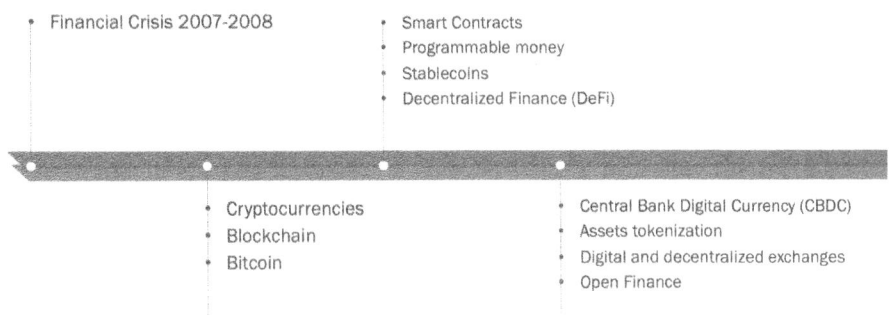

Figure 1.1: Recent innovations in the financial industry.

Examining closer the way information technology has influenced the financial industry in the past few years makes it difficult to ignore the "opportunities vs. risks" dichotomy that has emerged from the latest advances. On one hand, information technology has contributed to the evolution and efficiency in the provision of financial products and services. But on the other hand, it has also brought about some significant challenges. In fact, several difficulties experienced by the financial sector over the years are intertwined with technological issues.

In this thesis, we claim that many challenges faced by the financial industry due to recent innovations, have to do with a lack of conceptual clarity in the financial sector domain. For example, the lack of a shared conceptualization hinders the communication among the different actors in the financial industry, and consequently, the definition of *laws*, *regulations* and *proper governance models*. Also, without a common understanding about key concepts it is difficult to *integrate information* and provide *semantic interoperability*. Consequently, the lack of an integrated view to allow decision makers to figure out what is going on, hampers *risk management*, as well as the fight against money laundering and terrorism financing.

Making sense of a plethora of information in a dynamic and complex environment is paramount not only in the aforementioned examples, but also in a number of other activities performed to ensure the proper functioning of the financial system, such as the formulation of monetary policy, the safeguarding of financial stability and the maintenance of trust in the monetary system. However, having an integrated view that shares a common conceptualization regarding the domain of economics and finance is still a challenge, as the vast majority of initiatives developed to provide an unified view of these domains share two common limitations: (1) they are not specified using an ontologically well-founded conceptual modeling language, supported by expressive logical theories, which allows the representation of the subject domain with truthfulness, clarity and expressivity; consequently, they put forth a number of concepts without accurately characterizing them; (2) they were conceived in the light of the traditional finance paradigm, and consequently, do not address issues that have arisen with the introduction of decentralized technologies and other recent innovations, such as the emergence of new forms of trust, money and payment instruments, as well as new business models for digital economic exchanges.

In this thesis we address the problem of conceptual clarification in finance and economics with focus on the two limitations aforementioned. We defend the adoption of ontology-based conceptual models to make the nature of the conceptualizations explicit, as well as to safely establish the correct relations between them, thereby supporting semantic interoperability. Naturally, having a clear understanding of the ontological nature of the concepts is fundamental not only to proper address semantic interoperability but also to understand the evolution of the economy before innovations in the financial industry.

Reference ontologies have been widely recognized as a key enabling tool for providing conceptual clarification and capturing the shared consensus of a given community. They have been used on a wide range of domains, both in academic and industrial contexts. For instance, they have been successfully used to provide conceptual clarification in domains such as accounting (Blums and Weigand, 2016; Fischer-Pauzenberger and Schwaiger, 2017), bioinformatics (Gonçalves et al., 2011), competition (Sales, Porello, et al., 2018), decision making (Guizzardi, Carneiro, et al., 2020), digital platforms (Derave et al., 2021), legal issues (Griffo, Almeida, and Guizzardi, 2018), mulsemedia (Saleme et al., 2019), programming languages (Aguiar et al., 2019), services (Nardi et al., 2013), software requirements (Duarte et al., 2018), software engineering (Oberle et al., 2009), among many others. A reference ontology can be defined as a special kind of conceptual model constructed with the purpose of making the best possible description of the domain in reality, representing a model of consensus within a community, regardless of its computational properties (Guarino, 1998; Guizzardi, 2007). They are used for establishing a common conceptualization of the domain of interest to support communication, meaning negotiation, consensus establishment, as well as semantic interoperability and information integration. However, some domains are often too large and complex to be represented as a single, large and monolithic ontology. This is the case of finance and economics. We believe that an integrated ontological framework, built incrementally and in an integrated way, as a network, can improve ontology-based applications in finance and economics, as well as improve communication among the different actors in these sectors.

This thesis aims at addressing these issues by investigating the conceptual foundations of some intertwined concepts in finance and economics, namely those of money, trust, value, risk and economic exchanges, to propose an Ontology Network in Finance and Economics (OntoFINE), grounded in the Unified Foundational Ontology (UFO), based on the literature review of the most relevant economic theories and considering recent innovations in the financial industry (see figure 1.1). The reason why we have chosen these domains is threefold. Firstly, because they are ubiquitous in the finance domain. The financial system relies heavily on trust, which is the bedrock for the well-functioning of financial institutions, central banks, monetary authorities, and the whole monetary system — interestingly, as we shall see, at the same time that trust may create value, it also entails some risk. Similarly, from the operational perspective of economics, money and economic transactions are essential. Secondly because they are intertwined concepts, directly related to recent challenges faced by the financial industry due to emergence of new technologies (see figure 1.1), which introduce new forms of decentralized trust, digital money and decentralized exchanges. Finally, because despite the wide number of efforts to create an unified view of the reality related to economic and financial domains, no formal model, expressive enough, has been developed[10] to accurately describe the semantics of money and trust, as well as their relationships with value, risk and economic exchanges.

1.2 Scope and Objectives

In this thesis, we intend to contribute to conceptual clarification in finance and economics, with focus on helping the different actors[11] in the financial industry to promptly adapt to the evolution of the economy before the aforementioned innovations (see figure 1.1). Our main objective here is to provide ontological foundations for fundamental concepts in economics and finance to support communication, meaning negotiation, consensus establishment, as well as semantic interoperability and information integration. As previously mentioned, economic and finance are huge domains, which involve

---

[10] See related work on section 3.4 of chapter 3.

[11] Financial institutions, central banks, supervisory authorities, regulatory boards, monetary authorities, insurance corporations, payment service providers and citizens.

a large number of concepts from different subdomains. Therefore, in this work, we are focusing on a smaller subset, consisting of subdomains directly related to recent innovations in the financial industry (see figure 1.2), namely, money, trust, value, risk and economic exchanges.

In summary, the general objective of this thesis is:

Provide well-founded ontological accounts for the modeling of information in economics and finance, particularly that which is related to money, trust, value, risk and economic exchanges, in order to support economic and financial actors in reasoning with it and adapting to innovations in the financial industry.

From this general objective, we define the following specific objectives (SO):

SO.1 Develop solid conceptual foundations on trust, which can properly define and characterize the concept of trust and its different types, explain the relation between trust and risk, as well as describe the elements that can influence trust.

SO.2 Develop solid conceptual foundations on money and currencies, such that this knowledge can be used to make explicit the differences between currencies and virtual currencies, and to characterize recent innovations related concepts, such as criptocurrencies, stablecoins and central bank digital currencies.

SO.3 Develop solid conceptual foundations on economic exchanges that can explain how economic exchanges can be handled uniformly, regardless the environment and the object of the transaction.

SO.4 Provide solid conceptual foundations on value that can explain the concept of exchange value and its role in the universe of money, as well as how value emerges from trust relations.

SO.5 Provide solid conceptual foundations on risk that can explain the relation between trust and risk, and how risk emerges from trust relations.

SO.6 Apply the theoretical foundation in practice to (i) demonstrate its usefulness and relevance, by solving real-world problems in different areas, in the context of economics and finance; and (ii) validate the ontologies expressivity and capacity to represent real-world situations.

1.2. Scope and Objectives

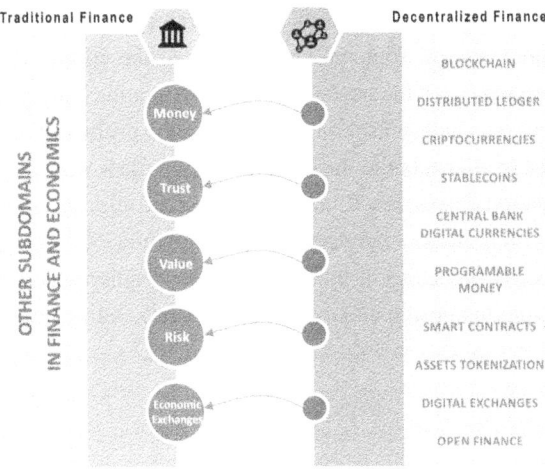

Figure 1.2: Research scope.

1.3 Methodological Aspects

For the development of this PhD project we conduct a design science project, inspired in the design science research paradigm, proposed by Hevner and Chatterjee (2010).

Hevner and Chatterjee (2010) define design science research as "a research paradigm in which a designer answers questions relevant to human problems via the creation of innovative artifacts, thereby contributing new knowledge to the body of scientific evidence. The designed artifacts are both useful and fundamental in understanding that problem.".

By analyzing our research objectives in light of this research paradigm, we can notice some correspondences. Our primary goal is the creation of an artifact, the Ontology Network in Finance and Economics, to address questions relevant to financial sector actors' problems, with respect to their need to promptly adapt to recent innovations in the financial industry (see sections 1.1 and 1.2). Furthermore, we demonstrate the artifact usefulness by applying it to solve real-world problems in different areas, in the context of finance and economics (e.g., requirements engineering, decentralized finance, enterprise modeling and game theory).

Hevner and Chatterjee (2010) emphasize the existence of three design science research cycles in any design research project, depicted in figure 1.3. The *relevance cy-*

cle bridges the contextual environment of the research project with the design science activities. The contextual environment corresponds to the application context, which provides the requirements for the research (e.g., opportunities and problems to be addressed) and defines acceptance criteria for the ultimate evaluation of the research results. The *rigor cycle* connects the design science activities with the knowledge base of scientific foundations, experience, and expertise that informs the research project. The central *design cycle* iterates between the core activities of building and evaluating the design artifacts and processes of the research. The requirements are input from the relevance cycle, while the design and evaluation theories and methods are drawn from the rigor cycle.

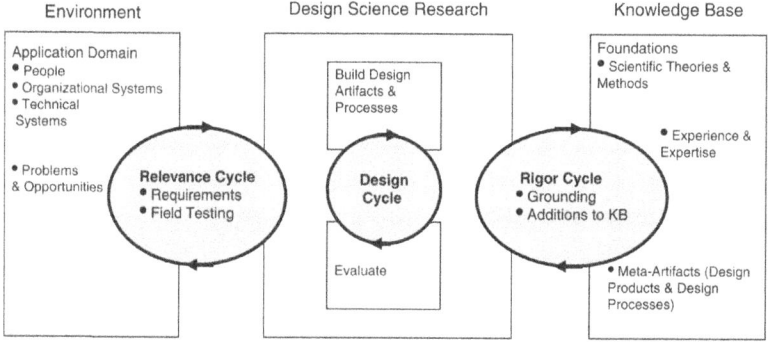

Figure 1.3: Design science research cycles proposed by (Hevner and Chatterjee, 2010).

Figure 1.4 presents the above-mentioned design science research cycles, applied to this thesis.

For the relevance cycle, we clarify the project environment. OntoFINE's application domain is conformed by diverse kinds of stakeholders of the financial sector, such as:

- Monetary authorities responsible for the formulation of monetary policy and the maintenance of trust in the monetary system.

- Regulatory entities responsible for defining the norms, rules and regulations that compose the regulatory framework of the financial industry.

- Legislators responsible for defining and adapting legislation frameworks to support innovations and new business models in the financial industry.

- Supervisory entities responsible for supervising the compliance of financial enti-

1.3. Methodological Aspects

ties with the legislation and regulations on anti-money laundering and combating the finance of terrorism.

- Supervisory entities working on the monitoring of financial systems, which need to identify and evaluate vulnerabilities that may impact the financial system and monitor the risks to which the supervised entities institutions are exposed, as well as the compliance to operational and prudential[12] limits.
- Entities responsible for ensuring the normal, safe and efficient functioning of payment systems.
- Financial institutions like banks, which need to comply with the regulatory framework, keep up to date with the innovations of the financial industry, manage risks efficiently, as well as be considered trustworthy and effectively promote well-placed trust.
- Financial-technology-intensive startups (Fintechs), which technologically enable financial innovation — new business models, applications, processes, or products — with an associated substantial effect on financial markets and institutions in the provision of financial services.
- Computer science academics like requirements engineering researchers, enterprise modeling researchers and ontology engineering researchers.
- Information technology practitioners in the financial sector, such as business analysts, requirements engineers, ontology engineers, enterprise architects, data scientists and data architects.

For the rigor cycle, we describe the knowledge context of this PhD project:

- The Ontology Network in Finance and Economics is composed of a set of well-founded reference ontologies. Their knowledge context is grounded on several theories from economics, theories of trust, theories on economic exchanges, as well as theories about money and related concepts. The reference ontologies are specified in OntoUML (Guizzardi, 2005) and thus, compliant with the meta-ontological commitments of the Unified Foundational Ontology (Guizzardi, 2005). The different applications of the Ontology Network are placed in the fields of requirements engineering, enterprise modeling, decentralized finance, game theory

---

[12] The prudential regulation orders financial institutions to comply with requirements to cope with risks associated with their financial activities. Prudential regulation is intended to prevent a "domino effect" on the financial system associated to one of its institutions bankruptcy.

and data science. In addition, the knowledge context contains our experience in the use of gUFO (Almeida, Guizzardi, et al., 2020), a lightweight implementation of the Unified Foundational Ontology suitable for Semantic Web OWL 2 DL applications. We also use our experience in design science research, NeOn (Suárez-Figueroa et al., 2012) — a methodology for building ontology networks — and SABiO (Almeida Falbo, 2014) — a systematic approach for building ontologies — to conduct the project activities.

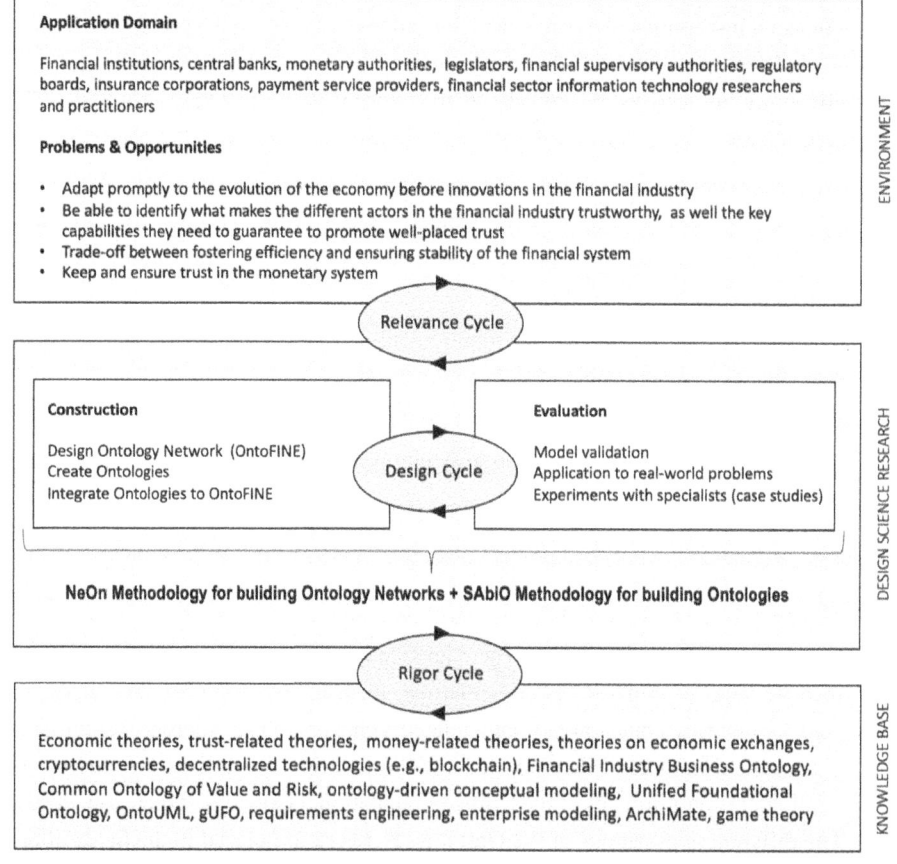

Figure 1.4: Research methodology (adapted from (Hevner and Chatterjee, 2010)).

To perform the the design cycle activities, we follow a customized version of the

1.3. Methodological Aspects

NeOn methodology (Suárez-Figueroa et al., 2012) for building ontology networks, combined with a customized version of the SABiO methodology (Almeida Falbo, 2014) for building ontologies, proposed in (Sales, 2019). We provide a detailed description of SABiO and NeOn in sections 1.3.1 and 1.3.2, respectively.

Finally, according to the Design Science Research Methodology (Peffers et al., 2007) mentioned by Hevner and Chatterjee (2010), the design science process includes six steps: (1) problem identification and motivation; (2) definition of the objectives for a solution; (3) design and development; (4) demonstration; (5) evaluation; (6) communication. In the sequel we present a brief description of these steps and relate them to this thesis achievements.

1. **Problem identification and motivation.** Define the specific research problem and justify the value of a solution. In this step, we identify and represent opportunities and problems in the application domain. We investigate reliable sources of information, such as business and scientific literature in finance and economics and interact with domain experts, including real practitioners directly working in the areas of economics and information technology, in the context of central banks and financial institutions. Section 1.1 describes the problems and motivation for this research. In each of the next chapters, we present an introduction section including a detailed discussion of problems and motivation behind the work reported in that chapter.

2. **Definition of the objectives for a solution.** Define the objectives for a solution. Infer the objectives of a solution from the problem definition and knowledge of what is possible and feasible. The overall research objectives are described in section 1.2. To define the objectives of each ontology developed in this thesis, we follow the activity *purpose specification* of the SABiO methodology (Almeida Falbo, 2014) for building ontologies, presented in section 1.3.1.

3. **Design and Development.** Create the artifact. In this research, the artifact is the Ontology Network in Finance and Economics. To design and implement each networked ontology proposed in this thesis, we follow the steps *knowledge acquisition* and *ontology formalization* of the SABiO methodology (Almeida Falbo, 2014) (see section 1.3.1). To integrate the ontologies to OntoFINE, use a customized version of the NeOn methodology (Suárez-Figueroa et al., 2012) for building ontology networks (see section 1.3.2), by following the best suited scenario for each context and needs (see section 3.1 of chapter 3). OntoFINE is

described in chapter 3. Its networked ontologies, namely, the Common Ontology of Value and Risk, the Reference Ontology of Trust, the Reference Ontology of Money and Virtual Currencies, the Core Ontology for Economic Exchanges and the Reference Ontology of Trustworthiness Requirements are described, respectively, in chapters 3, 4, 5, 6 and 7.

4. **Demonstration.** Demonstrate the use of the artifact to solve one or more instances of the problem. We demonstrate the use of OntoFINE by applying its networked ontologies in the solution of practical problems, in the context of requirements engineering (chapter 7), decentralized finance (chapters 8 and 9), enterprise modeling (chapter 10), game theory (chapter 11) and ontological analysis (chapter 12).

5. **Evaluation.** Observe and measure how well the artifact supports a solution to the problem. To evaluate each ontology developed in this thesis, we follow the activity *ontology evaluation* of the SABiO methodology (Almeida Falbo, 2014) for building ontologies, presented in section 1.3.1. We conduct case studies in the context of requirements engineering (chapter 7), decentralized finance (chapter 8) and enterprise modeling (chapter 10). We also use OntoFINE's networked ontologies to analyze and redesign an existing conceptual modeling language (ArchiMate) for representation adequacy of the concepts defined in the ontologies (chapter 10).

6. **Communication.** Communicate the problem and its importance, the artifact, its utility and novelty, the rigor of its design, and its effectiveness to researchers and other relevant audiences, such as practicing professionals, when appropriate. We report the achievements and results of this thesis in the publications listed in Apendix ??. Furthermore, for all case studies conducted, the results are shared with the participants.

1.3.1 The SABiO Methodology for building Ontologies

In this thesis, for building the ontologies, we follow a customized version of the SABiO[13] (Almeida Falbo, 2014) methodology, suited to our particular context and needs. SABiO defines a process that starts with the development of a reference conceptual model, which is then used to develop a data model. We adhere to the general steps proposed in the methodology, up to the point of developing a reference ontology. These general steps are depicted in figure 1.5. The process starts with the specification of the purpose

---
[13]SABiO stands for "Systematic Approach for Building Ontologies".

1.3. Methodological Aspects

of the ontology and then enters an iterative loop of knowledge acquisition, ontology formalization, and ontology evaluation. In the sequel we present a brief description of each step.

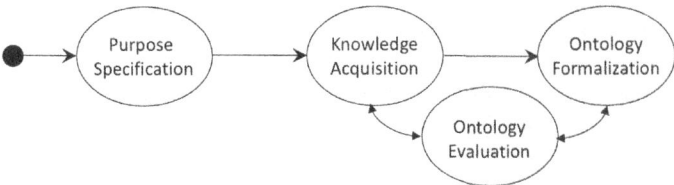

Figure 1.5: Adapted version of SABiO (Almeida Falbo, 2014) proposed by (Sales, 2019).

Purpose Specification. The first step in the ontology development process is to specify why the ontology is being built. At this stage, motivation statements should be explored to elicit a number of problems the ontology is meant to help users solve, i.e. actual valuable ways in which the ontology can support its intended users.

Knowledge Acquisition. The second step in the ontology development process is to acquire knowledge about the domain. This means understanding how domain experts would solve the problems previously elicited, identifying the most prominent theories on the domain, uncovering the most important terms and their respective definitions, and so on. One way in which this can be done is by surveying relevant literature on the topic. There are three types of publications that are particularly useful in this context. First, there are those that propose theories (sometimes called "conceptual frameworks") to describe the domain of interest. This type of publication usually introduces a number of concepts and definitions that can provide a lot of insight into how experts understand the domain. A second type of publication is one that introduces a proper ontology to conceptualize the domain (or a closely related one). These are obviously extremely useful, but they are not always available. Lastly, a third type of publication is one that proposes modeling languages to represent the domain of interest. Since every modeling language makes an ontological commitment (even if not explicitly), they can also help one to identify relevant concepts and relations. Another strategy (and undoubtedly the fastest) is to interact with domain experts, such as researchers and practitioners. By conducting interviews and exploring cases, knowledge about a domain can be obtained much quicker.

Ontology Formalization. The ontology formalization step consists in using a formal language to model domain concepts, along with their interrelations and properties, such that they form an ontology that can support the intended uses elicited in the beginning of the process. In this thesis, our ontology representation language of choice is OntoUML. We chose OntoUML both for its expressivity and because it provides such a complete ecosystem of tools and technologies to facilitate the ontology engineering process, such as ontological design patterns (Guizzardi, Graças, et al., 2011) and anti-patterns (Sales and Guizzardi, 2015), visual model simulation (Benevides, Guizzardi, et al., 2010), and transformations for codification technologies (Almeida, Guizzardi, et al., 2020; Barcelos et al., 2013; Rybola and Pergl, 2016) (for more details, see subsection 3.1). It is natural that, while building the ontology, a number of questions about the domain arise. Thus, the ontology formalization step often simultaneously occurs with that of knowledge acquisition.

Ontology Evaluation. Ontologies can be evaluated according to multiple criteria, each of which can be assessed using a particular set of methods and tools (Vrandečić, 2009). Three of them are particularly relevant for this research, namely accuracy, precision, and completeness. Accuracy regards whether an ontology appropriately covers the domain of interest by providing enough concepts to distinguish between desired and undesired state-of-affairs. For an ontology to be accurate, it does not need to contain every imaginable concept of a domain, but those that are necessary for the ontology to fulfill its purpose. The last two metrics, precision and completeness, regard how well an ontology actually captures the domain of interest. In a maximally precise ontology, every instantiation (logical model) corresponds to an intended domain structure, whilst in a maximally complete ontology, every intended domain structure is a model of the ontology.

There are several ways in which each of these three criteria can be assessed. In this research, we measure accuracy by means of cases we want the ontology to be able to handle. To assess precision and completeness, we use visual model simulation. Visual model simulation is an approach to automatically generated possible instances of an ontology in order to expose the consequences of modeling decisions (Benevides, Guizzardi, et al., 2010). By generating the allowed instances of our ontologies, we can confront them with the desired states-of-affairs, ruling out undesired instances. We can also intentionally request examples of instantiations we expect the ontology to allow. The comparison between admissible model instances, generated by the simulations, and the

1.3. Methodological Aspects

intended ones, obtained from domain experts or the conceptual model documentation, highlights possibly erroneous modeling decisions. A support for visual model simulation is available in the Menthor Editor (Moreira et al., 2016), an open-source platform for designing, evaluating and implementing ontologies using OntoUML.

Furthermore, we follow the so-called *application-based approach to ontology evaluation* (Brank et al., 2005), which proposes the evaluation of ontologies when they are put in practice. For this purpose, we conduct empirical experiments (e.g., case studies) with experts in the financial domain to apply the built theoretical foundation and the reference ontologies.

1.3.2 The NeOn Methodology for building Ontology Networks

In this thesis, for building the ontology network, we follow a customized version of the NeOn methodology (Suárez-Figueroa et al., 2012), suited to our particular context and needs. NeOn provides guidance for engineering networked ontologies, making available detailed processes, guidelines and different scenarios for collaboratively building networked ontologies.

By combining the NeOn methodology with the customized version of SABiO previously described (section 1.3.1), we defined the five flexible scenarios described below, for building ontologies in the context of our work (figure 1.6).

– **Scenario 1: From specification to implementation.** The networked ontology is developed without reusing available ontological resources, following the customized version of SABiO.

– **Scenario 2: Reusing ontological resources.** In this scenario, ontology developers reuse ontological resources (foundational ontologies, core ontologies, ontology design patterns) as they are, during the step "Ontology Formalization", defined in SABiO. The ontological resource reuse process includes the following activities: (1) search for candidate ontological resources that satisfy the requirements; (2) inspect the content of these ontological resources; (3) select the set of ontological resources that are the most appropriate for the ontology network requirements and define the reuse mode: reuse the ontological resources as they are, re-engineer the ontological resource before reusing it or merge the ontological resources to obtain a new one; and (4) integrate the selected ontological resources to the ontology network, following the customized version of SABiO.

- **Scenario 3: Reusing and re-engineering ontological resources.** This scenario is similar to Scenario 2, however, in this case, ontology developers both reuse and re-engineer ontological resources, during the step "Ontology Formalization", defined in SABiO. This scenario unfolds in those cases in which the selected resources are not exactly useful as they are, and should be modified (i.e., re-engineered) before being reused, to serve to the intended purpose or problem.
- **Scenario 4: Reusing and merging ontological resources.** This scenario is applicable when several ontological resources in the same domain can be selected for reuse and the ontology developer wishes to either create a new ontological resource from two or more (possibly overlapping, ontological resources) or just establish alignments among the selected ontological resources in order to create the ontology network. Firstly, ontology developers should perform the ontological resource reuse process to select the most suitable ontological resources that will be used for building the ontology network. Then ontology developers should decide how they will reuse the selected ontological resources selected. They have two different possibilities: (1) to establish the mappings among such selected resources—ontology alignment or (2) to establish the mappings and also to merge the selected resources—ontology alignment and ontology merging. Finally, ontology developers should use the resultant ontological resource as input to SABiO "Ontology Formalization" step.
- **Scenario 5: Reusing, merging, and re-engineering ontological resources.** This scenario is similar to Scenario 4, however, here developers decide not to use the set of merged resources as it is, but to re-engineer it, as it is not exactly useful as it is, and thus should be modified before being reused.

It is worth mentioning that the scenarios just described can be combined in different and flexible ways, and that any combination of scenarios should include Scenario 1, as this scenario is composed of the core activities that have to be performed in any ontology development.

1.3. Methodological Aspects

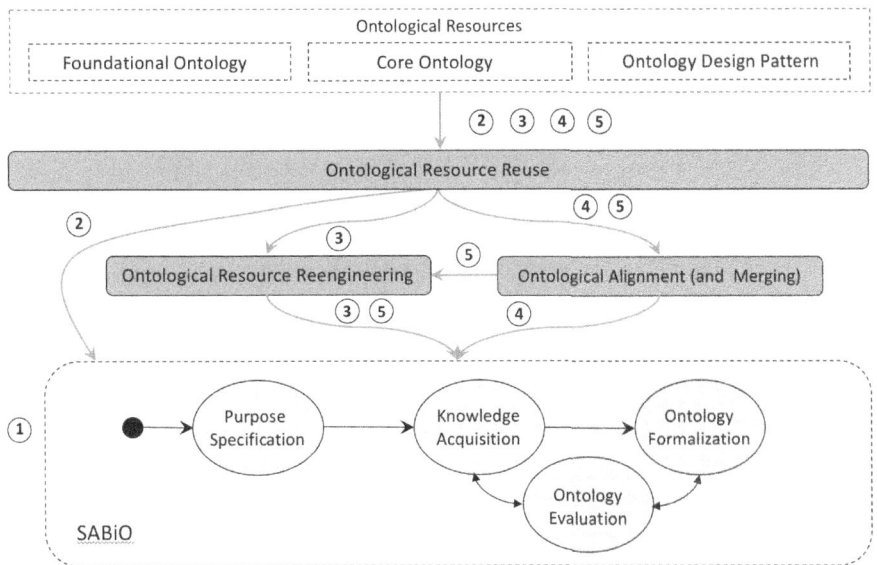

Figure 1.6: Overview of the ontology network development method (adapted from (Suárez-Figueroa et al., 2012) and (Sales, 2019)).

1.4 Thesis Structure

This thesis is further structured as follows:

Part II (chapter 2) presents the theoretical framework. Part III is organized in four chapters (3 to 6) that provide the ontological foundations for the Ontology Network in Finance and Economics. Part IV validates and demonstrates the usability and relevance of OntoFINE, by presenting six different applications of the ontology network (chapters 7 to 12). Finally, Part V (chapter 13) summarises our contributions and provides directions for future research.

Part II. Theoretical Framework

Chapter 2. Theoretical Framework

This chapter presents an overview of the theoretical background necessary for grounding the ideas of this thesis. The content comprises ontologies and their classifications, ontology networks and an introduction to the Unified Foundational Ontology, which provides the ontological foundations for our proposal. We describe a subset of UFO's ontological distinctions that are relevant for this thesis.

PART III. ONTOLOGICAL FOUNDATIONS

Chapter 3. The Ontology Network in Finance and Economics

This chapter introduces the Ontology Network in Finance and Economics, which provides the ontological foundation on money, trust, value, risk and economics exchanges, proposed in this thesis. We describe the architecture of OntoFINE and present an overview of its networked ontologies, namely, the Reference Ontology of Trust (ROT), the Reference Ontology of Money and Virtual Currencies (ROME), the Core Ontology for Economic Exchanges (COEX), the Common Ontology of Value and Risk (COVER), and the Reference Ontology of Trustworthiness Requirements (ROTwR). Then, we provide a detailed description of COVER, a core reference ontology on value and risk, proposed by (Sales, Baião, et al., 2018). Different from the other ontologies just mentioned, COVER was not created within the scope of this work. It is being reused in OntoFINE to provide the ontological foundations on value and risk. The detailed descriptions of ROT, ROME, COEX and ROTwR are presented in chapters 4, 5, 6 and 7, respectively. We finalize by presenting some related works found in the literature.

This chapter is related to the following author publication: (Amaral, Sales, and Guizzardi, 2021c).

Chapter 4. The Reference Ontology of Trust

This chapter presents the ontological foundations for trust proposed in this thesis, in the form of a well-founded core reference ontology, the Reference Ontology of Trust (ROT). We start by discussing the literature on the topic, then we present an ontological analysis that characterizes the general notion of trust, identifies different types of trust, and makes explicit the dynamic nature of trust, as well as the factors that can influence it. We also leverage the analysis of the behavioral aspect of trust to explain the implications of the decision to trust with respect to value and risk: at the same time that this decision creates value, it also implies some risk, as the trustor becomes dependent on the trustee, and consequently, more vulnerable. We reuse the ontological foundations on risk provided by COVER to model the emergence of risk from trust relations. The result of this analysis is formalized in an OntoUML reference model, whose use we demonstrate by means of three illustrative cases: (1) an example of social trust, using the case of a working mother who trusts a babysitter to take care of her children; (2) an example of institution-based trust, related to the trust of people in the monetary system; and (3) an example about trust in vaccines in the time of COVID-19. We conclude the chapter by presenting some related work on trust.

This chapter is related to the following author publications: (Amaral, Sales, Guizzardi, and Porello, 2019), (Amaral, Sales, and Guizzardi, 2021b) and (Amaral, Sales, and Guizzardi, 2022).

Chapter 5. The Reference Ontology of Money and Virtual Currencies

This chapter presents the ontological foundations for money proposed in this thesis, in the form of a well-founded core reference ontology, the Reference Ontology of Money and Virtual Currencies (ROME). We start by discussing the literature on money and currencies, as well as the notion of virtual currency. Then, we present an ontological analysis that characterizes the general notion of money and currencies. We leverage our analysis to characterize the concept of virtual currencies and make explicit the differences between them and official currencies. In addition, we discuss the relation between money and trust, arguing that money depends on trust, which is precondition for the proper functioning of any monetary system. The relation between money and trust is modeled by reusing the ontological foundations on trust, provided by ROT. The result of this analysis is formalized in an OntoUML reference model, whose working we illustrate by means of a case illustration that covers key concepts of the ontology. We finalize by presenting some related works on money, found in the literature.

This chapter is related to the following author publications: (Amaral, Sales, Guizzardi, Porello, and Guarino, 2020), (Amaral, Sales, Guizzardi, and Porello, 2020a) and (Amaral, Sales, and Guizzardi, 2021d).

Chapter 6. The Core Ontology for Economic Exchanges

This chapter presents the ontological foundations for economic exchanges proposed in this thesis, in the form of a well-founded core reference ontology, the Core Ontology for Economic Exchanges (COEX). We present an ontological analysis inspired by a recent view on this phenomenon, namely, the *Action Theory of Economic Exchanges* (Massin and Tieffenbach, 2016). According to this view, economic exchanges are based on an agreement on the actions that the agents are committed to perform. This view enables a unified treatment of economic exchanges, regardless the object of the transaction. The result of this analysis is formalized in an OntoUML reference model, whose use we demonstrate by means of a case illustration that covers key concepts of the ontology. We finalize the chapter by presenting some related work on economic exchanges.

This chapter is related to the following author publications: (Porello, Guizzardi, Sales, Amaral, and Guarino, 2020) and (Porello, Guizzardi, Sales, and Amaral, 2020).

PART IV. APPLICATIONS

Chapter 7. Ontology-based Modeling and Analysis of Trustworthiness Requirements

In this chapter, we demonstrate how OntoFINE can be used to support requirements engineering activities, by proposing a novel methodology for ontology-based requirements engineering (ObRE), which applies the Reference Ontology of Trust to define the class of trustworthiness requirements and their relation to concepts such as trust, capability, vulnerability and risk, among others. We also conducted a real case study to verify if the Reference Ontology of Trust is capable of properly representing real world situations. In this study, ROT was applied to help with the elicitation of trustworthiness requirements of software systems by analyzing the case of Pix, the Brazilian Instant Payments Ecosystem created and managed by the Central Bank of Brazil.

This chapter is related to the following author publications: (Amaral, Guizzardi, Guizzardi, et al., 2020) and (Amaral, Guizzardi, Guizzardi, et al., 2021).

Chapter 8. Modeling Trust Dynamics: The Case of Central Bank Digital Currency Ecosystems

This chapter presents an OntoFINE application that demonstrates how the ontology network can be used to support recent challenges faced by the financial industry, due to the advent of the decentralized finance (DeFi) paradigm. We rely on the Reference Ontology of Trust and on the Reference Ontology of Money and Virtual Currencies to analyse trust in light of the the new DeFi paradigm, by conducting a real case study, in collaboration with a national central bank. In this case study, ROT was used to model citizens' trust in central bank digital currency ecosystems.

This chapter is related to the following author publication: (Amaral, Sales, and Guizzardi, 2022).

Chapter 9. Modeling Payments and Linked Obligation Settlements

This chapter presents another OntoFINE application in the context of decentralized finance. In this initiative, we propose and ontology-based approach for the modeling of payments and linked obligation settlement mechanisms, aiming at providing conceptual clarification and supporting semantic interoperability in DeFi. Firstly, we create two domain-related ontology patterns by reusing pieces of knowledge extracted from the Core Ontology for Economic Exchanges and the Reference Ontology of Money and Virtual Currencies. Then, we systematically apply these patterns to model payments and linked obligations in OntoUML. Finally, we export the models to OWL using gUFO, a lightweight implementation of UFO in OWL.

This chapter is related to the following author publication: (Amaral, Sales, and Guizzardi, 2021a).

Chapter 10. Modeling Trust in Enterprise Architecture: A Pattern Language for ArchiMate

This chapter introduces the Trust Pattern Language (TPL) for ArchiMate, a standardized enterprise architecture modeling language that is adopted by many organizations worldwide. TPL defines a pattern language for trust modeling in ArchiMate, derived from the Reference Ontology of Trust and the Common Ontology of Value and Risk. The modeling of trust in the context of enterprise architecture is fundamental to bridge the gap between the stakeholders' trust concerns and the processes and other elements of the architecture that are needed to achieve the organization's goal of being trustworthy. TPL is designed in conformance with the ArchiMate 3.0.1, meaning it does not introduce any new construct to the language, but only specializes existing ones when necessary. As a pattern language, TPL introduces a catalogue of patterns and a process on how to combine them. We demonstrate the working of TPL by means of of a realistic case study about trust in a COVID-19 data repository.

This chapter is related to the following author publication: (Amaral, Sales, Guizzardi, Almeida, et al., 2020).

Chapter 11. Modeling the Emergence of Value and Risk in Game Theoretical Approaches

In this chapter, we apply OntoFINE to support the analysis of value and risk in game theoretical approaches. We conduct an ontological analysis characterizing some basic concepts in game theory, which make clear the emergence of value and risks from game outcomes. We make use of the concepts and relations defined in the Common Ontology of Value and Risk to analyze the payoffs of a game in terms of value and risk, as well as how they emerge from outcomes in game theory. We also propose a formalization of our analysis by means of an ontologically well-founded model, specified in OntoUML, and demonstrate its use by means of a *bank run* game example. Finally, to provide enterprise architects with a common ground to apply game theory notions in coherent enterprise architecture descriptions, we apply the results of our analysis to model game outcomes in the context of enterprise architectures.

This chapter is related to the following author publication: (Amaral, Porello, et al., 2020).

Chapter 12. Capability Agreements and Risk

In this chapter, we apply OntoFINE, more specifically the Common Ontology of Value and Risk, to conduct an ontological analysis on the emergence of value and risk in delegation relations, in capability agreements. Having a clear understanding of the influence of these forces over delegation networks is fundamental both for the management of risks and for the awareness of the value created through the complex network of interdependencies.

This chapter is related to the following author publication: (Amaral, Guizzardi, Guarino, et al., 2019).

PART V. CONCLUSIONS

Chapter 13. Conclusions

In the concluding chapter we outline the main contributions of this thesis, while arguing how they satisfy the goals we established for this doctoral research project. We also discuss why and how these contributions are relevant for the application domain. We finalize the chapter by revisiting the general limitations of our work and and describing our research agenda for the future.

Figure 1.7 presents an overview of the structure of this thesis and how the chapters can be related to the research specific objectives.

1.4. Thesis Structure

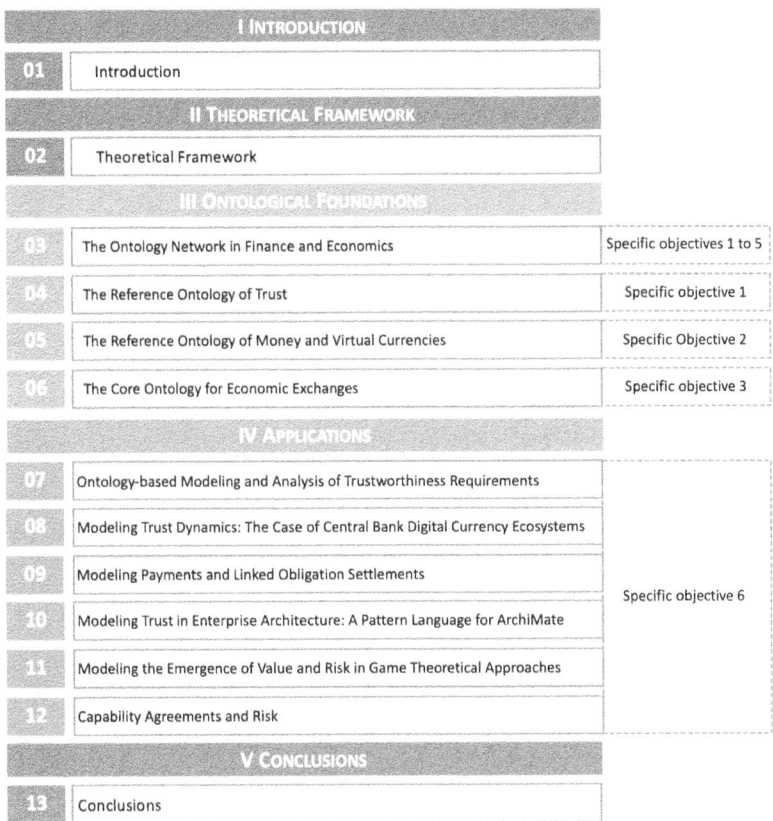

Figure 1.7: Overview of the thesis structure and related objectives.

Part II

Theoretical Framework

Chapter 2
Theoretical Framework

The main objective of this chapter is to set the conceptual basis of this work. We present the background knowledge on ontologies and ontology networks that is necessary for the work developed through this thesis. Section 2.1 elaborates on ontologies and their classifications. Section 2.2 presents our view of ontology networks. In section 2.3, we introduce the reader to the Unified Foundational Ontology (UFO), which servers as conceptual foundation for the ontologies developed in this thesis, and OntoUML, the ontology representation language we use to specify the ontologies. We present some final considerations in section 2.4.

2.1 Ontologies and their classifications

Ontologies have been applied in a multitude of areas in computer science. Two common trends in the traditional use of the term ontology in computer science are: (i) ontologies regarded as an explicit representation of a shared conceptualization, i.e., a concrete artifact representing a model of consensus within a community and a universe of discourse. In this sense of a reference model, an ontology is primarily aimed at supporting semantic interoperability in its various forms (e.g., model integration, service interoperability, knowledge harmonization, and taxonomy alignment); (ii) ontologies regarded as representation mechanisms for the construction of domain ontologies, typically centered on computational issues, not truly ontological ones.

The use of foundational concepts that take truly ontological issues seriously is especially important in domains with complex concepts, relations and constraints, and with potentially serious risks which could be caused by interoperability problems, as it (i) allows modelers to be explicit regarding their ontological commitments, thus minimizing the chances of running into a False Agreement Problem (Guarino, 1998), in which each modeler would come to a different interpretation of the same model and would not detect the conflict; and (ii) supports the user in justifying their modeling choices and providing a sound design rationale for choosing how the elements in the universe of discourse should be modeled in terms of language elements. In contrast, languages traditionally used in knowledge representation (e.g., RDF, OWL, UML, EER), and database languages (e.g., some instances of Description Logics), have been specifically designed to afford efficient automated reasoning and decidability. Thus, in general, they offer no support neither for helping the modeler on choosing a particular structure to model elements of the subject domain nor for justifying the choice of a particular structure over another. This duality poses a tradeoff between expressivity and computational tractability that should be addressed in different phases of an ontology engineering process.

In this thesis, we address this issue by using an ontologically well-founded conceptual modeling language, supported by expressive logical theories, which allows the representation of the subject domain with truthfulness, clarity and expressivity (regardless of computational requirements) and that, at the same time, drives the implementation of lightweight ontologies supported by efficient computational algorithms (e.g., OWL-DL, RDF, Alloy), thus satisfying the need for computational tractability. In particular, we make use of OntoUML as the ontology representation language. OntoUML is a general purpose ontology-driven conceptual modelling language designed to comply with the ontological distinctions put forth by the Unified Foundational Ontology (UFO) (Guizzardi, 2005). We describe both UFO and OntoUML (Guizzardi, 2005) in section 2.3.

2.1.1 Ontology Classifications

There are different classifications of ontologies in the literature. In the context of this thesis, we are interested in the ones that classify ontologies according to their generality levels and intended application. Regarding the generality level, ontologies can be classified into foundational, core and domain ontologies (Scherp et al., 2011). At the highest level of generality, there are the foundational ontologies. Foundational ontologies span across many fields and model the very basic and general concepts and relations that make up the world, such as object, event, parthood relation etc. (Borgo and Masolo, 2009; Guarino, 1998; Guizzardi, 2005). Domain ontologies, in turn, describe the conceptualization related to a given domain, such as infectious diseases in biomedicine and financial instruments in finance. With a level of generality between that of foundational

2.1. Ontologies and their classifications

and domain ontologies, there are core ontologies. Core ontologies provide a precise definition of structural knowledge in a specific field that spans across different application domains in this field. These ontologies are built based on foundational ontologies and provide a refinement to them by adding detailed concepts and relations in their specific field (Scherp et al., 2011). The different generality levels do not amount to a discrete classification, but to a continuum (Almeida Falbo et al., 2013), ranging from foundational ontologies that are totally domain-independent (such as DOLCE[1] (Borgo and Masolo, 2009), GFO[2] (Herre, 2010) and UFO (Guizzardi, 2005)), to domain ontologies, for a very particular domain. Finally, core ontologies, despite being more general than domain ontologies, are also domain-dependent. Higher-level ontologies can be used to support the development of lower-level ontologies, e.g., foundational ontologies can be used as basis for building core and domain ontologies, and core ontologies can support the development of domain ontologies. In fact, considering the continuous nature of the aforementioned classification, some ontologies can be used for supporting the development of more specific ontologies even within the same level of generality. For example, UFO-A (an ontology of endurants) (Guizzardi, 2005) and UFO-B (an ontology of events) (Guizzardi, Wagner, Falbo, et al., 2013), both of which are foundational ontologies, have been used as basis for building UFO-C (an ontology of social entities) (Guizzardi, Falbo, et al., 2008b; Guizzardi and Guizzardi, 2010). The latter, albeit being more specific, is still considered to be a foundational ontology. The Common Ontology of Value and Risk (COVER) (Sales, Baião, et al., 2018), is a core ontology grounded in UFO, while the Coronavirus Infectious Disease Ontology (CIDO)[3] in biomedicine is an example of domain ontology. Figure 2.1 illustrates the view of ontology generality levels as a continuum using the aforementioned ontologies.

Another relevant classification criterion concerns the intended application of ontologies. Guizzardi (2005) makes an important distinction between ontologies as conceptual models, known as reference ontologies, and ontologies as coding artifacts, called here operational ontologies. A reference domain ontology is constructed with the goal of making the best possible description of the domain in reality. It is a special kind of conceptual model, an engineering artifact with the additional requirement of representing a model of consensus within a community (Guizzardi, 2005). On the other hand, once users have already agreed on a common conceptualization, operational versions

---

[1] Descriptive Ontology for Linguistic and Cognitive Engineering (http://www.loa.istc.cnr.it/dolce/overview.html)

[2] General Formal Ontology (https://www.onto-med.de/ontologies/gfo)

[3] https://bioportal.bioontology.org/ontologies/CIDO

of a reference ontology can be created. Contrary to reference ontologies, operational ontologies are designed with the focus on guaranteeing desirable computational properties. In other words, when developing a reference ontology, the focus is on expressivity of the representation and truthfulness to the domain being represented (domain appropriateness), even at the expenses of computational characteristics such as tractability and decidability (Guizzardi, 2007).

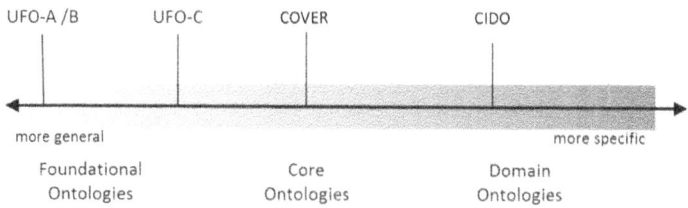

Figure 2.1: Ontology generality levels as a continuum.

2.2 Ontology Networks

Ontologies have been widely recognized as a key enabling tool for knowledge management. They are used for establishing a common conceptualization of the domain of interest to support knowledge representation, integration, storage, search and communication (O'Leary, 1998). However, domains like finance and economics are too large and complex to be represented as a single ontology. If we try to represent the whole domain as a single ontology, we will achieve a large and rigid artifact that is hard to manipulate, use, and maintain (Suarez-Figueroa et al., 2012). On the other hand, representing each subdomain separately would be too costly, fragmented, and again hard to handle.

d'Aquin and Gangemi (2011) point out a set of characteristics that are presented in "beautiful ontologies", from which we detach the following ones: having a good domain coverage; being modular or embedded in a modular framework; being formally rigorous; capturing also non-taxonomic relations; and reusing foundational ontologies. We believe that an integrated ontological framework, built considering the characteristics just mentioned, can improve ontology-based applications in finance. In such integrated ontological framework, there must be ways for creating, integrating and evolving related ontologies. Thus, we advocate that these ontologies should be built incrementally and in an integrated way, as a network.

An Ontology Network is a collection of ontologies related together through a variety of relationships, such as alignment, dependency, and modularization (Suárez-Figueroa et al., 2012), briefly described below.

- **Alignment.** The alignment mechanism allows modelers to declare which entities in one ontology are the same as those in another ontology, or a generalization or specialization. The main purpose of alignments is to ensure semantic interoperability, making it possible to merge ontologies in a meaningful way by representing information in one ontology in terms of the entities in another.
- **Dependency.** In order to define its own model, an ontology can refer to the definitions included in another ontology. In this case, we say that this ontology is dependent on the one containing the original concept.
- **Modularization.** Large, monolithic ontologies are hard to manipulate, use, and maintain. Modular ontologies on the contrary divide the ontological model in self-contained, interlinked components, which can be considered independently, while at the same time participate to the definition of a specific aspect of an ontology.

The term *networked ontology* is used to refer to ontologies included in a network ontology, sharing concepts and relations with other ontologies (Suárez-Figueroa et al., 2012). Hence, networked ontologies are not stand-alone artifacts. They relate to each other in ways that might affect their meaning, so that the whole (the network ontology) ends up being more meaningful than the sum of its parts (the networked ontologies).

2.3 The Unified Foundational Ontology

The Unified Foundational Ontology (UFO) is an axiomatic domain-independent formal theory, developed by consistently putting together a number of theories originating from areas such as formal ontology in philosophy, cognitive science, linguistics, and philosophical logic. Other examples of foundational ontologies include DOLCE (Borgo and Masolo, 2009) and GFO (Herre, 2010). DOLCE, GFO and UFO are all centered around the same notions of what is termed the *Aristotelian Square* (Guizzardi, 2005). So, in that respect, they are rather similar. In fact, UFO was created as an extension of the unification of DOLCE and GFO to deal with a number of specific phenomena that arise in Conceptual Modeling. For example, unlike DOLCE, UFO includes a rich *ontology of relations* (Guarino and Guizzardi, 2016). Moreover, unlike DOLCE, which is an ontology of particulars, UFO includes a number of formal distinctions among types of universals (e.g., kinds, phases, roles, mixins). Both these features have been shown to be fundamental for conceptual modeling (Guizzardi, 2005). Additionally, unlike GFO, UFO has a theory of relations that is finitely instantiable (Guizzardi, Wagner, Almeida, et al., 2015), which makes it practical to conceptual modeling applications. Furthermore, unlike DOLCE (but also SUMO[4] (Niles and Pease, 2001), GFO (Herre, 2010), BFO[5] (Masolo et al., 2003)), UFO is formally connected to a conceptual modeling language (OntoUML). OntoUML was designed such that its modeling primitives reflect the ontological distinctions of its underlying ontology, and its grammar is enriched with semantically-motivated syntactical constrains that mirror UFO's axiomatization. UFO is also formally connected to a number set of tools to facilitate the ontology engineering process, such as ontological design patterns and anti-patterns (Guizzardi, Graças, et al., 2011), visual model simulation (Benevides, Guizzardi, et al., 2010), automated model diagnosis and repair via learning (Fumagalli et al., 2020), and transformations for codification technologies (Barcelos et al., 2013; Rybola and Pergl, 2016). In particular, UFO has a partial translation to OWL termed gUFO (Almeida, Guizzardi, et al., 2020) (see section 2.3.1), which is suitable for knowledge graph applications. Finally, research shows that UFO is vastly more used in Conceptual Modeling — an area closely connected to the theme of this thesis — than the aforementioned foundational ontologies (Verdonck and Gailly, 2016).

UFO is organized in three incrementally layered compliance sets:

- UFO-A, an ontology of endurants (roughly, objects) (Guizzardi, 2005; Guizzardi, Botti Benevides, et al., 2021);

- UFO-B, an ontology of perdurants (roughly, events and processes) (Almeida, Falbo, et al., 2019; Guizzardi, Wagner, Falbo, et al., 2013);

- UFO-C, which is an ontology of social and intentional entities build on the foundations provided by UFO-A and UFO-B (Guizzardi, Falbo, et al., 2008b; Guizzardi and Guizzardi, 2010; Oliveira Bringuente et al., 2011)

In the remainder of this section, we focus our discussion on UFO, briefly explaining a subset of its ontological distinctions that are relevant for this thesis, which are depicted in figures 2.3, 2.4 and 2.5. For a fuller discussion on this ontology, one should refer to (Guizzardi, 2005; Guizzardi, Wagner, Almeida, et al., 2015).

---

[4]Suggested Upper Merged Ontology (https://www.ontologyportal.org)
[5]Basic Formal Ontology (https://basic-formal-ontology.org)

2.3. The Unified Foundational Ontology

UFO makes a fundamental distinction between individuals (particulars), and types (or universals), that is, patterns of features that are repeatable across individuals. Individuals can be concrete or abstract. Concrete individuals are further categorized into endurants (roughly, things or object-like entities) or perdurants (roughly, events, occurrences, processes). Within the category of endurants, UFO distinguishes substantials and moments (also termed aspects, abstract particulars, or variable tropes (Moltmann, 2020)). Substantials are existentially independent objects, such as the Moon, an enterprise, a person, a horse. Moments are existentially dependent entities and can only exist by inhering in other entities. They are distinguished into intrinsic moments and relators.

Intrinsic moments are existentially dependent on a single individual. These include qualities, i.e., reifications of categorical properties such as height, weight, age, electrical charge, color. Qualities are entities that can be directly projected into certain value spaces. The latter, termed quality structures, are abstract entities delimiting the space of possible values (qualia, singular quale) for qualities of a given quality type. Quality structures can be either one-dimensional, in which case they are termed quality dimensions, or composed of multiple co-dependent (or integral (Gärdenfors, 2004)) dimensions, in which case they are termed quality domains. While the former includes height and weight dimensions as examples (one-dimensional structures isomorphic to a subset of the positive half-line of real numbers), the later includes dates, which can be associated to a structure (a quality domain) formed by three dimensions, named day, month, and year. For example "being red" is a property that constrains the color quality of its subject to be in the red region of a color quality space (a chromatic map known as the color spindle) (see figure 2.2).

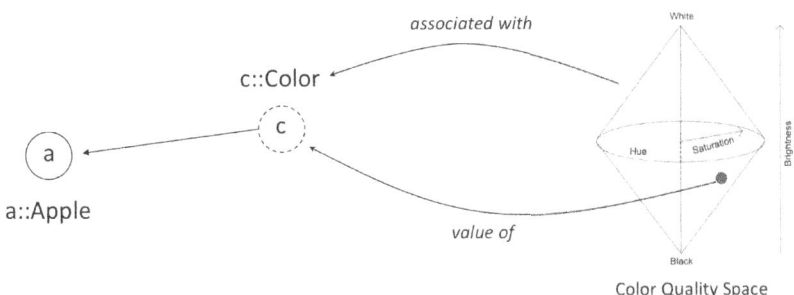

Figure 2.2: Quality Space example (color).

Intrinsic moments also include modes. Modes can bear their own moments, including their own qualities, which can vary in independent ways. The category of modes includes dispositions (e.g., functions, capabilities, vulnerabilities) as well as externally dependent entities (e.g., the trust of citizens in politicians, the commitment of John towards Mary to watch a film on Netflix on Saturday night).

Dispositions are dependent entities in the sense that depend on other objects to exist. We consider them as properties that are only manifested in particular situations on the occurrence of certain triggering events, and that can also fail to be manifested. When manifested, they are manifested through the occurrence of resulting events and state changes. Take for example the disposition of a magnet to attract metallic material. The magnet has this disposition even if it is never manifested, e.g., because the magnet was never close to any magnetic material. Capabilities and vulnerabilities are special types of dispositions. Capabilities[6] are usually understood as positive dispositions, in the sense that they enable the manifestation of events desired by an agent. Conversely, vulnerabilities are dispositions whose manifestation constitute a loss or can potentially cause a loss from the perspective of an agent.

Externally dependent modes inhere in an entity while being externally dependent on another entity. For example, the love of a mother for her child is a mode that inheres in the mother and externally depends on the child. Other examples are beliefs, desires, intentions, perceptions, symptoms, among many others.

Relators are moments existentially dependent on multiple individuals. They are individuals with the power of connecting entities. For example, an enrollment relator connects an individual playing the Student role with an Educational Institution. Every instance of a relator type is existentially dependent on at least two distinct entities. Moreover, relators are typically composed of modes, for example, in the way that the service agreement between John and Netflix is composed of their mutual commitments and claims.

As previously mentioned, UFO is an ontology of both individuals and types, i.e., patterns of features that are repeatable across different individuals. The hierarchy of types in UFO reflects on the one hand the existing distinctions among sorts of individuals. So, we have perdurant types, substantial types, moment types, etc. On the other hand, UFO employs a number of formal meta-properties to spawn a rich typology of endurant types (Guizzardi, Fonseca, Almeida, et al., 2021).

---

[6]Capabilities are usually perceived as beneficial, as they enable the manifestation of events desired by an agent. However, when the manifestation of a capability enables undesired events that threaten agent's abilities to achieve a goal, it can be seen as a threatening capability (Sales, Baião, et al., 2018)

2.3. The Unified Foundational Ontology

In the hierarchy of types in UFO, the taxonomy reflecting the existing distinctions among sorts of individuals (e.g., perdurant types, substantial types, moment types, etc) is orthogonal to the one reflecting meta-properties such as sortality, rigidity, etc.

An important characteristic of all endurants is that they exist in time keeping their identity, even if changing in a qualitative way (e.g., a flower's color which may change from red to brown while keeping its identity). The sorts of changes an endurant can undergo and still be the same is determined by its kind. By a kind, we mean an entity type that necessarily classify their instances, being responsible for their principle of identity. For this reason, all endurants classified by a kind cannot cease to instantiate it without ceasing to exist (e.g., a horse cannot cease to be a horse and keep existing). Kinds can be specialized in other subtypes that also necessarily classify their instances, named subkinds. For example, if we take 'Person' to be a kind then some of its subkinds could be 'Man' and 'Woman'.

Endurant kinds and subkinds are also termed rigid types as they represent essential properties of objects. There are, however, types that represent contingent or accidental properties of objects, named anti-rigid types. Examples of anti-rigid types are phases and roles. The former represent properties that are intrinsic to entities (e.g., teenager as a phase of person, tenured employment as a phase of employment), while the latter represent properties that entities have in a relational context, i.e., contingent relational properties (e.g., student as a role of a person in the scope of an enrollment relator, and wife as a role of a person in the scope of a marriage relator).

Kinds, subkinds, phases, and roles are categories of sortals. In the philosophical literature, a sortal is a type that provides a uniform principle of identity, persistence, and individuation for its instances (Guizzardi, 2005). In contrast with sortals, non-sortals are types that represent properties shared by entities of multiple kinds. These can be: (i) categories: rigid types that define essential properties for their instances, e.g., the category 'physical object' describing the properties of having a mass and a spatial extension, common to things of the kinds car, person, bridge, cow, etc.; (ii) phase mixins: anti-rigid types that define contingent properties for their instances. Their instantiation is characterized by intrinsic contingent conditions. For example, the phase mixin 'living animal' may apply to instances of the kinds person, dog, and horse; the phase mixin 'functional device' may characterize instances of the kinds computer, watch, and espresso machine; (iii) role mixins: anti-rigid types that define contingent properties for their instances. Their instantiation is characterized by relational contingent conditions. Examples include 'customer' for the kinds person and organization, but also 'insured legal relator' for the kinds employment and enrollment; (iv) mixins: semi-rigid types that define properties that are essential to some of their instances but accidental to some other instances (e.g., being a 'music artist' is essential to bands but accidental to people).

Beyond the *ontology of endurants*, UFO also comprises an *ontology of events* (UFO-B). An event (also called perdurant) is composed of a time interval that has a beginning (time point - beginpoint) and an end (time point - endpoint). Examples of events are a conversation, a football game, a symphony execution, a birthday party, or a particular business process. One first aspect of events is that they may be composed of other events. Thus, an event can be composed of a single event (atomic event) or of multiple events (complex event). A second characteristic of events is that they are ontologically dependent entities in the sense that they existentially depend on objects in order to exist, and objects participate of events. In fact, events can be seen as manifestation of particular endurants called dispositions (see figure 2.3), which can themselves inhere in other endurants. Finally, dispositions are said to be triggered by certain situations. Thus, events map the world from situations (that activate the dispositions of which they are manifestations) to situations (which are brought about the occurrence of that event). If an event E1 brings about a situation S that activates the dispositions that are manifested as event E2, then we say that: S triggers E2 and that E1 causes E2. Figure 2.4 summarizes these aspects of UFO-B. For a complete presentation and full formalization of this ontology, one please refer to (Almeida, Falbo, et al., 2019; Botti Benevides et al., 2019; Guizzardi, Wagner, Falbo, et al., 2013).

The third layer of UFO is an *ontology of social entities* (both endurants and perdurants). As shown in figure 2.5, one of the main distinctions made in UFO-C is between agents and (non-agentive) objects. An agent is a substantial that creates actions, perceives events and to which we can ascribe mental states (intentional moments). Agents can be physical (e.g., a person) or social (e.g., an organization). A distinction is made between human agent and artificial agent (both subkinds of physical agent), to differentiate humans agents from software (or hardware) agents. An object, on the other hand, is a substantial unable to perceive events or to have intentional moments. Objects can also be further categorized into physical (e.g., a book, a car) and social objects (e.g., money, language).

Agents can bear special kinds of moments named intentional moments. Intentional moments can be social moments or mental moments. Mental moments refer to the capacity of some properties of certain individuals to refer to possible situations of reality (Guizzardi, Falbo, et al., 2008b). Examples of mental moments include perceptions,

2.3. The Unified Foundational Ontology 41

beliefs, desires and intentions. Perception expresses how agents sense their environment and the things that happen around them. Beliefs have a propositional content that agents consider to be true. They can be justified by situations in reality. Examples include my belief that Rome is the Capital of Italy, and the belief that the Moon orbits the Earth. Beliefs can be formed by perceptions expressing how agents sense their environment and the things that happen around them. Desires and intentions can be fulfilled or frustrated. A desire expresses the will of an agent towards a possible situation (e.g., a desire that Brazil wins the next World Cup). Intentions (or internal commitments) express desired states of affairs for which the agent commits to pursuing (e.g., Mary's intention of paying a bill using an internet banking system). They cause the agent to perform actions. The propositional content of an intention is a goal. Besides internal commitments (intentions), there are also social commitments. A social commitment is a commitment of an agent A towards another agent B. As an externally dependent moment, a social commitment inheres in A and is externally dependent on B. The social commitments necessarily cause the creation of an internal commitment in A. Also, associated to this internal commitment, a social claim of B towards A is created. Commitments and claims always form a pair that refers to a unique propositional content. For example, when John rents a car at a car rental office, he commits (a social commitment towards that organization) to pay the rental fee according to the table of "vehicle categories and prices". Thus, it creates a social claim of the rental car office towards John with respect to this particular propositional content (the payment).

Finally, a normative description is a type of social object that defines one or more rules/norms recognized by at least one social agent and that can define social intrinsic and relational properties (e.g., social commitment types), social objects (e.g., the crown of the King of Spain) and social roles (e.g., president, or pedestrian). Examples of normative descriptions include the Italian Constitution and a set of directives on how to perform some actions within an organization. In the finance domain, the Treaty on the Functioning of the European Union ("Treaty on the Functioning of the European Union" 2012) is an example of normative description, which defines euro banknotes and coins as money in the countries of the euro area.

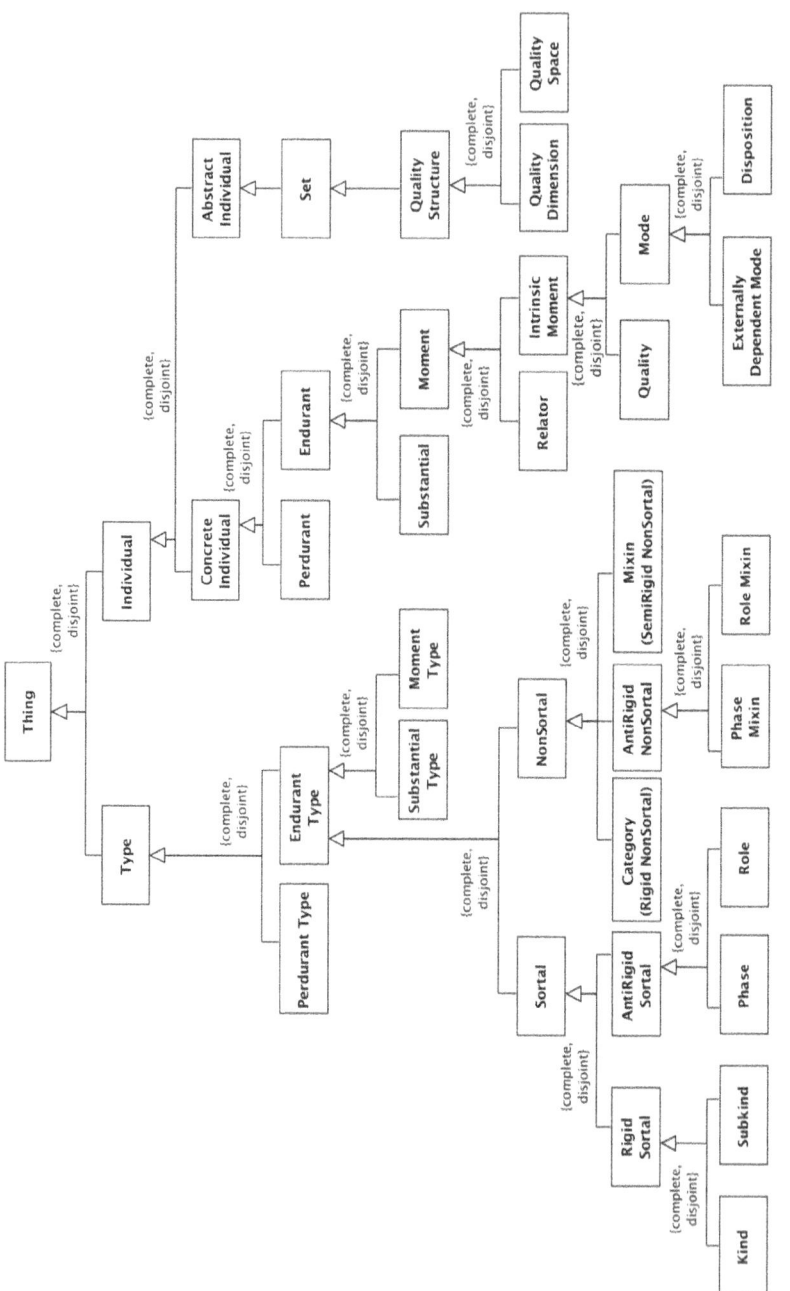

Figure 2.3: Fragment of UFO (Guizzardi, Botti Benevides, et al., 2021).

2.3. The Unified Foundational Ontology

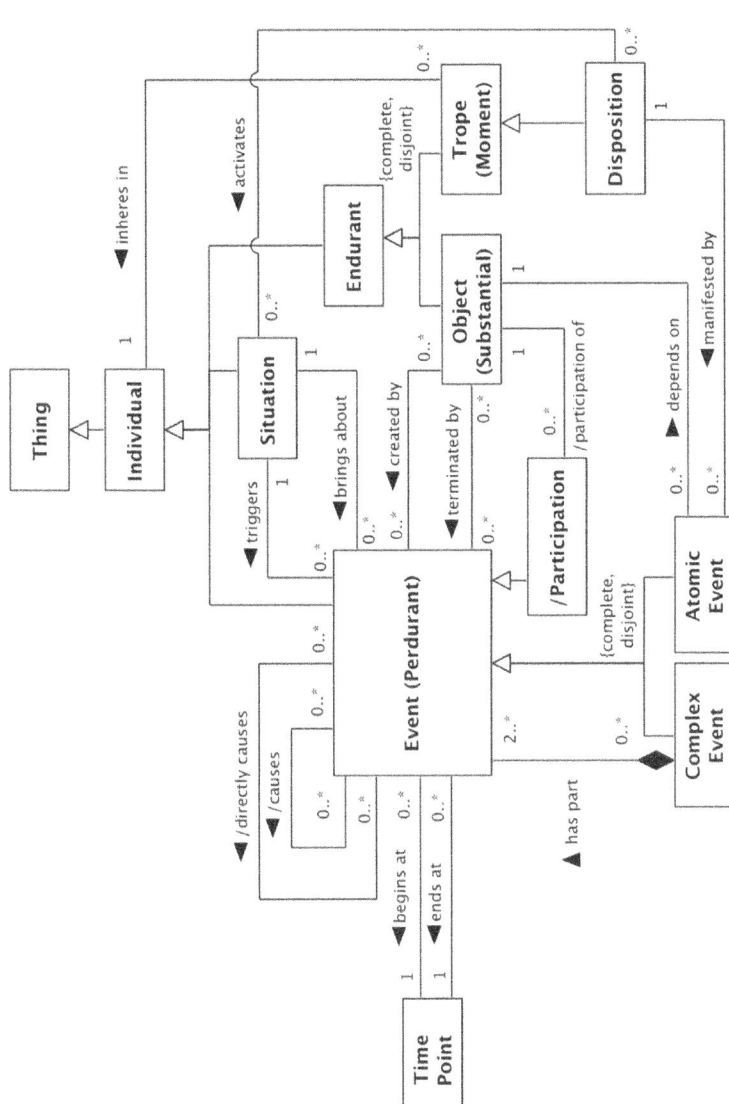

Figure 2.4: Fragment of UFO-B (Almeida, Falbo, et al., 2019).

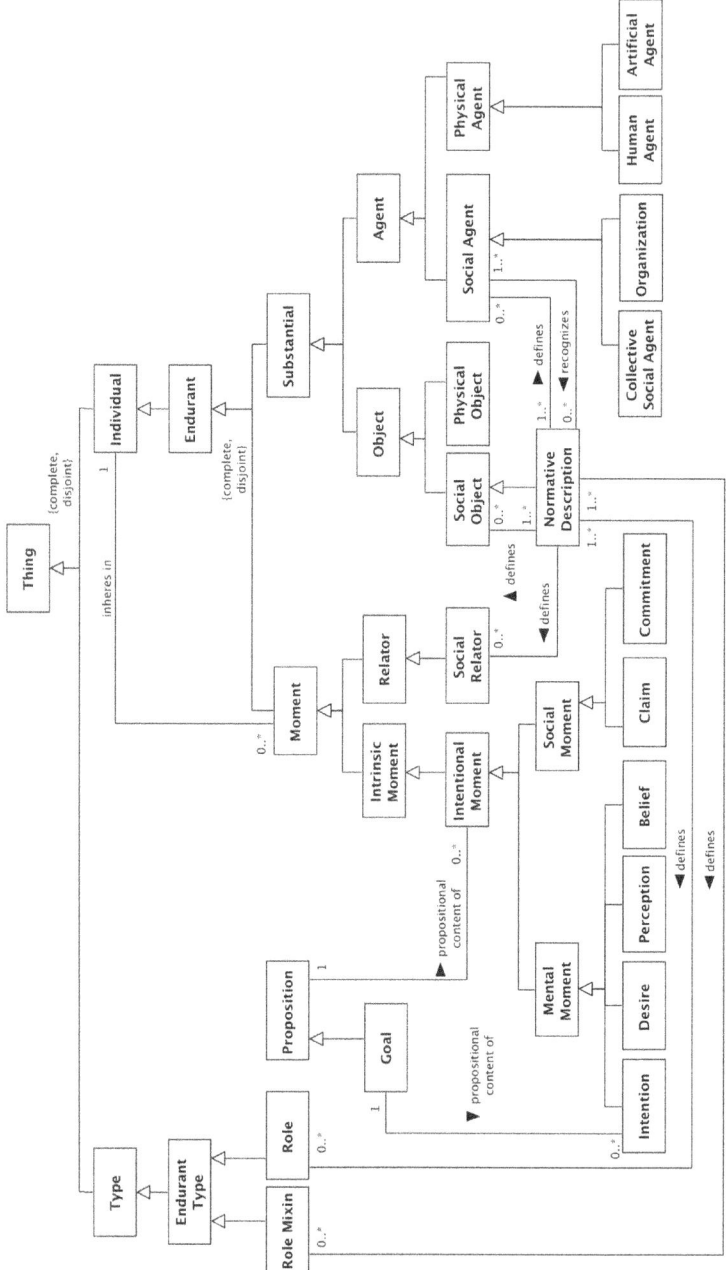

Figure 2.5: Fragment of UFO-C (Guizzardi, Falbo, et al., 2008b).

2.3.1 gUFO: A Lightweight Implementation of the UFO

gUFO[7] (Almeida, Guizzardi, et al., 2020) is a lightweight implementation of UFO suitable for Semantic Web OWL 2 DL applications, enabling the exploration of the technologies available in this field. In OWL, gUFO allows for the specification of both models and instances, the usage of reasoners and querying languages (e.g., SPARQL), integration with triple stores, and integration to other ontologies in the Semantic Web, for example. These gUFO/OWL concrete artifacts can contribute to semantic web related initiatives in finance (Bennett, 2013), as well as to the goal of transparency of financial data exchange according to FAIR principles[8] (Jacobsen et al., 2020). Intended users are those implementing UFO-based lightweight ontologies that reuse gUFO by specializing and instantiating its elements.

The objective of gUFO is to provide users with the key reusable concepts of UFO in a simple manner. gUFO can be directly imported in RDF/OWL based tools (such as Protégé[9] and TopBraid Composer[10]) and can be reused by specialization and instantiation of its elements. Reuse of gUFO consists in instantiating and/or specializing the various classes, object properties and data properties defined in the ontology, inheriting thus the domain-independent distinctions of UFO. This includes not only basic ontological distinctions (for example, objects vs. events) but also key reusable patterns (such as relationship reification through relators, quality reification, situation representation, among others).

For instance, the hierarchy of endurants captures specializations of endurant according to distinct ontological natures partitioning endurants into object (i.e., substantial), relator, mode, or quality (see figure 2.3). In order to define a class of endurants in a domain ontology identifying the ontological nature of its instances, the user must specify a rdfs:subClassOf statement towards one of the aforementioned specializations of endurant. For example, the Turtle fragment in listing 2.1 defines that Person and Student are classes of Objects (OntoUML model in figure 2.6), the former through direct specialization of Object and the latter through its indirect specialization via Person.

As for the hierarchy of endurant types, it captures specializations of EndurantType according to their modal properties (e.g., sortality and rigidity) partitioning them into

---

[7]The 'g' in gUFO stands for gentle. At the same time, "gufo" is the Italian word for "owl".
[8]The FAIR principles are intended as a guide to enable digital resources to become more Findable, Accessible, Interoperable and Reusable for machines and thus also for humans.
[9]https://protege.stanford.edu
[10]https://www.topquadrant.com/products/topbraid-composer/

Kind (i.e., ultimate sortals), SubKind, Role, Phase, Category, RoleMixin, PhaseMixin, or Mixin. In order to represent the modal properties of a class of endurants in a domain ontology, the user must specify a rdfs:type statement towards one of the aforementioned specializations of EndurantType. For example, in listing 2.2 the class Person represents an ultimate sortal and, thus, instantiates Kind with a rdf:type statement. Likewise, Student represents a role (i.e., an externally dependent anti-rigid sortal), as captured by the instantiation of Role.

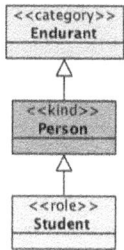

Figure 2.6: Example of classes specializing Endurant in UFO.

Listing 2.1: Example of classes specializing Endurant in gUFO-based UFO ontologies.
```
PREFIX gufo: <http://purl.org/nemo/gufo#>
PREFIX rdf: <http://www.w3.org/1999/02/22-rdf-syntax-ns#>
PREFIX rdfs: <http://www.w3.org/2000/01/rdf-schema#>

:Person rdfs:subClassOf gufo:Object .
:Student rdfs:subClassOf :Person .
```

Listing 2.2: Example of classes instantiating EndurantType in gUFO-based UFO ontologies.
```
PREFIX gufo: <http://purl.org/nemo/gufo#>
PREFIX rdf: <http://www.w3.org/1999/02/22-rdf-syntax-ns#>
PREFIX rdfs: <http://www.w3.org/2000/01/rdf-schema#>

:Person rdf:type gufo:Kind;
    rdfs:subClassOf gufo:Object .
:Student rdf:type gufo:Role;
    rdfs:subClassOf :Person .
```

For a detailed description and specification of gUFO, the reader is referred to (Almeida, Guizzardi, et al., 2020).

2.4 Final Considerations

Finance and economics are wide domains, in which ontologies are useful instruments for dealing with semantic interoperability and information integration problems, as well as improving communication and problem solving among people. In particular, reference ontologies have been widely recognized as powerful tools for representing a model of consensus within a community to support communication, meaning negotiation, consensus establishment, as well as semantic interoperability and information integration.

In domains like economics and finance, knowledge is diverse, interlinked and highly influenced by technology innovations. In such complex domains, representing its knowledge as a single ontology results in a large and rigid artifact, difficult to be managed. Conversely, representing each subdomain as a stand-alone ontology is a costly effort that leads to a very fragmented solution, equally hard to evolve and maintain. Therefore, for dealing with such rich scenarios, ontologies should relate to each other, forming a network of interlinked semantic resources, also known as an ontology network. Some benefits of ontology networks are: (i) knowledge is organized and structured and can be used as needed: whole or extracts of it; (ii) it is easier to reuse and extend; (iii) it is easier to figure out the "big picture" and at the same time have an understanding of each subdomain separately.

In chapter 3 we introduce OntoFINE, an Ontology Network in Finance and Economics that organizes and integrates knowledge in the realm on finance and economics, serving as a basis to several applications. As we shall see, OntoFine is grounded in the Unified Foundational Ontology and was built based on the literature review of the most relevant economic theories and considering recent innovations in the financial industry. We have experienced the benefits of ontology networks by using OntoFINE in applications in different areas, such as requirements engineering (chapter 7), decentralized finance (chapters 8 and 9), enterprise modeling (chapter 10), game theory (chapter 11) and ontological analysis (chapter 12).

Part III

ONTOLOGICAL FOUNDATIONS

Chapter 3

The Ontology Network in Finance and Economics

A central concern of this thesis is to provide solid ontological foundations for some intertwined concepts in finance and economics, namely those of money, trust, value, risk and economic exchanges, to support the different actors in the financial industry to properly understand the evolution of the economy before recent innovations in the financial industry (see figure 1.1 in chapter 1).

We address this problem by proposing the creation of an integrated ontological framework, with initial focus on the domains of money, trust, value, risk and economic exchanges. In this chapter, we introduce our proposal, the Ontology Network in Finance and Economics (OntoFINE), which aims at supporting communication, meaning negotiation, consensus establishment, as well as semantic interoperability and information integration in the financial industry. Furthermore, we demonstrate the benefits and usefulness of OntoFINE, by providing an overview of diverse applications of the ontology network, in different areas, in the context of finance and economics.

The construction of the building blocks that compose OntoFINE is presented in Part III of this thesis (chapters 3 to 6), while its applications in different scenarios are presented in Part IV (chapters 7 to 12). In this chapter, we start by introducing OntoFINE in section 3.1. In section 3.2, we present the Common Ontology of Value and Risk, which is one of OntoFINE's networked ontologies. Next, in section 3.3, we present an overview of the application scenarios where OntoFINE is used to solve practical problems. We discuss existing work on ontology networks in finance and economics in section 3.4 and conclude the chapter in section 3.5.

© The Author(s), under exclusive license to Springer Nature Switzerland AG 2025
G. C. Moura Amaral, *An Ontology Network in Finance and Economics*, LNBIP 532, 2025.
https://doi.org/10.1007/978-3-031-71082-7_3

3.1 The Ontology Network in Finance and Economics

OntoFINE aims at providing a solid ontological foundation on finance and economics. As previously mentioned, in this thesis, we are focusing on the domains of money, trust, value, risk and economic exchanges. OntoFINE was designed to continuously evolve, thus allowing that ontologies covering additional domains in finance and economics be incrementally added and integrated to it. Nevertheless, the development of ontologies regarding domains other than the ones just mentioned (namely, money, trust, value, risk and economic exchanges) and their integration to OntoFINE fall outside the scope of this thesis.

OntoFINE rises with three main premises: (i) being based on a well-founded grounding for ontology development; (ii) offering mechanisms to easy build and integrate new subdomain ontologies to the network; and (iii) promoting integration by keeping a consistent semantics for concepts and relations along the whole network.

Regarding the intended application, our main goal is to develop ontologies in the sense of reference conceptual models, which are meant to primarily support humans in tasks such as conceptual clarification, meaning negotiation and consensus establishment (Guizzardi, 2007). Furthermore, as discussed in chapter 2 , it is also our objective to enable the implementation of lightweight ontologies supported by efficient computational algorithms (e.g., OWL-DL, RDF, Alloy), to satisfy the need for computational tractability.

As previously mentioned, the ontology representation language of choice in this thesis is OntoUML, a version of UML class diagrams that has been designed such that its modeling primitives reflect the ontological distinctions put forth by UFO (described in detain in section 2.3), and its grammatical constraints follow UFO axiomatization. Our motivation for choosing OntoUML is twofold. Firstly, because of its expressivity. As argued in (Guizzardi, 2007), reference conceptual models in the sense that we are proposing here should be represented using a language that commits to a rich foundational ontology, so that one can create strongly axiomatized ontologies that approximate as well as possible to the ideal ontology of the domain. Research shows that UFO and OntoUML provide enough constructs to accurately describe complex social domains, while supporting the clarification and disambiguation of overloaded terms. Examples include ontologies for services (Nardi et al., 2013), legal relations (Griffo, Almeida, and Guizzardi, 2018), resources and capabilities (Azevedo, C.L.B. et al., 2015), organizational structures (Santos Jr et al., 2010), accounting (Blums and Weigand, 2016;

3.1. The Ontology Network in Finance and Economics

Fischer-Pauzenberger and Schwaiger, 2017), decision making (Guizzardi, Carneiro, et al., 2020), smart contracts (Sharifi et al., 2020), digital platforms (Derave et al., 2021), competition (Sales, Almeida, et al., 2018), value and risk (Sales, Baião, et al., 2018). Secondly, as presented in section 2.3, OntoUML provides such a complete ecosystem of technologies and in a way that is familiar to data modelers, which include libraries of patterns and anti-patterns (Guizzardi, Graças, et al., 2011; Sales and Guizzardi, 2015), automated model diagnosis and repair via learning (Fumagalli et al., 2020), and computational tools for model creation, verification, validation, verbalization, codification, and database generation (Almeida, Guizzardi, et al., 2020; Barcelos et al., 2013; Benevides, Guizzardi, et al., 2010; Guidoni et al., 2021; Rybola and Pergl, 2016). Furthermore, by choosing OntoUML as a modeling language, we follow a foundational approach for ontology representation. In this type of approach, domain concepts are defined in terms of broader concepts specified in a foundational ontology, either by specializing or instantiating them. It has been demonstrated in the literature that grounding a domain ontology in a foundational has a number of advantages (Arp et al., 2015; Guizzardi, 2006a; Guizzardi, Baião, et al., 2010; Guizzardi, Falbo, et al., 2008a; Keet, 2011; Schulz, 2018), including increase in quality, precision and expressiveness. One particularly important advantage is that it provides a conceptual basis from where to start the domain analysis. For instance, when developing an ontology about wedding, one can reuse the notion of event to define a wedding ceremony, and that of an endurant to define a church. In addition to these generic concepts, foundational ontologies define a number of meta-properties one can go through to investigate the ontological nature of a domain concept, such as rigidity and dependency. For instance, the concept of wife is anti-rigid, as it only contingently characterizes its instances — a person can become someone's wife given a relational context and can cease to be so while maintaining her identity.

As aforementioned, domains such as economics and finance are too large and complex to be represented as a single, large and monolithic ontology. Therefore, in this thesis, we propose the creation of OntoFINE as an ontological framework, built incrementally and in an integrated way, as a network. Having this in mind, OntoFINE architecture is organized considering three ontology generality levels[1] (figure 3.1):

Foundational Layer: The Unified Foundational Ontology lies in the foundational layer, providing the common grounding for all the networked ontologies. UFO's ontological distinctions are used for classifying OntoFINE concepts, e.g., as objects, events, commitments, agents, roles, goals and so on. In chapter 2, we presented a subset of UFO's

---
[1] More details on ontologies generality levels are given in section 2.1.1

ontological distinctions that are relevant for this thesis. For a fuller discussion on this ontology, the reader should refer to (Guizzardi, 2005; Guizzardi, Wagner, Almeida, et al., 2015).

Core Layer. In the center of the ontology network, core reference ontologies are used to represent the general domain knowledge, being the basis for the subdomain networked ontologies. In its current version, OntoFINE includes four core reference ontologies, focusing on the subdomains that are addressed this thesis, namely, trust, money, economic exchanges, value and risk. These core ontologies are briefly described below.

- **The Common Ontology of Value and Risk (COVER).**

    COVER is a well-founded ontology, specified in OntoUML, which makes the deep connections between the concepts of value and risk explicit (Sales, Baião, et al., 2018). It is grounded on several theories from marketing, service science, strategy and risk management. COVER characterizes and integrates different perspectives of value and risk. It proposes an ontological analysis of notions such as value, risk, risk event (threat event, loss event) and vulnerability, among others. Section 3.2 presents an overview of this ontology, by describing the COVER concepts that are relevant for this thesis. The reader interested in an in-depth description of the complete version of COVER is referred to (Sales, Baião, et al., 2018).

    COVER was integrated to OntoFINE by following the guidelines provided by the customized version of the NeOn methodology (Suárez-Figueroa et al., 2012) for building ontology networks, defined for this thesis, which is decribed in section 1.3.2. More specifically, we followed the activities defined in *Scenario 2*, which proposes the reuse of ontological resources.

- **The Reference Ontology of Trust (ROT).**

    ROT is a UFO-based ontology that formally characterizes the concept of trust, clarifies the relation between trust and risk, and represents how risk emerges from trust relations (Amaral, Sales, and Guizzardi, 2021b; 2022; Amaral, Sales, Guizzardi, and Porello, 2019). It also provides a deep account of the different factors that can influence trust, such as mental biases, trustworthy behavior indications provided by the trustee and pieces of evidence that suggest a trustee should be trusted. In its definition, ROT reuses concepts on the nature of risk from COVER. It was developed and integrated to OntoFINE by following the activities defined in *Scenario 3* of the customized version of NeOn (see section 1.3.2 of chapter 1), which proposes the reuse and re-engineering of ontological resources. *Scenario*

3.1. The Ontology Network in Finance and Economics   55

3 was chosen because some of the COVER entities that were reused had to be adapted to serve the intended purposes of ROT.

The development of ROT is within the scope of this thesis. The complete version of this ontology is presented in chapter 4.

– **The Reference Ontology of Money and Virtual Currencies (ROME).**

ROME is a reference model, grounded on the UFO, that formalizes the characterization of money, currency and virtual currencies, as well as its embedded concepts and relations (Amaral, Sales, and Guizzardi, 2021d; Amaral, Sales, Guizzardi, and Porello, 2020a; Amaral, Sales, Guizzardi, Porello, and Guarino, 2020). In its definition, ROME reuses concepts on the nature of trust from ROT. Therefore, it was developed and integrated to OntoFINE by following the activities defined in *Scenario 2* of the customized version of NeOn (see section 1.3.2 of chapter 1), which proposes the reuse of ontological resources.

The development of ROME is within the scope of this thesis. The complete version of this ontology is presented in chapter 5.

– **The Core Ontology for Economic Exchanges (COEX).**

COEX is a well-founded reference ontology, specified in OntoUML, that formally characterizes the concept of economic exchanges based on the Action Theory of Economic Exchanges (Massin and Tieffenbach, 2016; Porello, Guizzardi, Sales, and Amaral, 2020). In this theory, an economic exchange is based on an agreement in which agents commit to performing certain reciprocal actions. In its definition, COEX reuses concepts on the nature of value ascription from COVER. It was developed and integrated to OntoFINE by following the activities defined in *Scenario 3* of the customized version of NeOn (see section 1.3.2 of chapter 1), which proposes the reuse and re-engineering of ontological resources. *Scenario 3* was chosen because some of the COVER entities that were reused had to be adapted to serve the intended purposes of COEX.

The development of COEX is within the scope of this thesis. The complete version of this ontology is presented in chapter 6.

Domain-specific Layer. Over the foundational and core layers, OntoFINE places the domain ontologies. Each networked ontology is grounded in one or more core reference ontologies of the core layer and also in UFO, and encompasses a subdomain of

OntoFINE. Currently, this layer contains the Reference Ontology of Trustworthines Requirements (ROTwR) (Amaral, Guizzardi, Guizzardi, et al., 2020), a reference domain ontology grounded on UFO, and based on the trust-related concepts defined in ROT. In ROTwR, trustworthiness requirements are defined as non-functional requirements, where the desired states-of-affairs are stakeholder mental states that include an attitude of trust towards the system-to-be. Trustworthiness requirements are related to an intention that is part of a trust relation between a stakeholder (the trustor) and the system-to-be (the trustee). According ROTwR, the system can emit trust-warranting signals to ensure trustworthy behavior. For example, information about how privacy and security measures are implemented could be provided as signals of the trustworthiness of a system.

ROTwR reuses concepts from ROT and COVER and was created within the scope of this thesis, as an application of ROT in the context of requirements engineering (see chapter 7). It was developed and integrated to OntoFINE by following the activities defined in *Scenario 3* of the customized version of NeOn (see section 1.3.2 of chapter 1), which proposes the reuse and re-engineering of ontological resources. The complete version of ROTwR is presented in chapter 7.

Figure 3.1 shows the current status of OntoFINE. Each circle represents an ontology. Arrowed lines denote dependencies between networked ontologies.

It is important to notice that, even adopting a layered architecture, OntoFINE is a network and each new added node contributes for the whole network. When a new ontology is added, it should reuse existing elements (from a higher or the same layer). Other ontologies, in turn, may be adapted to keep consistency and share the same semantics along the whole network. Even the core ontologies can evolve to adapt or incorporate new concepts or relations discovered when domain ontologies are created or integrated.

OntoFINE specification is available at purl.org/krdb-core/ontofine, where machine processable lightweight versions of the ontologies implemented in gUFO/OWL are also available.

3.1. The Ontology Network in Finance and Economics

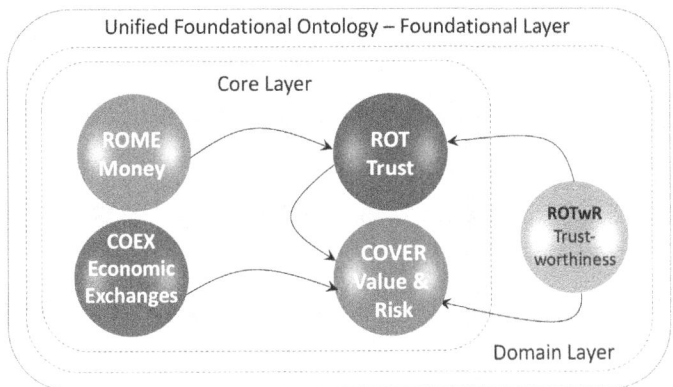

Figure 3.1: OntoFINE: the network view.

3.2 COVER: Common Ontology of Value and Risk

The Common Ontology of Value and Risk (COVER) (Sales, Baião, et al., 2018) is a well-founded ontology that makes the deep connections between the concepts of value and risk explicit. COVER is grounded on several theories from marketing, service science, strategy and risk management. It is specified in OntoUML (Guizzardi, 2005).

COVER proposes an ontological analysis of notions such as *value*, *risk*, *risk event* (*threat event*, *loss event*) and *vulnerability*, among others. This ontology characterizes and integrates different perspectives of value and risk.

COVER makes the following ontological commitments on the nature of value:

— Value emerges from impacts on goals. Value emerges from events that affect the degree of satisfaction of one or more goals of an agent.
— Value is relative. The same object or experience may be valuable to a person and of no value to another.
— Value is experiential. Even though value can be ascribed to objects, it is ultimately grounded on experiences. For instance, in order to explain the value of a smartphone, one must refer to the experiences enabled by it.
— Value is contextual. The value of an object can vary depending on the context in which it is used.

As for risk, COVER makes the following ontological commitments:

- Risk is relative. This means that an event might be simultaneously considered as a risk by one agent and not as a risk by another (it may even be considered as an opportunity by such an agent).
- A risk is perceived according to its impact on goals, i.e. in order to talk about risk, one needs to account for which goals are "at stake".
- Risk is experiential. This means that we ultimately ascribe risk to events, not objects.
- Risk is contextual. Thus, the risk an object is exposed to may vary even if all its intrinsic properties (e.g. its vulnerabilities) are the same.
- Risk is grounded on uncertainty about events and their outcomes.

Given the objectives of this thesis, we focus here on the perspective of value and risk as a chain of events that impacts an agent's goals, which the authors named Value Experience and Risk Experience, respectively.

COVER breaks down Value Experiences into "smaller" events, dubbed Value Events. These are classified into Impact and Trigger Events. The former are those that directly impact a goal or bring about a situation (named Impactful Outcome) that impacts a goal. On contrast, Trigger Events are simply parts of an experience that are identified as causing Impact Events, directly or indirectly. To formalize goals, COVER reuses the concept of Intention from UFO (Guizzardi, 2005), as a type of mental state that describes a class of state-of-affairs that an Agent is committed to bring about. Note that, since agents in UFO's view includes both physical and social agents, COVER is able to represent value being ascribed from the perspective of a customer and an employee, but also from that of a business unit or even a whole enterprise.

Risk Experiences focus on unwanted events that have the potential of causing losses and are composed by events of two types, namely Threat and Loss Events. A Threat Event is the one with the potential of causing a loss, which might be intentional or unintentional. A Threat Event might be the manifestation of a Vulnerability (a special type of disposition whose manifestation constitutes a loss or can potentially cause a loss from the perspective of a stakeholder). The second mandatory component of a Risk Experience is a Loss Event, which necessarily impact intentions in a negative way (captured by a hurts relation between Loss Event and Intention).

Figures 3.2 and 3.3 depict two COVER diagrams in OntoUML, which captures part of the aforementioned ontological notions.

3.2. COVER: Common Ontology of Value and Risk

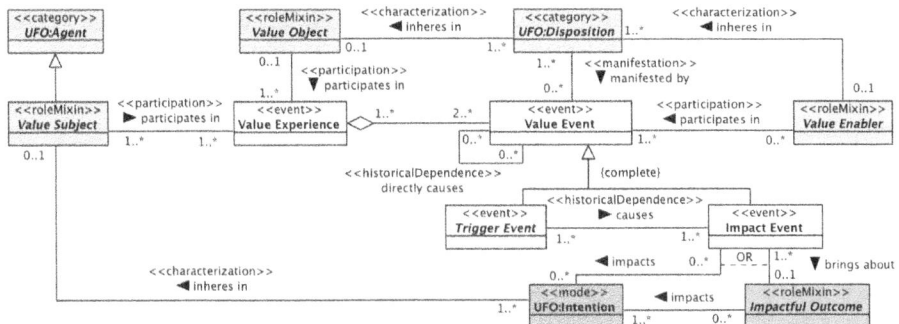

Figure 3.2: COVER fragment on value experiences (Sales, Baião, et al., 2018).

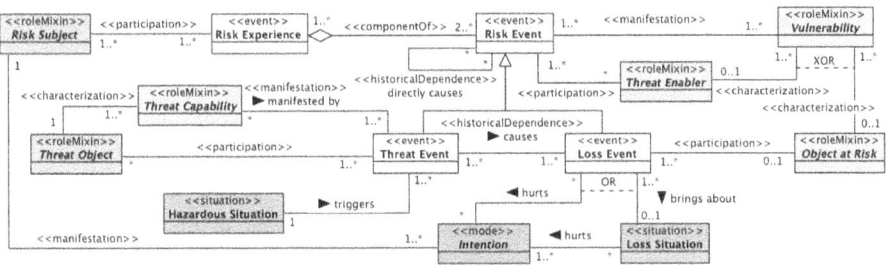

Figure 3.3: COVER fragment on risk experiences (Sales, Baião, et al., 2018).

3.3 OntoFINE Applications

As aforementioned, in this thesis we adopt a research strategy inspired in the combination of "theory and practice" as way of achieving our objectives. In this direction, we use the theoretical foundations provided by OntoFINE for solving practical problems in economics and finance. This strategy also allows us to apply the so-called *application-based approach to ontology evaluation* (Brank et al., 2005), which proposes the evaluation of ontologies when they are put in practice. In order to validate and demonstrate the relevance of OntoFINE, we applied it in several initiatives, conducted in different areas, in the context of economics and finance, namely, requirements engineering (chapter 7), decentralized finance (chapters 8 and 9), enterprise modeling (chapter 10), game theory (chapter 11) and ontological analysis (chapter 12). In the following, we discuss why these application domains were chosen.

Decentralized Finance (DeFi) (see chapters 8 and 9). As mentioned in chapter 1, one of the main objectives of OntoFINE is to provide ontological foundations in finance and economics to fill the conceptual gap between the traditional finance and the decentralized finance paradigms. Therefore, it is paramount to show its relevance and evaluate if it properly addresses issues that have arisen in the decentralized context, such as decentralized exchanges and new forms of digital money and payment instruments. As aforementioned, decentralized exchanges organize digital assets exchanges through blockchain smart contracts, without the need for a centralized trusted intermediary. This creates new forms of trust, such as trust in the computer code, and trust that the blockchain decentralized computer network will continue to enforce the code. These new variations of trust then coexist with earlier forms, such as trust in the (digital) currency used to make transactions, trust in the institutions that ensure the safety and integrity of the financial system, and ultimately, trust in the legal system to enforce contracts, laws, and regulations.

Requirements Engineering (see chapter 7). The advent of recent innovations in the finance industry like the above-mentioned (see figure 1.1) has broadened the scope of requirements engineering, which must now deal with new classes of challenging requirements, such as trustworthiness, fairness, ethics and privacy. In this context, a major challenge for RE is to propose concepts, tools and techniques that support requirements engineering activities for incorporating this kind of complex requirement. In this sense, OntoFINE can help by "semantically unpacking" concepts such as trustworthiness or ethics where the analysts may struggle in understanding, for example, which requirements can make the system under development trustworthy or ethical. For this reason, we consider the RE field a relevant application scenario for both validate OntoFINE and demonstrate its usefulness.

Enterprise Modeling (see chapter 10). Enterprise modeling plays a key role in addressing the need to align strategic decisions with their actual implementation at the level of processes, information technology systems and infrastructure. Currently, in the financial industry, a main challenge for incorporating notions related to high-level societal concerns and goals — such as trust and ethics — in enterprise architecture lies in identifying a precise conceptualization for these notions. Without such a precise conceptualization, rigorous definition of the semantics of the proposed modeling elements is problematic, and modeling and communication problems arise. OntoFINE constitutes a powerful tool to address this issue, as it provides adequate real-world and formal

3.3. OntoFINE Applications

semantics for concepts in the domain of finance and economics. This led us to consider enterprise modeling an appropriate scenario for applying the ontology network in practice. For example, in the case of trust, the modeling of this concept in the context of enterprise architecture enables to bridge the gap between the stakeholders' trust concerns and the processes and other elements of the architecture that are needed to achieve the organization's goal of being trustworthy.

Game Theory (see chapter 11). Game theory has become an important field of study and has been employed by practitioners of different disciplines, including economics and finance. Game theory is largely about interactions of agents whose decisions affect each other. The combination of agents' actions corresponds to outcomes, which may impact agents' goals, either positively or negatively. The analysis of the probable consequences and expected utilities of all possible outcomes is fundamental to support agents when deciding whether to engage in a certain strategy. The results of outcomes, represented by payoffs, may create value for agents as they can positively impact their goals, but they also entail some risk, as they can negatively impact an agent's goal. The relation between value and risk is the very focus of the Common Ontology of Value and Risk, which led us to consider game theory an interesting application area for our ontology network.

Ontological Analysis (see chapter 12). Ontological analysis enables a deep account of the meaning of a particular domain. The idea behind ontological analysis is to provide a sound foundation for modelling concepts, if assumed that such concepts are aimed at representing reality (Fettke and Loos, 2003). Several efforts have shown the benefits of ontological analysis (Rosemann et al., 2004; Shanks et al., 2003), which includes the rigorous definition of models, in terms of real-world semantics and the identification of problems in the definition, interpretation or usage of concepts. The reference ontologies proposed in this thesis play an important role in this scenario, by providing a frame of reference, i.e., to serve as conceptual tools for mastering the complexity and harmonizing possibly heterogeneous viewpoints and terminologies regarding the domains of finance and economics. They can serve a variety of purposes, such as to support the representation and analysis of complex problems, to make useful connections with different types of information, and to facilitate communication between stakeholders. This led us to consider ontological analysis an appropriate application scenario for OntoFINE.

Figure 3.4 depicts an overview of the different applications of OntoFINE, conducted within the scope of this thesis, which are briefly described below.

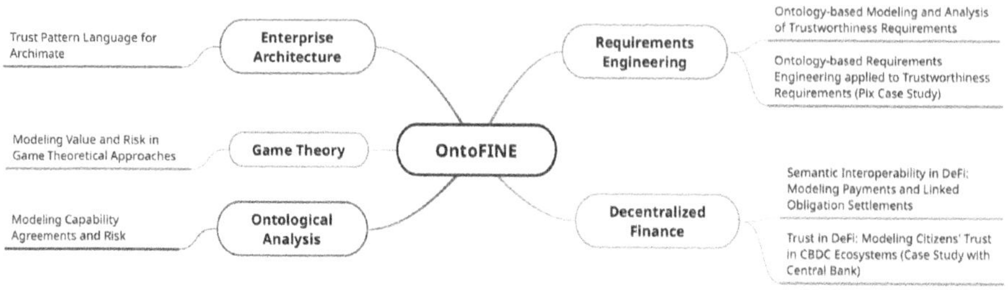

Figure 3.4: OntoFINE applications.

Requirements Engineering (see chapter 7). We propose a novel methodology for ontology-based requirements engineering, which applies ROT in a case illustration (Amaral, Guizzardi, Guizzardi, et al., 2020). In this work, we rely on ROT to define the class of trustworthiness requirements for software systems and their relation to concepts such as trust, capability, vulnerability and risk, among others. Then, in a second initiative, we conducted a real case study (Amaral, Guizzardi, Guizzardi, et al., 2021) to verify if ROT is capable of properly representing real world situations. In this study, ROT was applied to help with the elicitation of trustworthiness requirements of software systems by analyzing the case of Pix, the Brazilian Instant Payments Ecosystem created and managed by the Central Bank of Brazil.

Decentralized Finance (DeFi) (see chapters 8 and 9). In chapter 8, we conduct a real case study in collaboration with a national central bank (Amaral, Sales, and Guizzardi, 2022), in which we apply both ROME and ROT to support the modeling and analysis of citizens' trust in CBDC ecosystems. In chapter 9, we discuss how semantic interoperability can be addressed in the context of DeFi by proposing and ontology-based approach for the modeling of payments and linked obligation settlement mechanisms (Amaral, Sales, and Guizzardi, 2021a), aiming at providing conceptual clarification and supporting semantic interoperability in decentralized finance ecosystems. Firstly, we create two domain-related ontology patterns by reusing pieces of knowledge extracted from COEX and ROME. Then, we systematically apply these patterns to model payments and linked obligations in OntoUML. Finally, we export the models to OWL using gUFO.

Enterprise Modeling (see chapter 10). Driven by the need to align the vision and strate-

3.3. OntoFINE Applications

gic goals of enterprises with their business architectures, we specify a pattern language for trust modeling in ArchiMate (Amaral, Sales, Guizzardi, Almeida, et al., 2020), based on ROT and COVER, which can be used to model trust in the context of Enterprise Architecture (EA). The advantage of a pattern language (Buschmann et al., 2007) is that it offers a context in which related patterns can be combined, thus, reducing the space of design choices and design constraints (Falbo et al., 2016). In ROT, trust is modeled as a complex mental state of a trustor, composed of a set of beliefs about a trustee and her behavior. In the specification of the trust pattern language, we focus on the modeling and on the assessment of the beliefs that compose trust relations, in order to identify potential risks that can emerge from these relations. These models can be used, for example, in risk management to address the gap between trust concerns and the components that integrate the different layers of the enterprise architecture.

Game Theory (see chapter 11). We conduct an ontological analysis characterizing some basic concepts in game theory, which make clear the emergence of value and risks from game outcomes (Amaral, Porello, et al., 2020). We make use of the concepts and relations defined in COVER to analyze the payoffs of a game in terms of value and risk, as well as how they emerge from outcomes in game theory. We formalize our analysis by means of an ontologically well-founded model, specified in OntoUML. In addition, we apply these results to represent the emergence of value and risk from game outcomes in enterprise architecture models in ArchiMate.

Ontological Analysis (see chapter 12). In this initiative, COVER is used to analyze the emergence of value and risk from delegation relations, in capability agreements (Amaral, Guizzardi, Guarino, et al., 2019; Amaral, Sales, Guizzardi, and Porello, 2019). Briefly speaking, the decision to delegate may create value, as the focal agent is endowed with new capabilities, but also implies some risk, as it becomes dependent on the partner agent, and consequently, more vulnerable. Having a clear understanding of the influence of these forces over delegation networks is fundamental both for the management of risks and for the awareness of the value created through the complex network of interdependencies.

Table 3.1 relates the above-mentioned initiatives to their respective types of application.

Table 3.1: OntoFINE applications by type.

APPLICATION		ARTIF	TYPE
Requirements Engineering	Ontology-based modeling and analysis of trustworthiness requirements	ROT	Demonstration
	Ontology-based requirements engineering applied to trustworthiness requirements	ROT	Demonstration and Validation (Pix Case Study)
Decentralized Finance	Modeling citizen's trust in CBDC ecosystems	ROT ROME	Demonstration and Validation (CBDC Case Study)
	Modeling payments and linked obligation settlements	ROME COEX	Demonstration
Enterprise Modeling	Trust pattern language for ArchiMate	ROT	Demonstration and Validation (Lancet Case Study)
Game Theory	Modeling value and risk in game theoretical approaches	COVER	Demonstration
Ontological Analysis	Modeling capability agreements and risk	COVER	Demonstration

3.4 Related Work

There exists in the literature several initiatives aiming at the creation of an unified view of the reality related to finance and economics. In this section, we present some approaches that involve the use of interlinked ontologies and discuss how they are related to our research.

3.4.1 The Financial Industry Business Ontology (FIBO)

The Financial Industry Business Ontology (FIBO) (Enterprise Data Management Council, 2015) is a set of formal models that aims at defining unambiguous shared meaning for financial industry concepts (Bennett, 2013). FIBO proposes to be a representation of *things* of interest for financial business applications and how they relate to one another (Enterprise Data Management Council, 2015). It is developed as a set of ontologies specified using the Web Ontology Language (OWL) and, in general, can be seen as a kind of ontology network.

FIBO is organized in six domains, namely *Business Entities*, *Business Process*, *Corporate Actions and Events*, *Derivatives*, *Financial Business and Commerce*, *Foundations*, *Indices and Indicators*, *Loans*, *Market Data* and *Securities*. Each domain includes one or more specific subdomains, as well as several ontologies at the bottom level. In the sequel we present a brief description of these domains.

- **Business Entities.** Defines a range of business and legal entities that are considered by financial industry firms, regulators and other industry participants to be of relevance in the financial services domain, such as corporations, legal entities, government entities, partnerships, among others.
- **Business Process.** Includes ontologies that define financial process flows such as securities issuance and transaction workflows.
- **Corporate Actions and Events.** Covers events and actions that may occur during the life of a security, ranging from announcements regarding stock offerings, splits, dividends and so forth, as well as more general business events that are relevant to investors and regulators alike.
- **Derivatives.** Includes concepts that are common to derivative instruments, including but not limited to options, futures, forwards, swaps, and a wide range of other derivatives.

- **Financial Business and Commerce.** Defines business concepts that are common to a number of finance areas, such as loans, securities, and corporate actions, including products and services, financial intermediaries, regulators, and financial instruments and products.

- **Foundations.** Includes ontologies that define general purpose concepts required to support other FIBO domains, such as concepts and relationships about people, organizations, places, and contracts. The scope of the definitions provided in this domain is limited to coverage of exactly those concepts needed by other FIBO specifications. In particular, it is worth mentioning some ontologies included in this domain, due to their relevance to the work developed in this thesis. The first one is the *Agreements Ontology*, under the *Agreements* subdomain, which defines actual agreements between parties. The Agreements Ontology is connected to the *Products and Services Ontology* and to the *Payments and Schedules Ontologies*, both under the domain *Products and Services* and is related to the notion of economic exchanges. Another relevant ontology, related to the notion of money, is the *Currency Amount Ontology*, which is part of the FIBO *Accounting* subdomain. FIBO's Currency Amount Ontology defines currency and monetary amount related concepts, which are used to define other FIBO ontology elements. The ontology defines two distinct kinds of concepts that correspond to money and amounts: a concrete, actual amount of money, and the monetary measure of something denominated in some currency. Whereas "money amount" is defined as an amount of money, "monetary amount" is an abstract monetary measure. The definition of currency provided in this ontology is compliant with the definitions given in ISO4217 (ISO, 2015).

- **Indices and Indicators.** Defines market indices and reference rates including economic indicators, foreign exchange, interest rates, and other benchmarks.

- **Loans.** Provides a model of concepts that are common to loan contracts in various market categories including but not limited to commercial, small business, automobile, education and mortgage.

- **Market Data.** Contains ontologies that represent temporally variant concepts for financial instruments, loans and funds. It covers concepts represented in market data, such as prices, yields and analytics for debt and for pools of assets.

- **Securities.** Provides a model of concepts that are common to financial instruments that are also securities, including but not limited to exchange-traded securities and

3.4. Related Work

funds.

Although it is quite comprehensive, FIBO was created in light of the traditional finance paradigm and does not address issues that have emerged with the introduction of decentralized technologies and other recent innovations. These new developments, such as cryptocurrencies, blockchains and distributed ledger technologies, smart contracts (Schär, 2021), programmable money (Arner, Auer, et al., 2020), stablecoins (Arner, Auer, et al., 2020), and central bank digital currencies (Amaral, Sales, and Guizzardi, 2021d), involve new forms of trust, money, payment instruments and innovative forms of digital exchanges (tokenization of assets, smart contracts, programmable money, decentralized exchanges, etc). OntoFINE addresses these issues by providing sound ontological accounts on trust, money, economic exchanges as well as about the emergence of value and risk in this new scenario. For example, concepts related to digital currencies and cryptocurrencies are not present in FIBO. Furthermore, different from OntoFINE that includes a well-founded ontology on trust, FIBO does not explore the notion of trust, neither does it describe the fundamental role of trust as the bedrock for money and for the proper functioning of the whole financial system.

In fact, it is possible to state that FIBO and OntoFINE (in its current version) are complementary rather than mutually exclusive, as OntoFINE's networked ontologies were conceived aiming at filling the gap created with the advent of recent innovations, which is not addressed by FIBO. Although the integration of OntoFINE and FIBO falls outside the scope of this work, we believe that the integration of these ontology networks, in the future, is very promising.

Regarding their generality level, FIBO's ontologies can be classified either as core or as domain ontologies. For example, the *Currency Amount Ontology* is an example of core ontology, as it crosscuts several other subdomains. The *Financial Instruments Ontology*, under the *Financial Business and Commerce* domain, and the *European Government Entities and Jurisdictions Ontology*, under the *Derivatives* domain, are examples of FIBO's domains ontologies. However, different from our approach that proposes the use of UFO as conceptual foundation for building the networked core and domain ontologies, and OntoUML as the representation languange, FIBO's ontologies are specified in OWL and are not grounded on a foundational ontology, such as UFO (Guizzardi, 2005), GFO (Herre, 2010) or DOLCE (Borgo and Masolo, 2009). In (Guizzardi, 2006a), the author shows how a modeling language based on a foundational ontology can be used to address a number of semantic interoperability problems that cannot be handled by semantic web languages, such as OWL and RDF, nor by most other languages used for conceptual modeling (in general) and ontology representation (in particular), such as UML, ER and LINGO (Guizzardi, 2006a).

Finally, FIBO is developed and hosted by the Enterprise Data Management Council (EDMC) and is published in a number of formats for operational use and business definitions. It is also standardized through the Object Management Group (OMG). As previously mentioned, it was initially developed as a set of ontologies in OWL. To bridge the gap between semantic (ontologists) and conventional data management (data architects), the FIBO development team created the FIBO Data Model (FIB-DM), a complete transformation of FIBO into a conceptual data model, which derives FIB-DM entities from FIBO classes, associative entities from object properties, relationships from the domain, range, and class restrictions, and attributes from data properties. Similarly, to bridge the gap between data architects and business users and analysts, the FIBO team created the FIBO Conceptual Map (FIB-CM), a conceptual map with standardized icons for concepts and an agreed vocabulary for labels, which establish a direct correspondence between the map (FIB-CM) and the data model (FIB-DM). Comparing FIBO's development with our approach, we can observe that as OntoFINE is specified in OntoUML — a language that commits to a rich foundational ontology (UFO) thus allowing the creation of strongly axiomatized ontologies that approximate as well as possible to the ideal ontology of the domain (see section 2.3) — it is more expressive than FIBO, which is specified in OWL, a representation language for building lightweight ontologies. The problem of FIBO's approach is that OWL expressiveness is more focused on computational aspects, thus not being an appropriate form to present information for humans. Therefore, although this language provides the modeler with mechanisms for building conceptual structures, it offers no support neither for helping the modeler on choosing a particular structure to model elements of the subject domain nor for justifying the choice of a particular structure over another. Therefore, much of important domain knowledge is either lost in the OWL-DL[2] codification or remains tacit in the minds of the domain experts. Moreover, as presented in section 2.3, ontologies developed in OntoUML can be represented in OWL by making use of gUFO, a lightweight implementation of UFO that allows the representation of UFO's concepts in OWL, with the limitations imposed by the expressiveness of this language.

---

[2]Description Logic-based Web Ontology Language (https://www.w3.org/TR/owl-features/)

3.4. Related Work

3.4.2 The Financial Industry Regulatory Ontology (FIRO)

The Financial Industry Regulatory Ontology (FIRO) (Espinoza et al., 2014) is an ontology model composed of relevant and interlinked ontologies in the financial industry regulatory domain. FIRO captures regulatory vocabularies, compliance imperatives and rules into the OWL-DL codification. Basically, the objective of FIRO is to enable efficient access and smarter consumption of the wide and complex spectrum of legislation and regulatory rules governing the financial industry globally. The FIRO model is composed by the following ontologies:

- **FIRO-H.** Describes the high-level concepts and their relationships, based on the financial industry regulatory initiatives. Includes concepts, such as Obligation, Prohibition, Exemption or Sanction.
- **FIRO-S.** Models the general structure of a parliamentary, legislative and judiciary document.
- **FIRO-[Domain].** Describes the concepts and their relationships for domain-dependent regulations (e.g., FIRO-AML for the Anti-Money Laundering regulation).
- **FIRO-Op[Purpose].** This ontology merges all the three previous ones, in order to support a particular purpose and task in the regulatory change management process.

The FIRO model differs from our work in relation to the scope of the financial domain represented, as it is focused on the legislation and regulation domains and does not address the notions of money, trust, value, risk and economic exchanges.

3.4.3 The Financial Regulation Ontology (FRO)

The Financial Regulation Ontology (FRO) (Ziemer, n.d.) is a set of linked ontologies, specified in OWL, which aims at implementing "semantic compliance" in the financial industry. Regulatory compliance combines the domains of legal and finance. Therefore, FRO imports the FIBO (Enterprise Data Management Council, 2015) and the Legal Knowledge Interchange Format (Hoekstra et al., 2007), which represent information in the finance and in the legal domain, respectively. In addition, FRO integrates three operational ontologies, namely: the Bank Regulation Ontology, the Fund Regulation

Ontology, the Hedge Fund Regulation Ontology and the Insurance Regulation Ontology. Although the purpose of FRO is related to OntoFINE, it has a different objective, focusing on regulatory compliance aspects.

3.5 Final Considerations

This chapter has described the Ontology Network in Finance and Economics, along with an overview of how it has been applied in different areas, such as requirements engineering, decentralized finance, enterprise modeling, game theory and ontological analysis.

In its current version, OntoFINE includes core ontologies on money, trust, value, risk and economic exchanges, as well as a domain ontology on trustworthiness requirements, which results from an application of OntoFINE in requirements engineering. Being an ontology network, OntoFINE is is constantly evolving. In the future, other ontologies on complementary subdomains in economics and finance should be developed and/or integrated to OntoFINE to enlarge its coverage.

As aforementioned, one possibility would be integrate FIBO to OntoFINE, as the latter provides an ontological account of the concepts of money, trust, value and economic exchanges in the light of the recent innovations in the finance industry, which are missing in FIBO. In its turn, FIBO provides a comprehensive set of ontologies in finance, which could be revisited and grounded in UFO, thus improving their expressivity.

The development and integration of ontologies regarding domains other than money, trust, value, risk and economic exchanges, as well as FIBO's integration to OntoFINE is beyond the scope of this thesis.

In this chapter we also presented the Common Ontology of Value and Risk (Sales, Baião, et al., 2018), one of OnotoFINE's core ontologies. In chapters 4 to 6 we present the other core ontologies that are part of OntoFINE's core layer, respectively, the Reference Ontology of Trust, the Reference Ontology of Money and Virtual Currencies and the Core Ontology for Economic Exchanges. The Reference Ontology of Trustworthiness Requirements, which is at OntoFINE's domain layer, is presented in chapter 7.

Finally, in chapters 7 to 12, we present the different applications of OntoFINE, respectively in the areas of requirements engineering, decentralized finance, enterprise modeling, game theory and ontological analysis.

Chapter 4

The Reference Ontology of Trust

This chapter presents the Reference Ontology of Trust[1] (ROT), a UFO-based ontology, specified in OntoUML (Guizzardi, 2005; Guizzardi, Fonseca, Almeida, et al., 2021), that formally characterizes the concept of trust, clarifies the relation between trust and risk, and represents how risk emerges from trust relations (Amaral, Sales, and Guizzardi, 2021b; 2022; Amaral, Sales, Guizzardi, and Porello, 2019). ROT also provides a deep account of the different factors that can influence trust, such as mental biases, trustworthy behavior indications provided by the trustee and pieces of evidence that suggest a trustee should be trusted.

As a core reference ontology (Guizzardi, 2007; Scherp et al., 2011), ROT is designed to account for a conceptualization of trust that is independent of a particular application domain, and to be applied in an off-line manner to assist humans in tasks such as meaning negotiation and consensus establishment. ROT intends to address the notion of trust broadly, so that it can be applied to a number of disciplines and areas, such as requirements engineering, decentralized finance and enterprise modeling.

The chapter is organized as follows. Section 4.1 motivates the relevance of developing an ontology of trust. Section 4.2 discusses the ontological nature of trust in the literature. Section 4.3 presents the Reference Ontology of Trust. Section 4.4 applies the ontology to model and example of social trust (babysitter), and example of institution-based trust (monetary system) and a case illustration about trust in vaccines in the time of COVID-19. Section 4.5 discusses some related work. Finally, section 4.6 presents the conclusions of this chapter.

---

[1] The complete version of ROT in OntoUML and its implementation in OWL are available at http://purl.org/krdb-core/trust-ontology.

4.1 Introduction

Trust is a central component of social life. In the literature, trust is frequently referred to as the "glue of society", vital in economics, social cooperation, organizations, groups, etc. Because of its ubiquitous presence, the notion of trust appears in many contexts and has been defined in a wide number of ways throughout the years and across several areas (Cross, 2005; Giorgini et al., 2005; Rotter, 1967; Walterbusch et al., 2020; Williamson, 1993).

The term trust has been used to refer to different types of relationships, such as the trust between individuals, as well as between individuals and organizations, individuals and autonomous agents, between software systems operating in a network, the trust in the context of offline or online commercial relationships, among others. Regardless of the context, trust is generally the basis for decision making closely related to achieving a goal. Therefore, understanding the key factors that play a role in trust assessment is paramount to avoid exposing decision makers to the risk of loss from incorrect decisions due to misplaced trust. Since these factors are numerous, it is not trivial to select the key ones that maximize decision performance, and thus promote effective decision making.

From the perspective of trustees it is important to understand what characteristics they should have to be considered trustworthy and identify what they could do to increase trust levels. Moreover, as important as gaining trust is having the ability to maintain it, as trust is a highly dynamic entity. But what exactly is trust? What makes one trustworthy? And what factors can influence trust?

In technological contexts, many disciplines, such as human-computer interaction, distributed artificial intelligence, multi-agent systems and networked-computer systems, are working to integrate trust into technological infrastructures. In this scenario, the need for a technology able to deal with typical human cognitive and social features and phenomena, like trust, emerges. To support this, a precise and rigorous conceptualization, based on foundational ontologies, is needed, as well as some theoretical abstraction and some possible modeling of it.

Although much progress has been made to clarify the ontological nature of trust, the term remains overloaded and there is not yet a shared or prevailing, and conceptually clear definition for it (Castelfranchi and Falcone, 2010; McKnight and Chervany, 2001). In the light of the above, we advocate for the need of a reference ontology of trust to serve as a basis for communication, consensus and alignment among different approaches and perspectives, as well as to foster interoperability across the heterogeneous application domains.

4.2 On Trust

A wide number of definitions of trust have been proposed along the years, across several areas, such as psychology (Rotter, 1967; Tyler, 2006), sociology (Barber, 1983; Gambetta et al., 2000; Luhmann, 2018), economics (Williamson, 1993), law (Cross, 2005), and more recently, computer science (Giorgini et al., 2005; Moyano et al., 2012). Although much progress has been made to clarify the nature of trust, the term remains semantically overloaded and there is not yet a shared or prevailing, and conceptually clear notion of trust (Castelfranchi and Falcone, 2010).

A classic definition of trust, widely accepted in the literature, was proposed by the sociologist Diego Gambetta, who defines trust as "the subjective probability with which an agent expects that another agent or group of agents will perform a particular action on which its welfare depends" (Gambetta et al., 2000). In his definition it is clear the existence of both a *trustor* and a *trustee*, as well a belief of the trustor about the behavior of the trustee. Gambetta also relates trust to an intention of the trustor regarding her welfare and the uncertainty about the trustee's behavior, which reveals the existence of a certain degree of risk. In fact, this idea that trust presupposes a situation of risk is ubiquitous in the literature. For instance, Luhmann (Luhmann, 2018) argues that when people trust others, they act "as if they knew the future", and uncertainty is transformed into risk. Also, Castelfranchi and Falcone (2010) state that without uncertainty and risk there is no trust.

A similar concept of trust is proposed by Mayer, Davis, et al. (1995), who define trust as "the willingness of a party to be vulnerable to the actions of another party, based on the expectation that the other party will perform a particular action important to the trustor, irrespective of the ability to monitor or control that other party". Also here, the authors refer to the expectations (or beliefs) of the trustor regarding the trustee and correlates trust to the trustor's goals (the actions of the other party that are important to the trustor). According to the authors, by trusting another party, the trustor makes herself vulnerable and exposed to the occurrence of risk events.

Rousseau and colleagues relied on a large interdisciplinary literature and on the identification of fundamental and convergent elements to define trust as "a psychological state of a trustor comprising the intention to accept vulnerability in a situation involving risk, based on positive expectations of the intentions or behavior of the trustee"

(Rousseau et al., 1998). Note that, also in this definition, the authors reinforce the presence of the trustor's expectations regarding the trustee, as well as the relationship between trust and risk: by trusting, the trustor accepts to become vulnerable to the trustee in terms of potential failure of the expected action and result, as the trustee may not perform the expected action or the action may not have the desired result.

McKnight and Chervany (2001) compared sixty-five definitions of trust from different sources to propose an interdisciplinary model of conceptual trust types that takes into account several important aspects of trust and some of their mutual interactions. For example, the authors are able to distinguish between a belief and a behavioral component of trust, and to explain that the latter depends on the former. The belief component is related to cognitive perceptions about the attributes or characteristics of others, i.e., the trustor believes, with "feelings of relative security", that the trustee is willing and able to act in her interest. The behavioral component means that a person voluntarily takes actions that makes herself dependent on another person, with a feeling of relative security, even though negative consequences are possible. According to the authors, trust-related behavior comes in a number of subconstruct forms because many actions can make one dependent on another, such as cooperation, information sharing, informal agreements, decreasing controls, accepting influence, granting autonomy, and transacting business.

A further important aspect in the model of McKnight and Chervany (2001) is the distinction between *interpersonal trust* and *institution-based trust*. This distinction is also made by Luhmann (2018), who defines:

- **interpersonal trust** as that between individuals that frequently have face-to-face contact and become familiar with each other without substantially taking recourse to institutional arrangements; and

- **institution-based trust** as that in the reliable functioning of certain social systems, which no longer refers to a personally known reality, but is built on impersonal and generalized "media of communication", such as the monetary system and the legal system.

According to McKnight and Chervany (2001), institution-based trust affects interpersonal trust by "making the trustor feel more comfortable about trusting others, as she securely believes that protective structures (such as guarantees, contracts, regulations, promises, legal recourse, processes or procedures) are in place that are conducive to situational success". For example, people believe in the efficacy of a bank to take care of their money because of the existence of laws and institutions that insure them against loss. Lewis and Weigert (1985) argue that institution-based trust is indispensable for the effective functioning of "symbolic media of exchange", such as money and political power. They argue that "without public trust in the reliability, effectiveness, and legitimacy of money, laws, and other cultural symbols, modern social institutions would soon disintegrate".

More recently, Castelfranchi and Falcone (2010) analyzed the concept of trust as a composed and "layered" notion, relying on some key aspects: (i) a mental attitude and a disposition towards another agent; (ii) a decision and intention to rely upon the other, which makes the trustor vulnerable; (iii) the act of relying upon the trustee's expected behavior; and (iv) the consequent overt social interaction and relation between the trustor and the trustee.

In their definition of trust, Castelfranchi and Falcone (2010) emphasize the role of the trustor's goal by stating that an "agent trusts another only relative to a goal, i.e., for something she wants to achieve, that she desires or needs". They also reinforce the idea of trust consisting of beliefs about the trustee and his behavior: "the belief that the trustee is able and willing to do the needed action; the belief that the trustee will appropriately do the action, as the trustor wishes; and the belief that the trustor can make herself less defended and more vulnerable". As for the behavioral component of trust, Castelfranchi and Falcone (2010) argue that there may be mental trust without the corresponding behavioral part (i.e., without an action). That may happen because the level of trust is not sufficient; the level of trust is sufficient, but there are other reasons preventing the action (e.g. prohibitions); or trust is just potential, a predisposition (e.g. "the trustor would, might rely on the trustee, if/when..., but it is not (yet) the case").

In summary, what can be extracted from these different proposals is that there is a conceptual core to be enlightened in order to properly define trust. Therefore, to conceptualize trust, one must refer to: (i) *agents and their goals*; (ii) *agents' beliefs*; (iii) possibly executable *actions* of a given type; and (iv) *risk*.

4.3 ROT: Reference Ontology of Trust

This section presents the Reference Ontology of Trust (ROT) (Amaral, Sales, and Guizzardi, 2021b; 2022; Amaral, Sales, Guizzardi, and Porello, 2019), a well-founded ontology that formalizes the concept of trust as discussed in the previous section. We formalize the mental aspects of trust in the OntoUML² model depicted in figure 4.1, and the particular behavioral aspect of trust, as well as the relation between trust and risk in figure 4.10. In the OntoUML diagrams depicting the Reference Ontology of Trust, we represent types of substantials in pink, events in yellow, modes in blue and situations in orange.

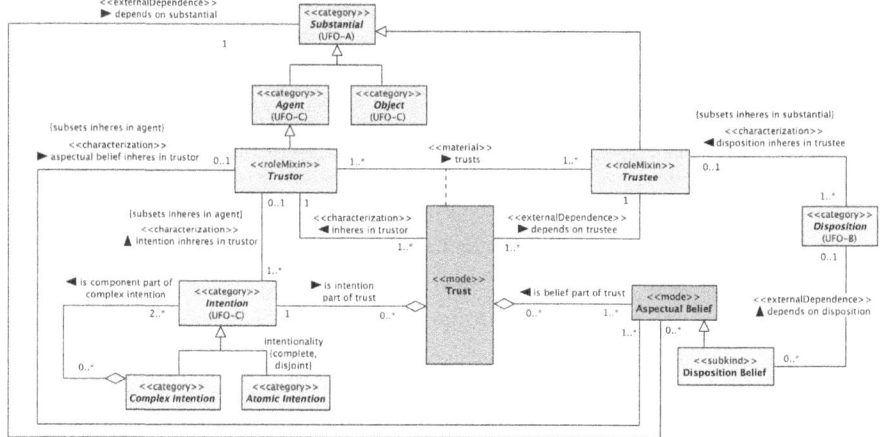

Figure 4.1: Trust.

In ROT, Trust is modeled as a complex mental state of a Trustor agent, composed of a set of Beliefs about a Trustee and its behavior. Trust is always about an Intention of the Trustor regarding a goal, for the achievement of which she counts upon the Trustee. Note that in the conceptualization of goal we propose here, the achievement of a goal does not necessarily require an action of the Trustee. Also omissions may be relevant in this context as the Trustor might precisely rely on the fact that the Trustee will not do an specific action or, more generally, that the Trustee will not do anything at all.

The Trustor may trust in the Trustee regarding a certain Intention, but may not trust it with respect to a different one. For example, I trust my dentist to fix a cavity in my tooth, but not to fix my computer. Furthermore, such an intention is not always atomic. For instance, in the trust relation "Bob trusts a certain airline to take him on his holiday trip comfortably and safely", trust is about a complex intention, composed of (i) Bob's intention of traveling; (ii) his intention of being safe; and (iii) his intention of

---

²Once more, OntoUML is a conceptual modeling language whose primitives reflect the ontological distinctions put forth by the UFO ontology (Guizzardi, 2005)

4.3. ROT: Reference Ontology of Trust

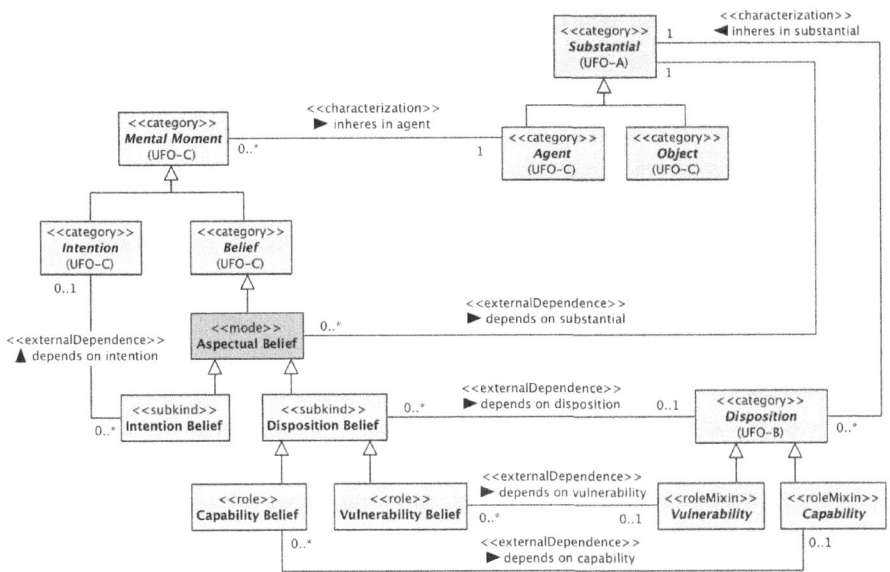

Figure 4.2: Aspectual Belief.

being comfortable. Let us now consider a situation in which Mary trusts an application provider for collecting her location data, except when she is in sensitive places such as a cancer treatment center for her medical treatment, since such information may lead to disclosing her disease. In this example, trust is also about a complex intention, composed of (i) Mary's intention of having her location data collected; (ii) Mary's intention of not having her diseased disclosed to others; and (iii) Mary's intention of preserving her location privacy when she is in sensitive places.

The Trustor is necessarily an "intentional entity", that is, a cognitive agent, an agent endowed with goals and beliefs. In UFO, a belief is a special type of mode, named mental moment, which is existentially dependent on a particular agent, being an inseparable part of its mental state. As for the Trustee, it is an entity capable of impacting one's intentions by the outcome of its behavior (Castelfranchi and Falcone, 2010), regardless if this involves an action or an omission (e.g. 'doing nothing', 'abstaining from doing X'). Moreover, note that the Trustee is not necessarily aware of being trusted. An example, given in Castelfranchi and Falcone (2010), is a person running to catch a bus. Even if this person is not seen by the bus driver and the people waiting for the bus at the stop, she may attribute to these people the intention to take the bus, and thus the intention to stop it. In such a case, the runner is trusting in the people at the bus stop to do so.

In our ontology, in accordance with Castelfranchi and Falcone (2010), the Trustee is not necessarily a cognitive system, or an animated or autonomous agent. It can also be a lot of things we rely upon in our daily activity: rules, procedures, conventions, infrastructures, technology and artifacts in general, tools, authorities and institutions, environmental regularities, as well as different types of social systems. Based on the nature of the Trustee, we have modelled two specializations of Trust, namely Social Trust and Institution-based Trust. The former stands for the "trust in another agent as an agent" (Castelfranchi and Falcone, 2010). Consequently, it is externally dependent of an Agent Trustee. For example, in a social trust relation between a mother that trusts a babysitter to take care of her kids, the babysitter is the Agent Trustee. The latter builds upon the existence of shared rules, regularities, conventional practices, etc. and is related to a Social System Trustee. In the case of the Intitution-based Trust, the Trustee is what we name here a Social System. This comes from the sociology tradition positing that people can rely on others because of structures, situations or assigned social roles that provide assurances that things will go well (Barber, 1983). Intitution-based Trust refers to beliefs about those protective structures, not about the people involved. In this thesis, we term these protective structures Social Systems. We adopt the interpretation of Social Systems as orderly arrangements of social entities that interact with each other, based on established and prevalent social rules that structure social interactions. Social Systems create a shared world of clear rules and reliable standards, which no longer refers to a personally known reality, but is built on impersonal and generalized "media of communication" (Luhmann, 2018) such as the monetary system and the legal system. Let us take the example of the monetary system as a Social System Trustee: in the society, individuals provide something of value in return for a token they trust to be able to use in the future to obtain something else of value, as well as they trust that the value of the instrument will be stable in terms of goods and services. An additional example, involving different types of trust, is the case of a person who buys a phone in an e-commerce platform. Here we can identify several trust relations: (i) the buyer's social trust in the seller about her delivering the phone in perfect state; (ii) the buyer's trust in the phone about it behaving as she expects; (iii) the buyer's and the seller's institution-based trust in the monetary system; (iv) the buyer's and the seller's institution-based trust in the legal system (in case of one of the parties does not fulfill its commitments); (v) the buyer's and the seller's trust in the online platform.

As shown in figure 4.1, we modeled Trust as a complex mode[3] composed of a

4.3. ROT: Reference Ontology of Trust

Trustor Intention, whose propositional content is a goal of the Trustor, and a set of beliefs about the Trustee that we name here Aspectual Beliefs. As previously mentioned, the Trustor Intention can be atomic or complex. While atomic intentions have no proper parts, complex intentions are aggregations of at least two disjoint intentions. We use the notion of *belief* defined in UFO (see section 2.3 of chapter 2) to model Aspectual Belief as a belief that inheres in the Trustor and is externally dependent on an external entity (Azevedo, C.L.B. et al., 2015; Guizzardi, Wagner, Falbo, et al., 2013), more specifically, the Trustee.

As illustrated in figure 4.2, Aspectual Belief is specialized into Disposition Belief and Intention Belief. Disposition Belief is a belief about a Disposition of the Trustee and therefore is externally dependent on a Disposition[3]. It is distinguished into Capability Belief and Vulnerability Belief. The former refers to a belief about a Trustee's Capability[3] — the Trustor believes that the Trustee is capable of performing a desired action or exhibiting a desired behavior — while the latter refers to a Trustee's Vulnerability[3] — the Trustor believes that the Trustee's vulnerabilities will not prevent it from performing the desired action or exhibiting the desired behavior. Note that the very same disposition may play the role of a capability, a vulnerability, or even a threat capability[4]. For example, in the scope of military operations, information can be seen both as a capability (as digital data and networks support and facilitate the achievement of military objectives) and a vulnerability (as confidential information can be disclosed as a consequence of a cyber-attack). For this reason, both capabilities and vulnerabilities are represented as roles of dispositions (figure 4.2) that inhere in the Trustee, which are manifested in particular situations, through the occurrence of events (Guizzardi, Wagner, Falbo, et al., 2013). We adopt here the interpretation of capability proposed by Azevedo, C.L.B. et al. (2015), who defined capability as the power to bring about a desired outcome.

Intention Belief is a belief about an Intention of the Trustee — the Trustor believes that the Trustee intends to perform a desired action or exhibit an expected behavior — and therefore is externally dependent on this Intention. For example, a mother who trusts a babysitter to take care of her kids believes that: (i) the babysitter has experience in caring for children and is First Aid trained (a belief about the babysitter's capabilities); (ii) the babysitter is well and probably is not going to have health issues (a belief

---

[3]The notions of mode, disposition, capability and vulnerability are defined and discussed section 2.3 of chapter 2 of this thesis.

[4]Capabilities are usually perceived as beneficial, as they enable the manifestation of events desired by an agent. However, when the manifestation of a capability enables undesired events that threaten an agent's abilities to achieve a goal, it can be seen as a threat capability (Sales, Baião, et al., 2018).

about the babysitter's vulnerabilities); and (iii) the babysitter is willing to take good care of her children (a belief about the babysitter's intention).

Social Trust is a specialization of Trust in which the Trustee is an Agent (figure 4.3). The Intention Belief is specific to this type of trust, as in this case the Trustee is a cognitive agent endowed with goals.

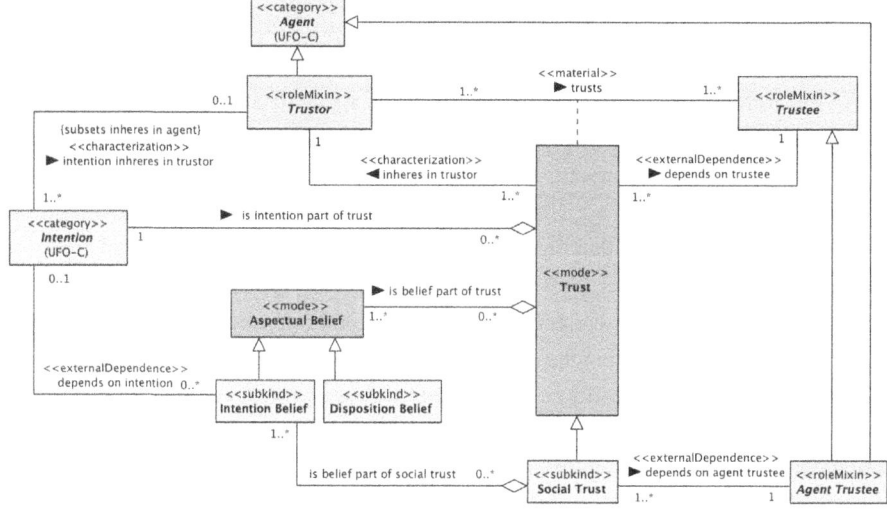

Figure 4.3: Social Trust.

A further specialization of Trust is that of Institution-based Trust, in which the Trustee is a *Social System* (figure 4.4). An important aspect, related to the nature of Social Systems, is that they can be seen as *integral wholes*, whose parts play particular *functional roles* that contribute in specific ways to the functionality of the whole (Guizzardi, 2005; Sales and Guizzardi, 2017). UFO includes micro-theories to address different types of *part-whole relations* (Guizzardi, 2005; Sales and Guizzardi, 2017) generally recognized in cognitive science (Gerstl and Pribbenow, 1995; Pribbenow, 2002). Social Systems embody one particular kind of such parthood relations, namely, *componentfunctional complex* (Sales and Guizzardi, 2017). In UFO's terminology, this "componentOf" relation is used to relate entities that are *functional complexes*. Some examples of functional complexes are an organization, a legal system or a monetary system and their corresponding "componentOf" relations (e.g., presidency-organization, law-legal system, currency-monetary system). Consequently, Social Systems can be defined as

4.3. ROT: Reference Ontology of Trust

functional complexes composed of social entities like the ones mentioned in section 2.3 (e.g. social roles, social objects, social relationships, normative descriptions and so on). An example of Social System is the legal system, which is an integral whole composed of a number of social entities, such as social roles (e.g. lawyer, judge, etc.), social objects (e.g. contract, court sentence), normative descriptions (e.g. laws, regulations) and others that contribute in complementary manners to the functionality of the whole.

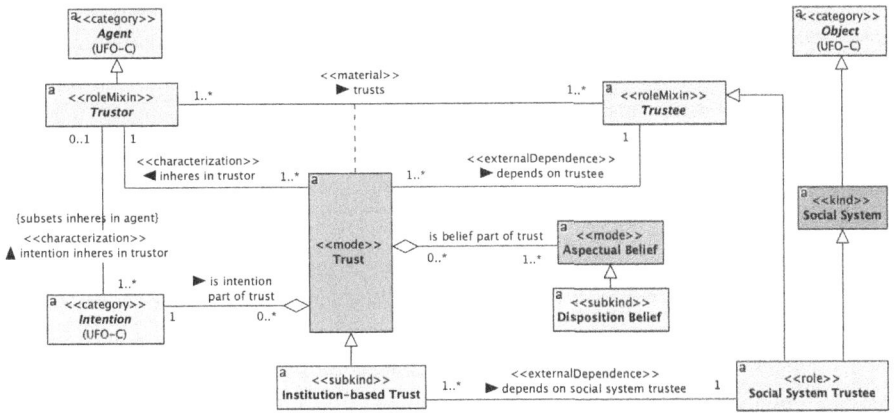

Figure 4.4: Institution-based Trust.

Finally, the trusts relation between the Trustor and the Trustee is a relation that is *non-symmetric*, *non-reflexive* and *non-transitive*. An example that evinces the non-symmetry is a child that trusts her father to lift a heavy object, but the father does not trust his child to do so. However, it is possible that the father trusts the mother to take care of their kids and vice-versa. Trust is non-reflexive because an agent may or may not trust herself to perform actions. For example, an athlete may trust herself to run one kilometer in ten minutes, but not to cook a sophisticated meal. Lastly, it is non-transitive because agents might have different evaluations about the same entity's trustworthiness. For instance, it is very well possible that Alice trusts Bob for performing certain actions and Bob trusts Charlie for performing the same actions, but it is not the case the Alice trusts Charlie to perform them.

4.3.1 Quantitative Perspective of Trust

As we mentioned before, Trust is a complex mental state of a Trustor regarding a Trustee and its behavior, which is composed of an Intention of the Trustor and a set of her beliefs about the Trustee. We begin the representation of the quantitative perspective of Trust by means of the Trust Degree moment (*quality*) that inheres in the Trust entity. In UFO, a quality is an objectification of a property that can be directly evaluated (projected) into certain value spaces (Guizzardi, 2005). Common examples include a person's weight, which can be measured in kilograms or pounds, and the color of a flower, which can be specified in the RGB or HSV color models. Thus, representing Trust Degree as a quality means that it can also be measured according to a given scale, such as a simple discrete scale like <Low,Medium,High> or a continuous scale (e.g. from 0.0 to 100.0).

In general, the trustor beliefs are not black and white, in the sense that a trustor needs to believe that a trustee either has a certain Disposition (or Intention) or not. In fact, they have an intrinsic quality that corresponds to the strength of a trustor belief (Jacquette, 2013). For instance, it may be the case that "Alice believes more strongly that Burger King is capable of making a good hamburger than it is capable of delivering orders on time". Another example, which considers the same capability and different trustees, is "people believe more strongly that an adult is capable of lifting a heavy object than a child". Note that in this case, we are not comparing the performance of an adult with that of a child when lifting a heavy object, because the child may not even be able to lift it. Nevertheless, performance levels are an important aspect to be considered with respect to capability beliefs. For example, a project manager may believe that both a junior and a senior analysts are capable of performing a particular task. However, he probably believes that the senior analyst is able to perform the task with a higher level of performance than the junior analyst. In (Castelfranchi and Falcone, 2010), the authors claim that the degree of trust is a function of (i) the estimated quantitative level of the trustee's quality on which the positive expectation is based and (ii) how much the trustor is sure of her evaluation about the trustee's quality. In our approach, the Belief Intensity and the Performance Level are analogous to, respectively, (ii) and (i) in Castelfranchi and Falcone's proposal (Castelfranchi and Falcone, 2010).

Finally, another important aspect to be considered, related to beliefs about trustee dispositions, is how strongly the trustor believes a disposition may be manifested through the occurrence of certain events. For example: "although Charlie believes that he can get a flat tire during a trip (which corresponds to a vulnerability belief about his car), he believes that the likelihood of this happening is very small".

Based on these considerations, we propose that the above-mentioned measures (belief intensity, performance level, and manifestation likelihood) be considered when quantifying trust. To account for the quantitative perspective of beliefs, we modeled these three belief-related measures (figure 4.5), representing them as qualities that inhere in Aspectual Beliefs (Belief Intensity) and Disposition Beliefs (Performance Level and Manifestation Likelihood). This means that they can be mapped into quality spaces, such as a discrete scale like <Low,Medium,High> or a continuous one like <0-100> (Agudo et al., 2008; Ennew and Sekhon, 2007; Marsh, 1994).

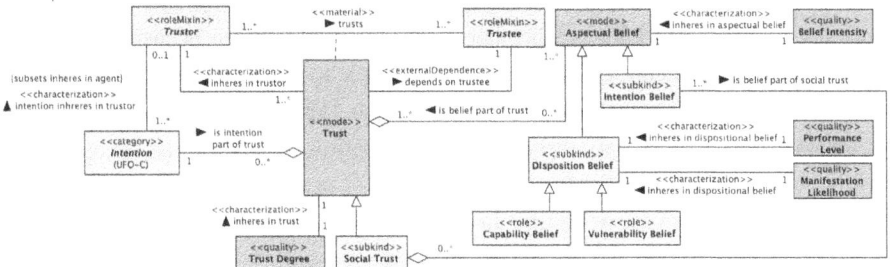

Figure 4.5: Quantitative Perspective of Trust.

4.3.2 Influences

Several factors that influence trust have been discussed in the literature (Mayer, Davis, et al., 1995). For instance, Castelfranchi and Falcone (2010) argue that "trust changes with experience, with the modification of the different sources it is based on, with the emotional or rational state of the trustor, with the modification of the environment in which the trustee is supposed to perform, and so on". They claim that trust is a dynamic entity because it depends on dynamic phenomena.

In this section, we categorize influence relations according to the ontological nature of the factors that explain them. These categories are: (F1) trust influencing trust; (F2) mental biases; (F3) trust calibration signals; and (F4) trustworthiness evidence.

F1: Trust Influencing Trust

This category represents the situation in which Trust is influenced by another trust relationship. According to Castelfranchi and Falconi (Castelfranchi and Falcone, 2010) "in the same situation trust is influenced by trust in several rather complex ways". In the same work they also discuss the phenomenon of trust creating reciprocal trust, as well as how trust relations can influence each other. In fact, countless examples can be found in real life about trust influencing trust, either positively or negatively. For instance, citizens' trust in the central bank positively influence their trust in the national currency. People's trust in the healthcare system, in the experts defining vaccination strategies, and more generally in government bodies influence their trust in vaccines.

McKnight and Chervany (2001) argues that Institution-based Trust affects Social Trust by making the Trustor feel more comfortable about trusting others in a given situation. For example, regulations and institutions may enable people to trust each other not because they know each other personally, but because licensing, auditing, laws or governmental enforcement bodies are in place to make sure the other person is either afraid to harm them or punished if they do so. This influence may also hold in the opposite direction. Social Trust may influence Institution-based Trust by generating positive beliefs about established social systems. For example, one's trust in the local police officer may increase one's trust in the "judiciary system".

F2: Mental Biases

This category represents situations in which Trust is influenced by *mental moments* (a concept from UFO) (chapter 2). Mental Moments refer to the capacity of some properties of certain individuals to refer to possible situations of reality (Guizzardi, Falbo, et al., 2008b). A Mental Moment is existentially dependent on a particular Agent, being an inseparable part of its mental state (figure 4.6). Examples of Mental Moments include Perceptions, Beliefs, Desires and Intentions. Perception expresses how agents sense their environment and the things that happen around them. Beliefs have a propositional content that agents consider to be true. They can be justified by situations in reality. Examples include my belief that Rome is the Capital of Italy, and the belief that the Moon orbits the Earth. Beliefs can be formed by perceptions expressing how agents sense their environment and the things that happen around them. Desires and intentions can be fulfilled or frustrated. A Desire expresses the will of an agent towards a possible situation (e.g., a desire that Brazil wins the next World Cup), while an Intention expresses desired states of affairs for which the agent commits to pursuing (e.g., Mary's intention of going to Paris). For an extensive discussion of mental moments, please refer to (Guizzardi, Falbo, et al., 2008b).

Mental Moments can significantly influence Trust. Let us consider the example of a person who really wants to travel but cannot. One day she receives an email containing an unbelievable offer for an exotic destination that is just about to expire. Although many will immediately think it is a scam, the person's desire to travel may influence

4.3. ROT: Reference Ontology of Trust

her to trust the email offer (Fischer et al., 2013). Another example would be people who are strongly committed to environmental preservation and tend to trust companies that support environmental sustainability (Chen and Chang, 2012). There is also the case of beliefs not related to specific trustees. An example discussed by McKnight and Chervany (2001) suggests that some religious beliefs, which prescribe honesty and mutual love, lead people to generally assume that others are usually honest, benevolent, competent, and predictable.

Another important aspect is the occurrence of events that can affect one's perception regarding a trustee. In (McKnight, Liu, et al., 2012), the authors discuss how trust changes in response to external events and propose a model that addresses the mental mechanisms people use as they are confronted by trust-related events, which "indicates that trust may be sticky or resistant to change, but that change can and will occur" (McKnight, Liu, et al., 2012). Falcone and Castelfranchi (2004) claim that the success of an action performed by the trustee in order to reach a goal of the trustor depends not only on the trustee's capabilities but also on external conditions that allow or inhibit the realization of the task. To illustrate this point, the authors use the case of a violinist that will give a concert in an open environment. In general, people trust the violinist to play well. However, if it is particularly cold during the concert, their trust will decrease if they infer that the cold can hinder her ability to play. Similarly, in financial systems, the emergence of detrimental information about a financial agent can negatively affect public trust in this agent, which can lead to considerable adverse effects on one or several other financial institutions that can ultimately propagate to the entire financial system.

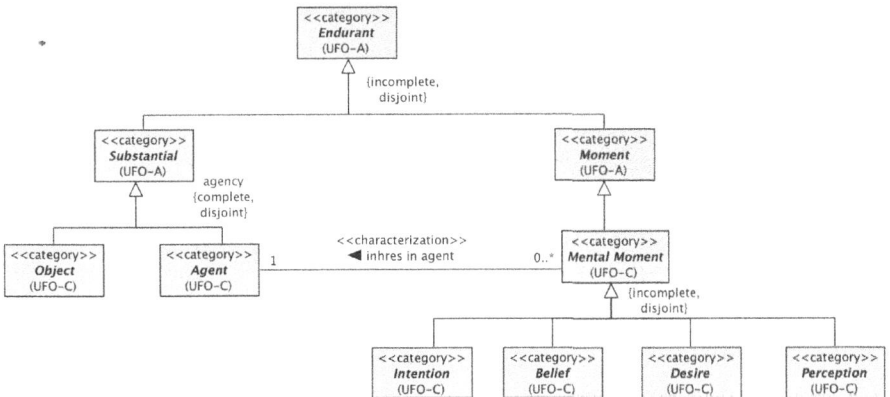

Figure 4.6: Mental Moment.

F3: Trust Calibration Signals

The emission of *trust-warranting signals*, that is, signals that indicate trustworthy behavior of a trustee, is one of the ingredients for building sustainable trust (Riegelsberger et al., 2005). In trust relations, once the trustee's capabilities and vulnerabilities related to the beliefs of the trustor are known, it is possible to reason about the signals that the trustee should emit to indicate that it can successfully realize its capabilities and prevent its vulnerabilities from being manifested. These signals are specifically created to indicate a trustworthy behavior on the part of the trustee and therefore can influence trust. For example, information about how privacy and security measures are implemented could be provided as signals of the trustworthiness of a system. Another example is the establishment of a universal brand to create visual identity, so that users can identify the system interface elements in a clear and unambiguous way, thus facilitating the understanding and adoption of its functionalities.

Equally important are *uncertainty signals*, i.e. signals that communicate uncertainties regarding the realization of capabilities and the prevention of vulnerabilities. Some examples are the publication of uncertainties about the accuracy of scientific findings, patient communication of uncertainties on the precision of medical diagnosis, investor communication of uncertainties in forecasting financial investments returns, communication to the public about uncertainties regarding the efficacy of vaccines, among others. While trust-warranting signals contribute to trust building, uncertainty signals allow trustors to adjust their trust level appropriately to the trustee's trustworthiness, thus avoiding misplaced levels of trust. Research show that communicating uncertainty can be beneficial for maintaining trust and commitment over time (Batteux et al., 2021; Tomsett, Richard et al., 2020). This is because building trust that is higher than the actual trustworthiness of the trustee might set trustors' expectations too high, which may result in disappointment sooner or later.

As illustrated in figure 4.7, the Trustee may emit Trust Calibration Signals regarding its Dispositions (either a Capability or a Vulnerability). Trust Calibration Signal is specialized into Trust-warranting Signal and Uncertainty Signal. The former represents trust-warranting signals that should be emitted by the trustee in order to ensure trustworthy behavior, while the latter represents uncertainty signals emitted by the trustee, which allow trustors to adjust their trust levels[5].

---

[5]Emits is grounded on a communicative act of the trustee (Guizzardi, Falbo, et al., 2008b) and, hence, a *historical* relation in the sense of (Fonseca, C. et al., 2019). The propositional content of this act refers to a disposition, thus, grounding the (derived) refers to relation between the latter and Trust Calibration Signal.

4.3. ROT: Reference Ontology of Trust

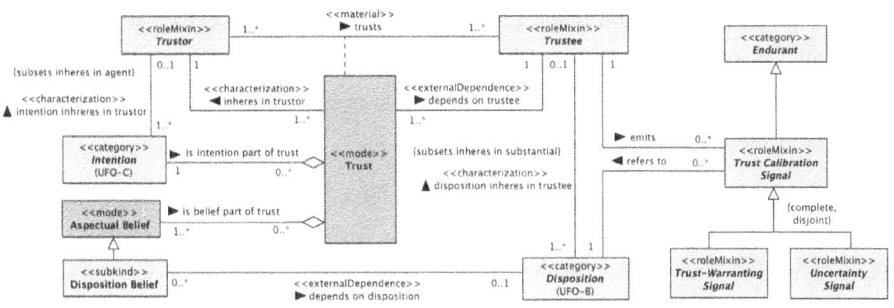

Figure 4.7: Trust Calibration Signal.

F4: Trustworthiness Evidence

Another trust influencing factor corresponds to *trustworthiness evidence*, pieces of evidence that suggest that a trustee should be trusted. Similarly to trust-warranting signals, they suggest that a trustee can realize its capabilities and shield its vulnerabilities. However, differently from signals, which are purposefully emitted to suggest trustworthiness, evidence result from trustees' trustworthy actions. Examples include:

- third-party certifications and credentials (e.g. John's TOEFL certification makes me believe that he can speak English, because I trust the certificate issued by a certain authority);
- performance history (e.g. accuracy of a medical diagnosis system);
- track record (e.g. reviews from service recipients and statistics on its experience);
- recommendations (e.g. my brother trusts a car mechanic and recommends his services to me);
- reputation records (e.g. positive evaluations received by an Uber driver);
- availability (e.g. a medical doctor you rarely succeed to make an appointment with is not trustworthy);
- past successful experiences (e.g. all the products I purchased at Amazon arrived on time and in perfect condition);
- transparency (e.g. offering information on what an artificial intelligence system is doing, as well as rationale for its decisions (aka explainability));

- longevity (e.g. indication that a vendor has been in the market for a long time and that it is interested in continued business relationship with the client); and
- risk mitigation measures, which indicate that one is actively trying to prevent the manifestation of one's vulnerabilities.

Ontologically speaking, a piece of Trustworthiness Evidence is a *social thing*, typically a *social relator*[6] (e.g. a relator binding the certifying entity, the certified entity and referring to a capability, vulnerability, etc.), but also documents (*social objects* themselves) that represent these *social entities* (e.g., in the way a marriage certificate documents a marriage as a social relator). As illustrated in figure 4.8 we modeled Trustworthiness Evidences as roles played by *endurants* (objects, relators, etc.) related to a Disposition of the Trustee[7].

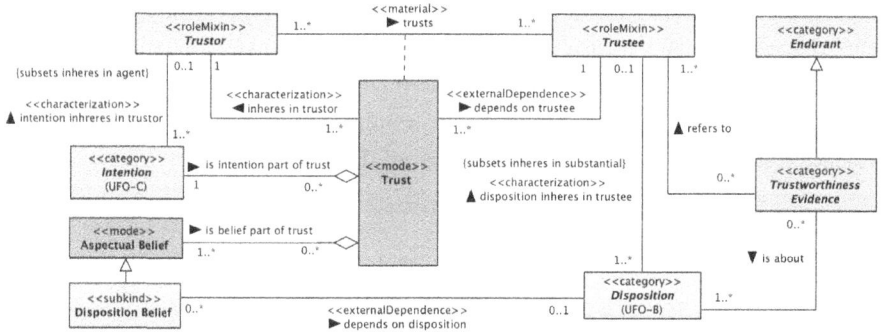

Figure 4.8: Trustworthiness Evidence.

To represent the role of influences in ROT, we included the Influence relator, which connects the sources of influence to the Aspectual Beliefs of the Trustor under their influence (figure 4.9). We distinguish Influence according to the source of influence into: (i) Trust Influence, associated to a Trust entity (F1); (ii) Mental Moment Influence, associated to a Mental Moment (F2); (iii) Trust Calibration Signal Influence, associated to a Trust Calibration Signal (F3); and (iv) Trustworthiness Evidence Influence, associated

---

[6]A relator (concept from UFO) is an entity that is existentially dependent on at least two individuals, thus, mediating or binding them (section 2.3.1). For a formalization of this notion, we refer to (Fonseca, C. et al., 2019).

[7]Playing of the "role" of Trustworthiness Evidence for a particular focal disposition is dependent on the belief of trustors, whose propositional content makes that connection between that player and that disposition. The is about relation in this model is, thus, derived from the propositional content of that belief. The refers to relation connected to the trustee is derived from the relation between that focal disposition and its bearer.

4.3. ROT: Reference Ontology of Trust

to a Trustworthiness Evidence (F4). The property weight corresponds to the weight of an influence over a particular belief, as certain influences may weight more heavily than others.

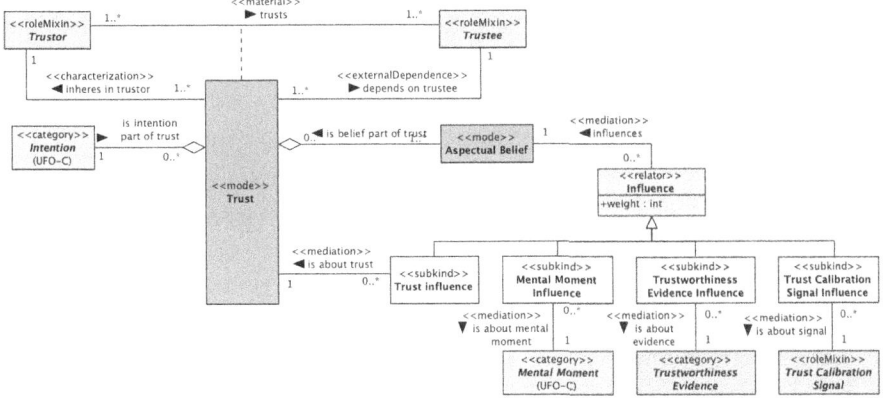

Figure 4.9: Influences.

4.3.3 The Emergence of Risk from Trust Relations

We analyze the relation between trust and risk, based on the Common Ontology of Value and Risk (see section 3.2 of chapter 3). COVER proposes an ontological analysis of notions such as Risk, Risk Event (Threat Event, Loss Event) and Vulnerability, among others. Given the objectives of this thesis, we focus here on the perspective of risk as a chain of events that impacts on an agent's goals, which the authors named Risk Experience. Risk Experiences focus on unwanted events that have the potential of causing losses and are composed by events of two types, namely threat and loss events. A Threat Event is the one with the potential of causing a loss, which might be intentional or unintentional. A Threat Event might be the manifestation of a Vulnerability (a special type of disposition whose manifestation constitutes a loss or can potentially cause a loss from the perspective of a stakeholder) or a threatening Capability (capabilities are usually perceived as beneficial, as they enable the manifestation of events desired by an agent. However, when the manifestation of a capability enables undesired events that threaten agent's abilities to achieve a goal, it can be seen as a threatening capability). The second mandatory component of a Risk Experience is a Loss Event, which necessarily impact intentions in a negative way (captured by a hurts relation between Loss

Event and Intention) (Sales, Baião, et al., 2018).

We represent the relation between trust and risk, together with its embedded concepts, in the OntoUML model depicted in figure 4.10. As part of the behavioral perspective of trust, the Trustor may take some Actions, motivated by her Intentions and based on her Trust in the Trustee. These Actions may involve the Trustee or not (some examples are cooperation, information sharing, informal agreements, decreasing controls, accepting influence, granting autonomy, and transacting business (McKnight and Chervany, 2001)), however they are taken considering that the Trustee will behave according to the Trustor's Beliefs. As previous mentioned, a Trustor may *trust* in a Trustee but not take any Action based on this Trust. For this reason, the relationship between Trust and the Trustor's Actions is optional.

Similarly, the Trustee may take some Actions aiming at performing Capabilities or preventing the manifestation of Vulnerabilities, as expected by the Trustor.

Actions performed by either the Trustor (based on her Trust in the Trustee) or the Trustee (regarding a Trust relation) brings about a Resulting Situation, which may satisfy the Trustor goals (and in this case it is considered a Successful Situation) or, in the worst case, may not have the desired result and the Trustor will not be able to achieve her goal. In this case, the Resulting Situation stands for a Threat Situation that may trigger a Threat Event, which may cause a loss. The Loss Event is a Risk Event that impacts intentions in a negative way, as it hurts the Trustor's Intentions of reaching a specific goal.

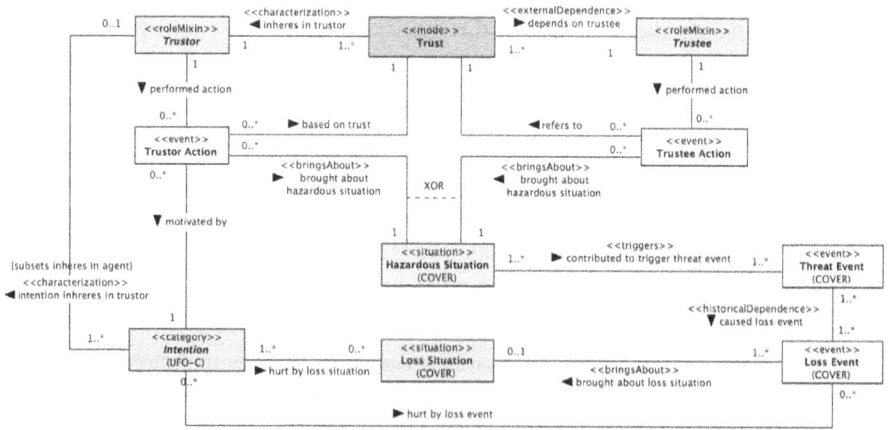

Figure 4.10: Trust and Risk.

4.4 Use Case Illustrations

In this section we apply the Reference Ontology of Trust to model three examples. First, in section 4.4.1, we model an instance of social trust using the case of a working mother who trusts a babysitter to take care of her children. Then, in section 4.4.2, we model an instance of institution-based trust related to the trust of a person in the monetary system. Finally, in section 4.4.3, we apply ROT to model an example about trust in vaccines in the time of COVID-19.

4.4.1 Social Trust Example: Babysitter

In this section we take the case of a mother who trusts a babysitter, to present an example of social trust. Firstly, we illustrate, in figure 4.11, the model regarding the mental aspect of trust, which is composed of a set of beliefs. In the example, the mother has the intention of "having an adult to take care of her kids while she is out" and she trusts in a specific babysitter to do this task. Her Trust is composed of a set of Beliefs regarding: (i) the Capabilities of the babysitter (the babysitter has experience in caring for children and is First Aid trained); (ii) the babysitter's Intentions (the mother believes that the babysitter is willing to take good care of her children); and (iii) the babysitter's Vulnerabilities (the babysitter is well and probably is not going to have health issues).

Secondly, in Fig 4.12, we illustrate the behavioral aspect of trust, i.e. the Actions that the Trustor performs relying on the behavior of the Trustee. In the example, the mother believes that the babysitter is a good candidate and decides to count on her to take care of the kids. The mother arrives at a decision that is based on trust and eventually expresses her trust through an official delegation, which is the action of hiring the babysitter.

Finally, also in figure 4.12, we illustrate the emergence of risk from the trust relation. When the mother hires the babysitter, the latter commits to take care of the former's children. With the commitment of the babysitter, the mother becomes vulnerable and may be exposed to unanticipated risks. Considering a situation in which the babysitter gets sick during the term of the employment contract, it can be considered a Threat Situation that may trigger a Threat Event if, for example, the babysitter does not go to work because she is no feeling well. In this case, the babysitter not going work is a Threat Event that may trigger a Loss Event, which would be the children getting unattended while the mother was out. This Lost Event hurts the mother's Intention of having an adult to take care of her kids while she is out.

4.4.2 Institution-based Trust example: Monetary System

This section illustrates the trust of a person in the monetary system, which is a case of institution-based trust. In this example, a person has the Intention of "selling a house and use the money to buy an apartment" and she Trusts the monetary system as a protective structure, which assures that things will go well. Hinged on her Institution-based Trust in the monetary system, the individual provides something of value in return for a "token" she trusts to be able to use in the future to obtain something else of value.

Figure 4.13 illustrates the model regarding the mental aspect of Trust, which is composed of a set of Beliefs about:

(i) the Capabilities of the monetary system:

- **the function of money as a medium of exchange**: related to the capability of money (which is a social object and a component of the monetary system) to function as a means of payment with a value that everyone trusts.

- **the function of money as a unit of account**: related to the capability of money to function as a standard numerical unit for the measurement of value and costs of

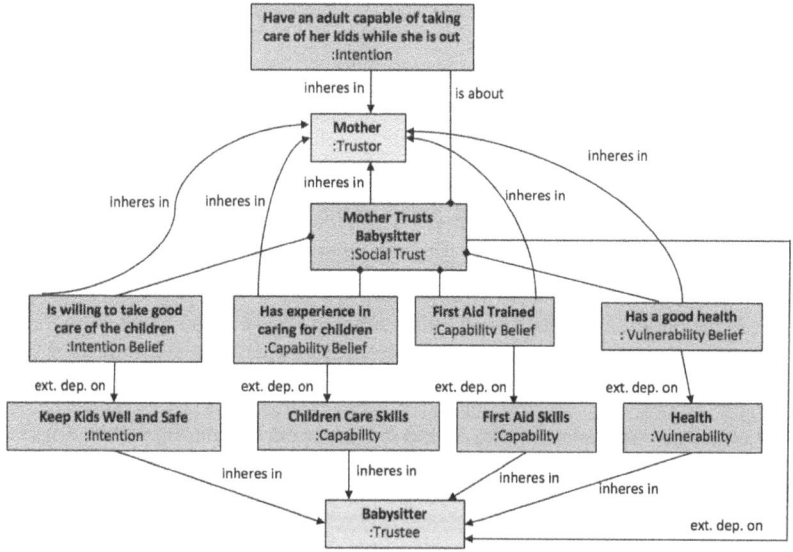

Figure 4.11: Social Trust: Mother trusts a babysitter.

4.4. Use Case Illustrations

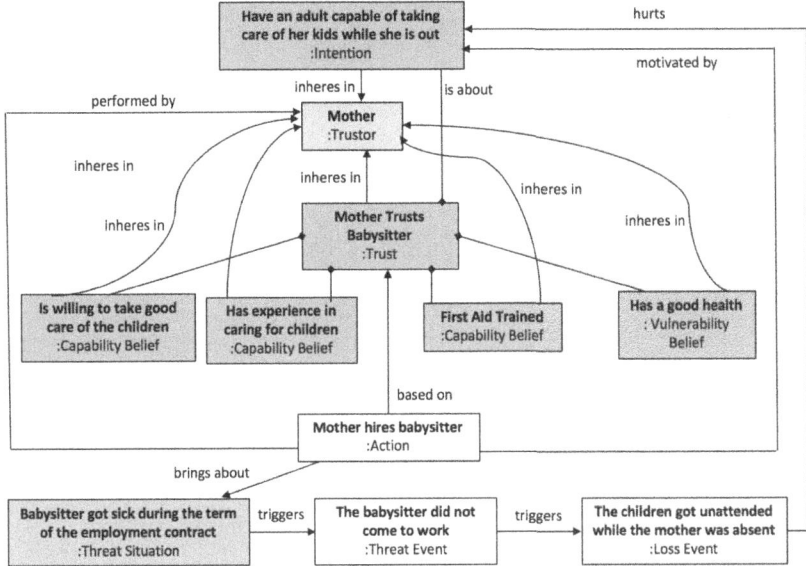

Figure 4.12: Social Trust: Risk emerging from the trust relation.

goods, services, assets and liabilities.

- **the function of money as a store of value**: related to the capability of money that allows it to be saved and retrieved in the future.

- **inflation is controlled**: related to the capability of the monetary system to have structures and mechanisms to maintain price stability and inflation control.

- **the value of money is stable**: related to the capability of the monetary system to ensure the stability of the currency's purchasing power.

(ii) the Vulnerabilities of the monetary system:

- **economy is healthy**: related to changes in the economy that may impact the monetary system.

- **the international scenario is favorable**: related to changes in the international scenario that may impact the monetary system.

In the sequel, Fig 4.14 illustrates the behavioral aspect of trust, i.e. the Actions that the Trustor (the person) performs relying on the Trustee (the monetary system). In the

94   Chapter 4. The Reference Ontology of Trust

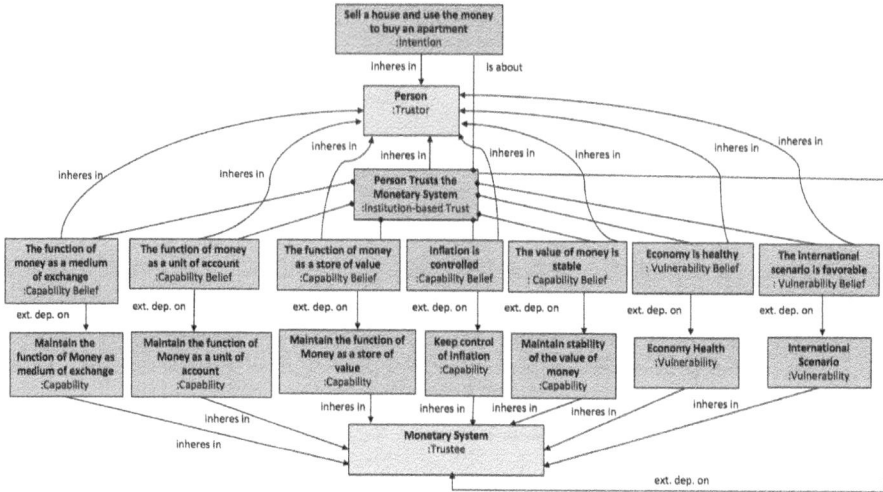

Figure 4.13: Institution-based Trust: Person trusts the monetary system.

example, the person believes in the stability and efficiency of the monetary system and decides to sell the house to buy an apartment. The person arrives at a decision based on her Institution-based Trust in the monetary system and eventually expresses her Trust through the Action of selling the house.

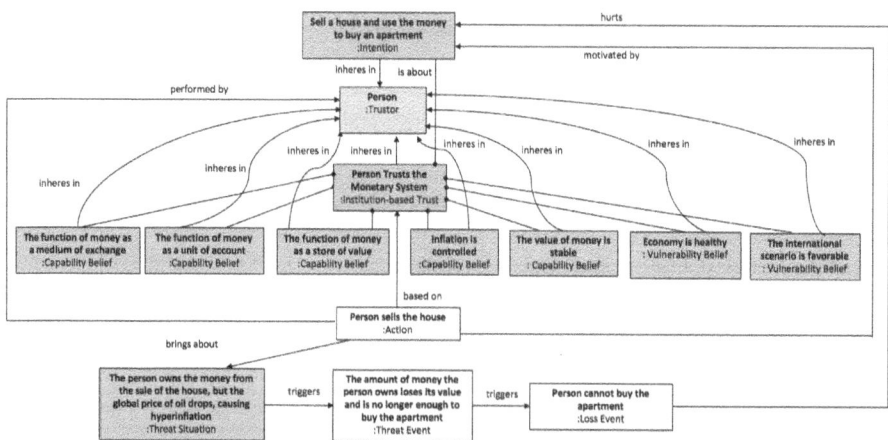

Figure 4.14: Institution-based Trust: Risk emerging from the trust relation.

The person sells the house in exchange for an amount of money she trusts to be able to use in the future to buy an apartment. By selling the house, the person becomes vulnerable to the stability of the monetary system (which in turn has its own vulnerabilities) and may be exposed to unanticipated risks. In order to illustrate the emergence of risk, let us consider that in this example the economy is highly dependent on oil exports. Thus, the price of oil can be considered a Vulnerability of the monetary system regarding the international scenario. If the global price of oil falls to the point of causing a disruption in the economy, currency may lose value and the price of goods goes up. In this case, the situation in which "the person owes a large amount of money at the time when the global price of oil drops, causing hyperinflation" can be considered a Threat Situation that may trigger a Threat Event if, for example, the amount of money the person owns loses its value and is no longer enough to buy the apartment. In this case, the amount of money loosing its value is a Threat Event that may trigger a Loss Event, which would be the person no longer being able to buy the apartment. This Lost Event hurts the person's Intention of selling the house and use the money to buy an apartment.

4.4.3 The Case of Vaccines in the Time of COVID-19

By the end of 2020, there were more than fifty COVID-19 vaccine candidates in trials, according to the World Health Organization (WHO) (World Health Organization, 2020). Naturally, each of them may present differences when it comes to efficacy. A study found that Pfizer-BioNTech vaccine efficacy was 52% after the first dose and 95% after the second (Polack et al., 2020). This stands for a trustworthiness evidence that can positively influence people's trust in the vaccine (a trustworthiness evidence influence), as it can lead people to believe that Pfizer-BioNTech vaccine is capable of protecting from COVID-19 (capability belief) with a high performance level. Let us suppose that another study shows that the efficacy of a second candidate is lower. This is a trustworthiness evidence that may lead people to believe that the performance level of the second candidate's capability of protecting from COVID-19 is lower than Pfizer-BioNTech's. Consequently people's trust degree will be higher in their trust relationship with Pfizer than in their trust relationship with the second candidate. Considering that Pfizer and BioNTech are, respectively, from the USA and Germany, it is possible that citizens of these two countries have more trust in the Pfizer-BioNTech vaccine than in the ones produced by pharmaceutical companies from other countries. That is because people's trust in the science and technology capacity of a particular country positively influences their trust in the pharmaceutical companies from that country (a trust influence).

Now let us consider the case of two friends, Tom and Jerry (trustors), who trust Pfizer-BioNTech COVID-19 vaccine (trustee) with different trust degrees. They trust the vaccine to safely protect them from COVID-19. Note that their trust is about a complex intention, composed of (i) the intention of being protected from getting COVID-19; and (ii) the intention of not experiencing side effects from the vaccine. Tom does not have any health issues. He strongly believes (belief intensity) that the vaccine can protect him from COVID-19 (a capability belief) and that its side effects (a threat capability) will not harm him (a capability belief). Jerry is allergic. His trust degree in the vaccine is lower than Tom's, as he believes that there is a small likelihood (manifestation likelihood) that the side effects (a threat capability) will harm him (a capability belief). Unfortunately, Jerry saw on the news that three Alaska health care workers had an allergic reaction after receiving a dose of the new Pfizer COVID-19 vaccine (Firger and Caldwell, 2020). His perception about this event negatively influenced his trust in the vaccine (a mental moment influence), as he started to believe that there is a high likelihood (manifestation likelihood) that the vaccine side effects will harm him. Conversely, people been vaccinated around the world and reporting just mild side effects are events that can be perceived by people in a positive way and consequently, positively influence people's trust in the vaccine (a mental moment influence). Hopefully, in Jerry's case, the influence weight of "people having just mild side effects" will be higher than the influence weight of the news about "the Alaska health care workers having allergic reactions". If we consider the case of people who opposes vaccines, their anti-vaccination beliefs (a mental moment) negatively influence their trust in a COVID-19 vaccine (a mental moment influence).

Finally, the US President-elect Joe Biden receiving the first dose of COVID-19 vaccine on live television and stating that " I'm doing this to demonstrate that people should be prepared when it's available to take the vaccine" (Sullivan, 2020) is an event that can be perceived by people in a positive way, thus positively influencing people's trust in the vaccine (a mental moment influence).

4.5 Related Work

Several trust-modeling approaches have been proposed over the years. In the context of the semantic web and social networks, most approaches focused simply on the representation of trust relations. One example is the work of Golbeck et al. (2003), which proposes an extension of the Friend of a Friend (FOAF) ontology to allow users to

4.5. Related Work

state and represent their trust in individuals they know. Another example is the Proof Markup Language Trust Ontology (PML-T) (McGuinness et al., 2007), which provides an extensible set of primitives for encoding trust information associated with information sources. PML-T was created as part of the Proof Markup Language, a standard developed by the Stanford University that defines primitive concepts and relations for representing knowledge provenance (McGuinness et al., 2007). It defines trust and belief relations involving a trustor, a trustee (the information source), and pieces of information. Although providing a framework for encoding trust relations, PML-T does not prescribe a way for representing trust itself.

Dokoohaki and Matskin (2008) propose a trust ontology for the design of trust networks on semantic web-driven social systems. The main component of their ontology is the trust relation that represents the connection between entities on the network. Every relation has a set of main properties that describe its nature and purpose, such as a topic and a value that represents the trust level. The authors also define a set of auxiliary properties for the trust relation, such as a goal that stands for the reason for establishing the relation and a recommender, which is a person on the network that has recommended the trustee. Furthermore, the relation between trust and risk is not mentioned. An important difference between these ontologies and our proposal is that they are not based on foundational ontologies, but are built on semantic web languages that give precedence to computational tractability over expressiveness. As discussed in Guizzardi (2006a), a number of semantic interoperability problems that cannot be handled by semantic web languages, such as OWL and RDF, as their expressivity is purposefully limited so that they remain computationally tractable.

Huang and Fox (2006) proposed a logical theory of trust in the form of an ontology that gives formal and explicit specification for the semantics of trust. The authors define two types of trust, namely, trust in belief and trust in performance. In the former, the trustor believes that something the trustee believes is true (for example: Mary wants to order a product and her friend John suggests she buys it from an online store he believes always delivers the orders on time. Mary does not know the online store at the time, but she believes what John believes, which is that the store delivers the orders on time). In the latter, the trustor believes in a piece of information created by the trustee or in the performance of an action committed by the trustee, both in a context within the trustor's context of trust. These two types refer to the general form of trust. The institution-based trust is not represented in Huang and Fox's ontology (Huang and Fox, 2006) nor is the relation between trust and risk.

Viljanen (2005) surveyed and classified thirteen computational trust models to create an ontology of trust. In his proposal, trust is represented as a relation between a trustor and a trustee, which depends on the action that the trustor is attempting and on the competence of the trustee. Additionally, Viljanen defines an element of confidence attached to the trust relationship, as well as a set of third party opinions in the form of reputation information. The author uses the concept of business value to represent both value and risk associated to the trustor's action. By attaching business values to the action, the ontology is able to represent the potential impact, positive or negative, of the action that the trustor is attempting. However, the representation of the relation between trust and risk lacks a more detailed description. For example, the ontology does not make it explicit how risk events are triggered, nor how they affect the trustor.

Secure Tropos (Giorgini et al., 2005) is a security-oriented extension of the agent-oriented software development methodology Tropos (Bresciani et al., 2004) that adds both security and trust as part of the software development process. In Secure Tropos the concepts of trust and delegation are combined to represent dependence relations between agents. Their constructs for trust refer to existent trustworthiness between actors along trust relations rather than specify the nature of the concept of trust. Secure Tropos differs from our approach not only regarding this particularity, but also because it does not represent the close relation between trust and risk. Moreover, although supporting a role-based approach to trust (Giorgini et al., 2005), in which the trustee is represented by roles or positions rather than by individual agents, it does not address explicitly the notion of institution-based trust.

Riegelsberger et al. (Riegelsberger et al., 2005) propose a framework on the mechanics of trust, in which they identify contextual (temporal, social, and institutional embeddedness) and intrinsic (ability and motivation) properties that warrant trust in another actor, which they name trust-warranting properties. They also describe how the presence of these properties can be signaled. Their analysis focus on correctness of trust-decisions. According to them, signals of trust-warranting properties are the basis for trust. In their model, they identify two broad categories of signals: symbols and symptoms, which are analogous to the ROT concepts of trust-warranting signals and trustworthiness evidence, respectively. Despite this similarity, their work differs from what we propose here, as they do not consider uncertainty signals and other factors that may influence trust, such as other trust relations and the mental state of the trustor. Also, they do not provide an ontological account for the concepts represented in their model.

Castelfranchi and Falcone (2010) made an important contribution with their theory of trust. In their work, they investigate what kind of beliefs and goals are necessary for trust to formulate several necessary conditions, such as the trustor having a goal and the belief that the trustee is competent and willing to achieve this goal. They also consider a behavioral aspect of trust, which is related to the notion of acting on trust. In our proposal we rely largely on their theory to formalize the general concept of trust, as well as the concept of social trust. As for the institution-based trust, Castelfranchi and Falcone (2010) state that it "builds upon the existence of shared rules, regularities, conventional practices, etc. and relies on this, in an automatic, non-explicit, mindless way", however the authors do not formalize this aspect of trust. Likewise, the relation between trust and risk is emphasized in their theory, but is not formalized. Finally, in the same work, they present trust dynamics in different aspects: (i) how trust changes on the basis of the trustor's experiences, which is related to the ROT concepts of *trustworthiness evidence* and *influence*; (iii) how trust is influenced by trust; how diffuse trust diffuses trust (that is how A's trusting B can influence C trusting B or D, and so on); and (iv) how trust can change using generalization reasoning (the fact that it is possible to predict how/when an agent who trusts something/someone will therefore trust something/someone else, before and without a direct experience). These last three aspects are related to *trust influences* in ROT. Although it is rather comprehensive, their proposal does not mention the emission of signals to communicate uncertainties nor to indicate trustworthy behavior on the part of the trustee.

4.6 Final Considerations

This chapter presented ROT, a core reference ontology of trust grounded in the Unified Foundational Ontology (Guizzardi, 2005; Guizzardi, Botti Benevides, et al., 2021) and that reuses concepts from the Common Ontology of Value and Risk (see section 3.2 of chapter 3).

The ontology proposed was developed through an ontological analysis based in a number of results in the literature of computer science, sociology, psychology, cognitive and behavioral sciences. It formalizes the general concept of trust and characterizes two types of trust, namely social trust and institution-based trust. ROT also provides an ontological account for the quantitative perspective of trust and for the factors that can influence trust. Lastly, it leverages the analysis of the behavioral aspect of trust to explain the emergence of risk from trust relations.

In chapter 7, ROT is applied and validated in the context of requirements engineering. We propose a novel methodology for ontology-based requirements engineering, which applies ROT as ontological foundation for the modeling of trustworthiness requirements (Amaral, Guizzardi, Guizzardi, et al., 2020). In this work, we rely on ROT to define the class of trustworthiness requirements and their relation to concepts such as trust, capability, vulnerability and risk, among others. As part of the ontology validation, we conducted a real case study to verify if ROT is capable of properly representing real world situations. In this study (Amaral, Guizzardi, Guizzardi, et al., 2021), ROT is applied to help with the elicitation of trustworthiness requirements of software systems by analyzing the case of Pix, the Brazilian Instant Payments Ecosystem created and managed by the Central Bank of Brazil.

In chapter 8, ROT is applied and validated in the context of decentralized finance, in a real-world case study on citizens' trust in central bank digital currency (CBDC) ecosystems, which was conducted in close collaboration with a national central bank (Amaral, Sales, and Guizzardi, 2022). This case study is also part of the ontology validation.

In chapter 10, ROT is applied and validated in the context of enterprise modeling. Driven by the need to align the vision and strategic goals of enterprises with their business architectures, ROT is used as the foundation for the specification of a pattern language for trust modeling in ArchiMate (Amaral, Sales, Guizzardi, Almeida, et al., 2020), which can be used to model trust in the context of enterprise architecture. These models can be used to address the gap between stakeholders' trust concerns and the components that integrate the different layers of the enterprise architecture.

Chapter 5

The Reference Ontology of Money and Virtual Currencies

This chapter presents the Reference Ontology of Money and Virtual Currencies[1] (ROME), a UFO-based ontology, specified in OntoUML (Guizzardi, 2005; Guizzardi, Fonseca, Almeida, et al., 2021), that formalizes the characterization of money, currency and virtual currencies, as well as its embedded concepts and relations (Amaral, Sales, and Guizzardi, 2021d; Amaral, Sales, Guizzardi, and Porello, 2020a; Amaral, Sales, Guizzardi, Porello, and Guarino, 2020).

ROME is a core reference ontology (Guizzardi, 2007; Scherp et al., 2011), designed to account for a conceptualization of money that is independent of a particular application domain, and to be applied in an off-line manner to assist humans in tasks such as meaning negotiation and consensus establishment. ROME intends to address the notion of money broadly, so that it can be applied to a number of disciplines and areas in finance and economics. Nonetheless, the codification of ROME models in gUFO (a partial translation of UFO to OWL) (Almeida, Guizzardi, et al., 2020) contributes to dealing with semantic interoperability issues, to semantic web related initiatives in finance (Bennett, 2013), as well as to the goal of transparency of financial data exchange according to FAIR principles (Jacobsen et al., 2020).

The chapter is organized as follows. Section 5.1 motivates the relevance of developing an ontology of money. Section 5.2 presents some characteristics of money and virtual currencies, as discussed in the literature. Section 5.3 presents the Reference On-

---
[1] The complete version of ROME in OntoUML and its implementation in OWL are available at http://purl.org/krdb-core/money-ontology.

tology of Money and Virtual Currencies. Section 5.4 applies the ontology to model and instantiation example. Section 5.5 discusses some related work. Finally, section 5.6 presents the conclusions of this chapter.

5.1 Introduction

It is a curious paradox that some entities are so ever-present in our daily life that we tend to be oblivious to the importance of the mechanisms that support their operation, as well as to the vital role they play in our lives. One example is breathing. We breathe all the time without even thinking about it, but when unexpected events occur, like the recent worldwide spread of a virus with the potential to threaten our respiratory capacity, we realize the importance of ensuring the proper functioning of our respiratory system.

The same goes for money. Money permeates most aspects of life in modern societies, however, the infrastructures that support the monetary system "remain invisible as long as they operate and fulfill their functions. In case of accident, disruption or crisis, their breakdown makes them visible and raises concerns and questions about their operation" (Papadopoulos, 2015). The financial crisis of 2007-2008 was an urgent reminder about the importance of money and finance.

Making sense of a plethora of information in a dynamic and complex environment is paramount in many activities realized to ensure the proper functioning of the financial system (Basel Committee, 2013; Scholes et al., 2010), such as the formulation of monetary policy, the safeguarding of financial stability, and the maintenance of *trust* in the monetary system. Moreover, having a clear understanding of the ontological nature of key concepts is fundamental to understand the evolution of the economy before innovations in the finance industry. This can be seen in the case of the advent of cryptocurrencies (European Central Bank, 2012). Despite their increasing popularization and the impacts they may have on the wider economy, research on this subject still lacks conceptual and semantic rigor, and the definition of a formal concept of cryptocurrencies and their relationship with money is still an open issue. Semantic interoperability is a fundamental aspect for a number of applications in this context in which, for example, values referred to in cryptocurrencies need to be integrated with values referred to in official currencies. For instance, in applications such as for anti-money laundering, one must analyze information from multiple and heterogeneous sources to detect unusual patterns, such as large amounts of cash flow at certain periods, by particular groups of agents.

5.1. Introduction

Despite several efforts to create a unified view of our economic and financial reality (Blums and Weigand, 2017; Enterprise Data Management Council, 2015; Fischer-Pauzenberger and Schwaiger, 2017), no formal model, comprehensive enough, has been developed to accurately describe the semantics of money and currencies. In this thesis we advocate for the need of a reference conceptual model that provides an ontological account to the concept of money and related concepts, to serve as a basis for communication, consensus and alignment among different approaches and perspectives, as well as to foster interoperability across different applications in the financial industry.

5.2 On Money and Virtual Currencies

5.2.1 The Origins of Money

Different theories about the origin of money are reported in the literature and until today this topic is a matter for debate. Regarding the emergence of money in society, two leading schools of thought present fundamentally different arguments on its origins. A classic theory, known as the *commodity theory of money* or the *catallactic theory* (Von Mises, 2013), was defended by many classical economists like Carl Menger (Menger, 2009), Georg Simmel (Simmel, 2004) and Ludwig von Mises (Von Mises, 2013). They claim that money is an institution that spontaneously evolved in society, from some commodities — such as tobacco (Simmel, 2004), salt (Simmel, 2004) and cattle (De Bonis and Vangelisti, 2019; Simmel, 2004)) — until the current stage of fiat money that is designated and issued by a central authority (Searle, 2017) and cannot be redeemed for a commodity. Its value is based on the trust that the issuer will keep its value relatively stable and not on it being redeemable or not (Zelmanovitz, 2015).

Alternatively, there are those who argue that money is a social construction (De Bruin et al., 2018; Innes, 1913; Keynes, 1971; Knapp, 1924; Mann, 1938), "an instrument representative of a debt owed by the state or even a token created and accepted by it as an instrument to pay taxes" (Zelmanovitz, 2015, p 12). This view is known as *chartalism* or the *state theory of money* (Knapp, 1924). According to the chartalist school, money is what is stated in law (Zelmanovitz, 2015).

In line with the state theory's argument that money represents a debt owed by the state, is the position defended by the *credit theory of money*, (a.k.a. *debt theory of money*), which states that money is merely a token of a credit/debt relationship (Innes, 1913; Macleod, 1890).

Questions about the commodity theory versus the state theory of money have been the subject of intense debate in the literature. In the current state of research, the state theory view seems to have stronger arguments than the commodity theory (De Bonis and Vangelisti, 2019). One of these arguments is that the value of the first metal coined money was too high for everyday consumption, so it is not plausible to think that it was intended to be used in exchanges between private individuals, while it makes sense to conclude that it was issued by city-states for administrative purposes (Zelmanovitz, 2015). Another noticeable argument of the state theorists is the difficulty the commodity theorists have in explaining the decreasing value of money over time (simply put, inflation) (De Bruin et al., 2018).

5.2.2 The Multiple Functions of Money

Although the format of money has changed considerably over time, its functions remain unchanged. From the wide number of definitions proposed in the literature on economics, it is possible to deduce a consensus about three main functions, namely:

- **medium of exchange**: a means of payment with a value that everyone trusts. For example, the statement "I bought this shirt for 20 euros" (from (Searle, 2017)) refers to this function. Note that here is also included the ability to make payments that have nothing to do with buying anything, like taxes and donations.
- **a unit of account**: money acts as a standard numerical unit for the measurement of prices and costs of goods, services, assets, and liabilities. For example, the statement "My car is worth 10,000 euros" (from (Searle, 2017)) refers to this function.
- **a store of value**: "money can be saved and retrieved in the future" (European Central Bank, 2012, p. 10). For example, the statement "I have 1,000 euros in my bank account" (again from (Searle, 2017)) refers to this function.

It is generally accepted in the literature that money performs its functions in virtue of the collective recognition of a certain status that makes it valuable and guarantees its acceptability (De Bruin et al., 2018; Innes, 1913; Keynes, 1971; Knapp, 1924; Mann, 1938; Papadopoulos, 2015; Searle, 1995). When this status is recognized for a certain object, it acquires a function known as *status function*, which "is not performed in virtue of the physical features of the person or object, but in virtue of the fact that a certain status has been assigned to the person or object" (Searle, 2017, p. 1457). This function can be performed only in virtue of the collective acceptance or recognition of that status in the community in question. Status functions are created by a certain type of speech act that Searle (Searle, 1995; Searle, 2017) terms *declaration*, where "you make something the case by declaring it to be the case" (Searle, 2017, p. 1458). According to Searle (Searle, 2017, p. 1455) "money always requires a *declaration* whereby some representation makes it the case that it is money".

Currently, the status function of money is defined by law. For example, a twenty-euros banknote fits this definition because it does have a definite status of being a twenty-euros banknote in Europe, as defined in the Treaty on the Functioning of the European Union ("Treaty on the Functioning of the European Union" 2012). People are willing to accept it in exchange for goods and services because they *trust* the monetary system that supports this status function. In (Castelfranchi and Falcone, 2010), the authors state that trust is the presupposition of money: originally money relies on the trust of the individuals accepting a monetary item as an instrument to indirectly acquire a certain amount of desirable goods (Zelmanovitz, 2015). Trust is therefore a crucial element of every monetary system.

5.2.3 Currency

The Oxford Dictionary ("Oxford English Dictionary" 1989) defines *currency* as "the system of money that a country uses". Generally, the national government is the only party authorized to produce and distribute physical currency in its geographical area of control. The government also regulates the production of non-physical currency by banks through its monetary policy, usually implemented via the central bank. In some countries, alternate currencies are permissible (e.g., Ethiopian Birr and US dollar in Ethiopia), but only the nationally sponsored currency has the status of legal tender. And in still other countries a foreign produced currency is both acceptable currency and legal tender (e.g. US dollar in Ecuador). For example, in the countries of the euro area, only euro banknotes and coins are legal tender and therefore, by law, they must be accepted as payment for a debt within those countries. According to the Article 128 of the Treaty on the Functioning of the European Union ("Treaty on the Functioning of the European Union" 2012): "The European Central Bank (ECB) shall have the exclusive right to authorise the issue of banknotes within the Union. The ECB and the national central banks may issue such notes. The banknotes issued by the ECB and the national central banks shall be the only such notes to have the status of legal tender within the Union".

5.2.4 On the notion of Central Bank Digital Currency

Central banks issue money as physical cash and electronic central bank deposits (aka reserves or settlement balances) and provide infrastructure to support a third type, namely commercial bank deposits (Bank for International Settlements et al., 2020). While cash and reserves are a liability of the central bank (in the sense that they represent a claim on the central bank), commercial bank deposits are a liability of the bank that issues them. Central Bank Digital Currency stands for a new type of money issued by central banks, which is different from cash and reserves or settlement balances.

Central banks have been actively researching the pros and cons of offering a digital currency to the public (Bank for International Settlements et al., 2020) and a number of definitions for this term have been proposed in the literature. Kochergina and Yangirovab (2019) define CBDC as "an electronic obligation of the central bank expressed in a national monetary unit and acting as a means of exchange and store of value". In (Committee on Payments and Market Infrastructures, 2018), CBDC is defined as "a central bank liability, denominated in an existing unit of account, which serves both as a medium of exchange and a store of value". According to Mancini-Griffoli et al. (2018) "CBDC is a new form of money, issued digitally by the central bank and intended to serve as legal tender". In the context of the European Union, CBDC is referred in the European Central Bank publications by the term *digital euro*. According to the ECB (European Central Bank, 2020) "the term digital euro denotes a liability of the Eurosystem recorded in digital form as a complement to cash and central bank deposits". They also state that "a digital euro would be just another way to supply euro, not a parallel currency" and "it should be convertible at par with other forms of the euro, such as banknotes, central bank reserves and commercial bank deposits".

Recently, aiming at coordinating and consolidating the investigation on CBDCs, the central banks of Canada, Japan, Sweden, Switzerland, the United Kingdom and the United States have come together, along with the European Central Bank and the Bank for International Settlements to produce a report (Bank for International Settlements et al., 2020) that summarises where they collectively stand. In this work, CBDC is defined as "a digital form of central bank money that is different from balances in traditional reserve or settlement accounts. A CBDC is a digital payment instrument, denominated in the national unit of account, that is a direct liability of the central bank" (Bank for International Settlements et al., 2020).

In general, in the literature, the concept of CBDC has been characterized based on several properties and design choices, explained as follows.

Liability. Currently money can represent a liability of the central bank (cash, reserves and settlement balances) or a liability of the bank that has emitted it (commercial bank deposits). While in the former the end user holds a claim on the central bank, in the latter she holds a claim on the issuing entity. CBDC is a liability of the central bank (Bank for International Settlements et al., 2020).

Form. While cash (such as coins and banknotes) is physical, central bank deposits, commercial bank deposits and CBDCs are digital.

Denomination in official currency. CBDC is another way to supply official money. It is denominated in the official currency and must be convertible at par to official currency, in the same way as cash, central bank deposits and commercial bank deposits (European Central Bank, 2020).

Functions of Money. CBDC is just a different manifestation of the same unit of account, store of value and medium of exchange already offered by central banks (Bank for International Settlements et al., 2020).

Scope. Payments are generally distinguished into retail and wholesale. While the former refers to relatively low-value transactions (in the form of, for example, credit transfers and direct debits), the latter corresponds to large-value and high-priority transactions, such as interbank transfers (Committee on Payments and Market Infrastructures, 2018). Wholesale CBDCs limit access to a predefined group of users (such as financial institutions), while the general purpose ones (aka retail CBDCs) are widely accessible to the general public.

Technology. A common distinction found in the literature is that between "token-based" and "account-based" CBDCs (Committee on Payments and Market Infrastructures, 2018). According to the authors that support this classification, a key difference between them is regarding the form of verification needed when CBDCs are exchanged. While token-based CBDC relies on the ability of the payee to verify the validity of the object used to pay, account-based CBDCs requires verifying the identity of the payer. Examples of token-based systems are cash (physical) and CBDCs stored in digital wallets. In both cases, the payee does not need to know anything about the payer. In the case of cash, the main concern is about counterfeiting (e.g. if the banknote is fake). With CBDC, the worry is both whether the token is genuine and whether it has already been spent (Committee on Payments and Market Infrastructures, 2018). A good example of account-based systems are bank deposits, which can be used to make payments. Similar to bank deposits, account-based CBDCs depend on the ability to verify the account holder's identity. A key concern here is identity theft, which allows transfers or withdraws from accounts without permission (Committee on Payments and Market Infrastructures, 2018).

Recently, some authors have questioned this distinction, arguing that, different from banknotes stored in one's physical wallet, CBDCs stored in digital wallets cannot be considered pure token-based. According to them, a CBDC is not just a token stored locally in the digital wallet provided to the user by the bank, but also an account entry on the central bank's blockchain ledger. This position can be explained as follows: Digital wallets have associated a private key and a corresponding public key address, where balances of CBDCs are stored. Although the bank offers to the user a digital wallet to facilitate the management of CBDC holdings and payments, the user's account (or public key) related to the CBDC resides on the central bank's blockchain where its CBDC is issued. Only someone who knows the private key can spend CBDCs associated with the corresponding public key address. In this sense, the private key is the proof of identity needed to transact from the account. Since digital tokens need an account (public key address) to send and receive transactions, some authors claim that pure token-based CBDC do not exist.

As the terms "token" and "account" can be used to refer to different concepts across different fields, to avoid confusion, in this thesis we use the term *object-based* to refer to CBDCs associated to an object stored somewhere and controlled by a user, which is the case of CBDCs held in digital wallets, and the term *registry-based* to refer to CBDCs associated to stored balances tied to the identity of the owner, just as in a bank account. The former is analogous to the "token-based" category mentioned above, while the latter is analogous to the aforementioned "account-based" category.

Transfer mechanism. The transfer of cash is conducted on a peer-to-peer basis (decentralized), while deposits are transferred through an intermediary (centralized) (Committee on Payments and Market Infrastructures, 2018). CBDC may be transferred either on a peer-to-peer basis or through an intermediary, which could be the central bank, a commercial bank or a third-party agent (Committee on Payments and Market Infrastructures, 2018).

Anonymity Users' privacy can be protected to various degrees, depending on the preferred balance between individual rights and public interest. Although cash transactions are anonymous, regulations (mainly related to money laundering and terrorist financing) do not allow anonymity in electronic transactions and thus CBDCs must in principle comply with such regulations (European Central Bank, 2020).

5.2. On Money and Virtual Currencies

Availability. Currently, access to reserves and settlement balances is limited to central bank operating hours. CBDCs could be available 24/7 or only during certain specified times. So far there is considerable agreement amongst the central banks in the sense that CBDCs should be available available 24/7 (European Central Bank, 2020).

The prevalence of one or other property or design choice to characterize the concept of CBDC is driven by the particularities and circumstances of each country or area. Although so far there is no "one size fits all" conceptualization of CBDC, we argue that it is possible to deduce a consensus in the literature on a core set of essential properties that define what a CBDC is. In summary, what can be extracted from these different definitions is that a CBDC necessarily: (i) is a digital form of money; (ii) is a liability of the central bank; (iii) is denominated in the official currency; (iv) is convertible at par with other forms of official money, such as banknotes, central bank reserves and commercial bank deposits; (v) serves as a medium of exchange, an unit of account and a store of value; and (iv) is subjected to legal and regulatory frameworks that specify and regulate it.

An important aspect is that the different types of official money (cash, central bank deposits and commercial bank deposits) also have the same above-mentioned essential properties, except for cash w.r.t. form (as it is physical) and commercial bank deposits w.r.t. liability (as they are a liability of the issuing bank). CBDCs can be further distinguished into different subcategories (such as retail object-based, retail registry-based, wholesale object-based and wholesale registry-based) according to different design choices. Table 5.1 provides a comparison of some design choices across existing (cash, central bank deposits and commercial bank deposits) (ISO, 2013) and potential (CBDC) (Bank for International Settlements et al., 2020) types of money.

Table 5.1: Design choices by money type.

	Scope	Technology	Transfer Mechanism	Anonymity	Availability
Cash	General purpose	Object-based	Decentralized	Yes	24/7
Central bank deposit	Restricted	Registry-based	Centralized	No	Restricted
Commercial bank deposit	General purpose	Registry-based	Centralized	No	Restricted
CBDC Retail Object-based	General purpose	Object-based	Decentralized	Possible[2]	24/7 (possible)
CBDC Retail Registry-based	General purpose	Registry-based	Centralized	No	24/7 (possible)
CBDC Wholesale Object-based	Restricted	Object-based	Decentralized	Possible[2]	24/7 (possible)
CBDC Wholesale Registry-based	Restricted	Registry-based	Centralized	No	24/7 (possible)

5.2.5 Virtual Currencies (VC)

The ECB defines virtual currency as "a digital representation of value, not issued by a central bank, credit institution or e-money institution, which in some circumstances can be used as an alternative to money" (European CentralBank, 2015, p. 4). We could go a little bit further and include non-digital forms of virtual currencies in this definition such as tokens used in casinos.

From the point of view of central banks and regulatory authorities, virtual currencies cannot be regarded as full forms of money at the moment (European CentralBank, 2015). Also from a legal perspective, they are not considered money, nor have a legal tender capacity backed by law. From an economic perspective, the virtual currencies currently known do not fully meet all three functions of money defined in economic literature (European CentralBank, 2015). In some cases they "have a limited function as a medium of exchange because they have a very low level of acceptance among the general public" (European CentralBank, 2015, p. 23). In addition, due to the high volatility

---

[2] Although object-based CBDC supports anonymity, it must take into consideration anti-money laundering and counter terrorist financing regulations, as well as security policies.

of their exchange rates to currencies, they are not considered suitable to be used as store of value. Lastly, "both the low level of acceptance and the high volatility of their exchange rates and thus purchasing power make them unsuitable as a unit of account" (European CentralBank, 2015, p. 24).

However, virtual currencies are similar to money within their user community. They necessarily have their own rules and processes enabling the transfer of value, as well as their payment systems (European CentralBank, 2015). These systems of rules and processes are called *virtual currency schemes*, and are organized into three categories:

1. **closed virtual currencies**, which have almost no link to the real economy, as they can only be spent by purchasing virtual goods and services offered within the virtual community and, at least in theory, they cannot be traded outside it.

2. **virtual currencies with unidirectional flows**, in which "units can be purchased using real money at a specific exchange rate but cannot be exchanged back to the original currency" (European CentralBank, 2015, p. 6), and trading with other users is not allowed. Examples are loyalty programmes like airlines' points programmes and the Pokemon Go's PokeCoins (Stanley-Smith and Schwanke, 2016) (which can be bought using real money and can be exchanged with in-game items).

3. **virtual currencies with bi-directional flows**, in which units can be bought and sold according to (floating) exchange rates. Examples include private cryptocurrencies (Mukhopadhyay et al., 2016), such as Bitcoin and Ethereum, and stablecoins (cryptocurrencies with values tied to official fiat currencies or other assets).

5.3 ROME: Reference Ontology of Money and Virtual Currencies

5.3.1 Analyzing Money, Currency and Related Concepts

In general, we are in line with the widespread position defended by some authors in the literature, which assume that money depends on the collective acceptance or recognition of its status as money (De Bruin et al., 2018; Innes, 1913; Keynes, 1971; Knapp, 1924; Mann, 1938; Papadopoulos, 2015; Searle, 1995). This dependence is straightforward in the case of fiat money, but is also true for commodity money, as it requires a status function "precisely to the extent that it is collectively recognized as money and not just as a commodity" (Searle, 2017, p. 1460). In contemporary society the status function of money is constituted by the law that creates it. For example, in Europe, the Treaty on the Functioning of the European Union ("Treaty on the Functioning of the European Union" 2012) describes the status function that defines euro banknotes and coins as legal tender money in the countries of the euro area. Note that the law specifies both the currency and the objects that are considered legal tender in a particular country or region. It also defines a structure for the currency value domain. Examples of structures are: one-dimensional structure of numbers with two decimal places defined for euros, and one-dimensional structure of integers defined for Paraguay's Guarani (ISO, 2015).

According to the literature on the history of money, different types of objects have been used as money in all its manifestations, such as (i) tobacco and salt, used as *commodity money*; (ii) banknotes and paper certificates, used as *commodity backed money*; and (iii) banknotes, coins and bank deposits in electronic format, used as *fiat money*. In our analysis we are focusing on the objects currently used as fiat money, such as banknotes and coins. We shall refer to these objects as *monetary objects* henceforth.

Every monetary object has a nominal value (also known as face value) denominated in the currency defined in the law that describes its status function. Only in exceptional cases in history (generally in times of crisis) there has been temporary reutilization of banknotes, "overstamped" with a nominal value different from the original one. For example, in 1986, in Brazil, the prevailing currency Cruzeiro was replaced by an new currency, named Cruzado, at a rate of 1 Cruzado to 1000 Cruzeiros. For a short period of time, some denominations of Cruzeiro banknotes were "overstamped" with the equivalent nominal value denominated in Cruzados (Central Bank of Brazil, 2007).

During their life cycle, monetary objects can be considered either valid or not valid. For example, new banknotes are not considered valid until they are released and put into public circulation. Likewise, damaged banknotes fulfilling certain criteria defined in law are not considered valid (for example, an euro banknote is not considered valid if 50% or less of the banknote is presented and there are no proofs that the missing parts have been destroyed (European Central Bank, 2013)). Obviously, only valid monetary objects can be exchanged for goods and services in the economy. In modern economies, money emerges a standard unit of account in which all other commodities express their exchange values. A valid monetary object has an exchange value that is equal to its nominal value; and an agent holding control of it is endowed with the capacity of making economic transactions in the amount corresponding to its exchange value. For example, a twenty-euros banknote has an exchange value of twenty euros. If the price of a Big Mac is five euros, an agent holding control of a valid twenty-euros banknote is capable of exchanging it for four Big Macs.

Money also presupposes the existence of a credit/debt relation (Innes, 1913; Macleod, 1890). Monetary objects establish this relation between the agent holding control of them and the monetary authority (e.g. central bank), which ultimately represents the State. As for bank deposits, they correspond to an electronic monetary credit denominated in a certain currency. In this case, the credit/debt relation involves also the financial institution in charge of the bank account, as intermediary.

Agents holding control of monetary objects or owing electronic monetary credits are endowed with the capacity of making economic transactions in the amount corresponding to the exchange value of the monetary object or the electronic monetary credit value, respectively. This capacity is closely related to the *media of exchange* function of money. In this thesis we name it exchange power. Moving in this direction, if we consider the exchange power resulting from the total of electronic monetary credits and monetary objects controlled by an agent, we obtain a kind of aggregated exchange power that corresponds to the total value in economic transactions the agent is capable to carry out.

As previously mentioned, goods and services have their prices expressed in terms of currencies. As the price of goods and services can change, influenced by the economic environment and the dynamic of the system of prices, the purchasing power associated with these aggregated exchange powers also changes. The purchasing power describes the quantity of goods an amount of money can buy. It is related to the concepts of inflation and price indexes. The inflation rate means an increase in general price level, measured by the variation in a price index during a period. When there is inflation, the purchasing power decreases. It means that the exchange value of the transactions that the agent manages to carry out remains the same (and is equal to the aggregate exchange value), however, the quantity of goods and services that he manages to get with that value will vary, depending on the price of the commodities.

Let us consider an example in which an agent named Mary has twenty euros in her bank account and a ten-euros banknote in her wallet. In this case, she has an aggregated exchange power of thirty euros and is able to carry out economic transactions in the amount corresponding to this value. Considering that the price of a Big Mac is five euros, the purchasing power of Mary is equivalent to six Big Macs. If the Big Mac's price rises to six euros, Mary's aggregated exchange power remains the same, but her purchasing power is no longer the same because now she's able to buy only five Big Macs.

It is worth mentioning that monetary objects can also be traded in the economy as regular commodities, like collectible items. For example, some rare banknotes are traded by banknote collectors at far more than their nominal (or face) value. Even valid banknotes in circulation can be traded as collectible items at a value above their face value. However, for the acquisition of goods and services in the economy, a banknote functions as a means of exchange and will always be worth its face value.

Finally, another important aspect is money's dependence on trust (Amaral, Sales, and Guizzardi, 2021b; 2022; Amaral, Sales, Guizzardi, and Porello, 2019). It is clearly recognized in the literature that trust is a crucial element for the well functioning of any monetary system (Castelfranchi and Falcone, 2010; Papadopoulos, 2015; Searle, 2017; Zelmanovitz, 2015). A precondition for the system to work is trust that the monetary objects and credits will be generally accepted, as well as that both price and financial stability will be maintained. Even in this day and age, in which the legal tender status of money is enforced by law, money depends on the trust of society in the monetary system, which guarantees that mechanisms, infrastructures and protective structures (such as law, regulations, processes, procedures and government enforcement bodies) are in place to ensure that money is widely accepted, transactions take place, contracts are fulfilled and, above all, agents can count on that happening.

Nonetheless, as trust relations are highly dynamic (Amaral, Sales, and Guizzardi, 2022), the decreasing level of trust in a particular monetary system can lead money to gradually lose its functions. When inflation rates are very high, money does not function as an effective store of value and people tend to spend it immediately rather than hold it (Wolla, 2013). Also, as prices start to rise rapidly, the function of money as unit of account diminishes. Finally, inflation reduces the function of money as a medium of exchange. In situations of hyperinflation, people may abandon the use of one currency for a more stable one (Wolla, 2013). For example, in 2007, hyperinflation was so problematic in Zimbabue that "people abandoned the Zimbabwean dollar, preferring to conduct transactions in U.S. dollars or South African rands. The Zimbabwean currency became nearly useless as money and was removed from circulation in 2009" (Wolla, 2013, p 2).

5.3.2 Similarities and Differences between Money and VC

Virtual currencies have been the subject of intense policy debates, however there is currently no international agreement on how they should be defined. In this section, we elaborate on evidences that motivate us to advocate the position put forth by the European Central Bank (European CentralBank, 2015), according to which virtual currencies

5.3. ROME: Reference Ontology of Money and Virtual Currencies

are neither money nor official currencies. In particular, we explore the roles of status function, legal tender status and trust, in the conceptualization of both VC and money.

Status Function. Virtual currencies are similar to money in the sense that both have their value grounded on a collective recognition of a certain status that makes them valuable. In the case of money this status function is defined by law. As for virtual currencies, it is part of their specification and dedicated retail payment systems, also known as *virtual currency schemes*.

Legal Tender Status. According to the ECB (European Central Bank, 2012, p 5) "virtual currency schemes differ from electronic money schemes insofar as the currency being used as the unit of account has not a counterpart with legal tender status". In a virtual currency scheme, all digital representations of value map to "tokenised" representations of virtual currencies, which are not regulated by law. The lack of a legal framework leads to problems for redeeming funds, as the link between virtual currencies and currencies with legal tender status is not regulated by law (European Central Bank, 2012).

Trust. Another similarity between money and virtual currencies is that both are dependent on trust. A precondition for the proper functioning of both the monetary and the VC system is trust that money and virtual currencies will be accepted, respectively. While in the case of money this acceptance comprises the whole society and trust includes the belief that both price and financial stability will be maintained, virtual currencies still have a limited level of acceptance among the general public, probably due to the high volatility of their exchange rates to currencies and to the "lack of a proper legal basis for virtual currency schemes" (European Central Bank, 2012, p 42). As currently virtual currencies do not have a legal tender capacity nor are backed by law, "users do not benefit from legal protection such as redeemability or a deposit guaranty scheme, and are more exposed to the various risks that regulation usually mitigates" (European CentralBank, 2015, p 21).

5.3.3 Representing the Ontology of Money in OntoUML

In this section, we present the Reference Ontology on Money and Virtual Currencies (ROME) (Amaral, Sales, and Guizzardi, 2021d; Amaral, Sales, Guizzardi, and Porello, 2020a; Amaral, Sales, Guizzardi, Porello, and Guarino, 2020), a well-founded ontology that formalizes the characterization of money and currency, as well as its embedded concepts and relations. In the OntoUML diagrams depicting this ontology, we adopt the following color coding: types are represented in purple, objects in pink, qualities and modes in blue, relators in green, and datatypes in white.

Figure 5.1 depicts the concept of Money Status Function Description as a type of Normative Description (concept from UFO-C, see section 2.3). The Money Status Function Description defines a Currency and the Monetary Object Types that have the status of money. For example, the "Treaty on the Functioning of the European Union" ("Treaty on the Functioning of the European Union" 2012) is an example of Money Status Function Description, which defines euro banknotes and coins as legal tender money in the countries of the euro area. In this case, "euro" is the Currency, while "euro banknote" and "euro coin" are Monetary Object Types. The Money Status Function Description also defines a Currency Quality Space Structure for the Currency Quality Space. The former corresponds to a Social Object (concept from UFO-C, see section 2.3) that prescribes a structure for the domain of values (eg. number with two decimal places), while the latter corresponds to the value domain itself (see (Guizzardi, 2005) for *quality spaces*).

In the ontology, Monetary Objects represent instances of Monetary Object Types. For example, a "twenty-euros banknote" is a Monetary Object and corresponds to an instance of the "euro banknote" Monetary Object Type, defined in the "Treaty on the Functioning of the European Union" ("Treaty on the Functioning of the European Union" 2012). We classify Monetary Object in Physical Monetary Object (e.g. banknotes and coins) and Digital Monetary Object (e.g. object-based CBDC). Physical Monetary Objects are distinguished into Valid Monetary Object and Not Valid Monetary Object, which represent two different phases of the Physical Monetary Object's life cycle. The distinction between "valid" and "not valid" allows for the representation of the life cycle of a physical monetary object. It is particularly important in the context of central banks, because they need to control the movement of monetary objects, such as banknotes, since they are printed until their destruction. For example, new banknotes are not considered valid until they are released and put into public circulation.

The nominal_value property corresponds to the Monetary Object's nominal value, defined by the issuing authority. The property exchange_value is specific to Valid Monetary Objects and Digital Monetary Objects as only they can be exchanged for goods and services in the economy. The exchange value of a Valid Monetary Object is equal to its nominal value. In UFO, properties can be directly evaluated (projected) into certain value spaces (Guizzardi, 2005). Both the exchange value and the nominal value of a Monetary Object are modeled as properties that have a value in a Currency Quality

5.3. ROME: Reference Ontology of Money and Virtual Currencies

Space, which is structured according to a particular Currency Quality Space Structure. For example, euro has a measurable value in one-dimensional structure of numbers with two decimal places (ISO, 2015) (figure 5.2).

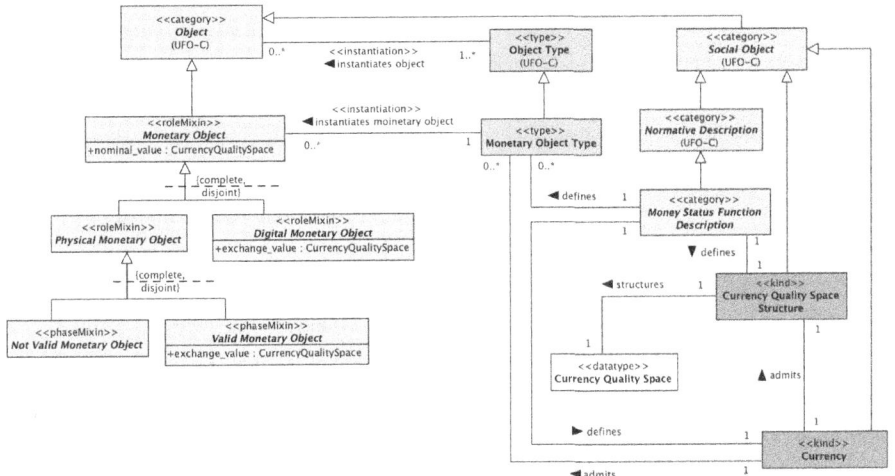

Figure 5.1: Money and Status Function.

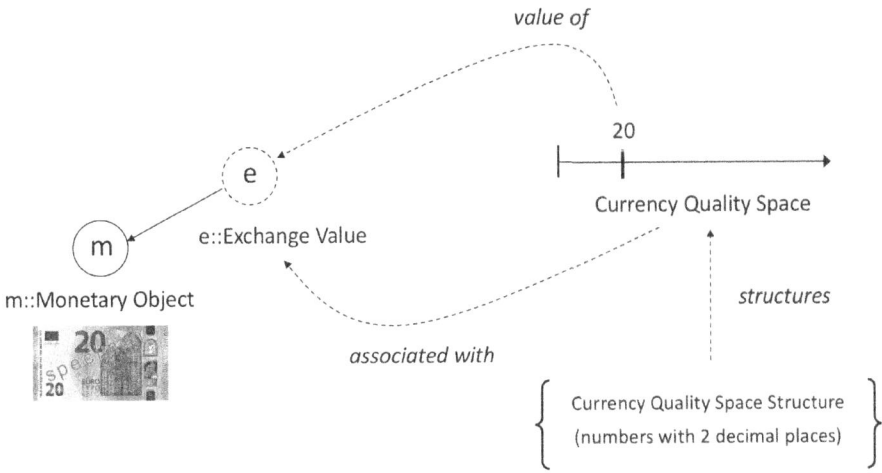

Figure 5.2: Currency Quality Space.

Figure 5.3 depicts monetary objects and monetary credit/debt relations.

Money represents a credit/debt relation between an Agent that holds control of a monetary object (cash or object-based CBDC) or has credit in an account (commercial bank deposit, central bank deposit or registry-based CBDC), and either a Monetary Authority such as a central bank (in the case of cash, central bank deposits and CBDC) or a Financial Institution (in the case of commercial bank deposits). In other words, money represents a liability of either a Monetary Authority (for cash, central bank deposits and CBDC) or a Financial institution (for commercial bank deposits). We have extended ROME to distinguish between Financial Institution Credit/Debt Relation and Monetary Authority Credit/Debt Relation. The former refers to commercial bank deposits and represents a liability of a financial institution. It is composed of a monetary credit (FI Monetary Credit) and a monetary debt (FI Monetary Debt), which have their values projected in a particular Currency Quality Space, and inhere in the Agent (creditor) and in the Financial Institution (debtor), respectively. The latter refers to cash, central bank deposits and CBDC, and represents a liability of a monetary authority such as a central bank. Similarly, it is composed of a Monetary Credit and a Monetary Debt, which have their values projected in a particular Currency Quality Space, and inhere in the Agent (creditor) and in the Monetary Authority (debtor), respectively.

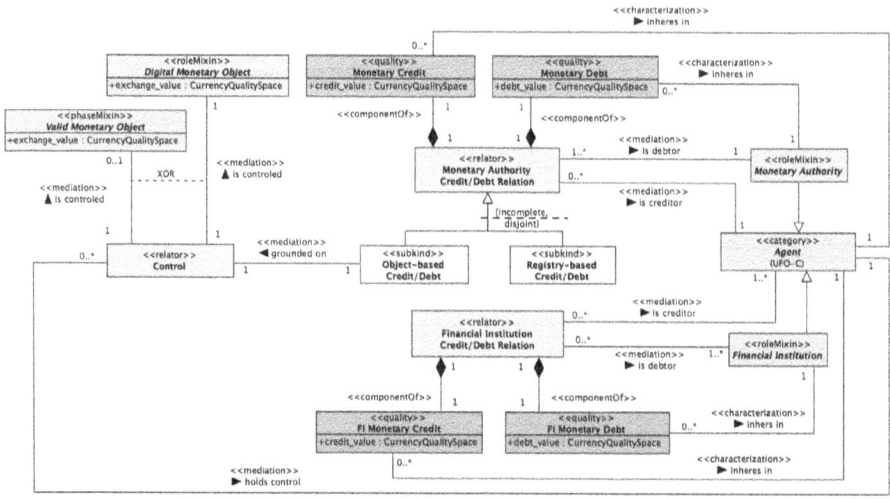

Figure 5.3: Monetary Objects and Monetary Credit/Debt.

The Monetary Authority Credit/Debt Relation is further specialized into Object-

5.3. ROME: Reference Ontology of Money and Virtual Currencies

based Credit/Debt and Registry-based Credit/Debt. The former represents the credit/debt relation that a Valid Monetary Object (e.g. banknotes and coins) or a Digital Monetary Object (e.g. object-based CBDC) establishes between the Agent that holds Control of it, and the Monetary Authority. As for the Registry-based Credit/Debt relation, it represents central bank deposits and registry-based CBDCs.

When an Agent plays the role of creditor in a Monetary Authority Credit/Debt Relation or in a Financial Institution Credit/Debt Relation, she is endowed with the power to make economic transactions in the amount corresponding to this credit (figure 5.4). This power is termed here exchange power. The Exchange Power to carry out economic transactions inheres in the Agent and is grounded either on a Monetary Authority Credit/Debt Relation or in a Financial Institution Credit/Debt Relation, in which the Agent is the creditor. The Exchange Power's property exchange_power_value assumes a value in a Currency Quality Space, which is equal to the value of the monetary credit. We model the exchange power resulting from the sum of monetary credits by means of the entity Aggregated Exchange Power, which is represented as a kind of capability inhering in the Agent. Finally, the Aggregated Exchange Power has an underlying Purchasing Power that corresponds to the quantity of goods and services the Agent manages to get with this Aggregated Exchange Power (figure 5.4). As previously discussed, the Purchasing Power depends on the Price of goods and services. We model Price as a quality value that is "attached" to an Object, as a result of an assessment made by an Agent. The relationship Pricing represents this assessment. We are aware that ROME does not provide a deep analysis of pricing. This analysis fall outside the scope of this thesis, as our focus is the modeling of the relationship between money and prices.

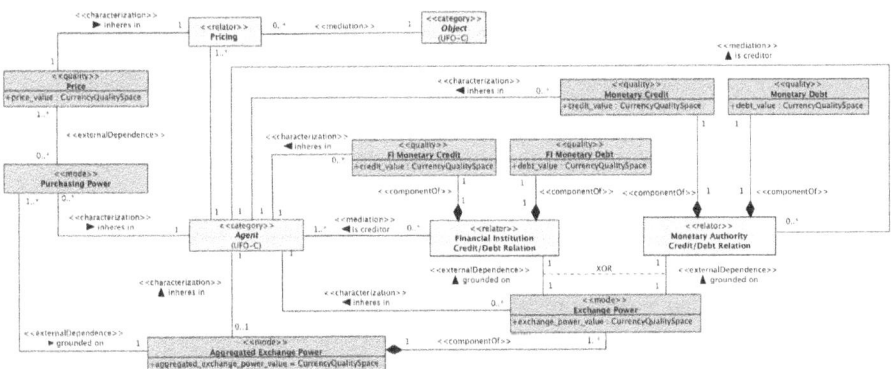

Figure 5.4: Money, Exchange Power and Purchasing Power.

We make use here of the concepts and relations defined in the Reference Ontology of Trust (see chapter 4) to model the relation between money and trust, presented in figure 5.5. ROT formalizes the general concept of trust and distinguishes between two types of trust, namely, social trust and institution-based trust. The latter builds upon the existence of shared rules, regularities, conventional practices, etc. and is related to social systems (Amaral, Sales, Guizzardi, and Porello, 2019), like the Monetary System. According to ROT, Institution-based Trust is a specialization of Trust in which the Trustee is a social system. In our ontology the entity Institution-Based Trust represents the Trust of the society (a social Agent) in the Monetary System.

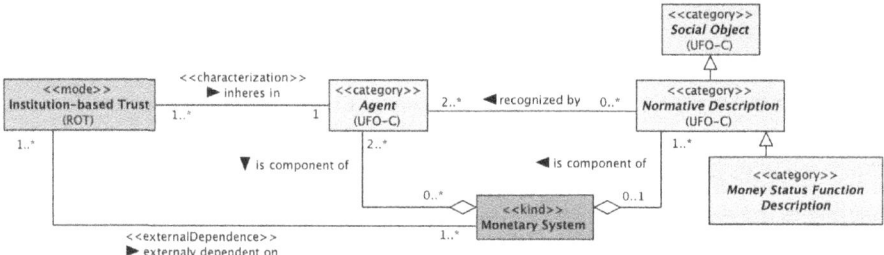

Figure 5.5: Money and Trust.

5.3.4 Modeling Virtual Currencies in OntoUML

Similar to money, virtual currencies have their value grounded on a status function, which is defined in their underlying virtual currency scheme. In Fig 5.6, the entity Virtual Currency Scheme Description, which defines the Virtual Currency and the Virtual Currency Token Type, represents this concept. As well as for money, the Virtual Currency Scheme Description also defines a Virtual Currency Quality Space Structure for the Virtual Currency Quality Space. Frequent flyer program points and private cryptocurrencies, such as Bitcoin and Ethereum are examples of Virtual Currencies.

In the ontology, Virtual Currency Token represents instances of Virtual Currency Token Type. The property vc_token_value represents the token value and is projected in a Virtual Currency Quality Space.

As aforementioned, virtual currencies are similar to money regarding the role played by trust. As we did for money, we made use of the concepts defined in the Reference Ontology of Trust (see chapter 4) to model the relation between virtual currencies and trust. Therefore, in figure 5.7, the entity Institution-Based Trust represents the Trust of

5.3. ROME: Reference Ontology of Money and Virtual Currencies

Agents in the Virtual Currency System.

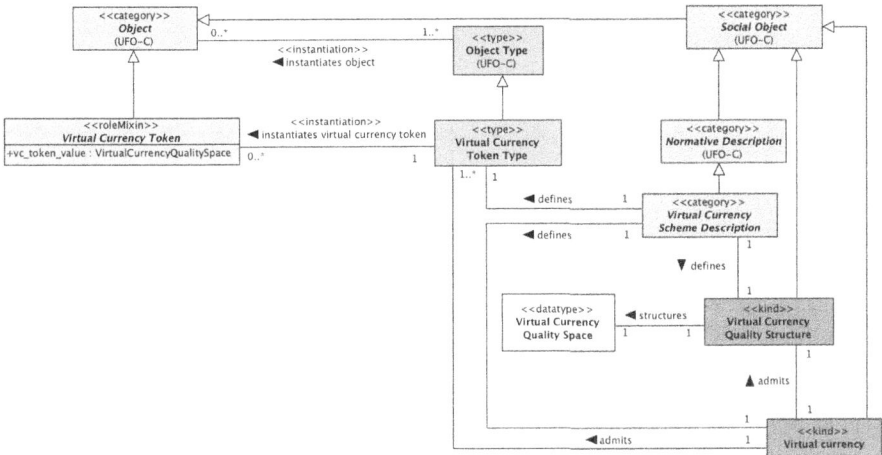

Figure 5.6: Virtual Currency.

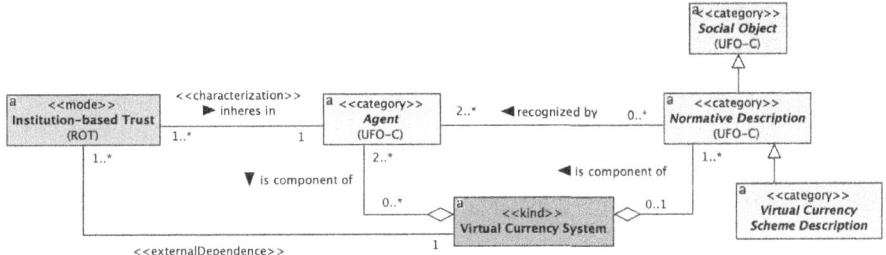

Figure 5.7: Virtual Currency and Trust.

Following the categorization proposed by the ECB (European CentralBank, 2015), in figure 5.8 we distinguish Virtual Currency Token into Closed VC Token and Purchasable VC Token. Closed VC Tokens cannot be purchased nor converted to legal tender currencies. Differently, Purchasable VC Tokens can be purchased using legal tender currencies at a specific exchange rate. For this reason, they have an associated price value that is represented by means of the property vc_token_price, which takes a value in a Currency Quality Space. Within the category of Purchasable VC Token we can further distinguish into Unidirectional Flow VC Token and Bidirectional Flow VC Token. The difference between then is that only Bidirectional Flow VC Tokens can

122   Chapter 5. The Reference Ontology of Money and Virtual Currencies

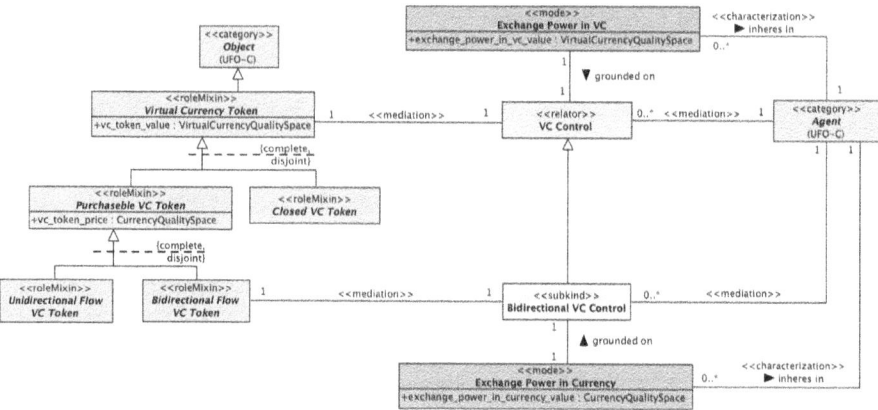

Figure 5.8: Virtual Currency and Exchange Power.

be exchanged to legal tender currencies. Therefore, Agents holding control of Bidirectional Flow VC Tokens have the power to exchange it to legal tender currencies, as well as to real goods and services. We model this capacity by means of the entity Exchange Power in Currency, which inheres in the Agent and is grounded on the control relation Bidirectional VC Control, between the Agent and Bidirectional Flow VC Token. Finally, every Agent holding control of a Virtual Currency Token has an exchange power to carry out economic transactions denominated in that particular virtual currency in the amount correspondent to the value of the Virtual Currency Token. The entity Exchange Power in VC represents this capacity.

5.4 Use Case Illustration

In this section, we apply ROME to model a case illustration that covers key concepts of the ontology. Let us consider the example described as follows: *Lorenzo has a fifty euro banknote in his pocket and one thousand euros in his bank account at the Medici Bank, a large commercial bank in Italy. At that time the digital euro has already been launched in Europe. Lorenzo has twenty digital euros (a CBDC, issued by the Banca d'Italia) stored in his digital wallet. He also has ten bitcoins, a privately issued cryptocurrency with no status of money.*

Figures 5.9, 5.10 and 5.11 present the ROME instantiation for this example. In figure 5.9, the "Treaty on the Function of the European Union" ("Treaty on the Functioning of

5.4. Use Case Illustration

the European Union" 2012) is a Money Status Function Description that defines euro banknotes and digital euro CBDC as money in the countries of the euro area. It also defines "euro" as the official Currency and prescribes "numbers with 2 decimal places" as the structure for the Currency domain of values (Currency Quality Space Structure). The "50 euro banknote" is a Valid Monetary Object that corresponds to an instance of the "euro banknote" Monetary Object Type, defined in the "Treaty on the Functioning of the European Union". Both its nominal value and its exchange value are equal to 50. Likewise, the "20 digital euro CBDC" is a Digital Monetary Object that corresponds to an instance of the "digital euro CBDC" Monetary Object Type, also defined in the "Treaty on the Functioning of the European Union". Both its nominal value and its exchange value are equal to 20.

As presented in figure 5.10 "Lorenzo" (an Agent) controls the "50 euro banknote", which establishes an Object-based Credit/Debt relation between him and the "Banca d'Italia" (the Monetary Authority). This relation is composed of "Lorenzo's Credit" of 50 euros and the "Banca d'Italia's Debt" of the same amount. "Lorenzo" also controls the "20 digital euro CBDC", which also establishes an Object-based Credit/Debt relation between him and the "Banca d'Italia" (the Monetary Authority), composed of "Lorenzo's Credit" of 20 euros and the "Banca d'Italia's Debt" of the same amount. Figure 5.11 also shows the credit/debt relation between "Lorenzo" (the creditor) and the "Medici Bank" (the debtor), associated to Lorenzo's bank account. This relation is composed of "Lorenzo's Credit" of 1000 euros and the "Medici Bank Debt" of the same amount.

In figure 5.11 we can observe that "Lorenzo" is endowed with the power to make economic transactions in the amount corresponding to the credits he has (aka Exchange Power), namely "50 euros" (the banknote exchange power), "20 euros" (the CBDC exchange power) and "1000 euros" (the exchange power of the credit in the bank account). Therefore, in total, Lorenzo has an Aggregated Exchange Power of 1070 euros, which has an underlying Purchasing Power that corresponds to the quantity of goods and services Lorenzo manages to get with this Aggregated Exchange Power (1070 euros).

Figure 5.12 shows "Bitcoin" as a Virtual Currency that is defined and operates according to the "Bitcoin Rules and Algorithms" (an instance of Virtual Currency Scheme Description). The "10 Bitcoin Token" is a Bidirectional Flow VC Token that corresponds to an instance of the "Bitcoin Token" Virtual Currency Token Type, as defined in the "Bitcoin Rules and Algorithms". We can observe in figure 5.13 that "Lorenzo" controls the "10 Bitcoin Token" (a Bidirectional VC Control relation) and, consequently, he is endowed with an exchange power of 10 bitcoin (Exchange Power in VC) that corresponds to an exchange power in currency of 50 euros (Exchange Power in Currency) — which is the value of bitcoin in an official currency (euros, in this case).

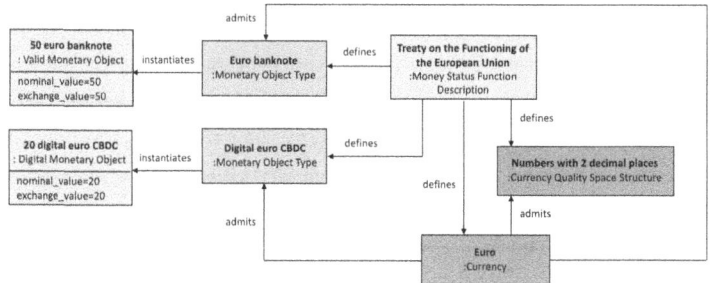

Figure 5.9: Money and Status Function Instantiation.

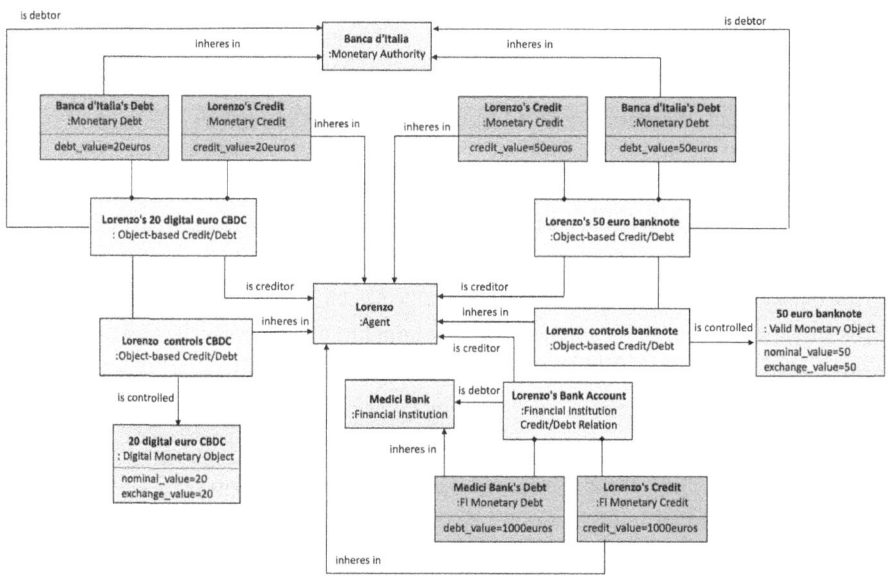

Figure 5.10: Monetary Objects and Monetary Credit/Debt.

5.4. Use Case Illustration

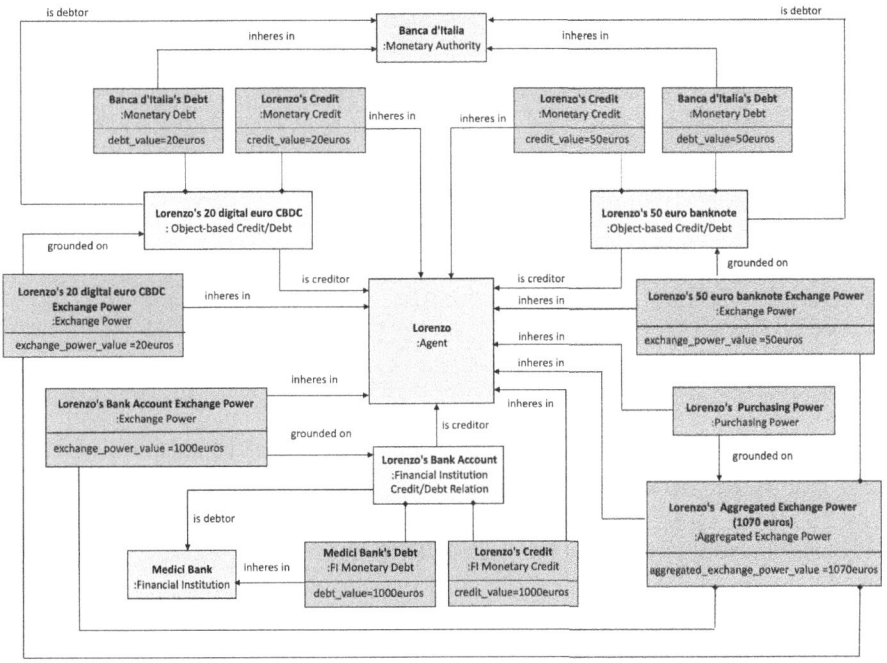

Figure 5.11: Exchange Power and Purchasing Power Instantiation.

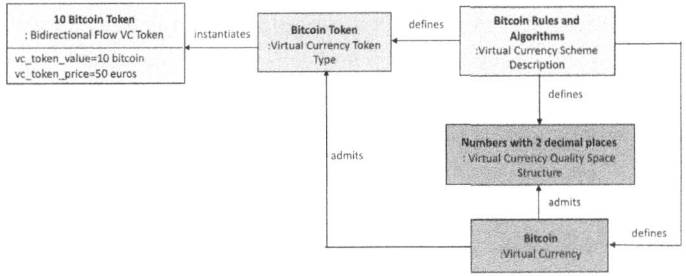

Figure 5.12: Virtual Currency Instantiation.

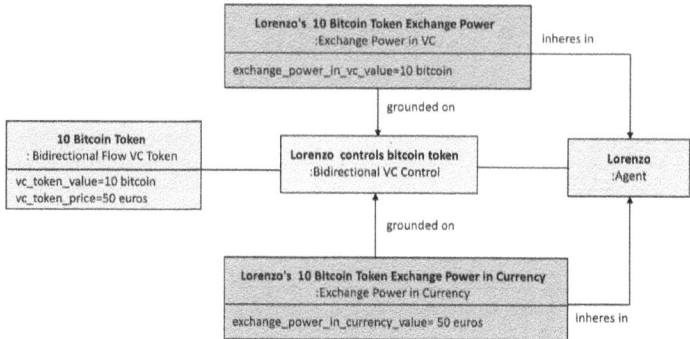

Figure 5.13: Virtual Currency and Exchange Instantiation.

5.5 Related Work

The Financial Industry Business Ontology (FIBO) (Enterprise Data Management Council, 2015) is an industry standard resource for the definition of business concepts in the financial services industry. It is developed and hosted by the Enterprise Data Management Council (EDMC) and is published in a number of formats for operational use and business definitions. It is also standardized through the Object Management Group (OMG). FIBO is developed as a series of ontologies in the Web Ontology Language (OWL) and proposes to be a representation of the "things in the world" of financial services. The use of logic ensures that each real-world concept is framed in a way that is unambiguous and that is readable both by humans and machines. With respect the universe of discourse of money, FIBO includes a Currency Amount Ontology that defines currency and monetary amount related concepts, which are used to define other FIBO ontology elements. The ontology defines two distinct kinds of concepts that correspond to money and amounts: a concrete, actual amount of money, and the monetary measure of something denominated in some currency. Whereas "money amount" is defined as an amount of money, "monetary amount" is an abstract monetary measure. The definition of currency provided in this ontology is compliant with the definitions given in ISO4217 (ISO, 2015).

Although it is quite complete in terms of financial industry concepts, when it comes to the money domain, FIBO is considerably less comprehensive than our proposal. For example, different from ROME, FIBO does not elaborate on the distinctions between physical and digital currencies nor provides an account for the latter. Concepts related

5.5. Related Work

to virtual currencies such as private cryptocurrencies are not covered by this ontology. Making explicit the distinction between official and virtual currencies is important, for example, for generating analytical data, as different rules and conditions (such as taxes and anti-money laundering measures) may apply for official money and virtual currencies. Although virtual currencies resemble official money within the communities where they are used, their relationship to regulatory frameworks and governance models can be quite different, and for this reason it is important to be able to make this distinction. Another main difference between the FIBO's approach and the one proposed here is with respect to the relation between money and trust. Money depends on trust, which is the basis for the proper functioning of the whole monetary system. Despite this importance, FIBO does not define trust, nor makes explicit its role in the universe of money.

Seeking to provide some clarity on the concept of central bank digital currency, Bech and Garratt (2017) propose a a taxonomy of money that identifies two types of CBDCs – retail and wholesale – and differentiates them from other forms of central bank money such as cash and reserves. In their work, they discuss the different characteristics of CBDCs and compares them with existing payment options. The taxonomy, which the authors name "Money Flower" (figure 5.14), is based on four key properties: issuer (central bank or other); form (electronic or physical); accessibility (universal or limited); and transfer mechanism (centralised or decentralised).

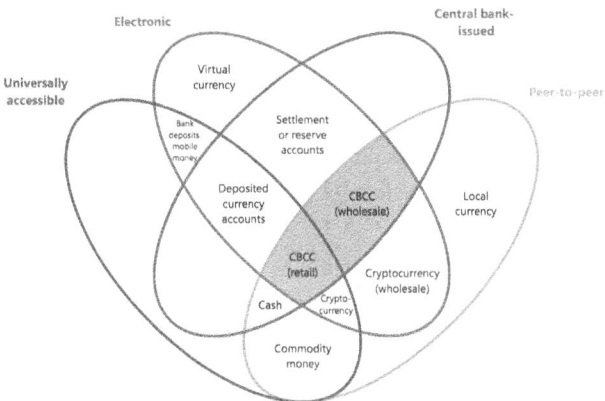

Figure 5.14: The money flower proposed by (Bech and Garratt, 2017).

By defining a taxonomy, the authors manage to provide a classification that accommodates various digital money proposals, however they do not conduct an ontological analysis to make explicit the ontological nature of money and related concepts. Furthermore, differently from ROME, the Money Flower taxonomy does not describe the relation between money and trust, nor explore its relation with exchange power and purchasing power.

5.6 Final Considerations

This chapter presented ROME, a core reference ontology of money and virtual currencies grounded in the Unified Foundational Ontology (Guizzardi, 2005; Guizzardi, Botti Benevides, et al., 2021) and that reuses concepts from the Reference Ontology of Trust (see chapter 4).

The ontology proposed was developed through an ontological analysis of money, currency, virtual currencies and related concepts, based on a literature review of the most relevant economic theories, and considering recent innovations in the financial industry. In particular, this analysis shows and important result, namely, that money is a polysemic term that might refer to several distinct, but related meanings. Consequently, it cannot be represented just as an entity, but as bunch of objects and relations that compose the concept of money. For example, when people say "I have some money in my bank account" they are referring to a credit, which ontologicaly speaking is a (credit) *relator*. Now, let us consider that someone states the following to refer to a ten euros banknote in her pocket: "This is the only money I have with me". In this case, the person is referring both to a physical *object* (the banknote) and to the underlying credit (a *relator*) — as discussed in section 5.3 banknotes establish a credit/debt relation between the agent holding control of them and the monetary authority (e.g. central bank). Finally, if one says "He made a lot of money investing on stocks", the person is probably referring to profit.

Another important observation is that things that are currently not considered money, may acquire this status in the future and be instantiated as such in the ontology. For example, currently, private cryptocurrencies are not considered money and are instantiated as virtual currencies in ROME. However, if they acquire the status of money in the future, they can instantiate the part of the ontology that describes money.

In chapters and 8 and 9, ROME is applied and validated in the context of decentralized finance. In chapter 8, ROME is applied to support the modeling and analysis of citizens' trust in central bank digital currency ecosystems, in a a real case study, which was conducted in close collaboration with a national central bank. In order to model

model citizens' trust in CBDC ecosystems, it is fundamental to properly understand the notion of central bank digital currency and its associated concepts and relations, which are provided by ROME. In chapter 9, ROME is used in an ontology-based approach for the modeling of payments and linked obligation settlement mechanisms, aiming at providing conceptual clarification and supporting semantic interoperability in multiple distributed ledger technology / blockchain networks.

Chapter 6

The Core Ontology for Economic Exchanges

This chapter presents the Core Ontology for Economic Exchanges[1] (COEX), a UFO-based ontology, specified in OntoUML, that formally characterizes the concept of economic exchanges based on the Action Theory of Economic Exchanges (Massin and Tieffenbach, 2016; Porello, Guizzardi, Sales, and Amaral, 2020).

As a core reference ontology (Guizzardi, 2007; Scherp et al., 2011), COEX is designed to account for a conceptualization of economic exchanges that is independent of a particular application domain, and to be applied in an off-line manner to assist humans in tasks such as meaning negotiation and consensus establishment. COEX intends to address the notion of economic exchanges broadly, so that it can be applied to a number of disciplines and areas. The codification of COEX models in gUFO (a partial translation of UFO to OWL) (Almeida, Guizzardi, et al., 2020) contributes to dealing with semantic interoperability issues, to semantic web related initiatives in economics and finance (Bennett, 2013), as well as to the goal of transparency of economics data exchange according to FAIR principles (Jacobsen et al., 2020).

The chapter is organized as follows. Section 6.1 motivates the relevance of developing an ontology for economic exchanges that enables a unified treatment of economic exchanges, regardless the object of the transaction. Section 6.2 presents the Action Theory of Economic Exchanges, which serves as conceptual foundation for the proposed ontology. Section 6.3 presents the Core Ontology of Economic Exchanges. Section

---
[1] The complete version of COEX in OntoUML and its implementation in OWL are available at http://purl.org/krdb-core/economic-exchanges-ontology.

6.4 applies the ontology to model an instantiation example. Section 6.5 discusses some related work. Finally, section 6.6 presents the conclusions of this chapter.

6.1 Introduction

The nature of economic exchanges has been thoroughly debated in philosophy, economics, and social sciences, since at least the XVIII century, when the epistemological status of the main concepts of the economic theory was intensively discussed in search of a solid foundation (Herzog, 2017). Two important issues regarding the nature of economic exchanges —which are quite pressing for a fruitful ontological understanding of economic interactions— are the nature of the things being exchanged and the matter of the agreement between the transacting agents. Do we transact goods, services, objects, actions, events, or promises? Are we motivated to transact because of converging or inverse interests? To approach these delicate points, we shall rely on the *Action Theory of Economic Exchanges* (ATE) (Massin and Tieffenbach, 2016), a recent perspective from the area of philosophy of economics. The motivation for this choice is three-fold. Firstly, it allows for a quite general view of economic exchanges concerning heterogeneous items (e.g. both goods and services). Secondly, the ATE explains why and under which conditions an economic exchange takes place. Finally, the ATE models economic exchanges from the perspective of both agents involved in a transaction, the so-called "helicopter view" (Laurier et al., 2018). For the above-mentioned reasons, we claim that ATE is more apt to guide a foundational analysis of economic exchanges than, for instance, the ISO standard for Accounting Information Systems REA (Resource-Event-Action) (McCarthy, June 2007). In particular, REA focuses mainly on exchanges of resource items, and it does not explain why a transaction happens.

In the subsequent sections, we shall develop an ontological account of economic transactions using the ATE as a guide to lay down the main aspects of a core ontology of economic interactions. To make our investigation precise and applicable to designing well-founded information systems, we shall place our analysis within the Unified Foundational Ontology (UFO) (Guizzardi, 2005; Guizzardi, Fonseca, Benevides, et al., 2018; Guizzardi, Wagner, Almeida, et al., 2015). One of the reasons for using UFO is its rich treatment of relations (Fonseca, C. et al., 2019), a compelling feature, as we shall see, for modeling concepts in economics.

6.2 The Action Theory of Economic Exchanges

The core assumption made by the Action Theory of Economic Exchanges (ATE) (Massin and Tieffenbach, 2016) is that, in any economic transaction, the "object" of the transaction is a pair of *actions* to be performed by the relevant agents involved in it. The main assumptions of the ATE are summarised below:

Definition 6.2.1. Agents a and b are transacting about actions ϕ and ψ iff

1. *Preferences and beliefs*:

    1.1 a prefers that a does ϕ and b does ψ, to a does not ϕ and b does not ψ.

    1.2 b prefers that a does ϕ and b does ψ, to a does not ϕ and b does not ψ.

    1.3 a believes that promising to b to do ϕ on condition that b does ψ is a way to make b to do ψ.

2. *Offer and acceptance*:

    2.1 Because of 1.1. and 1.3, a promises to b that a will do ϕ, if b does ψ

    2.2 Because of 1.2, b accepts the offer.

3. *Provisions*:

    3.1 Because of 2.2, b does ψ. Therefore, a is obliged to do ϕ.

    3.2 Because of 2.1 and 3.1, a does ϕ.

Three points are worth noticing. Firstly, by viewing the object of transactions as actions, the ATE is capable of accounting for economic transactions about goods as well as services. In the case of services, the agreement is about the respective actions to be performed by the relevant parties. E.g. a customer and a delivery company agree on the pair of actions ϕ : "a pays the agreed amount to company b" and ψ: "The company b delivers the requested service to a". In the case of goods, the preferred pair of actions can be expressed in terms of the transfer of ownership, the action of transferring the ownership of an item: e.g. ϕ : "a transfer the ownership of her laptop to b" and ψ : "b pays the agreed amount to a".

Secondly, the assumption about the *convergence* of the agents' preferences to the same pair of actions is an important bit here, as it is capable of explaining why two agents are in fact transacting with each other (and not with other parties). The actions to which the agents commit explicitly mention the relevant agents of the actions, which are in fact the very agents involved in the transaction: when an actual transaction between a and b happens, a is intending to transact precisely with b, and not to an other agent.

Thirdly, the ATE is a quite rich reconstruction of the steps happening in an economic exchange. If the preconditions in point 1 of Definition 6.2.1 are met, an economic transaction starts with an offering, cf. point 2.1, which is based on the preference of one agent for a certain course of action and on the belief that, by promising something to another agent, this course of action can take place. Moreover, an economic offering generates obligations, i.e. commitments. In point 2.1, a promises to (commits to) do ϕ, if b does ψ (a conditional commitment). In point 3.1, since b has accepted the offer, b is committed to do ψ, then once B has done ψ, a is obliged to do ϕ (an unconditional commitment). Thus the ATE's mechanism for explaining why economic transactions happen works by turning a conditional commitment into an unconditional commitment, under the suited conditions. For this reasons, ATE also provides an explanation of why and under which circumstances an economic exchange happens.

6.3 COEX: Core Ontology for Economic Exchanges

The core ingredients for representing the ATE in UFO are: *agents, preferences, actions, beliefs and commitments, economic offerings, and economic exchanges*. The focus here is on economic offerings and transactions.

Agent is a rigid non-sortal type, i.e., a type that essentially classifies individuals of different *kinds*, i.e., individuals that have different ontological natures (Guizzardi, 2005). The class Agent may include individual or collective agents (e.g. organisations, companies, etc.), with their specific ontological differences (Ferrario et al., 2018; Porello, Bottazzi, et al., 2014).

Since agents (i.e. entities with *intentionality*) are necessarily agents (in the modal sense), we stereotype the type Agent as an OntoUML *Category*. Agents can play the "role" of Value Beholder in a value ascription relation, the relation by which an agent assigns a value to an entity. We represent the type Value Beholder as a *role mixin* because: (i) it classifies entities only contingently, (ii) one is a value beholder due to a relational condition; (iii) it is a *Non-Sortal*, i.e., it can classify entities of multiple kinds.

A Value Ascription is a *mode* (Guizzardi, 2005; Sales, Guarino, et al., 2017b). As we discussed, a mode is an existentially dependent entity that, as such, can only exist by inhering in some other individual. In particular, a value is a *externally dependent*

6.3. COEX: Core Ontology for Economic Exchanges

mode, i.e., a mode that inheres in an individual but which is also externally dependent on a different entity. So, a value ascription is a sort of mental state inhering in the value beholder that is also externally dependent on a number of entities in Value Entity. A value ascription mode takes a value in at least one (but possibly several) Value Magnitude Spaces, via the *quality* of Value (a quality of the value ascription). These spaces have, in OntoUML, the semantics of abstract conceptual spaces, delimiting the possible values a property can be projected into, cf. (Guizzardi, 2005) (e.g. we can account for cardinal or ordinal measures of value).

Finally, a Preference (Porello and Guizzardi, 2018), of an agent between two entities is a relational mode (between the agent and the two entities) but a complex one (i.e., a complex mental state). A (binary) preference concerning two entities is a mode inhering a value beholder that is essentially composed of exactly *two* existing value ascriptions (it is the mereological sum of them), inhering in that very same value beholder: *i*) the value of the first entity given the second entity and *ii*) the value of the second entity given the first entity.[2]

A relational sentence expressing that an agent has a preference between two entities is then captured by means of the (ternary) relation *prefers* (a relational type in UFO, cf. (Fonseca, C. et al., 2019; Porello and Guizzardi, 2018)): "*i* prefers *x* over *y*" connects the Value Beholder *i* with two other entities, Preferred Entity *x* and Deprecated Entity *y*. The entity whose ascribed value is higher plays the role of Preferred Entity; the one with the lower magnitude then plays the role of Deprecated Entity.

To apply this view of preferences to ATE (step 1.1 and 1.2 of Definition 6.2.1), we need to understand ontologically what are the entities about which the agents have preferences. In ATE, preferences are definitely about *pairs of actions* (cf. point 1.1.).

Actions are particular types of events in UFO, so preferences are *prima facie* about events that are composed of two actions.[3]

This point is however quite delicate mainly for three reasons. Firstly, preference relations may be about events that may never occur. For instance, if I prefer to have pasta tonight at my place over pizza, and I have the means to satisfy my goal, then the event of me eating pizza tonight at my place in fact never happens. Thus, by defining preference over events, we are lead to include in our model instances of events that may

---

[2]The preference depends on the context of comparison between the entities, cf. (Sales, Guarino, et al., 2017b; Vajda et al., 2019).

[3]By assuming a mereology of events (Almeida, Falbo, et al., 2019), the event "A doing ϕ and B doing ψ" is defined as the mereological sum of the two events "A doing ϕ" and "B doing ψ".

never happen.[4]

Secondly, ATE includes preference over *negative* actions, or omissions, e.g. "*A does not ϕ and B does not ψ*". The ontological status of negative actions as events is debated, cf. (Casati and Varzi, 2015). Some authors endorse ontological commitments to negative events, whereas others identify the negative event with the (positive) action that one performs while omitting, cf. (Varzi, 2007).

Thirdly, by defining preferences over events, we are lead to view the object of the preference as fully determinate. That is, an agent must know to maximal detail the courses of actions that she or he is comparing. For instance, if I am preferring the particular event of having dinner at an Italian restaurant to the event of having dinner at a Chinese restaurant, I am implicitly comparing which waiter is assigned to my table, the exact moment in which the dinners start and end, the outfit that I am wearing, etc, at least if we consider events as *thick* entities.

The solution adopted here is to view preferences as being about *types* of actions. By viewing preferences as defined on types of events we can accommodate the three previous points as follows.

Concerning the first point, a type of event may have no instances in a model while still existing as a type. Types must have *possible* (in the modal sense) instances in UFO, which does not exclude that there are worlds where a type has no instances (Guizzardi, Fonseca, Benevides, et al., 2018). So we can talk about types of events that do not happen at a world, without introducing a special class of possible events.

Concerning the second issue, by defining preferences over types, we can avoid to take a position on the existence of negative events (or omissions): a type classifying negative actions may have instances that are either positive action (i.e. the actions that are performed while omitting) or truly negative actions, in case we commit to their existence.

Concerning the third point, defining preferences over types enables us to have preferences over sets of events, preventing the maximal determination of the agents' preferences. For instance, when I prefer the type of event "going out to an Italian restaurant"

---

[4]An analysis of *future* and *ongoing* events has been discussed in particular in (Guarino, 2017). However, they would not suffice for modelling preferences, as we need to discuss events that may never happen in the actual world. Here, we only notice that a class of *possible* events is in fact compatible with the formal theory of UFO, which is phrased within a first-order modal logic where the definition of modalities entails the *possibilia* view of the particulars in the domain of the ontology (events included). That is, we may in principle assume events that never happen in the actual world, while happening in some other possible world. See (Benevides, Almeida, et al., 2019) for a formalisation of events occurring in different time lines.

6.3. COEX: Core Ontology for Economic Exchanges

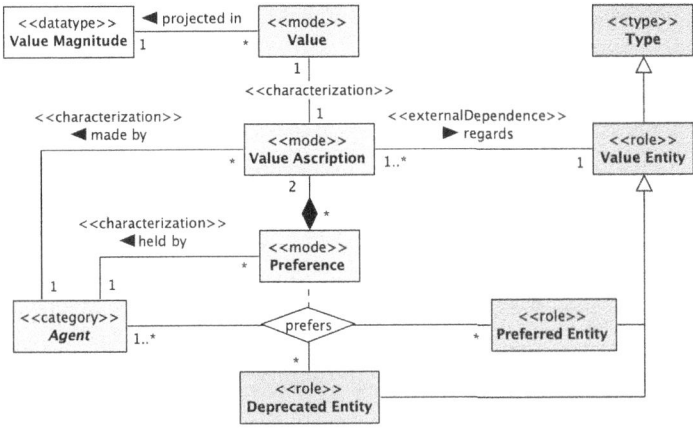

Figure 6.1: OntoUML model of preference relations.

to the type "going out to a Chinese restaurant", I prefer any event of the former type to any event of the latter type, regardless of all the aspects that single out a particular event of each type.

Summing up, an OntoUML module for preferences is depicted in figure 6.1, where Preferred Entity and Deprecated Entity are thus to be intended as types of types of events.

6.3.1 Economic offering and economic transactions

We can finally approach the modeling of economic transactions. We start from the offering event (Offering). This event is the foundation (cf. creation in OntoUML (Almeida, Falbo, et al., 2019)) of a relator Economic Offering which is composed of the (mereological) sum of (the externally dependent modes given by) the conditional commitment of the offerer and of the offeree. Offerer and Offeree are again rolemixins here. The important aspects is that, at this point, the commitments and claims are *conditional*, which corresponds to stage 2.1 of Definition 1. According to our discussion in section 6.2 about the entities that are related by preferences in ATE, the conditional commitments are about types of actions, cf. commits to in OntoUML. The Offered Contribution Type and the Counterpart Contribution Type are in fact types of types of events. The offering is based on the preferences of the offerer, according to stage 2.1 of Definition 6.2.1. Notice that here is where we changed Massin and Tieffenbach's model from ATE by viewing preferences as defined on *types* of actions. Accordingly, an instance of the class Economic Exchange Type is a type of event constructed by means of two types of events: the Offered Contribution Type and the Counterpart Contribution Type. We are modeling the constructed type by means of the relation requires. The idea is that a type in Economic Exchange Type classifies events that have two components: a component classified by a type in Offered Contribution Type and a component in Counterpart Contribution Type.[5]

The relation participate to events of type models the fact that the offerer participates in all the events of the offered contribution type and the offeree participates in all the events of the counterpart contribution type. This point accounts for the fact that the convergent preferences of the two agents, even in the case of preferences defined on types, mentions the agents involved in the transaction.[6] Figure 6.2 represents the OntoUML modeling of economic offerings.

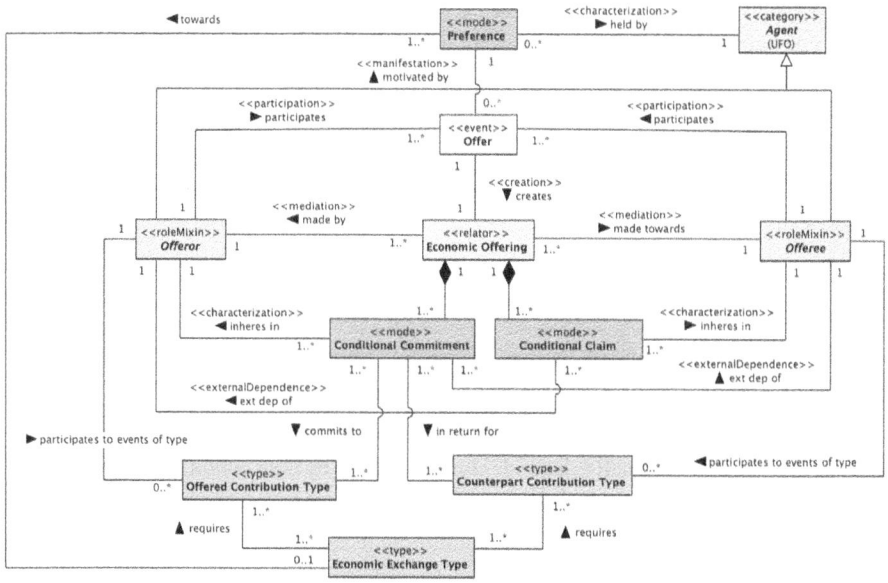

Figure 6.2: OntoUML diagram depicting economic offerings.

To shorten the exposition, here we model the situation where the offer proposed by

---

[5]We leave a proper treatment of the requires relation for a dedicated work.

[6]For the sake of simplicity, we omit some aspects of ATE. E.g. the economic offer is also based on beliefs, cf. point 1.2 and 1.3. We can easily integrate beliefs as in (Nardi, J. et al., 2015).

the offerer is immediately accepted, and no negotiation takes places between the parties, see figure 6.3. If the offer is accepted by the offeree, then the event of the offering founds a new relator of Economic Agreement between the two agents. This step provides the ontological counterpart of stage 2.2. of Definition 6.2.1. The new relator complies with the previously created economic offering relator. This new relator has parts the new (now) *unconditional* commitments of the agents to fulfill the promised courses of actions (of the required type). This step realises the final outcome of Definition 6.2.1, namely the actualisation of steps 2.1 and 2.2 based on the provisions 3.1 and 3.2. The actual event of Economic Exchange is required then to have as parts the event (action) of fulfilment of the offerer commitments as well as the event (action) of the fulfilment of the requested counterparts. Those events are of the right type, i.e. the Offered Contribution and the Counterpart Contribution match the type in Offered Contribution Type and Counterpart Contribution Type (respectively), cf. the relation instantiation.

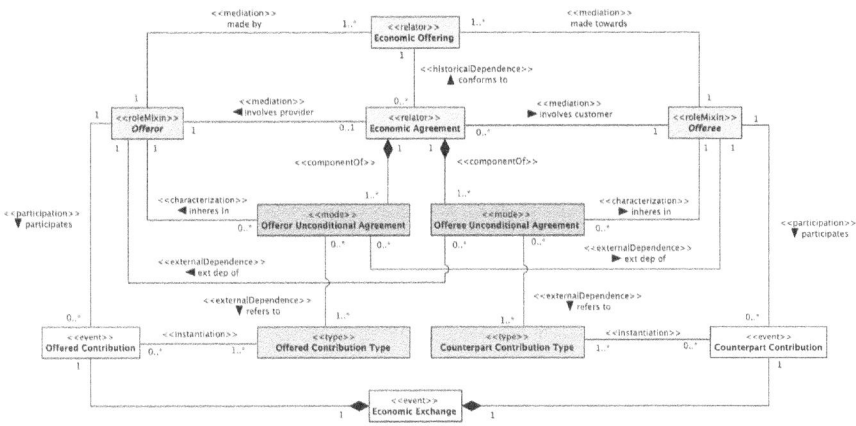

Figure 6.3: OntoUML diagram depicting economic exchanges.

6.4 Use Case Illustration

In this section, we apply COEX to model a case illustration that covers key concepts of the ontology. Let us consider the following example: *Leonardo tells Elon that he will paint his portrait if Elon takes him on a trip to the Moon.*

Figures 6.4 and 6.5 present the COEX instantiation for this example.

Figure 6.4 concerns the economic offering phase in which Leonardo (the Offeror) offers to "paint Elon's portrait" (the Offeree) in exchange for "Elon taking him on a trip to the Moon". In this example, the event of Leonardo saying this to Elon (Offer) is considered to create an Economic Offering.

The Economic Offering includes the Conditional Commitment that Leonardo establishes towards Elon, namely "Leonardo paints Elon's portrait as long as Elon takes Leonardo on a trip to the Mon", and its counterpart Conditional Claim, namely "Elon has his portrait painted by Leonardo in return for taking him on a trip to the Moon".

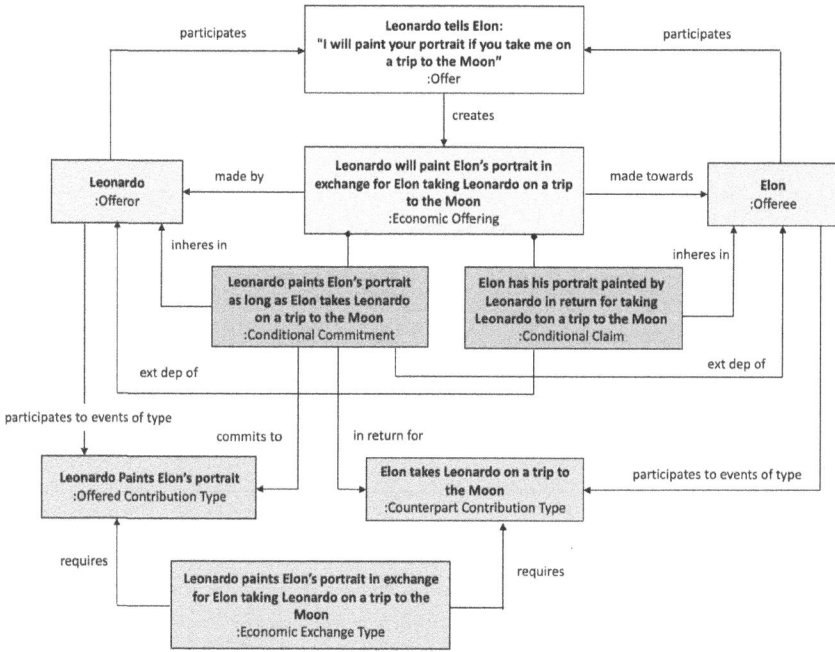

Figure 6.4: Economic Offering instantiation.

Considering that the offer proposed by Leonardo is immediately accepted by Elon, and no negotiation takes place, them the event of the offering founds a new relator of Economic Agreement between Leonardo and Elon (figure 6.5), which has as parts the unconditional commitments of the agents to fulfill the promised courses of actions (of the required type).

The event of Economic Exchange ("Leonardo paints Elon's portrait and Elon takes

Leonardo on a trip to the Moon") has as parts the event (action) of fulfilment of the offeror commitment ("Leonardo paints Elon's portrait") as well as the event (action) of the fulfilment of the requested counterparts ("Elon takes Leonardo on a trip to the Moon"). Those events are of the right type, i.e. the Offered Contribution and the Counterpart Contribution match the type in Offered Contribution Type and Counterpart Contribution Type (respectively), cf. the relation instantiation.

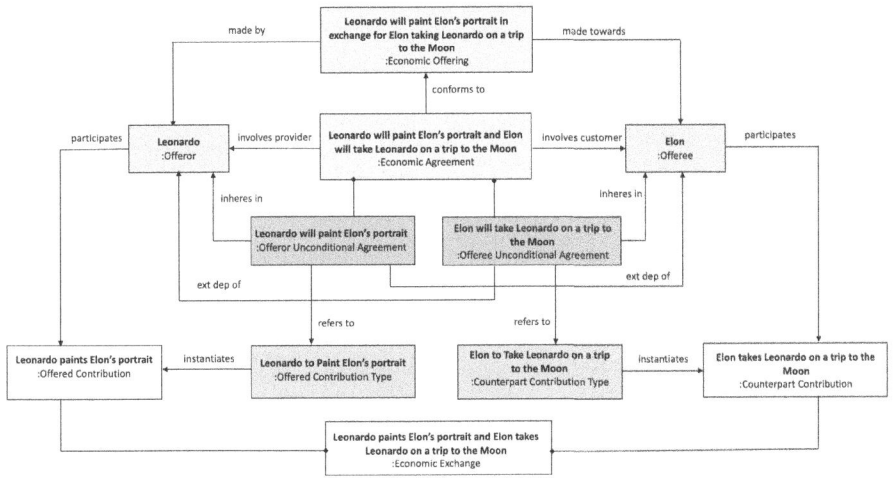

Figure 6.5: Economic Exchange instantiation.

6.5 Related Work

Economic exchanges are a central notion in frameworks such as the Resource-Event Action (REA) ISO Standard (McCarthy, June 2007) and service core ontologies such as UFO-S (Nardi, J. et al., 2015). We start by discussing the relationship between our ontological account of the ATE in COEX, UFO-S, and REA.

REA focuses mainly on exchanges of resource items. It does not explain why a transaction happens. As we shall see, the REA modeling style can indeed be retrieved within the ATE, which is in fact a richer perspective.

In REA economic transactions are intended as events, i.e. as "occurrences in time wherein ownership of an economic resource is transferred from one person to another person" (McCarthy, June 2007). Confronting this view with ATE, we can see that this aspect is captured by the realisation of the economic transaction, i.e. the part of our model where the commitments are fulfilled and trigger the relevant events (figure 6.3). Another interesting aspect to be considered is that (1) REA seems to view resources (e.g. endurants) as objects of the transaction; (2) however, what is brought about in economic exchanges is the transferring of ownership of an item, which is in fact an event, see (Guarino, Guizzardi, and Sales, 2018a); (3) therefore, in line with (2), the transferring of ownership of an item is, in fact, a specific type of action, which can be straightforwardly accounted by ATE. For instance, suppose that agent a is selling a bike to agent b. In our view of ATE, we can specify the relevant types of actions involved as follows: a and b both prefer the type of actions "a transfer the ownership of the bike to b and b pays the agreed price" to the type of actions "a does not transfer the ownership of the bike to b and b does not pay the agreed amount". In the analysis of REA in (Laurier et al., 2018), the economic agreement is captured by means of the duality relations, (e.g. transfer duality) (Laurier et al., 2018, p. 16). In (Laurier et al., 2018), transfer duality relations are modelled as relators, as we do here. This enables a direct comparison with our framework: in REA, transfer duality relators can be seen as a specific type of our Economic Agreement, restricted to agreement on types of actions that require, e.g. transfer of ownership. Hence, regarding this aspect, REA modelling can be seen as a submodel of our OntoUML version of ATE in COEX. Therefore, our modelling provides, on the one hand, a generalisation of REA to transactions involving any type of services and, on the other hand, an explanation of why the transaction occurs: it is based, as we have seen, on the convergent preferences of the agents and on the commitment generated by the offering steps.

UFO-S is a core ontology of services, which has been shown to be able to harmonize different views of service, ranging from marketing-oriented views (e.g., Service Dominant Logic) to a capability-oriented views in service science, to technology-oriented views (as in ArchiMate) (Nardi, J. et al., 2015). Moreover, it was successfully employed to analyze a number of prominent mainstreams service modeling languages (e.g., SoaML, USDL, ArchiMate) (Nardi, J. et al., 2019). Finally, it influenced the efforts towards defining a federal government ontology of services for the national infrastructure of open data in Brazil. As we show here, both REA and UFO-S can be seen as a special case of COEX.

We confront now our OntoUML model of ATE with UFO-S. The mechanism of turning conditional commitment into unconditional commitments is at the core of UFO-S. There, commitments are generated by the service offering (Nardi, J. et al., 2015), as in ATE are generated by the economic offering. In this perspective, ATE provides a

6.5. Related Work

simple generalisation of UFO-S from service offering to any kind of economic offering. Service offering are reinterpreted, in our view of ATE, as offering about types of actions, which serves to accommodate the ontological worries about committing to possible or negative events. Moreover, ATE nicely complements the model of UFO-S by providing an explanation of why the offering is proposed in the first place and of why it can be accepted by the counterpart. The beginning of the offering is grounded in ATE on the assumptions concerning the converging preferences. So ATE integrates UFO-S by providing an explanation of why the service offering is proposed and under which conditions it can be accepted: the proposal of the offering is based on the preferences of the offerer and on the belief that the offeree may agree on the proposal, as she or he has convergent interests. In practice, we can integrate the model of UFO-S of the relator of service agreement (Nardi, J. et al., 2015, p.181) with our model of figure 6.2.

Another related work is (Vajda et al., 2019), which starts the development of an ontology of commercial exchanges in the foundational ontology BFO. In comparison to this work, by levaraging on UFO's theory of relations, our work is able to capture the nature of economic offering and agreements as full-fledged endurants (Guarino and Guizzardi, 2015) and, as such, as entities capable of genuine changes in time (as opposed to modeling only the events and descriptions related to this phenomenon). This benefit is also present (for the same reason) in (Blums and Weigand, 2019), another closely related work to the one presented in this chapter. In their proposal, a Core Ontology for Financial Reporting Information Systems (COFRIS), the authors also approach economic exchanges in UFO with the goal of providing foundations for Financial Reporting Information Systems. COFRIS elaborates on the establishment and fulfillment of commitments and claims between exchange participants along the whole exchange life cycle — exchange offer, acceptance, and delivery or incurring obligations. When compared to our approach, COFRIS is deeper and more comprehensive in its coverage of the exchange life cycle. COEX is intended to provide a general conceptualization of economic exchanges, flexible enough to allow further extensions and the integration of domain ontologies to the network. Thus, it was designed to cover the backbone of an economic exchange, enabling a unified treatment of economic exchanges, regardless the object of the transaction (goods or services). COFRIS goes further, by adding the delivery process steps, incurring and settling obligations, and economic resources. Our main difference with respect to that approach is our explicit connection to the notion of economic preference and its explicit grounding on a modern philosophy theory of economic exchange (ATE).

6.6 Final Considerations

This chapter presented COEX, a core reference ontology for economic exchanges, grounded in the Unified Foundational Ontology (Guizzardi, 2005; Guizzardi, Botti Benevides, et al., 2021). In particular, we provided here the main elements for a well-founded ontological analysis of economic exchanges based on the Action Theory of Economic Exchanges. We developed our analysis in UFO, which provides a very expressive ontology to discuss relational dependencies, and we introduced the basic elements of an OntoUML modelling of economic transactions.

Our analysis highlights the dependency of economic offerings and transactions on the converging preferences of the agents and illustrates the mechanism of replacement of conditional with unconditional commitments that are in place in this forms of agents interaction. We proposed to view preferences and economic agreements about types of actions to avoid a number of ontological worries of directly dealing with events. This view of economic exchanges is very general and provides a unified treatment of a wide range of economic phenomena. In particular, as we demonstrated here, both the ISO Standard REA and the Core Ontology of Services UFO-S can be seen as special cases of COEX.

In chapter 9, COEX is applied in the context of decentralized finance, in an ontology-based approach for the modeling of payments and linked obligation settlement mechanisms, aiming at providing conceptual clarification and supporting semantic interoperability in multiple multiple distributed ledger technology / blockchain networks.

Part IV

APPLICATIONS

Chapter 7

Ontology-based Modeling and Analysis of Trustworthiness Requirements

In this chapter we apply the Reference Ontology of Trust (see chapter 4) and the Common Ontology of Value and Risk (see section 3.2 of chapter 3) in the area of requirements engineering. Firstly, we use ROT and COVER as ontological foundation in the ontology-based modeling of trustworthiness requirements for software systems (Amaral, Guizzardi, Guizzardi, et al., 2020). As a result, we propose a Reference Ontology of Trustworthiness Requirements (ROTwR) (Amaral, Guizzardi, Guizzardi, et al., 2020), which relies in ROT and COVER to define the class of trustworthiness requirements and their relation to concepts such as trust, capability, vulnerability and risk, among others. Then, we propose a novel methodology for Ontology-based Requirements Engineering (ObRE), which applies ROTwR in a real-world case study (Amaral, Guizzardi, Guizzardi, et al., 2021). In this study, ROTwR is applied to help with the elicitation of trustworthiness requirements of software systems by analyzing the case of Pix, the Brazilian Instant Payments Ecosystem created and managed by the Central Bank of Brazil. The main objective is to verify if ROTwR, and consequently, ROT and COVER, are capable of properly representing real world situations.

This chapter is organized as follows. Section 7.1 motivates the relevance of modeling and analyzing trustworthiness requirements for software systems. Section 7.2 presents the Non-functional Requirements Ontology (NFRO) (Guizzardi, R. et al., 2014), an ontological interpretation of non-functional requirements, based on the Unified Foundational Ontology. Section 7.3 provides an ontological account for the notion of trustworthiness requirements and related concepts, and section 7.4 presents our proposal, a *Reference Ontology of Trustworthiness Requirements*. Following, section 7.5 presents the ObRE method, which aims to systematize the elicitation and analysis of requirements, by using an ontology to conceptually clarify the meaning of a class of requirements, such as privacy, ethicality and trustworthiness. We illustrate the working of ObRE by applying it to a real case study concerning trustworthiness requirements, in which we use ROTwR to analyse the trustworthiness requirements of Pix. Finally, related work can be found in section 7.6, and section 7.7 concludes this chapter.

7.1 Introduction

Trust is an essential ingredient of everyday life. We relate to people, organizations and things because we trust them to deliver on a certain goal, task or asset. Trust is especially important in the case of safety-critical services that can directly affect human lives, such as medical diagnosis, autonomous driving, military technology, terrorism detection, and other situations that pose risks to human life and health. And although we tend to be tolerant if a "translation service produces grammatically incorrect sentences or if a cell phone camera misses to recognize a person" (Nassar et al., 2020), tolerating the possibility of a single wrong decision in "critical decision-making systems such as security, healthcare, or finance, where human lives or significant assets are at stake" (Nassar et al., 2020), is not acceptable. As systems are being developed, with or without artificial intelligence (AI) technologies, that do make critical decisions, it is essential that their users trust them in the same way they trust their doctors, drivers and police. In the context of AI systems this was a key conclusion of the High-Level Expert Group on Artificial Intelligence (AI HLEG), which elaborated a set of ethics guidelines for trustworthy AI, as part of the European Strategy on Artificial Intelligence (Hleg, A.I., 2019). A similar conclusion was drawn in the "Explainable AI" initiative launched by the United States Defense Advanced Research Projects Agency (DARPA) (Gunning and Aha, 2019), with the objective of making deep learning systems more trustworthy and controllable. These considerations call for studying a new class of requirements, namely, *trustworthiness requirements*, so that we can understand their nature and develop proper analysis techniques.

But what exactly is trust? And what makes a system trustworthy? We answer these questions in terms of the Reference Ontology for Trust (see chapter 4). Then, we combine ROT with the Non-Functional Requirements Ontology (NFRO) (Guizzardi, R. et al., 2014), which has the basic concepts to allow the definition of functional and non-functional requirements. This combination allows us to define the class of trustworthiness requirements and their relation to concepts such as trust, capability, vulnerability and risk, among others.

7.2 The Non-functional Requirements Ontology (NFRO)

Requirements can be functional and non-functional, but the latter are most relevant to trustworthiness requirements, so we focus on them by adopting NFRO (Guizzardi, R. et al., 2014). In (Guizzardi, R. et al., 2014), the authors propose a UFO-based ontological interpretation of non-functional requirements. In NFRO, requirement is defined as a Goal. Requirements are specialized into non-functional requirement (NFRs) — also named Quality Goals — and Functional Requirements (FRs). FRs refer to a Function (a capability, capacity) that has the potential to manifest certain behavior in particular situations, while NFRs refer to desired Qualities taking Quality Values in particular Quality Regions. For example, a software system is considered to have good usability if the value associated to its "usability" Quality (non-functional requirement) maps to the "good" Quality Region in the "usability" Quality Space.

This ontological account delineates different kinds of requirements, and clarifies the nature of NFRs as qualities that map a system artifact into a quality region (Guizzardi, R. et al., 2014). Figure 7.1 depicts a selected subset of the NFRO that is relevant for our discussions on trustworthiness requirements. For an in-depth discussion and formal characterization of Qualities, Quality Universals, Quality Regions, and Quality Spaces, we refer the reader to (Guizzardi, 2005).

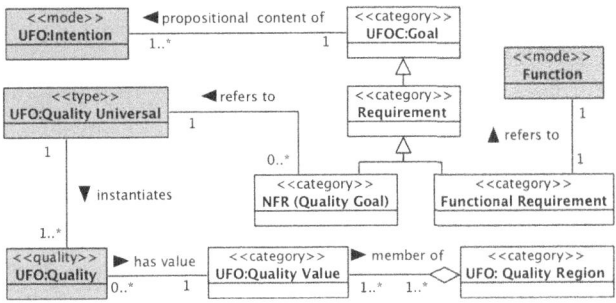

Figure 7.1: A fragment of the Non-functional Requirements Ontology (adapted from (Guizzardi, R. et al., 2014)).

7.3 Trustworthiness Requirements

Requirements are prescriptions of intended states-of-affairs that the system-to-be should bring about. Traditionally, these states-of-affairs were system-related, such as functions the system should deliver, or qualities it should possess with respect to performance, reliability, usability etc. Social requirements and physical requirements have been introduced in the literature more recently with the advent of socio-technical and cyber-physical systems (Mohammadi, 2019; Paja et al., 2013). For example, "schedule meeting" is a social requirement because the desired state-of-affairs is one that includes a new meeting, where meeting is a social artifact (a bundle of rights, commitments, powers, etc. binding a number of participants). On the other hand, "distance from nearby physical objects $\geq$ 50cm" is a physical requirement for an autonomous vehicle. Personal requirements constitute a forth category of requirements where the desired states-of-affairs involve attitudinal (mental) properties of (some of) the system's stakeholders. For example, "$\geq$70% of departments members are using the meeting scheduling system" is a personal requirement (more specifically, an acceptance requirement) in that the system-to-be has to bring members of the department to a state of mind where they are willing to use the system. Trustworthiness requirements are personal requirements as well in that their desired states-of-affairs are ones where some of the stakeholders trust the system.

But how can an agent earn the trust of the recipients of its services? Firstly, the agent can make available to its users its credentials (degrees, accreditations, certificates, awards) that suggest that "it knows its craft", "it is doing a good job", and the like. The agent can also make available information on its track record, such as reviews from service recipients and statistics on its experience. Moreover, all information that is used must be true (no half-truths and no lies). Politicians are able to convince a certain segment of their electorate to trust them. However, if done through the use of half-truths and lies in the process, this can make them trusted but unworthy of trust, or untrustworthy.

Trustworthiness means more than trust in other ways as well. A trustworthy agent must be delivering its service in a professional and effective manner. For example, a medical doctor agent may be trusted by most of its patients because of its accreditations and its affiliation with a healthcare organization, but it is not trustworthy unless it also delivers reliable healthcare services to its patients. Reliability here includes availability, the good doctor is available when you need it, but also effectiveness in its diagnoses

7.3. Trustworthiness Requirements

and treatments of its patients. A medical doctor you rarely succeed to make an appointment with isn't trustworthy, nor is one whose diagnoses are often contradicted by expert colleagues.

Another element of trustworthiness is transparency in the delivery of an agent's services. Transparency is influenced by many factors (Leite and Cappelli, 2010). In the context of an agent delivering a service, transparency includes offering information on what the agent is doing, as well as rationale for its decisions (aka explainability).

On the basis of these considerations, a trustworthiness requirement can be AND-refined into a *reliability requirement*, a *truthful information communication requirement* and a *transparency requirement* for the service being delivered.

Trustworthiness requirements are quality requirements (Guizzardi, R. et al., 2014). This means that they constrain the level of presence of a quality in its subject. For example "being red" is a property that constrains the colour quality of its subject to be in the red region of a color quality space (a chromatic map known as the color spindle). Likewise "being trustworthy" is a constraint for agents or services to fall in the trustworthiness region of a space that also includes an untrustworthiness region (figure 7.2).

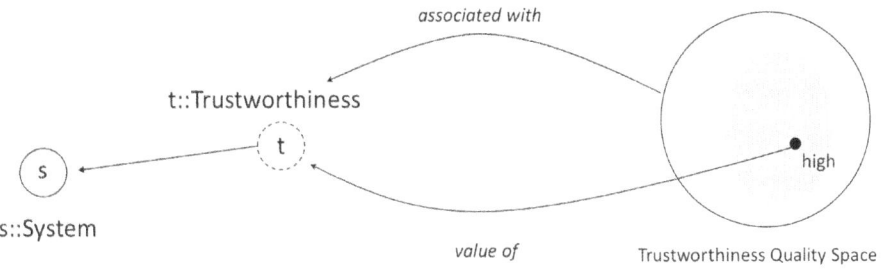

Figure 7.2: Trustworthiness Quality Space.

Of course, trustworthiness isn't only a black-and-white quality requirement. It also includes weaker versions that can be defined by refinement operators (Guizzardi, R. et al., 2014):

– Probabilistic refinements: These consider what percentage of the uses of the system's services were deemed trustworthy by the recipients of these services. For example, for a diagnostic system, a trustworthiness requirement could be "$\geq 80\%$ of uses were found trustworthy";

- Fuzziness refinements: Here, we weaken the notion of trustworthiness by making it fuzzy to include things that are "almost trustworthy","fairly trustworthy", "definitely not untrustworthy".

- Subjectivity refinements: These are requirements of the form "$\geq$N% of users asked consider the system trustworthy". Note that unlike probabilistic refinements, subjectivity refinements focus on users, not uses.

These refinement operators can also be applied to the sub-goals of a trustworthiness requirement, to yield a full space of requirements concerning the trustworthiness quality.

7.4 ROTwR: Reference Ontology of Trustworthiness Requirements

In this section, we present an ontological interpretation of requirements with focus on the conception of trustworthy systems and on the potential risks that can be posed by some technologies. We address this issue by proposing a reference model of a well-founded ontology that characterizes the concept of trustworthiness requirements in the context of software systems, as well as the emergence of risks in this scenario.

There are different definitions for the concept of requirement (Jureta et al., 2009; Letier and Van Lamsweerde, 2004; Ross and Schoman, 1977). In general, we are in line with the ontological interpretation of Non-Functional Requirements (NFRO) proposed by Guizzardi, R. et al. (2014) that models requirement as a goal. NFRO defines non-functional requirements as quality requirements related to qualities that take values in particular quality regions. We use this ontology to model *Trustworthiness Requirement* as a quality requirement that takes quality values in a trustworthiness space region (which includes an untrustworthiness region).

We rely in the concept of trust presented in ROT (see chapter 4) to characterize the trust of stakeholders in a system. In this scenario, the stakeholders and the system can be mapped, respectively, to ROT's concepts of trustor and trustee. Furthermore, in the same way as it is defined in ROT, the trust of a stakeholder in the system can be represented as a complex mental state of the stakeholder, composed of her intention w.r.t. the system, her belief that the system has the capability to perform the desired actions in order to reach her goals, as well as her belief that the system's vulnerabilities will not prevent it from exhibiting the desired behavior.

Understanding the elements of stakeholder trustworthiness towards the system to be is important because they reveal the qualities and properties the system should have in order to be considered trustworthy and effectively promote well-placed trust. Note that as trust is contextually dependent (the trust degree of a trustor in a trustee may vary from a context to another) the implementation of trustworthiness requirements depends on the specific application. For example, a user trusts a system in collecting her location data but not when she is in sensitive places, such as when she is being treated at a hospital, since such information may lead to disclose a health issue.

Another advantage of making the components of trust explicit is that this knowledge can be used as input to the definition of trust-warranting signals that ensure trustworthy behavior. In other words, once the system's capabilities and vulnerabilities related to the trust of the stakeholder are known, it is possible to reason about the signals that the system should emit to indicate that it is capable of successfully realizing the capabilities and prevent the manifestation of the vulnerabilities. For example, information about how privacy and security measures are implemented could be provided as signals of the trustworthiness of a system. Other relevant examples of trust-warranting signals are data certificates and data provenance information, both relevant for systems dealing with large amounts of data, to avoid bias and unfair results.

Finally, the identification of trust components is equally important to the assessment of risks related to the capabilities and vulnerabilities, which are the focus of stakeholders' beliefs. As previously discussed, *capabilities* are dispositions that inhere in an agent and, as such, are manifested in particular situations, through the occurrence of events (Guizzardi, Wagner, Falbo, et al., 2013). As defined in the Common Ontology of Value and Risk (see section 3.2 of chapter 3), a *threat event* is a type of *risk event* that may be the manifestation of a capability of the system, in case it fails to realize this specific capability in order to bring about an outcome desired by the stakeholder. According to COVER, the threat event may lead to a *loss event*, which negatively influences the stakeholder's intention. For example, suppose that a network malfunction prevents a medical system to access the server containing patient data and, as a result of that, it cannot deliver its capability of providing a diagnosis. In this case, the network malfunction is a threat event, which leads to a lack of diagnosis loss event.

Similarly, *vulnerabilities* are also a special type of disposition, whose manifestation causes or can potentially cause a loss, under the perspective of a stakeholder. Therefore, a threat event may be the manifestation of a vulnerability and eventually trigger a loss event. To illustrate this point, let us imagine that our medical system has a security vulnerability and is thus hacked, leading to the leak of patient data. In this case, the hacking threat event, resulting from the manifestation of the system's security vulnerability, triggered the patient privacy loss event.

We represent the concepts related to Trustworthiness Requirements in the OntoUML model depicted in figure 7.3, and the emergence of risks in this scenario in figure 7.4.

As shown in figure 7.3, we modeled Requirement as a Goal, which is the propositional content of an Intention of a Stakeholder. Quality Requirement is a type of Requirement, and Trustworthy Requirement is a type of Quality Requirement. Stakeholders are represented as Agents that play the role of trustor, while the System is an existentially independent object that plays the role of trustee. The System intends to satisfy the Trustworthiness Requirements.

As pointed out in section 7.3, the analysis of the trustworthiness requirement may involve its decomposition in other quality requirements, such as *reliability requirement*, *truthful information communication requirement* and *transparency requirement*. Thus, we include in the model of figure 7.3, a composition relation between Trustworthiness Requirement and Quality Requirement. Additionally, this model supports the representation of the mentioned sub-requirements as instances of the Quality Requirement concept. All Quality Requirements are such that they restrict the value of the qualities at hand to a particular set of values of the corresponding Quality Region. Trustworthy Requirement restrict the values of qualities referring to reliability, transparency and information truthfulness to particular set of values accordingly.

As for Trust, we represent it as a complex mode composed of a Stakeholder's Intention, whose propositional content is a Goal of the Stakeholder, and a set of Beliefs that inhere in the Stakeholder and are externally dependent on the dispositions (Azevedo, C.L.B. et al., 2015; Guizzardi, Wagner, Falbo, et al., 2013) that inhere in the System. These beliefs include: (i) the Belief that the System has the Capability to perform the desired action (Capability Belief); and (ii) the Belief that the System's Vulnerabilities will not prevent it from exhibiting the desired behavior (Vulnerability Belief). The System's Vulnerabilities and Capabilities are dispositions that inhere in the System, which are manifested in particular situations, through the occurrence of events (Guizzardi, Wagner, Falbo, et al., 2013). We adopt the interpretation of capability proposed by Azevedo, C.L.B. et al. (2015), who defined capability as the power to bring about a desired outcome. As previously discussed, the System can emit Trust-Warranting Signals in order to indicate that it is capable of successfully realizing the capabilities and prevent the manifestation of the vulnerabilities. Another important aspect is the role played by pieces of evidence that indicate that a trustee (System) is trustworthy, named here Trustworthiness Evidence. Examples of trustworthiness evidences are certifications

7.4. ROTwR: Reference Ontology of Trustworthiness Requirements

by trusted third parties, history of performance, recommendations, past successful experiences, among others. Ontologically speaking, Trustworthiness Evidences are social entities, typically social relators (e.g., a relator binding the certifying entity, the certified entity and referring to a capability, vulnerability, etc.), but also documents (social objects themselves) that represent these social entities (e.g., in the way a marriage certificate documents a marriage as a social relator). They are modeled as roles played by endurants (objects, relators, etc.) related to a Disposition of the System.

All these ontological concepts play an important role in helping us understand if the system is compliant to the sub-requirements that compose the trustworthiness requirement. For example, for *reliability*, we must understand how much of the Stakeholder's Capability Belief is actually met by the results of the system's operation (i.e., by system actions); regarding *truthful information communication*, the System Capability of providing truthful information may be validated, by comparing the information generated by the system with information known to be real; and finally, regarding *transparency*, we must make sure that the Trust-Warranting Signals are enough to make the Stakeholder satisfied w.r.t how often and how well the system explains its decision-making process.

We represent the emergence of trustworthiness-related risks in the OntoUML model depicted in figure 7.4. In order to realize the Capabilities, the System performs some Actions that bring about a Resulting Situation. The Resulting Situation may satisfy the Stakeholder's Goals (and in this case it is considered a Successful Situation) or, in the worst case, it may not have the desired result and the Stakeholder will not be able to achieve her goal. In this case, the Resulting Situation stands for a Threat Situation that may trigger a Threat Event, which may lead to a Loss Event that impacts intentions in a negative way, as it hurts the Stakeholder's Intentions of reaching a Goal. Analogously, System's Vulnerabilities may enable the occurrence of Risk Events that, in the worst case, may cause a Loss Event which will hurt the Stakeholder's Intentions of reaching her Goal.

156 Chapter 7. Ontology-based Modeling and Analysis of Trustworthiness Requirements

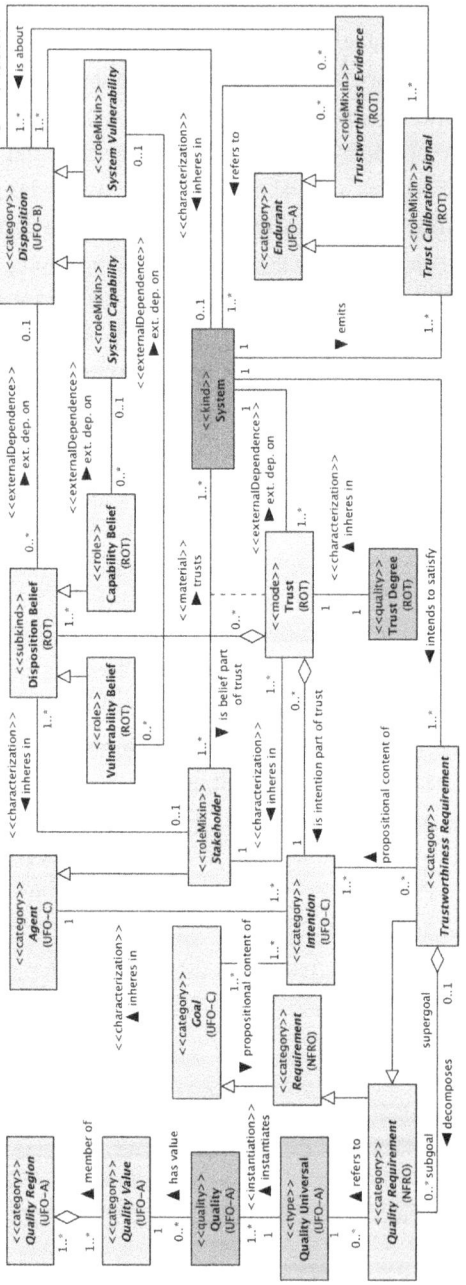

Figure 7.3: Modeling trustworthiness requirements in OntoUML.

7.4. ROTwR: Reference Ontology of Trustworthiness Requirements

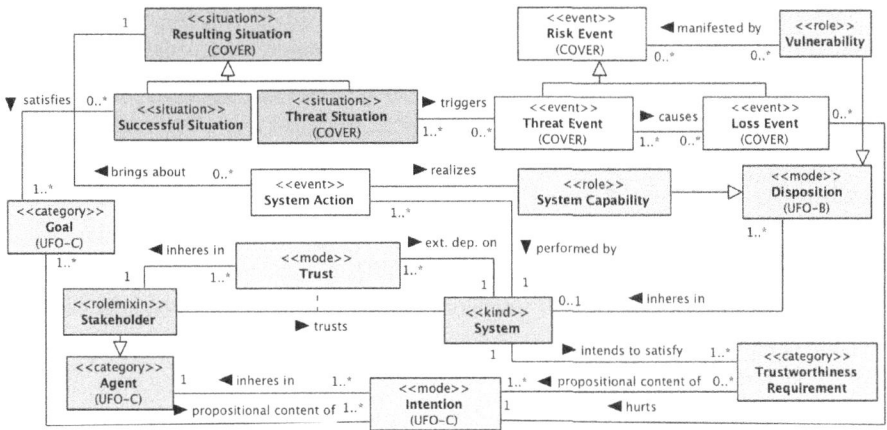

Figure 7.4: Modeling the emergence of trustworthiness-related risks.

7.5 Trustworthiness Requirements and ObRE: The Pix Case Study

Requirements Engineering (RE) is a critical system development activity that makes or breaks many software development projects (Hussain et al., 2016). A myriad of RE methods, following different paradigms, have been around for at least four decades. Early methods focused on 'what' stakeholders need, resulting in a list of system functionalities directly indicated by stakeholders or inferred by requirements analysts. In the early nineties, goal-oriented RE (GORE) inaugurated a new paradigm that focused on 'why' a system was needed and 'how' needs of stakeholders can be addressed (Van Lamsweerde, 2009). Also around this time, the realization that not only functionalities but also *qualities* are important to shape the system-to-be led to newfound attention on non-functional requirements (e.g., privacy, security, etc.) (Chung et al., 2000). In the 2000s, the agile software engineering paradigm emerged, leading to new RE methods focusing on incremental software delivery and teamwork (e.g., capturing requirements via user stories (Cohn, 2004))[1]. Generally, RE has evolved in response to an ever-increasing system complexity that today spans not only system concerns, but also social (e.g., security, privacy), physical (as in cyber-physical systems), and personal (e.g., eth-

---

[1] This is a brief historical account intended to highlight the evolution of ideas and methods in RE. This account is not meant to be exhaustive; we acknowledge the existence of many other high impact RE methods, such as feature-based RE, recent methods based on CANVAS.

ical concerns for artificial intelligence systems) ones. A major challenge for RE today is to propose concepts, tools and techniques that support requirements engineering activities for incorporating high-level societal concerns and goals, such as privacy, fairness and trustworthiness, into the software development processes as explicit requirements.

We address this challenge by proposing a novel method named Ontology-based Requirements Engineering (ObRE). The method aims to systematize the elicitation and analysis of requirements, by using an ontological account for a class of requirements, such as privacy, fairness and trustworthiness. ObRE is intended to help by "semantically unpacking" concepts such as trustworthiness or fairness where the analysts may struggle in understanding, for example, which requirements can make the system under development trustworthy or fair.

Ontological analysis provides a foundation for ObRE as it enables a deep account of the meaning of a particular domain. The notions of *ontology* and *ontological analysis* adopted here are akin to their interpretations in philosophy (Berto and Plebani, 2015). In this view, the goals of *ontological analysis* are: (i) characterize what kinds of entities are assumed to exist by a given conceptualization of a domain; (ii) the metaphysical nature of these kinds of entities. An *ontology*, in turn, is a collection of concepts and relationships that together address questions (i) and (ii).

This section presents in detail the ObRE method and illustrates its working by applying it to a real case study concerning trustworthiness requirements. In this study, ObRE was applied to help with the elicitation of the trustworthiness requirements of a recently released real system, named Pix. Pix is an instant payment solution, created and managed by the Central Bank of Brazil (BCB), which enables its users to send or receive payment transfers in few seconds at any time. The success achieved by Pix has led us to consider it an appropriate case study for our approach. In the case study, the Reference Ontology of Trustworthiness Requirements (section 7.4) served as ontological foundation for the ObRE method, by enabling a deep account of the notion of trustworthiness requirement.

First, in section 7.5.1 we present the ObRE method. In section 7.5.2 we present the Pix case study and in section 7.5.3 we use ObRE to analyse the trustworthiness requirements of Pix. Then, in section 7.5.4, we discuss on the case study results and on the implications of our proposal to the requirements engineering practice.

7.5.1 Ontology-based Requirements Engineering

In ObRE, we address the challenge of dealing with non-functional requirements, such as trustworthiness, by relying on ontological analysis. Ontological analysis provides a foundation for our proposal as it enables a deep account of the meaning of a particular domain, thus allowing to "semantically unpack" the requirements concepts at-hand, thereby facilitating requirements activities. Figure 7.5 illustrates the process of the ObRE method, showing the three activities that compose it, which are described below.

1. Adopt or develop an ontology for conceptualizing a class of requirements: In this step, requirements analysts and ontology engineers can choose between reusing an existing ontology or performing ontological analysis for the particular class of requirement. Having the requirements explicitly defined and understood, the analyst may proceed to the next step.

2. Instantiate the ontology for a system-to-be, resulting in a domain model: In this step, key concepts of the ontology can be used as a guide to define the right questions to be asked to the stakeholders during requirements elicitation (e.g., table 8.1). The answers can be used as input to instantiate elements of the ontology. This is intended to serve as a domain model for conducting requirements analysis.

3. Analyze requirements based on the domain model: In this step, the analyst uses the domain model to define and analyze system requirements. For instance, she may simply define a requirements table, listing the requirements instantiated with the help of the ontology. Or if she prefers a more sophisticated analysis methodology, she may use goal modeling, defining the contribution of different choices to accomplish a particular goal (i.e., requirement), and specifying how goals relate to each other, as well as to relevant stakeholders' resources and tasks. Or yet, she may create user stories based on the identified ontological instances. From this point on, the requirements analysis may progress as the chosen method prescribes, however, with the benefit of having the ontology and ontological instances as guides.

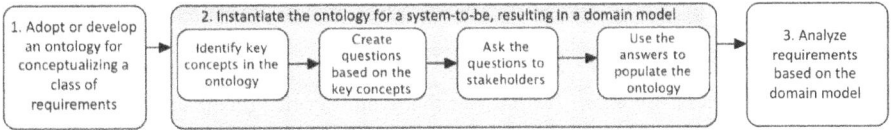

Figure 7.5: Ontology-based Requirements Engineering Method.

7.5.2 Case Study

Research Method

To evaluate and demonstrate the contribution of our ontology-based method for the analysis of trustworthiness requirements, we conducted a case study in the Central Bank of Brazil (BCB), in the context of the Brazilian Instant Payments Ecosystem.

The research procedure was adapted from (Yin, 2008). The initial stage involved the planning and designing of the case study. We defined the purpose of the case study - *evaluate the feasibility of the application of ObRE for the analysis and elicitation of Pix's trustworthiness requirements* - and held a planning meeting to identify different areas of interest and select the interviewees.

In the collect stage, we gathered information from documentation and interviews. Firstly, documents describing and documenting the project were collected from the BCB's website[2] to deepen the knowledge about Pix. Then, we conducted interviews with the stakeholders responsible for the areas of interest, namely communication, instant payment systems, communication interfaces, transaction accounts identifier directory, security and infrastructure. The questions in the interviews were based on the notions of trust and trustworthiness requirements described in the adopted ontology, namely, ROTwR (see section 7.4) (step 1 of ObRE method, in figure 7.5). The interviews were recorded and transcribed to facilitate and improve the analysis. In the analyze stage, the interviewers examined the transcripts and searched for the elements to instantiate the ontology of trustworthiness requirements (step 2 of ObRE method, in figure 7.5). Then, we used the ontology instantiation as a domain model to define and analyze trustworthiness requirements (step 3 of ObRE method, in figure 7.5).

The Brazilian Instant Payments Ecosystem (Pix)

The Central Bank of Brazil is a special nature agency, characterized by the absence of ties or hierarchical subordination to any Ministry. Among the main tasks of the BCB are the regulation and supervision of the National Financial System and the administration of the payments system.

Pix is the instant payment solution, created and managed by the BCB, having two kinds of stakeholders: *financial institutions* that want to offer this instant payment service, and *end users*, i.e. the clients of the financial institutions, aiming at exchanging

---
[2]https://www.bcb.gov.br/en/financialstability/pix_en.

money through such service. A Pix transaction will typically be initiated through the usage of a predefined Pix Key or a QR code associated with the beneficiary's transactional account. The Pix key is a 'nickname' used to identify the user account, which can be a cell phone number, an email, a taxpayer number or a random key. The key links one of these basic items of information to the complete information that identifies the customer's transactional account. Once started, Pix transactions are irrevocable and processed individually in a few seconds. Pix can be processed between: Person-to-Person (P2P), Person-to-Business (P2B), Business-to-Business (B2B), Person-to-Government (P2G), or Business-to-Government (B2G).

Pix operates through a centralized framework comprising messaging communication among the various participants and BCB. All transactions take place through digitally signed messages exchanged, in encrypted form, through a private network apart from the Internet. In order to promote public awareness, BCB created the Pix's brand, whose principles — Design, Sonority, Governance — aim at promoting an easily identifiable brand that should be displayed by all participating financial institutions.

7.5.3 Using ObRE to Analyze Pix's Requirements

This section presents the results of the case study. As aforementioned, our findings are based in the analysis of the documentation and the interviews conducted with stakeholders responsible for Pix key areas. Our analysis took into account the whole ecosystem in which the system is included, whose main stakeholders are the *Pix ecosystem participants* (financial and payment institutions that offer transaction accounts) and *end users* (individuals and organizations).

Domain Ontology Development or Adoption

We reused our previous Reference Ontology on Trustworthiness Requirements (see section 7.4) to unpack the notions of trust and trustworthiness requirements (step 1 of ObRE method, in figure 7.5). Then, we defined the initial questions that would guide the interviews with the stakeholders (table 8.1). The ontology served as guidance for our work from the beginning of the case study, helping us focus on the domain being investigated and supporting the creation of the interview questions. As can be seen on table 8.1, these questions are actually formulated based on the concepts from ROTwR (see column 2).

162   Chapter 7. Ontology-based Modeling and Analysis of Trustworthiness Requirements

Table 7.1: Questions related to key ontology concepts.

Question	ROTwR Concept
Stakeholders trust the system to...	Intention
Stakeholders trust the system because they believe that it is capable of...	Capability Belief / System Capability
Stakeholders trust the system because they believe that it has mechanisms to prevent...	Vulnerability Belief / System Vulnerability
How can the system indicate that it is trustworthy?	Trust-warranting Signal
What pieces of evidence show that the system is trustworthy?	Trustworthiness Evidence

Domain Ontology Instantiation

We adopt the following coding to refer to instances of key ROTwR concepts hereafter: **INT** for intentions; **BEL** for disposition beliefs; **TS** for trust-warranting signals; **TE** for trustworthiness evidences; and **TR** for trustworthiness requirements.

The interviews showed that, in general, *end users trust Pix to send or receive payment transfers safely and easily, in few seconds on a 24/7 basis* (INT1). According to an interviewee, "users want to be sure that the system will access their money only when they want, and in the way they want". In other words, users who trust the system believe that *it is safe* (BEL1) and that *it will be available when they need* (BEL2). Interviewees also expressed that it is important that Pix participants feel safe to perform transactions in the ecosystem . It was a consensus among the interviewees that *security* (TR1), *availability* (TR2) and *instantaneity* (TR3) are essential to build sustainable trust in the system.

As stated by the Pix project team and explained in the documentation, *security* has been a part of Pix design since its inception, and it is prioritized in all aspects of the ecosystem, including transactions, personal information and the fight against fraud and money laundering. The requirements for the *availability*, *confidentiality* (TR4), *integrity* (TR5) and *authenticity* (TR6) of the information were carefully studied and several controls were implemented to ensure a high level of security. All transactions take place through digitally signed messages that travel in encrypted form, over a protected network, apart from the Internet. In addition, user information is also encrypted and protected by mechanisms that prevent scans of personal information in the sole and centralized proxy database, an addressing database that will store Pix keys information. There are also *indicators that assist the ecosystem participants in the process of pre-*

7.5. Trustworthiness Requirements and ObRE: The Pix Case Study

vention against fraud and money laundering (TS1). Another important aspect related to security is *traceability* (TR7). All Pix operations are fully traceable, which means that the Central Bank and the institutions involved can, at the request of the competent authorities, identify the origin and destination account holders of any and all payment transactions in Pix. Thus, in a situation of kidnapping or other means of unlawful coercion, the recipient of a financial transfer is fully identified. In addition, *all participants must comply with basic regulation on operational and liquidity risk management framework* (TE1); *cybersecurity policy* (TE2); a *service level agreement that establishes high availability parameters and processing time limits* (TE3); among others.

Another aspect that emerged from the interviews is the importance of providing a simple experience for end users. Interviewees mentioned that "people are more likely to trust in something they understand" and "simplicity leads to trust". Simply put, users who trust the system believe that *it is simple and easy to use* (BEL3). The general consensus is that *usability* (TR8) is of paramount importance for effectively promoting trust in the system. *Visual identity* (TS2) was mentioned by interviewees as an important attribute to facilitate the understanding and adoption of the functionality. According to them, the establishment of a universal brand was essential for users to identify the new way of making/receiving payments and transfers, in a clear and unambiguous way. Equally important was the definition of a *manual with minimum usability requirements* (TE4), which must be followed by all participants of the Pix ecosystem.

Still in this direction, actions focusing on *explainability* (TR9) have been taken since the beginning of the project. Some examples mentioned during the interviews are: *advertising campaigns in the media and social networks using everyday examples* (TS3); *documentation available on the BCB website*[2] (TS4); *provision of information at dissemination events* (held in virtual mode, due to the COVID-19 pandemic) *for different market sectors* (TS5); (iv) partnership with the press and digital influencers for advertising, as well as for monitoring and preventing the spread of fake news about the system.

Finally, *transparency* (TR10) was another attribute mentioned by a number of interviewees. One of the reasons for the prioritization of *transparency*, as explained by several interviewees, is that "if the participants are involved in the discussions from the beginning, *they believe that their needs will be considered and that they will not be taken by surprise, consequently, they feel safe and trust the system*" (BEL4). Interviewees also mentioned that "participants' trust in the Pix ecosystem contributed to foster end users' trust". In this direction, the Pix operational framework development has been an open and transparent process, with intense participation from market agents and potential users. In order to foster a collaborative implementation process, BCB created a specific forum, named *'Pix Forum'* (TE5), which has about 200 participating institutions. Lastly, as previously mentioned, an extensive documentation about the Pix project and the Pix ecosystem is available at the BCB website[2], providing information such as a Pix regulations, Frequently Asked Questions, and Pix statistics[3], which contribute to *transparency* at different levels. Pix statistics include indicators, such as number of registered Pix keys, number of Pix transactions, number of users transacting Pix, among others. We identified that, in general, *these indicators* positively exceeded the initial expectations, thus demonstrating the success of the project. In this case, they can be seen as pieces of evidence (TE6) that indicate that the Pix ecosystem is trustworthy.

Figures 7.6, 7.7, 7.8 and 7.9 present the resulting models of the ontology instantiation.

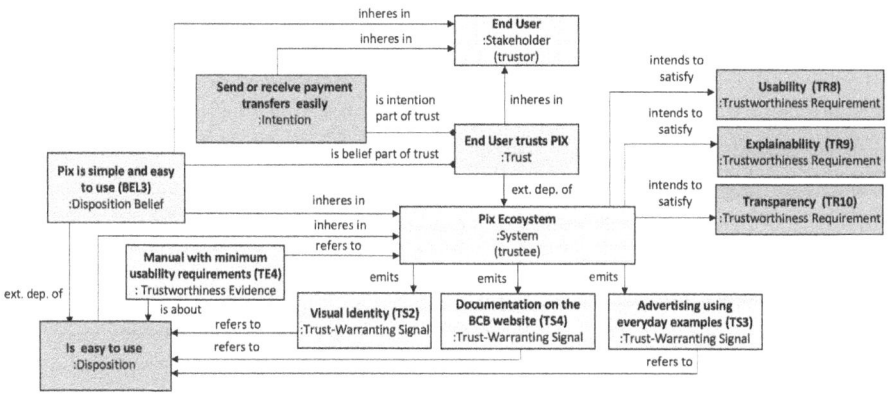

Figure 7.6: Ontology instantiation focusing on usability.

---

[3]https://www.bcb.gov.br/en/financialstability/pixstatistics

7.5. Trustworthiness Requirements and ObRE: The Pix Case Study

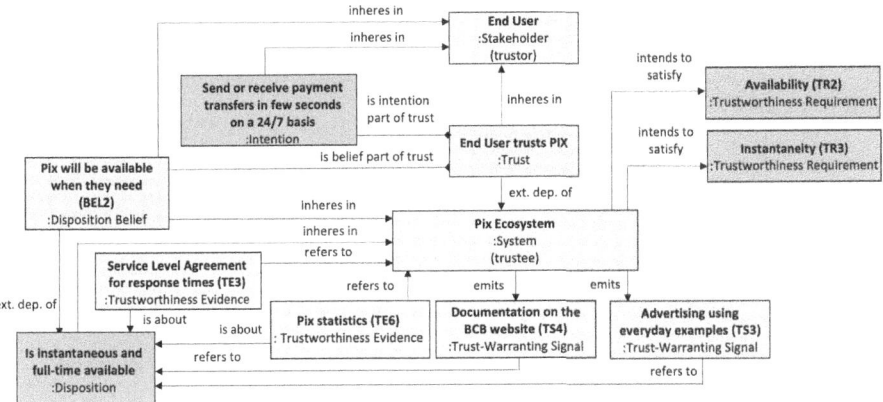

Figure 7.7: Ontology instantiation focusing on availability.

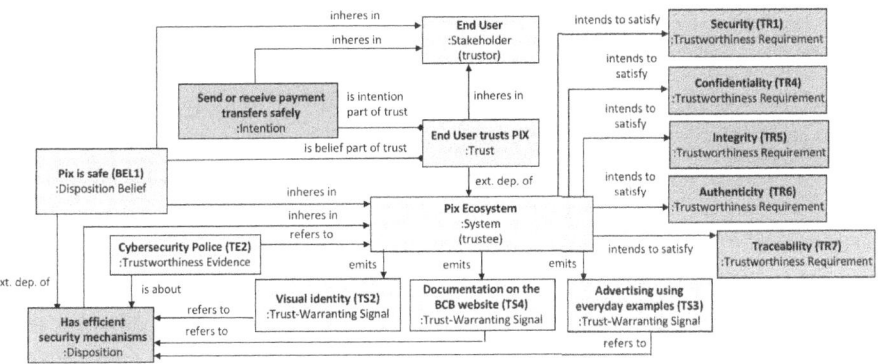

Figure 7.8: Ontology instantiation focusing on security (end users' perspective).

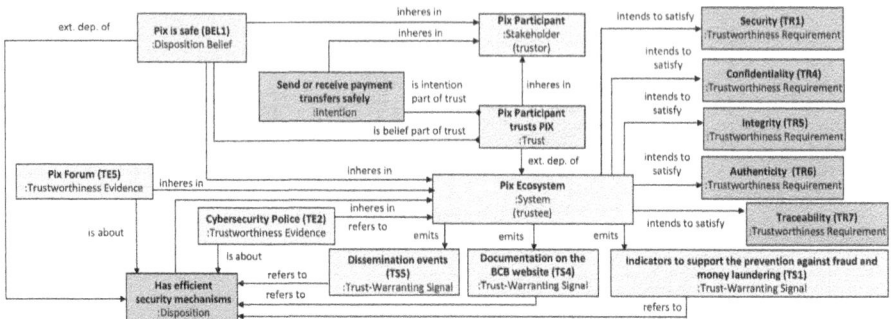

Figure 7.9: Ontology instantiation focusing on security (participants' perspective).

Requirements Analysis Method Execution

We exemplify the step 3 of ObRE method (figure 7.5) by analyzing the requirements of Pix. In particular, we present both a requirements table and a goal model for this case.

We start by presenting table 7.2, showing how a requirements table may be enriched with the inclusion of columns representing some of ROTwR concepts. All words highlighted in boldface in table 7.2 refer to ontological concepts analyzed in section 7.4, while the ontological instances are written as non-emphasized text. For the sake of simplicity, we focused only on security. To build a requirements table such as table 7.2, we first capture the elements that compose the trust of stakeholders in Pix, namely their intentions and beliefs about Pix dispositions, and then we come up with particular requirements for the system-to-be to fulfill these goals and beliefs. In particular, these are requirements for the developing capabilities (i.e. system's functionalities) needed to accomplish the desired requirements.

Table 7.2: Requirements table of Pix focusing on security.

Stakeholder	Intention	Capability Belief	Trustworthiness Requirement	Capability
End Users, Participants	Send and receive payment transfers safely	Pix is Safe (BEL1)	Security (TR1)	has security mechanisms
			Confidentiality (TR4)	make info traffic in protected network
				encrypt info and messages
			Integrity (TR5)	encrypt info and messages
			Authenticity (TR6)	digitally sign messages
			Traceability (TR7)	use traceability mechanisms

7.5. Trustworthiness Requirements and ObRE: The Pix Case Study

As an alternative, consider a requirements analysis for the Pix case using goal modeling. To illustrate, we present, in figure 7.10, a fragment of goal model for this case using the *i** framework (Dalpiaz et al., 2016). The model shows the goals that the stakeholders referred to in table 7.2 delegate to the Pix Ecosystem (through the *i** dependency relation). Besides dependencies, the goal model depicts the internal perspective of Pix, assisting in the analysis of the system's requirements. Note that security (TR1), availability (TR2), instantaneity (TR3), confidentiality (TR4), integrity (TR5), authenticity (TR6), traceability (TR7), usability (TR8), explainability (TR9), transparency (TR10) were represented as qualities and goals that contribute to (help) the ultimate goal of being trustworthy. Then, for each of them, more specific goals and qualities were identified and related to them by contribution links. For instance, the *protecting information confidentiality* goal helps the achievement of *being secure*.

The goal model also allows the requirements analyst to progressively identify more concrete requirements and solutions and the resources needed to accomplish them. For example, *making the information traffic in a protected network* contributes to the *protecting information confidentiality* goal, and the *protected network itself* is a resource needed in this task. To accomplish the higher level of *being secure*, other tasks, qualities and goals are involved.

We emphasize that ObRE does not subscribe to a specific RE method, leaving this choice for the requirements analyst, based on their particular preference or skill.

168 Chapter 7. Ontology-based Modeling and Analysis of Trustworthiness Requirements

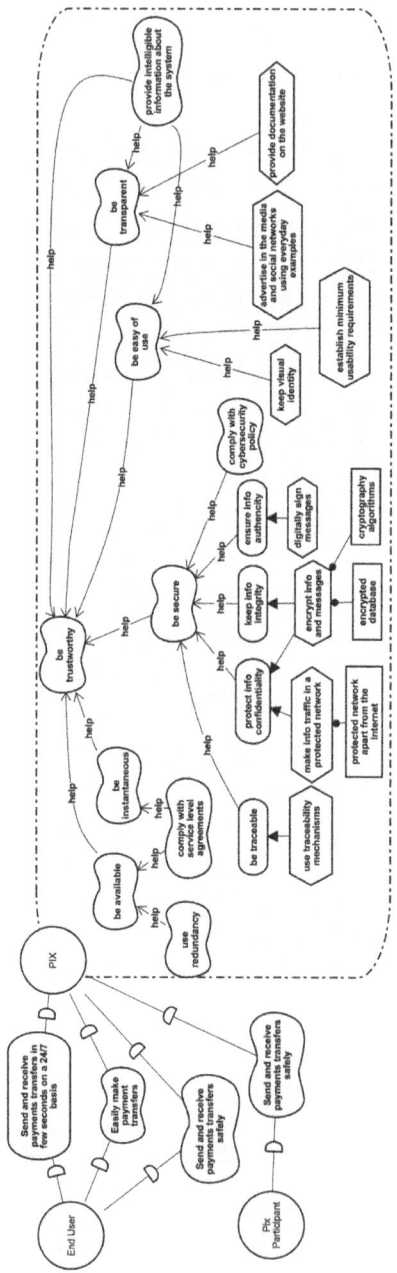

Figure 7.10: Goal Model of the Pix Ecosystem.

7.5.4 Discussion

The case study experience confirmed that the ontology-based method proposed here can have a positive impact in the requirements engineering activities of requirements related to high-level societal concerns and goals, such as trustworthiness, and suggests that this approach could be used to systematize the elicitation of other abstract requirements, such as privacy, fairness and ethical requirements.

The case study helped us reflect on which non-functional requirements are related (and can lead) to trustworthiness. For example, trustworthiness for Pix goes beyond reliability, transparency and security, including also availability, instantaneity and usability. We believe that the notion of trustworthiness involves different requirements, depending on the context.

An interesting finding of the case study was that once we understand what trustworthiness means and how it relates to other important concepts, we can address trustworthiness since the system's inception thus enabling trustworthiness by design. This allows the identification of potential risks in advance and the definition of risk mitigation strategies. Another interesting finding is that trustworthiness requirements may need constant monitoring, as the system is embedded in a dynamic environment, which is constantly changing. And changes in the environment can influence user's trust. In this case, the ObRE method can iteratively assist the analyst throughout the requirement life cycle.

We acknowledge that our case study has some limitations in terms of evaluating the use of ObRE. First, the interviews and analysis were made by the developers of the method. Moreover, only members of the Pix project team were interviewed, and not Pix's stakeholders. However, for the latter, the results shown by the Pix statistics confirm the team's perception regarding Pix's trustworthiness and indicate that they are going in the right direction.

The ObRE method has important implications for RE research and practice. For RE research, it suggests first and foremost that for a host of requirements families, including security, privacy, ethicality, trustworthiness and fairness, we need ontologies that capture relevant concepts. Many such ontologies have been proposed for security and privacy. For other families that only recently became prominent because of advent of AI systems, such ontologies are currently being developed. Secondly, we need tools for domain building by instantiating relevant ontologies for a particular system-to-be. Thirdly, for RE practice such tools need to be made available to practitioners who can't be expected to be knowledgeable in these fancy requirements in order to conduct requirements analysis for their next project.

7.6 Related Work

The elicitation of trust requirements has been broadly studied and different approaches have been proposed in the literature to support the capture and implementation of trust requirements in the context of software systems (Giorgini et al., 2005; Hleg, A.I., 2019; Mohammadi, 2019; Rosemann, 2019). Despite the wide number of efforts to properly analyse trustworthiness requirements and trust-related issues, little has been said about what constitutes the stakeholders' trust in the system, what it depends upon and how trustworthiness-related risks can be identified. Differently from other approaches, our proposal analyses the components of the trust complex mental state of the trustor in order to identify what the system should have for stakeholders to trust it. These elements are fundamental for a better understanding and proper elucidation of trustworthy requirements. Moreover, they are key for the identification of trustworthiness-related risks that may arise when the requirements are not fulfilled accordingly.

7.7 Final Considerations

In this chapter we applied and validated two networked ontologies of OntoFINE, namely ROT and COVER, in the context of requirements engineering. We used ROT and COVER as ontological foundation for the modeling of trustworthiness requirements and conducted a real case study, in collaboration with the Central Bank of Brazil, in which the proposed Reference Ontology of Trustworthiness Requirements was applied to help with the elicitation of trustworthiness requirements of Pix — the Brazilian Instant Payments Ecosystem created and managed by the BCB.

The success of RE activities largely depends on the creation of a shared understanding between stakeholders and analysts for a system-to-be (Charaf et al., 2013; Glinz and Fricker, 2015). Werner et al. (2020) conducted an empirical study to find out why a shared understanding NFRs is so difficult in software organizations. Their study shows that two of the main problems were lack of domain knowledge and inadequate communication. Reference ontologies have been widely recognized as powerful tools for representing a model of consensus within a community to support communication, meaning negotiation and consensus establishment. By applying ROT and COVER to "semantically unpack" the notion of trustworthiness requirements, we exemplify how reference ontologies can address the subjective and ambiguous nature of many classes of requirements, especially so ones that have become prominent recently with the advent of AI systems, such as ethicality, fairness, privacy and trustworthiness. As demonstrated in the case study presented in section 7.5, such artifacts facilitate the communication between analysts and stakeholders, besides assisting in the identification of requirements.

Chapter 8

Modeling Trust Dynamics: The Case of CBDC Ecosystems

In this chapter, we apply and validate the Reference Ontology of Trust (see chapter 4) and the Reference Ontology of Money and Virtual Currencies (see chapter 5) in the context of decentralized finance. We validate both ROT's capacity to represent real-world situations and ROME's expressivity on money-related concepts, by conducting a real case study, in close collaboration with a national central bank (Amaral, Sales, and Guizzardi, 2022), in which we model and analyse citizens' trust in central bank digital currency ecosystems.

This chapter is organized as follows. Section 8.1 motivates the relevance of modeling and analyzing the dynamics of citizens' trust in central bank digital currency ecosystems. Section 8.2 introduces the research method we followed in the case study, and section 8.3 describes the research context. We apply ROT to model citizens' trust in CBDC ecosystems in section 8.4 and discuss the case study results in section 8.5. Finally, section 8.6 concludes the chapter with some final considerations.

8.1 Introduction

New and disruptive technologies have been developed at a rapid pace, affecting almost every area of our lives. Industrial robots, artificial intelligence algorithms, machine learning, big data, decentralized technologies, just to cite a few, have the power to accelerate the production and delivery, improve the quality, and reduce the costs of goods and services, as well as to contribute to individual and collective well-being. However, the adoption of these innovative technologies relies largely on user trust. And trust is highly dynamic. Trust is generally said to be one of the easiest things to lose and one of the most difficult things to win back. It may break in an instant or erode gradually. Therefore, it is important to build sustainable trust that is not easily lost. In the case of information technology systems and ecosystems, building sustainable trust involves addressing stakeholders' trust concerns from the system (or ecosystem) inception to their constant monitoring, as trust changes with time.

In recent years, innovations in the financial industry, which include cryptocurrencies, blockchains and distributed ledger technologies, smart contracts (Schär, 2021), programmable money (Arner, Auer, et al., 2020), stablecoins (Arner, Auer, et al., 2020), and central bank digital currencies (Amaral, Sales, and Guizzardi, 2021d), have fostered the creation of financial products and services on top of decentralized technologies, giving rise to the concept of decentralized finance (DeFi) (Schär, 2021; Zetzsche et al., 2020)—the decentralized provision of financial products and services. This new paradigm has revolutionized the world money, payments, and economic exchanges, as they create new forms of trust, digital money and digital exchanges.

In DeFi ecosystems, central bank digital currencies (CBDC) emerge as an advanced representation of money for the digital economy with the potential to enable the improvement of financial products and services. However, the successful implementation of a CBDC crucially depends on citizens' motivation to adopt this new digital form of public money, which is directly related to their trust in the CBDC ecosystem.

In this chapter, we rely on ROT and ROME to model and analyse citizens' trust in CBDC ecosystems, by conducting a real case study in close collaboration with a national central bank. Due to the sensitivity of this topic (the development of CBDC ecosystems is in full swing, and their design is not finished yet) and specific request of the central bank, the only information we can disclose is that the contributing central bank's context is a country with between 50 and 300 million citizens. Our aim is twofold: a) to apply and validate ROT's capacity to proper represent real world situations, by modeling citizens' trust in CBDC ecosystems; and b) to validate ROME's expressivity as a tool to provide a correct and common understanding of the domain of money and, more specifically, of the notion of CBDC and related concepts, as the proper understanding of citizen's trust in CBDCs is only possible if the notions of money, currency and CBDC are clear.

8.2 Research Method

We conducted a case study, in collaboration with a national central bank, regarding citizens' trust in CBDC ecosystems. This methodological approach is particularly appropriate when the focus is investigating a contemporary phenomenon in depth and within its real-life context, and the investigator has no control over actual behavioral events (Yin, 2008). The research procedure we employed was adapted from (Yin, 2008).

We started by planning the case study. We defined its purpose — *to verify if the Reference Ontology of Trust can properly represent real world situations, or more specifically if it can model citizens' trust in CBDC ecosystems* — identified the areas of interest, namely, economics, financial citizenship and information technology, and selected the interviewees. We also obtained the necessary authorizations from the central bank to carry out the study.

In the collect stage, we gathered information from documentation and interviews. First, documents describing and documenting information on citizens' trust in CBDC ecosystems were collected from the literature (Bank for International Settlements et al., 2021b; Bijlsma et al., 2021; Boar, Holden, et al., 2020; Boar and Wehrli, 2021; European Central Bank, 2021; Söilen and Benhayoun, 2021) and from the central bank's website, to deepen our knowledge about the topic. Based on this documentation, we created an initial version of the ontology instantiation, to be validated and complemented at the interviews stage. Then, we conducted interviews with central bank experts in the areas of interest, namely, economics, financial citizenship and information technology. The questions that would guide the interviews with the stakeholders (table 8.1) were defined based on the main concepts of the Reference Ontology of Trust (see chapter 4). The ontology served as guidance for our work from the beginning of the case study, helping us focus on the domain being investigated and supporting the creation of the interview questions. As shown in table 8.1, these questions are actually formulated based on the concepts from ROT (see column 2).

We conducted three individual interviews in the form of guided conversations, one for each expert of the areas of interest, namely, economics, financial citizenship and information technology. During the interviews we presented the initial version of the ontology instantiation to be validated and gathered information based on the aforementioned questions (table 8.1). The interviews were recorded (audio) and with their feedback and validation we have improved both the ontology and the ontology instantiation, and presented them again to the central bank in a validation meeting. We had in total

Table 8.1: Questions related to key ontology concepts.

Question	ROT Concept
Citizens trust the CBDC ecosystem to...	Intention
Citizens trust the CBDC ecosystem because they believe that it can...	Belief
	Capability
Citizens trust the CBDC ecosystem because they believe that it has mechanisms to prevent...	Belief
	Vulnerability
How can the CBDC ecosystem indicate that it is trustworthy?	Trust Calibration Signal
What pieces of evidence show the CBDC ecosystem is trustworthy?	Trustworthiness Evidence
What can influence citizens' trust in the CBDC ecosystem?	Influence

four sessions with the central bank, in which the modeling of citizens' trust in CBDC ecosystems were discussed in detail.

In the analyze stage, we concluded the final version of the ontology instantiation. In addition, to demonstrate the contribution and applicability of our ontology to the modeling practice, we used the ontology instantiation as a domain model to create a goal model for this case using the *i** framework (Dalpiaz et al., 2016). Finally, we shared the results with the central bank team.

8.3 Research Context: CBDC Ecosystems

A CBDC is a form of digital money, denominated in the national unit of account, which is a direct liability of the central bank, such as physical cash and central bank settlement accounts (Amaral, Sales, and Guizzardi, 2021d) (see section 5.2.4). In general, a CBDC ecosystem would comprise elements and functions similar to traditional payment systems, with central banks facing many of the practical policy questions around access, services and structure they currently do. According to Bank for International Settlements et al. (2021a), at the center of any CBDC ecosystem would be a CBDC "core rulebook" outlining the legal basis, governance, risk management, access and other requirements of participants in the CBDC ecosystem. Participants in the CBDC system could include banks, payment service providers, mobile operators and fintech or big tech companies, which would act as intermediaries between the central bank and end users. This broader ecosystem would be complemented by a legal and supervisory framework and contractual arrangements between end users and their intermediaries

(Bank for International Settlements et al., 2021a). Currently, all CBDC ecosystems are still under design. The initiatives around the world are either at the stage of experimentation, proof-of-concept, or pilot arrangements.

Consumer demand for CBDC is an important element that determines how widely a CBDC would be used. Therefore, the successful implementation of a CBDC crucially depends on citizens' motivation to adopt this new digital form of public money, which is directly related to their trust[1] in the CBDC ecosystem.

8.4 Modeling Citizen's Trust in CBDC Ecosystems

8.4.1 Ontology Instantiation

We adopt the following coding to refer to instances of key ROT concepts hereafter: **INT** for intention; **BEL** for disposition belief; **CAP** for capability; **VUL** for vulnerability; **TS** for trust-warranting signal; **US** for uncertainty signal; **TE** for trustworthiness evidence; and **INF** for influence.

Both the literature research and the interviews showed that *citizens trust the CBDC ecosystem to preserve their privacy* (INT1). Privacy emerges as a key feature, which can be confirmed both indirectly — by the presence of comments on the importance of privacy — and directly — by ranking privacy first, among many other features (European Central Bank, 2021). Citizens who trust the CBDC ecosystem believe that *it safeguards their privacy* (BEL1.1). This belief is related, for example, to the *CBDC ecosystem's capability to comply with the General Data Protection Regulation (GDPR)[2] and other privacy laws and regulations* (CAP1.1).

Interviewees also expressed that it is important that citizens feel safe to perform digital transactions in the ecosystem. *Citizens trust the ecosystem to safely make transactions using CBDCs* (INT2). They believe that *the ecosystem is safe* (BEL2.1) and that *it will be able to prevent security breaches* (BEL2.2). The former belief (BEL2.1) is related to the *ecosystem's capability to have security mechanisms* (CAP2.1), while the latter (BEL2.2) is related both to *possible security breaches* (VUL2.1)— which correspond to a vulnerability — and to the *ecosystem's capability to quickly react to risk*

---

[1] Agustín Carstens, the General Manager of the Bank for International Settlements, in a recent speech at the Goethe University's ILF conference on "Data, Digitalization, the New Finance and Central Bank Digital Currencies: The Future of Banking and Money" explicitly defended that "the soul of money is trust." (https://www.bis.org/speeches/sp220118.htm)

[2] https://gdpr-info.eu/

events on security (CAP2.2). In addition, *the existence of a cybersecurity policy* (TE2.1) is an example of trustworthiness evidence related to the capability CAP2.1.

Another aspect that emerged from the interviews and the literature is the importance of providing a simple experience for end users. *Citizens trust the CBDC ecosystem to make transactions using CBDCs easily* (INT3) and they believe both that *the ecosystem is easy to access and use* (BEL3.1) and that *it is easy to onboard the CBDC ecosystem* (BEL3.2). A possible capability of the ecosystem, related to these beliefs, is *to meet minimum usability criteria* (CAP3.1). The *existence of a manual with minimum usability requirements, which must be followed by all participants of the ecosystem* (TE3.1) is an example of trustworthiness evidence related to the capability CAP3.1. *The establishment of a universal brand to create visual identity* (TS3.1), *advertising campaigns in the media and social networks using everyday examples* (TS3.2), and *documentation available* (TS3.3) are examples of trust-warranting signals related to capability CAP3.1.

Low cost was another attribute mentioned both in the literature and by the interviewees. *Citizens trust the CBDC ecosystem to make transactions using CBDCs at a low cost* (INT4) and they believe both that *it will be offered at a low cost to its users* (BEL4.1) and that *they will not need to buy a new device to make transactions in the CBDC ecosystem* (BEL4.2). The former belief (BEL4.1) is related to the *ecosystem's capability to have lower costs for consumers and merchants* (CAP4.1), while the latter (BEL4.2) is related to the *ecosystem's capability to operate using existing, accessible technology* (CAP4.2).

An additional valuable feature identified in the collect phase is the ability to make offline payments. This feature might be particularly relevant during outages and in environments where internet availability is limited or unreliable (Bank for International Settlements et al., 2021b). *Citizens trust the CBDC ecosystem to make transactions wherever they need* (INT5) and they believe that *they will be able to access the system from any place* (BEL5.1). This belief is related to the *ecosystem's capability to support offline transactions* (CAP5.1). Note that intention INT5 (offline access) conflicts with intention INT4 (low cost), as technology to support offline capacity may incur additional costs.

The interviews also showed that *citizens trust the CDDC ecosystem to make transactions instantly on a 24/7 basis* (INT6). In other words, users who trust the ecosystem believe that *it is able to make instantaneous transactions* (BEL6.1) and that *it will be available when they need* (BEL6.2). These beliefs are related to the ecosystem's capability to *meet high availability parameters and processing time limits* (CAP6.1). Exam-

8.4. Modeling Citizen's Trust in CBDC Ecosystems

ples of trustworthiness evidence related to this capability are the existence of *a service level agreement that establishes high availability parameters and processing time limits* (TE6.1) and *statistics on the functioning of the ecosystem showing that this service level agreement has being fulfilled* (TE6.2). Information about *instability* (US6.1) and *low response times* (US6.2) are examples of uncertainty signals.

A further important aspect identified both in the literature and in the interviews is currency acceptance. *Citizens trust the CDBDC ecosystem to make transactions using a widely accepted currency* (INT7). And they believe that *the CBDC ecosystem operates with a digital currency widely accepted* (BEL7.1). This relates to the *capability to operate using a legal tender currency* (CAP7.1).

Equally important is the stability of the currency purchasing power. *Citizens trust the CDBDC ecosystem to make transactions using a stable currency* (INT8). And they believe that *the CBDC purchasing power has stability* (BEL8.1). This belief relates to the ecosystem's *capability to have proper mechanisms to ensure stability of CBDC purchasing power* (CAP8.1).

Finally, it was also mentioned that *citizens trust the CBDC ecosystem to have access to better financial products and services offerings* (INT9). Therefore, they believe that *they will have access to more product and service offers customized to their needs* (BEL9.1). This relates to the *ecosystem's capability to provide better customized services and products offerings* (CAP9.1). Once more, it is possible to observe the existence of conflicting intentions: the intention just mentioned (INT9) conflicts with privacy preservation (INT1), as to propose better financial services offerings, financial institutions in the ecosystem need to have access to more (private) information about the citizen.

It is important to note that in the trust relation between citizens and the CBDC ecosystem, trust is about a complex intention, composed of the aforementioned intentions (table 8.2).

Furthermore, it is possible to observe the existence of trust influences. For example, *citizens' trust in a country's monetary system* (INF1) positively influences their trust in the CBDC ecosystem, just as *their trust in the central bank* (INF2) does.

Table 8.2: Citizens' trust in the CBDC Ecosystem - Intentions.

	Citizens' Intentions
INT1	Have their privacy preserved
INT2	Make transactions using CBDC safely
INT3	Make transactions using CBDC easily
INT4	Make transactions using CBDC at low cost
INT5	Make transactions using CBDC wherever they need
INT6	Make transactions using CBDC instantly on a 24/7 basis
INT7	Make transactions make transactions using a widely accepted currency
INT8	Make transactions make transactions using a stable currency
INT9	Have access to better financial products and services offerings

Figures 8.1, 8.2, 8.3, 8.4, 8.5, 8.6, 8.7, 8.8, 8.9 show a graphical representation of the ontology instantiation focusing on privacy (INT1), security (INT2), usability (INT3), cost (INT4), location (INT5), availability (INT6), acceptance (INT7), stability (INT8) and product/service offerings (INT9), respectively.

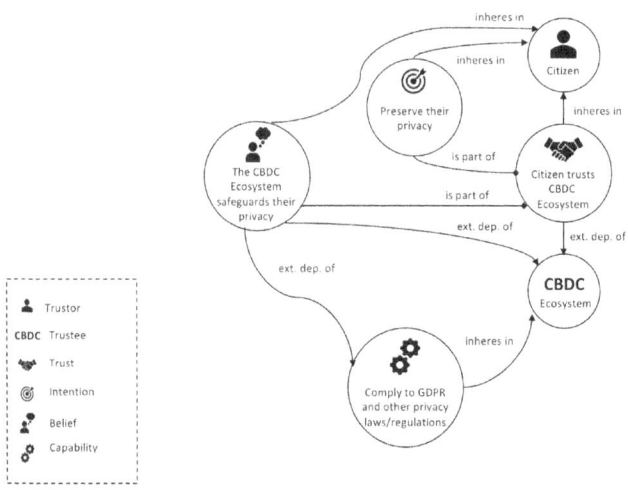

Figure 8.1: Ontology instantiation - Privacy (INT1).

8.4. Modeling Citizen's Trust in CBDC Ecosystems

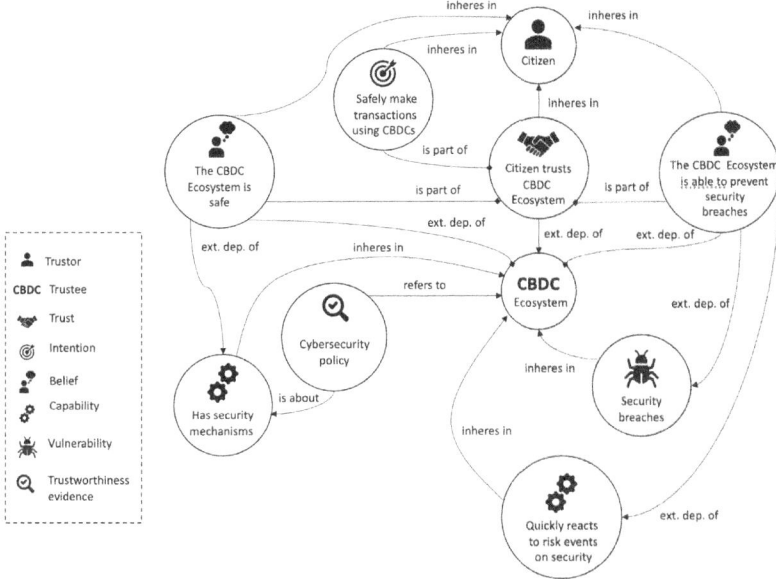

Figure 8.2: Ontology instantiation - Security (INT2).

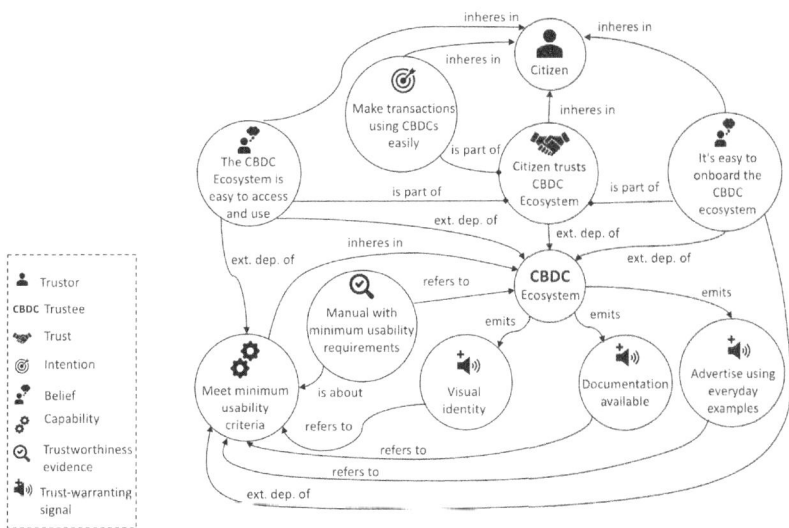

Figure 8.3: Ontology instantiation - Usability (INT3).

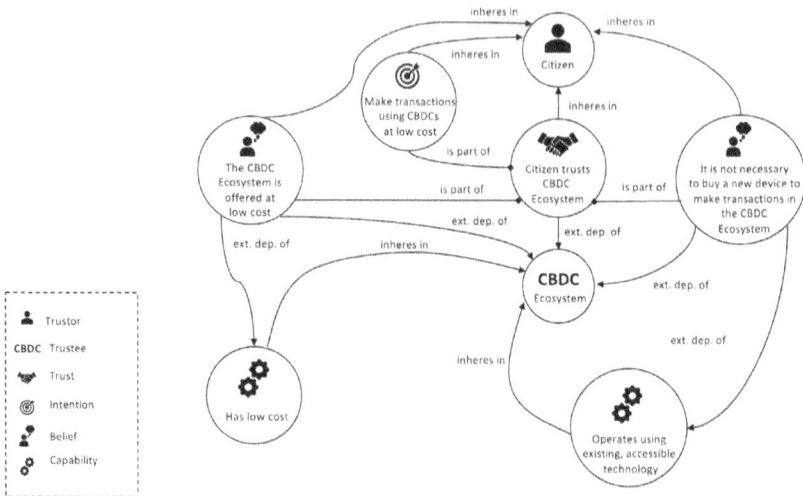

Figure 8.4: Ontology instantiation - Cost (INT4).

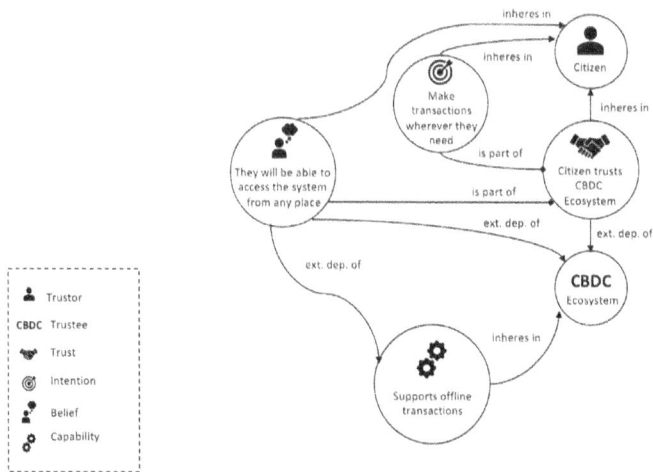

Figure 8.5: Ontology instantiation - Location (INT5).

8.4. Modeling Citizen's Trust in CBDC Ecosystems

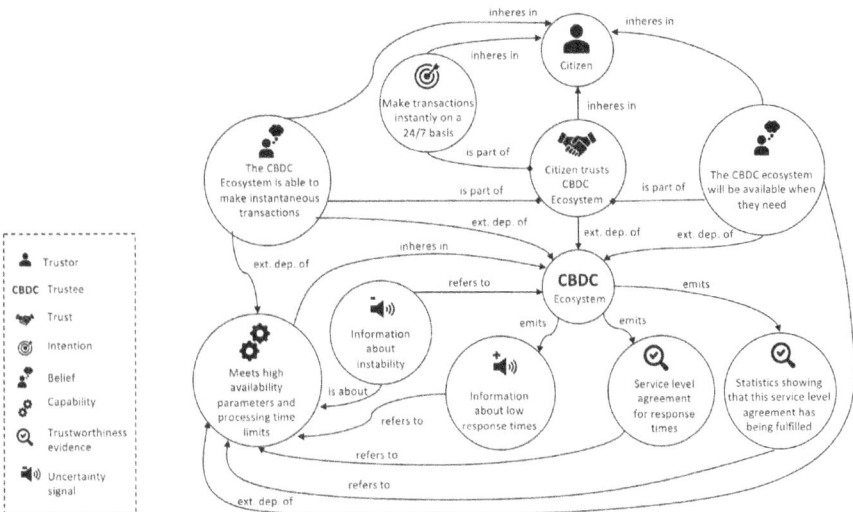

Figure 8.6: Ontology instantiation - Availability (INT6).

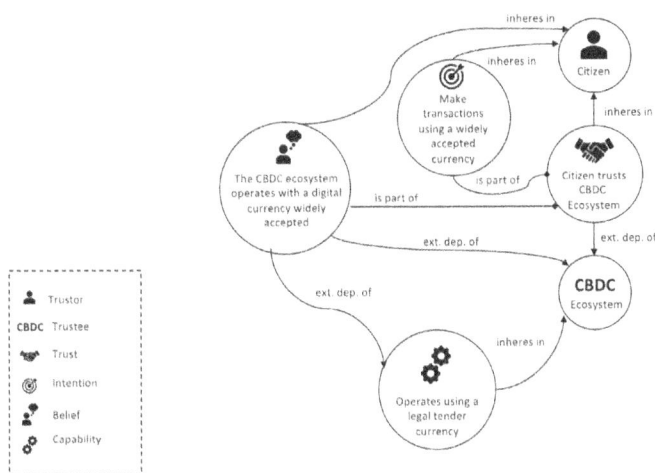

Figure 8.7: Ontology instantiation - Currency acceptance (INT7).

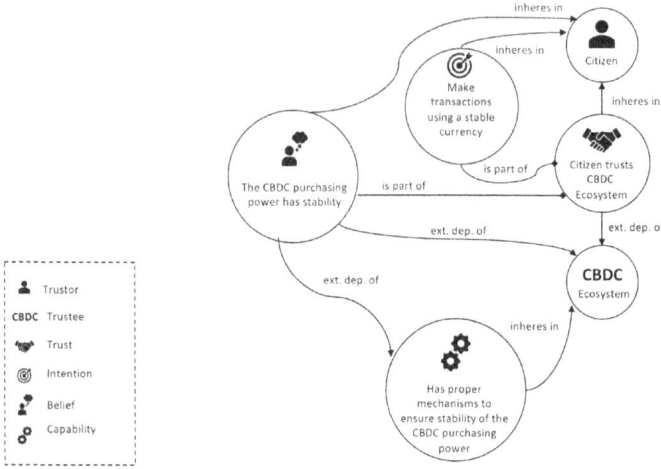

Figure 8.8: Ontology instantiation - Currency stability (INT8).

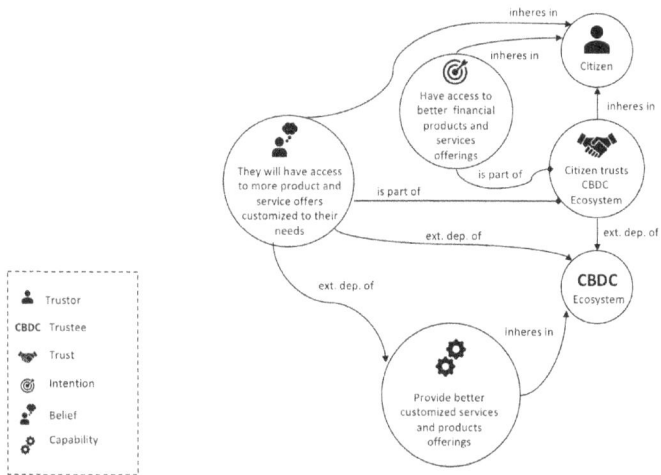

Figure 8.9: Ontology instantiation - Product and service offering (INT9).

8.4.2 Goal Model

We use the ontology instantiation as a domain model to create a goal model for this case using the *i** framework (Dalpiaz et al., 2016), presented in figure 8.10. The model shows the goals that citizens delegate to the CBDC ecosystem (through the i* dependency relation). Citizens and the CBDC ecosystem are represented as actor and agent, respectively. Citizens' intentions are represented as quality dependences. Conflicting intentions are represented in yellow, circled by a red dashed line. Entities represented in green and yellow were obtained directly by mapping elements from the ontology instantiation. For each of them, more specific goals, qualities, tasks and resources were identified and are represented in blue. Besides dependencies, the goal model depicts the internal perspective of the CBDC ecosystem. Beliefs are represented as goals or qualities that contribute to (help) the achievement of higher level goals. For example, beliefs such as *the ecosystem is safe* (BEL2.1), *the ecosystem is easy to use* (BEL3.1), *the CBDC is widely accepted* (BEL7.1) were represented as qualities that contribute to the ultimate goal of *being trustworthy*. Capabilities, trust calibration signals and trustworthiness evidence are represented as goals, qualities, tasks or resources that contribute to (help) the achievement of higher level goals. For example, the goal *support offline transactions* (CAP5.1) helps the achievement of *be available*. The tasks *meet minimum usability criteria* (CAP3.1) and *keep visual identity* (TS3.1) help the achievement of *be easy to use*. The resource *cybersecurity policy* (TE2.1) contributes to *comply with cybersecurity policy*. The resource *manual with minimum usability requirements* (TE3.1) contributes to the task *meet minimum usability criteria*, which in turn contributes to *be easy of use*. Conversely, vulnerabilities can be represented as goals, qualities, tasks or resources that negatively impact (hurts) the achievement of higher level goals. Finally, influences are represented as contribution links that help or hurt the achievement of higher level goals (help for positive influences and hurt for negative ones). The mapping between the ROT concepts and their representation in the i* Goal Model is presented in table 8.3.

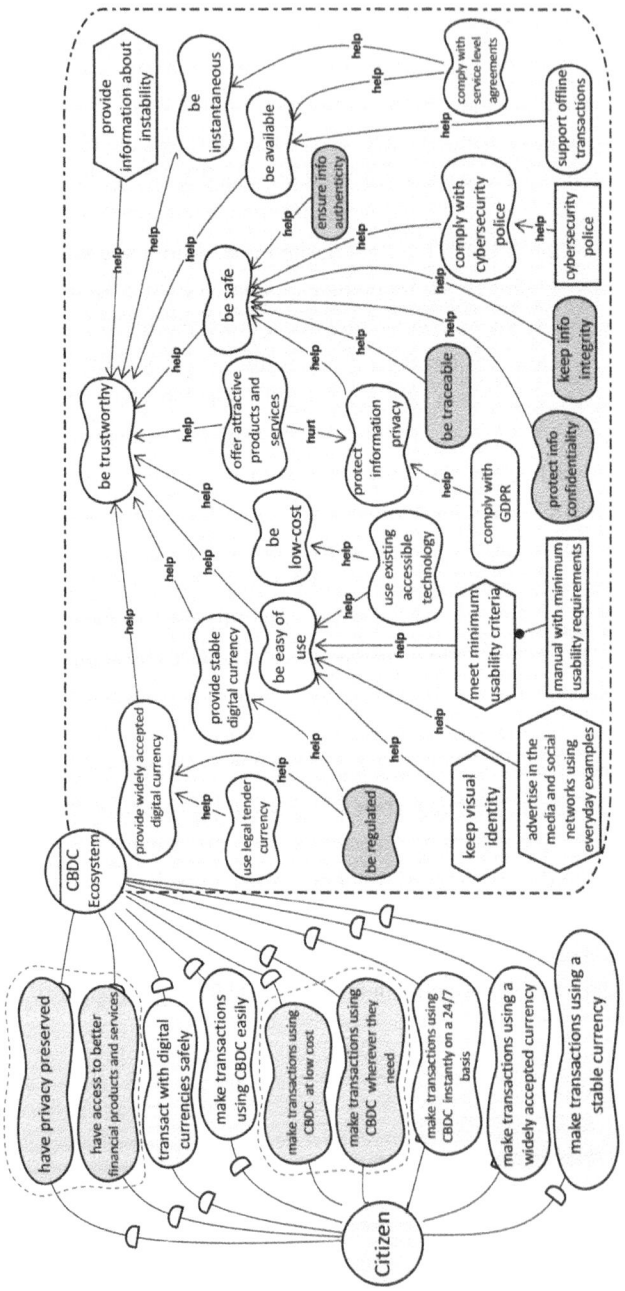

Figure 8.10: A fragment of the goal model of the CBDC ecosystem.

Table 8.3: Representation of ROT concepts in i* Goal Model.

ROT Concept	Representation in i* Goal Model
Trustor	Actor, Agent, Role
Trustee	Actor, Agent, Role
Intention	Goal dependence, Quality dependence
Belief	Goal, Quality
Capability	Goal, Quality, Task, Resource
Vulnerability	Goal, Quality, Task, Resource
Trust Calibration Signal	Goal, Quality, Task, Resource
Trustworthiness Evidence	Goal, Quality, Task, Resource
Influence	Contribution link

8.5 Discussion

In the validation session, the central bank experts of the aforementioned areas of interest were unanimously of the opinion that the ontology was capable of capturing all the important aspects of citizens' trust in CBDC ecosystems (perceived *usability* and *usefulness* of the approach). It was also mentioned by the interviewees that, when designing the CDBD ecosystem, it is useful to understand the intentions of the users that are related to their trust in the ecosystem, so that we can identify, at a very early stage, capabilities required to create a trustworthy and efficient environment, possible vulnerabilities that should be dealt with, as well as how to properly communicate about the ecosystem trustworthiness. Being able to identify citizens' goals provides a broad view of how CBDC can be successfully implemented, from a trustworthiness perspective. By eliciting goals, we can also identify the conflicting goals, and consequently we can be more proactive in resolving possible design issues.

An interesting finding was that once we understand what composes citizens' trust and which factors may influence it, we can take these requirements into account since the ecosystem's inception, thus enabling trustworthiness by design. Furthermore, it allows the identification of potential risks in advance and the definition of risk mitigation strategies. This is because if we know which capabilities and vulnerabilities are related to the trustor beliefs, we can reason about what can go wrong with the realization of the capabilities and the manifestation of the vulnerabilities, which will hurt the intentions of the trustor. These unwanted events correspond to risk events for which mitigations strategies may be defined in advance. Another interesting finding is that trust relations require constant monitoring as the ecosystem is very dynamic and is constantly changing. And changes in the environment can influence user trust.

8.6 Final Considerations

Knowledge in economics and finance is diverse, interlinked and highly influenced by technology innovations. Having a clear understanding of the ontological nature of the concepts is fundamental to understand the evolution of the economy before recent innovations in the financial industry, which involve new forms of money and trust, as well as new business models for digital exchanges.

In this chapter we conducted a real case study concerning citizens' trust in CBDC ecosystems. The case study experience confirmed that ROT can properly represent trust in this context, and suggests it could be used to represent other real cases.

Furthermore, the use of reference ontologies has proven to be useful for helping both researchers and practitioners in their communication and decision making, by establishing a common understanding and conceptualization of the domain.

Chapter 9

Modeling Payments and Linked Obligation Settlements

In this chapter, we apply and validate the Reference Ontology of Money and Virtual Currencies (see chapter 5) and the Core Ontology for Economic Exchanges (see chapter 6) in the context of decentralized finance. We apply ROME and COEX in and ontology-based approach for the modeling of payments and linked obligation settlement mechanisms (Amaral, Sales, and Guizzardi, 2021a), aiming at providing conceptual clarification and supporting semantic interoperability in DeFi ecosystems. Firstly, we create two domain-related ontology patterns by reusing pieces of knowledge extracted from COEX and ROME. Then, we systematically apply these patterns to model payments and linked obligations in OntoUML (Guizzardi, 2005). Finally, we export the models to OWL using gUFO (Almeida, Guizzardi, et al., 2020).

This chapter is organized as follows. Section 9.1 motivates the relevance of an ontology-based approach for the modeling of payments and linked obligation settlements. In section 9.2, we provide an overview of payments and linked obligation settlements. Then, in section 9.3, we present our approach and use it to model payments and linked obligation settlements. We demonstrate our approach by modelling an application example in section 9.4, and present some related work on section 9.5. Finally, section 9.6 presents the conclusions of this chapter.

9.1 Introduction

Digital innovation has revolutionized the world of payments and settlement services. Innovative technologies, such as the tokenization of assets, as well as new forms of digital payments, have challenged both current business models and the existing models of regulation. In this scenario, semantic transparency is fundamental not only to adapt regulation frameworks, but also to support information integration and semantic interoperability.

An important aspect of interoperability in this scenario is related to the role played by central banks and regulatory authorities, which need to integrate a plethora of information from dynamic and complex decentralized environments to perform advanced analytics. This integrated view allows supervisors and regulatory entities to figure out what is going on, so they can ensure financial stability, manage financial risks, support anti-money laundering, combat the financing of terrorism, etc. In order to be properly integrated and analyzed, data needs to be clearly conceptualized and understood.

In this context, interoperability relies upon three interacting "layers" (Lemieux and Feng, 2021, p. 3):

(i) a *social layer*, in which social actors interact to determine business models, regulatory frameworks and governance models;

(ii) an *information layer*, which supplies data stored both on-chain and off-chain; and

(iii) a *technical layer*, in which social actors interact to create, store, and obtain information via applications, networks, and consensus mechanisms.

In this chapter, we deal with issues related to conceptual clarification (interoperability in the social layer) and semantic interoperability (interoperability in the information layer) in DeFi. We focus on the integration of DeFi data (Zetzsche et al., 2020) and traditional finance data (Zetzsche et al., 2020) that could be used in advanced analytics for regulation and supervisory purposes. It is important to note that DeFi ecosystems, as proposed by many countries, are ongoing systems under design, and the outcome is not clear yet. The initiatives around the world are at the stage of experimentation, proof of concept or pilot arrangements. Therefore, research on the integration of DeFi data and traditional finance is still in its infancy. To the best of our knowledge, the semantic-level integration of DeFi data and traditional finance data has not yet been addressed in the literature and is still an open issue.

9.1. Introduction

We address this problem by proposing an ontology-driven conceptual modeling approach in which we (i) extract fragments of knowledge from reference ontologies to (ii) create ontology-based modeling patterns, which are (iii) systematically applied to represent concepts in the realm of money, payments, and economic exchanges. We first specify the models grounded on the Unified Foundational Ontology (UFO) (Guizzardi, 2005), via the OntoUML (Guizzardi, 2005) language, thus contributing to improving communication, problem-solving, and meaning negotiation among people. Then, we codify the models in gUFO (Almeida, Guizzardi, et al., 2020), an implementation of UFO suitable for linked data applications, which contributes to dealing with semantic interoperability issues in heterogeneous scenarios.

We illustrate our approach by applying COEX (see chapter 6) and ROME (see chapter 5) to model payments and linked obligation settlements. Among many innovations, decentralized technologies allow financial and real tradeable assets to be digitally represented by what is known as digital tokens (Bech, Hancock, et al., 2020; Laurent et al., 2018). An important aspect in this scenario is the utilization of settlement mechanisms that can prevent the risk that one counterparty irrevocably transfers the ownership of an asset, but does not receive the corresponding payment. A common way to mitigate this risk is to link the delivery and the payment legs, so that the asset moves if and only if the corresponding funds transfer occurs (Bank for International Settlements / International Organization of Securities Commissions, 2012). This settlement mechanism (a.k.a. *Delivery versus Payment*) is an example of a linked obligation settlement, a type of exchange transaction that must be performed atomically.

Although payments and linked obligation settlements have been modeled for decades (Bank of International Settlements, 2021; Blums and Weigand, 2017; Enterprise Data Management Council, 2015; Fischer-Pauzenberger and Schwaiger, 2017; McCarthy, June 2007), making sense of data in these new decentralized ecosystems is still a challenge. How to properly do analytics on financial data from different sources in decentralized heterogeneous ecosystems? The position defended here is that, in order to properly integrate data, it is necessary to make explicit their underlying ontological commitments. Let us take the example of two different ecosystem participants A and B that record information about payments. A and B may conceptualize the notion of payment in different ways. We cannot assume that just because the same term (e.g., payment) is used in both structures that they mean the same thing. For instance, Payment-A can refer to events, while Payment-B may refer to reified relationships (Guarino and Guizzardi, 2016). In this case, the relation between Payment-A and Payment-B is one of manifestation, that is, instances of payment in one case (A) are manifestations of properties of payments as a bundle of relational aspects (B). For this reason, we advocate the use of ontology-based models, so that the nature of real world entities can be properly understood and represented. In this direction, one of our objectives is to raise awareness of the importance of making explicit the ontological commitments of financial data, so that data from different sources in decentralized heterogeneous ecosystems can be properly and safely integrated.

9.2 Linked Obligation Settlements

In general, transactions involving the acquisition of goods, financial assets, or services have two settlement components: (i) the delivery of the good or service; and (ii) the transfer of funds (European Central Bank, 2010). According to the European Central Bank (ECB) (European Central Bank, 2010), a payment is "a transfer of funds which discharges an obligation on the part of a payer vis-à-vis a payee". In this case, the payer is the party to a payment transaction which issues the payment order or agrees to the transfer of funds to the payee, while the payee is the final recipient of funds. When a payment is successfully made, the obligation between the payer and the payee is discharged. In the context of payments, settlement is an act that discharges obligations between two or more agents. For a payment instruction in a payment system, settlement occurs when funds are transferred from the payer's bank to the payee's bank. According to the ECB (European Central Bank, 2010) "settlement discharges the obligation of the payer's bank vis-à-vis the payee's bank in respect of the transfer".

As explained in (Bank for International Settlements, 2016), a financial transaction involving two linked obligations may be settled by different mechanisms:

- **Payment versus Payment (PvP).** A settlement mechanism that ensures that the payment in one currency occurs if and only if the counterpart payment in another currency occurs as well (Bank for International Settlements, 2016). This mechanism is typically used to mitigate settlement risk in foreign exchanges, which is the risk of delivering the currency sold without receiving the currency purchased (or vice versa).

- **Delivery versus Payment (DvP).** A settlement mechanism that links a securities transfer and a funds transfer in such a way as to ensure that delivery occurs if and only if the corresponding payment occurs (Bank for International Settlements,

2016).

- **Delivery versus Delivery (DvD).** A settlement mechanism that links two securities transfers in such a way as to ensure that the delivery of one security occurs if and only if the security in the other transfer is also delivered (Bank for International Settlements, 2016).

Recently, the European Central Bank and the Bank of Japan conducted a proof-of-concept, in the context of Project Stella (European Central Bank, Bank of Japan, 2018), to explore how the settlement of two linked obligations, such as DvP, could be conceptually designed and operated in an environment based on the distributed ledger technology (DLT). In fact, such DLT-based Delivery versus Payment settlement can be applied not only in the context of financial assets but rather for all DLT use cases where assets, such as immovable property, goods, or services, are bought with money or exchanged with other assets.

9.3 Ontology-based Modeling of Payments and Linked Obligation Settlements

9.3.1 The Ontology-based Modeling Approach

In this section we present our ontology-based modeling approach and apply it to represent payments and linked obligation settlements, aiming at providing conceptual clarification and supporting semantic interoperability in the integration of DeFi off-chain data and traditional finance data. The three activities that compose our approach are described below.

1. **Extract knowledge fragments from reference ontologies**: In this step, we identify and extract fragments of core/domain reference ontologies, containing pieces of knowledge that describe the portion of reality that is intended to be represented, and that constitutes a well-proven modeling solution for the problem.

2. **Create ontology-based modeling patterns**: According to Buschmann et al. (2007), "a pattern describes a particular recurring design problem that arises in specific design contexts and presents a well-proven solution for the problem". In this step, we reuse the model fragments extracted in step 1 to create ontology-based modeling patterns to represent recurrent structures in the domain.

3. **Apply the ontology-based modeling patterns to represent specific concepts in a particular domain**: In this step, we effectively apply the ontology-based modeling patterns identified in step 2 to model the problem at hand.

Our approach was inspired in the customized version of the NeOn methodology (Suárez-Figueroa et al., 2012), presented in section 1.3.2 of chapter 2. NeOn provides guidance for the main activities in ontology engineering, making available detailed processes, guidelines and different scenarios for collaboratively building ontologies. In particular, we applied some of NeOn methodological guidelines regarding reusing and reengineering ontological resources, which in our case are reference ontologies. One of the benefits of this approach is that pieces of knowledge from reference ontologies can be reused as needed: whole or extracts of it.

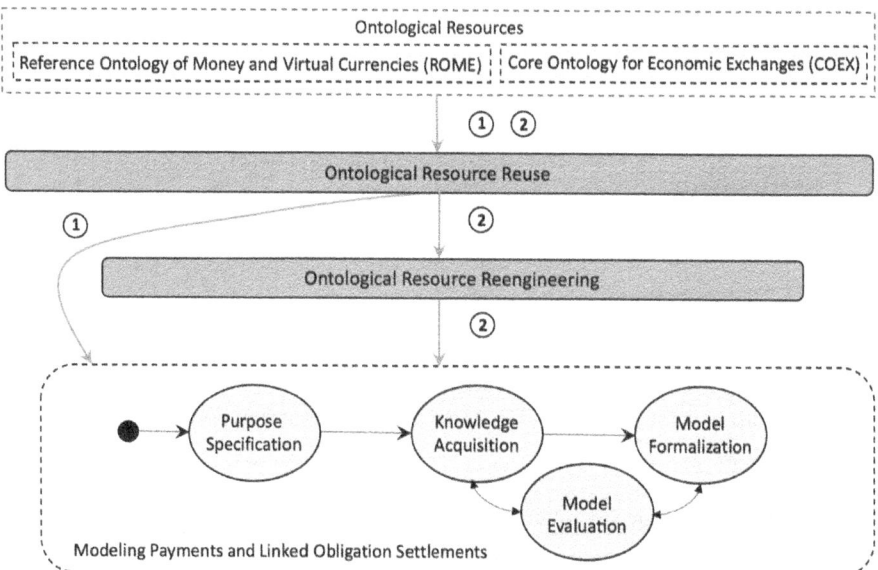

Figure 9.1: Overview of the ontology-based modeling approach inspired in the NeOn methodology (adapted from (Suárez-Figueroa et al., 2012)).

Figure 9.1 presents the customized version of the NeOn methodology (Suárez-Figueroa et al., 2012), suited to our particular context and needs. We defined two flexible scenarios, in which we applied some methodological directions of NeOn for reusing and reenginnering ontological resources, namely reference ontologies.

9.3.2 Modeling Payments and Linked Obligation Settlements

For the modeling of payments and linked obligation settlements, we reuse concepts and relations defined in COEX (see chapter 6) and ROME (see chapter 5) (step 1). As a result, we propose two ontology patterns (step 2) and apply them to model payments and different types of linked obligation settlements (Bank for International Settlements / International Organization of Securities Commissions, 2012) (step 3), namely, Delivery versus Payment, Delivery versus Delivery and Payment versus Payment. We extend the notion of Delivery versus Payment and Delivery versus Delivery to consider not only financial assets (securities), but also any digital representation of assets (such as a share in a company, ownership of a piece of real estate, ownership of a car, or participation in an investment fund), which we name here *digital asset*. An example of digital asset is a token created on top of a blockchain network to represent the ownership of a real tradeable asset.

We start by defining a *digital transfer* as an event (action), in which the ownership of a digital object is transferred from one agent to another agent. By a *digital object* we mean a monetary amount or a digital asset (Kud, 2019). For example, a digital payment is a digital transfer, in which a monetary amount is transferred from one agent to another. Similarly, a digital asset transfer is a digital transfer, in which a digital asset is transferred from a sender to a receiver. We define *digital exchanges* as events that have as parts two or more digital transfer events of: transferring a digital object to fulfill a commitment and transferring back another digital object to fulfill the requested counterpart. Confronting this view with COEX, we can see that this aspect is captured by the occurrence of an Economic Exchange event (figure 9.2), which is composed of two events that represent the fulfillment of an economic agreement, namely the Offered Contribution and Counterpart Contribution (figure 9.2). Moreover, what is brought about in digital transfers is the transferring of ownership of a digital object, which is in fact an event, see (Guarino, Guizzardi, and Sales, 2018b). This is indeed a specific type of action, which can be straightforwardly accounted by either an Offered Contribution or a Counterpart Contribution in COEX. Therefore, digital exchanges can be seen as a specific type of economic exchange, in which the Offered Contribution and Counterpart Contribution are digital transfers between agents. This fragment of knowledge can be retrieved by isolating a part of the OntoUML (Guizzardi, 2005) model that represent economic exchanges in COEX (area circled in green dotted lines, in figure 9.2).

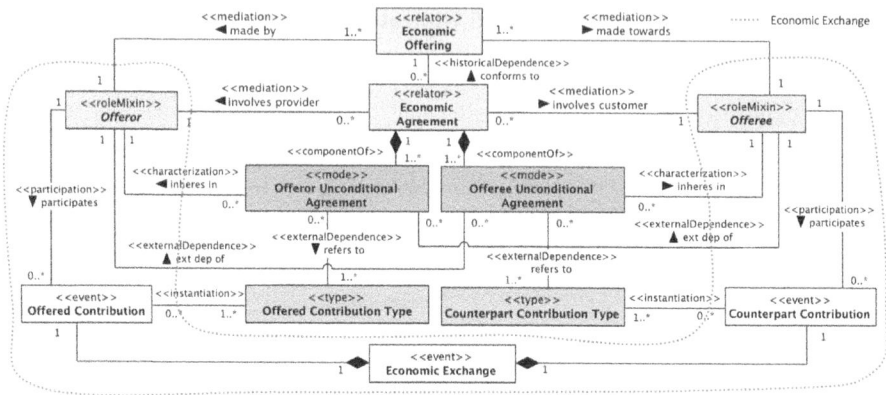

Figure 9.2: A fragment of COEX (chapter 6) depicting economic exchanges.

Based on these considerations, in figure 9.3, we propose the Digital Transfer Pattern, represented in OntoUML (Guizzardi, 2005). In this pattern, a Digital Transfer is modeled as an event, which represents the action of transferring the ownership of a digital object (Exchanged Digital Object) from a Sender to a Receiver. As in COEX (figure 9.2), both the Sender and the Receiver are UFO *agents* (Guizzardi, 2005). According to UFO, agent can be categorized into *human* (i.e. a person), *artificial* (i.e. artificial systems, such as information systems, cyber-physical systems, etc.) and *institutional* (i.e. organization). For reasons of space, we do not include a figure showing this agent categorization, but we refer the reader to (Guizzardi, 2006b)(chap.3), for details. In the Digital Transfer Pattern, Sender and Receiver are modelled as *rolemixins* because they represent roles played by entities of different kinds (e.g., information systems and organizations). The same goes for Exchanged Digital Objects, which represent roles that can be played either by monetary amounts or by different kinds of digital assets. In figure 9.4, we use the Digital Transfer Pattern to construct the Digital Exchange Pattern, which represents digital exchanges. It consists of a Digital Exchange event, composed of two or more Digital Transfer events.

9.3. Ontology-based Modeling of Payments and Linked Obligation Settlements 197

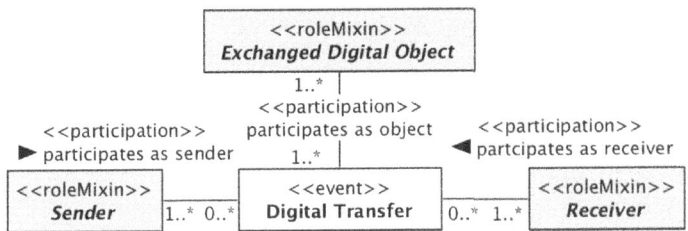

Figure 9.3: The Digital Transfer Pattern.

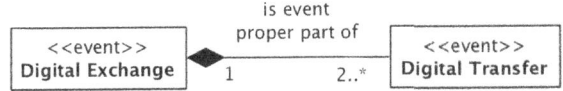

Figure 9.4: The Digital Exchange Pattern.

In the sequel, we systematically apply and reuse both the Digital Transfer Pattern and the Digital Exchange Pattern to build a set of models that characterize the concepts and relations involved in the representation of payments and linked obligation settlements. Firstly, we specify the models using the OntoUML language (Guizzardi, 2005). Then, we generate their representation in gUFO.

Digital Asset Transfer. Digital asset transfer concerns the execution of actions aiming at transferring some sort of ownership rights to an asset from an agent to another agent. In figure 9.5 we use the Digital Transfer Pattern (figure 9.3) to model a Digital Asset Transfer as an action (an UFO event (Almeida, Falbo, et al., 2019)), in which a Sender agent transfers the ownership of a Digital Asset to a Receiver agent. The Turtle[1] fragment in Listing 9.1 shows the representation of a digital asset transfer in gUFO. This representation reproduces, with the limitations imposed by the expressiveness of the OWL language, the concepts presented in the OntoUML model in figure 9.5. Figure 9.6 presents an instantiation example of the OntoUML model.

---
[1] https://www.w3.org/TR/turtle/.

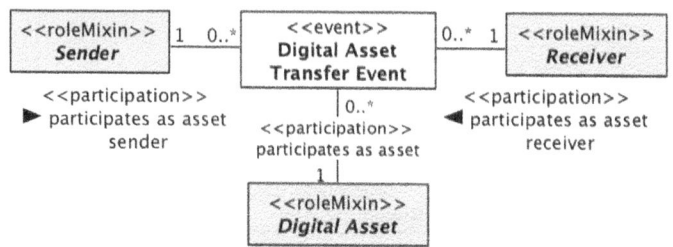

Figure 9.5: Digital asset transfer in OntoUML.

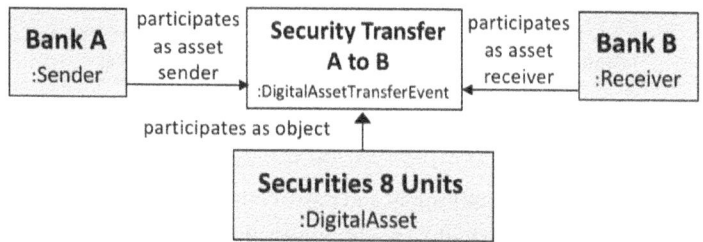

Figure 9.6: Instantiation example of digital asset transfer.

Listing 9.1: Digital asset transfer represented in gUFO.

```
:DigitalAsset              rdf:type gufo:RoleMixin ;
                           rdfs:subClassOf gufo:FunctionalComplex .

:DigitalAssetTransferEvent rdf:type gufo:EventType ,
                           rdfs:subClassOf gufo:Event .

:Receiver                  rdf:type gufo:RoleMixin ;
                           rdfs:subClassOf gufo:FunctionalComplex .

:Sender                    rdf:type gufo:RoleMixin ;
                           rdfs:subClassOf gufo:FunctionalComplex .

:participatesAsAssetSender   rdfs:subPropertyOf gufo:participatedIn ;
                             rdfs:domain  :Sender ;
                             rdfs:range   :DigitalAssetTransferEvent .

:participatesAsAssetReceiver rdfs:subPropertyOf gufo:participatedIn ;
                             rdfs:domain  :Receiver ;
                             rdfs:range   :DigitalAssetTransferEvent .

:participatesAsObject        rdfs:subPropertyOf gufo:participatedIn ;
                             rdfs:domain  :DigitalAsset ;
                             rdfs:range   :DigitalAssetTransferEvent .
```

9.3. Ontology-based Modeling of Payments and Linked Obligation Settlements

Payment. Payment concerns the transfer of a monetary amount in one currency from an agent to another. As explained in the modeling of Monetary Amount (figure 9.9), we are considering here payments made both in official currencies and in virtual currencies.

In figure 9.7 we use the Digital Transfer Pattern (figure 9.3) to model a Payment as an action (an UFO event (Almeida, Falbo, et al., 2019)), in which a Sender agent transfers a Monetary Amount to a Receiver agent. Figure 9.8 presents an instantiation example of this model. The Turtle fragment in Listing 9.2 shows the representation of a payment in gUFO.

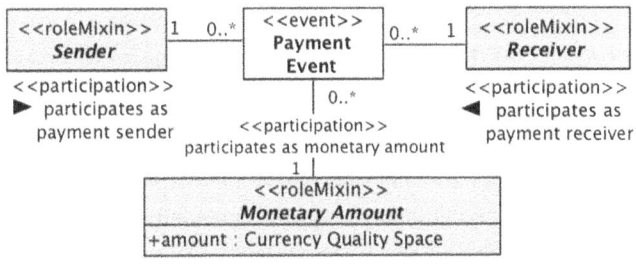

Figure 9.7: Payment model in OntoUML.

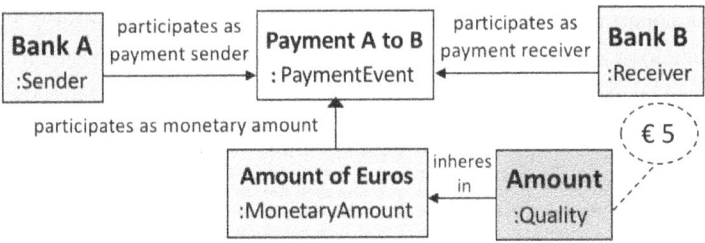

Figure 9.8: Instantiation example of payment.

Listing 9.2: Payment represented in gUFO.

```
:MonetaryAmount              rdf:type gufo:RoleMixin ;
                             rdfs:subClassOf gufo:FunctionalComplex .

:Receiver                    rdf:type gufo:RoleMixin ;
                             rdfs:subClassOf gufo:FunctionalComplex .

:PaymentEvent                rdf:type gufo:EventType ;
                             rdfs:subClassOf gufo:Event .

:Sender                      rdf:type gufo:RoleMixin ;
                             rdfs:subClassOf gufo:FunctionalComplex .

:participatedsAsPaymentSender    rdfs:subPropertyOf gufo:participatedIn ;
                                 rdfs:domain :Sender ;
                                 rdfs:range  :PaymentEvent .

:participatesAsPaymentReceiver   rdfs:subPropertyOf gufo:participatedIn ;
                                 rdfs:domain :Receiver ;
                                 rdfs:range  :PaymentEvent .

:participatedsAsMonetaryAmount   rdfs:subPropertyOf gufo:participatedIn ;
                                 rdfs:domain :DigitalAsset ;
                                 rdfs:range  :PaymentEvent .
```

Monetary Amount. To cope with the wide range of public and private payment means that emerged in recent times, our proposal considers not only payments made with real money and thus denominated in an official currency (e.g. Euro), but also payments using virtual currencies (eg. privately-issued cryptocurrencies like ETH). We rely on the notions of money, currencies, and virtual currencies defined in ROME (see chapter 5) and on the concept of monetary amount defined in the Financial Industry Business Ontology (FIBO) (Enterprise Data Management Council, 2015). According to FIBO, monetary amount corresponds to an amount of money specified in a currency. We extend FIBO's definition of monetary amount to consider also amounts specified in virtual currencies. Figure 9.9 shows an OntoUML diagram depicting the main concepts and relations involved in the representation of monetary amount.

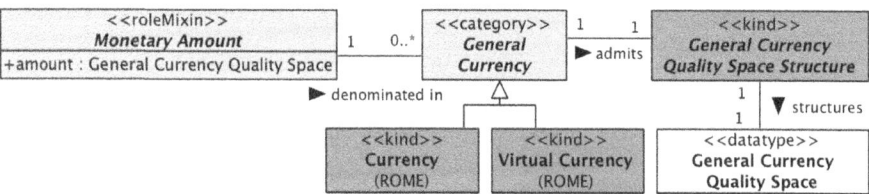

Figure 9.9: Monetary amount in OntoUML.

9.3. Ontology-based Modeling of Payments and Linked Obligation Settlements

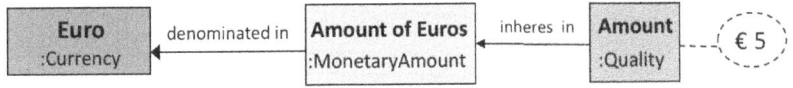

Figure 9.10: Instantiation example of monetary amount.

In Monetary Amount, the property amount represents the quantity, which has a value in a Currency Quality Space (see section 5.3). For example, euro has a measurable value in one-dimensional structure of numbers with two decimal places. A Monetary Amount is denominated in a General Currency, which is specialized into Currency (see chapter 5) and Virtual Currency (see chapter 5). For an extensive discussion on money, currency and virtual currencies, please refer to chapter 5. Figure 9.10 presents an instantiation example of the OntoUML model. The Turtle fragment in Listing 9.3 shows the representation of monetary amount in gUFO.

Listing 9.3: Monetary amount represented in gUFO.
```
:MonetaryAmount      rdf:type gufo:RoleMixin ;
                     rdfs:subClassOf gufo:FunctionalComplex.

:GeneralCurrency     rdf:type gufo:Category ;
                     rdfs:subClassOf gufo:FunctionalComplex.

rome:Currency        rdf:type gufo:Kind ;
                     rdfs:subClassOf :GeneralCurrency .

rome:VirtualCurrency rdf:type gufo:Kind ;
                     rdfs:subClassOf :GeneralCurrency .

:amount              rdfs:domain :MonetaryAmount ;
                     rdf:type owl:DatatypeProperty ;
                     rdfs:subPropertyOf gufo:hasQualityValue .

:denominatedIn       rdf:type owl:ObjectProperty ;
                     rdfs:domain :MonetaryAmount ;
                     rdfs:range :GeneralCurrency .
```

Delivery versus Payment. DvP can be seen as a specific type of digital exchange, in which the linked obligations are one or more digital asset transfers and the corresponding payment (or payments).

In figure 9.11 we use the Digital Exchange Pattern (figure 9.4) to model the Delivery versus Payment as an action (an UFO event (Almeida, Falbo, et al., 2019)), composed of one or more Digital Asset Transfers (figure 9.5) and one or more Payments (figure 9.7). Figure 9.12 presents an instantiation example of this model. The Turtle fragment in Listing 9.4 shows the representation of the Delivery versus Payment in gUFO.

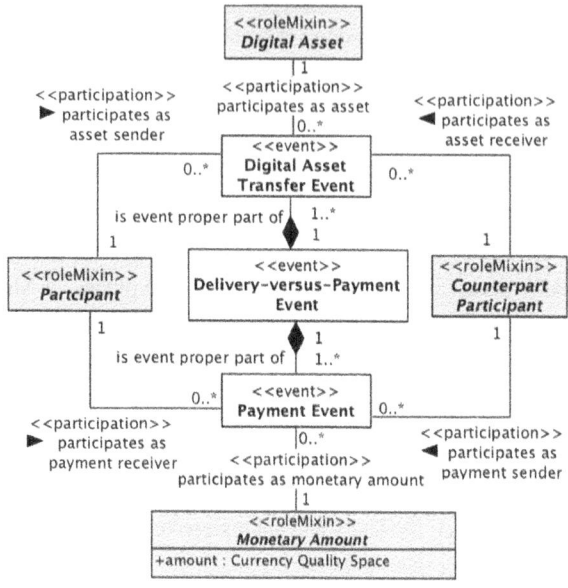

Figure 9.11: Delivery versus Payment in OntoUML.

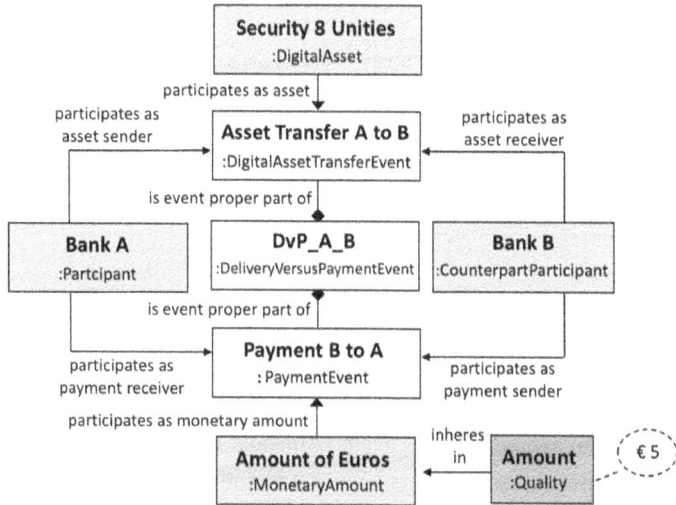

Figure 9.12: Instantiation example of Delivery versus Payment.

9.3. Ontology-based Modeling of Payments and Linked Obligation Settlements

Listing 9.4: Delivery versus Payment represented in gUFO.

```
:DeliveryVersusPaymentEvent    rdfs:subClassOf gufo:Event .
:DigitalAssetTransferEvent     rdfs:subClassOf gufo:Event ;
                               gufo:isEventProperPartOf :
                               DeliveryVersusPaymentEvent .
:PaymentEvent                  rdfs:subClassOf gufo:Event ;
                               gufo:isEventProperPartOf :
                               DeliveryVersusPaymentEvent .

:DigitalAsset                  rdf:type gufo:RoleMixin ;
                               rdfs:subClassOf gufo:FunctionalComplex .
:MonetaryAmount                rdf:type gufo:RoleMixin ;
                               rdfs:subClassOf gufo:FunctionalComplex .
:Partcipant                    rdf:type gufo:RoleMixin ;
                               rdfs:subClassOf gufo:FunctionalComplex .
:CounterpartParticipant        rdf:type gufo:RoleMixin ;
                               rdfs:subClassOf gufo:FunctionalComplex .

:participatesAsAssetSender     rdfs:subPropertyOf gufo:participatedIn ;
                               rdfs:domain :Partcipant ;
                               rdfs:range :DigitalAssetTransferEvent .
:participatesAssetReceiver     rdfs:subPropertyOf gufo:participatedIn ;
                               rdfs:domain :CounterpartParticipant ;
                               rdfs:range :DigitalAssetTransferEvent .
:participatesAsAsset           rdfs:subPropertyOf gufo:participatedIn ;
                               rdfs:domain :DigitalAsset ;
                               rdfs:range :DigitalAssetTransferEvent .
:participatesAsPaymentSender   rdfs:subPropertyOf gufo:participatedIn ;
                               rdfs:domain :CounterpartParticipant ;
                               rdfs:range :PaymentEvent .
:participatesAsPaymentReceiver rdfs:subPropertyOf gufo:participatedIn ;
                               rdfs:domain :Participant ;
                               rdfs:range :PaymentEvent .
:participatesAsMonetaryAmount  rdfs:subPropertyOf gufo:participatedIn ;
                               rdfs:domain :DigitalAsset ;
                               rdfs:range :PaymentEvent .
```

Payment versus Payment. PvP can be seen as specific type of digital exchanges, in which the linked obligations are two payments. In figure 9.13 we use the Digital Exchange Pattern (figure 9.4) to model the Payment versus Payment as an action composed of two Payments (figure 9.7). Figure 9.14 presents an instantiation example of this model. The representation of PvP in gUFO is analogous to the representation of DvP (Listing 9.4).

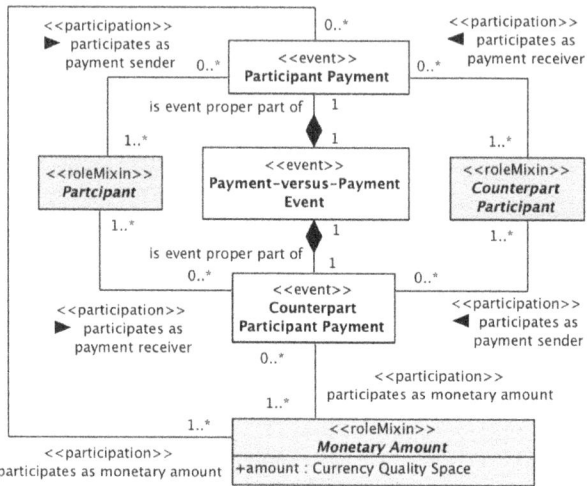

Figure 9.13: Payment versus Payment in OntoUML.

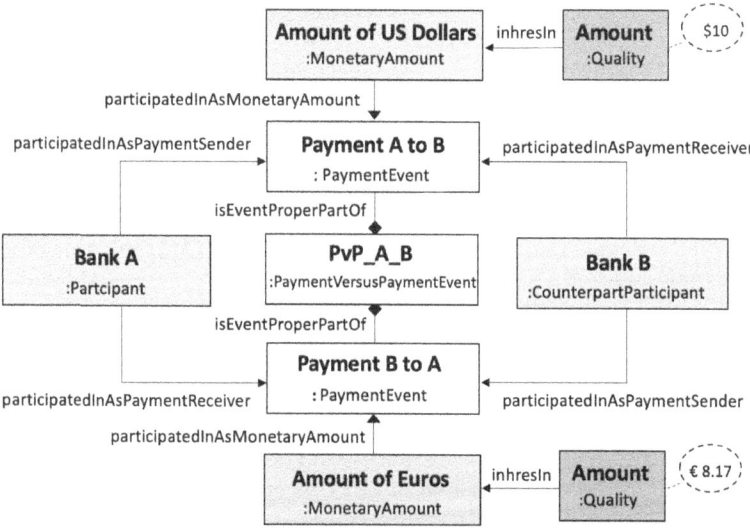

Figure 9.14: Instantiation example of Payment versus Payment.

9.3. Ontology-based Modeling of Payments and Linked Obligation Settlements

Delivery versus Delivery. DvD can be seen as specific type of digital exchanges, in which the linked obligations are two digital asset transfers. In figure 9.15 we use the Digital Exchange Pattern (figure 9.4) to model the Delivery versus Delivery as an action composed of two Digital Asset Transfers (figure 9.5). Figure 9.16 presents an instantiation example of this model. The representation of DvD in gUFO is analogous to the representation of DvP (Listing 9.4).

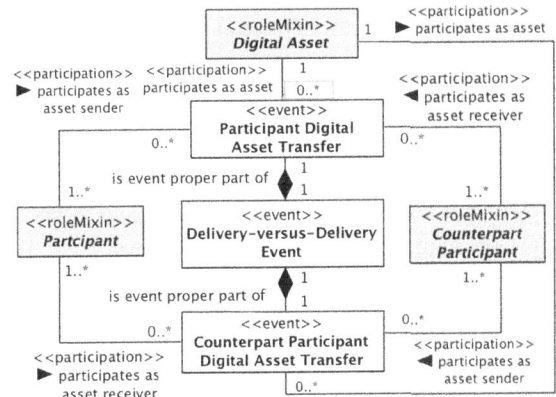

Figure 9.15: Delivery versus Delivery in OntoUML.

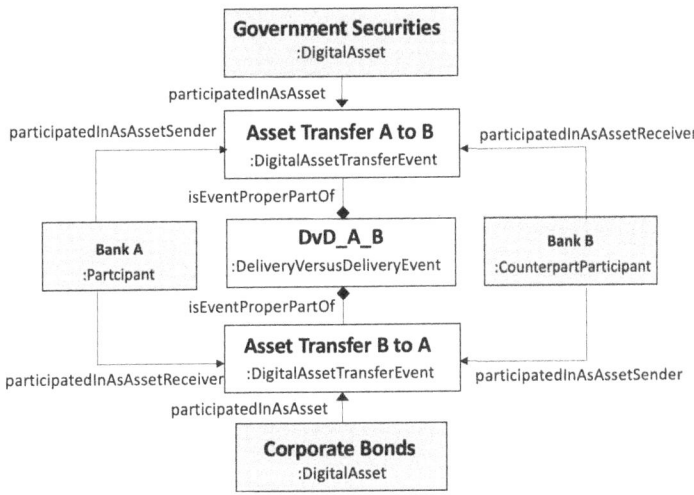

Figure 9.16: Instantiation example of Delivery versus Delivery.

9.4 Application Example

A major concern of regulators is the use of digital money for illegitimate activities, like money laundering, terrorist financing, and tax evasion. Digital solutions for anti-money laundering and counter financing of terrorism based on artificial intelligence and data analytics can potentially help to identify risks and respond to, communicate, and monitor suspicious activity. Semantic interoperability is a fundamental aspect for applications in this context, as information from multiple and heterogeneous sources must be analyzed to detect unusual patterns, such as large amounts of cash flow at certain periods by particular groups of agents. Let us take as an example the assessment of a company named "Orange Corporate" regarding suspicious transactions. In order to detect unusual patterns, it is important to analyze all payment transfers performed by Orange Corporate. As the company operates in multiple ecosystems, it may be necessary to integrate DeFi on-chain and/or off-chain data with traditional finance data. Furthermore, from the perspective of the prevention of tax evasion, it is also important to be able to distinct payment transfers denominated in official currencies from the ones denominated in virtual currencies as different controls and rules may apply in each case. Figure 9.17 illustrates the application of the Payment and the Monetary Amount models (Listing 9.2 and 9.3) to support information integration in data analytics, for the example just described.

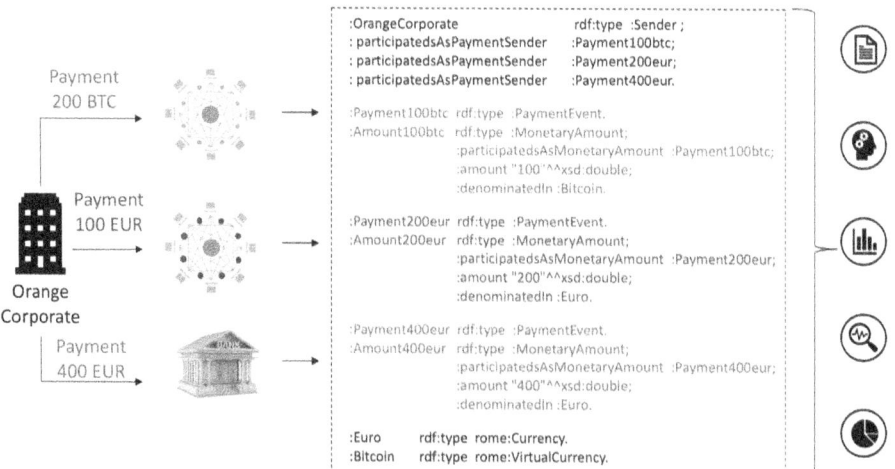

Figure 9.17: Regulatory data analytics example.

9.5 Related Work

The notions of payments and settlement services have been addressed by financial standards such as the Financial Industry Business Ontology (FIBO) (Enterprise Data Management Council, 2015), which includes the modeling of payments and monetary amounts. However, these standards usually represent only payments made in official currencies. Payments made in virtual currencies such as privately-issued cryptocurrencies are not considered in their models.

Economic exchanges are a central notion in the Resource-Event Action (REA) ISO Standard (McCarthy, June 2007). In fact, as shown in (Porello, Guizzardi, Sales, and Amaral, 2020), REA can be seen as subsumed by the Common Ontology for Economic Exchanges (see chapter 6), on which the proposal presented in this chapter is based. However, REA does not address the particularities of linked obligation settlement mechanisms (DvP, DvD and PvP) nor does it provide an ontological account of payments.

Another approach related to the notion of economic exchange is e3-value (Gordijn and Akkermans, 2001), an ontology-based methodology, commonly used for the modeling value exchanges. It adopts the economic value perspective by representing what is exchanged and by whom. The e3value ontology is based on the principle of reciprocity, denoting that every actor offers something of value, such as money, goods, services, etc., and gets a value in return. However, e3-value focuses on the exchanged value among actors in a generic way, leaving out the the particularities of linked obligation settlement mechanisms as well as the ontological distinctions between assets and payments.

Fischer-Pauzenberger and Schwaiger (Fischer-Pauzenberger and Schwaiger, 2017) proposed the OntoREA Accounting and Finance Model, which constitutes an ontology-based conceptualization of the accounting and finance domain, grounded on UFO. Similarly, Blums and Weigand (Blums and Weigand, 2017) proposed a Reference Ontology of Complex Economic Exchanges for Accounting Information Systems, grounded on UFO, which is a commitment-based economic exchange ontology, whose conceptualization is based on the establishment and fulfillment of commitments and claims between exchange participants (enterprise and counterparty) along the exchange lifecycle. In (Weigand et al., 2020), the same authors proposed a comprehensive approach for implementing economic exchanges in DLT. These three approaches are similar to ours in the sense that it uses a well-founded language to represent concepts in the realm of economic exchanges. However, they differ from our work as they do not consider the ontological distinctions between money and virtual currencies in the modeling of payments.

Finally, the Project Ellipse, launched by the Bank for International Settlements Innovation Hub (Bank of International Settlements, 2021) proposes the creation of an integrated regulatory data and analytics platform to support regulatory oversight. Although they rely on "common data models" to provide a common understanding and properly integrate information, their models do not consider the ontological distinctions between the concepts.

9.6 Final Considerations

In this chapter, we applied two networked ontologies of OntoFINE, namely ROME and COEX, in the context of decentralized finance. We proposed an ontology-based approach for the modeling of payments and linked obligation settlements, aiming at providing conceptual clarification and improving semantic interoperability in the integration of heterogeneous decentralized finance data to be used in advanced analytics. Firstly, we created two domain-related ontology patterns by reusing pieces of knowledge extracted from reference ontologies. Then, we applied these patterns to model payments and linked obligations settlements in OntoUML. Finally, we exported the models to OWL using gUFO. These gUFO/OWL concrete artifacts can contribute to semantic web related initiatives in finances (Bennett, 2013), as well as to the goal of transparency of financial data exchange according to FAIR principles (Jacobsen et al., 2020). As illustrated in the modeling of payments and liked obligation settlements, OntoFINE's networked ontologies can be used as powerful tools to provide semantic transparency, supporting information integration and semantic interoperability. As reference ontologies specified in OntoUML, they benefit from OntoUML's tooling support for model transformation for codification technologies that can be used to improve semantic interoperability and information integration among software applications.

Chapter 10

Modeling Trust in Enterprise Architecture: A Pattern Language for ArchiMate

This chapter presents a pattern language for trust modeling in ArchiMate (Amaral, Sales, Guizzardi, Almeida, et al., 2020), based on the Reference Ontology of Trust (see chapter 4) and on the Common Ontology of Value and Risk (see section 3.2 of chapter 3), which consists of a set of interrelated modeling patterns that can be used to model trust in the context of Enterprise Architecture (EA). ArchiMate was chosen as it is a widely used modeling standard in the EA field, which is also aligned to the TOGAF standard (The Open Group, 2018).

This chapter is organized as follows. Section 10.1 presents the motivation for developing a pattern language for trust modeling in ArchiMate. Section 10.2 provides an overview of ArchiMate modeling elements that are relevant to our proposal (section 10.2.1) and of the set of requirements identified for the language (section 10.2.2). Afterward, the individual modeling patterns that compose TPL are presented (section 10.2.3) together with a method for combining them (section 10.2.4). In section 10.3, we demonstrate how TPL can be used by presenting a real case of trust in a COVID-19 data repository. We conclude in section 10.4 with some final considerations.

10.1 Introduction

Trust is a vital ingredient in productive relationships. According to Castelfranchi and Falcone (2010), "trust in its intrinsic nature is a dynamic phenomenon" that changes with time. In times of crisis, such as the financial crisis of 2008 and the recent COVID-19 health crisis, it becomes even more evident how fragile trust is. Therefore, the understanding of the building blocks that compose the trust of agents in a given trustee (such as an organization) is of paramount importance, as they reveal the qualities and properties the trustee should have in order to be considered trustworthy and effectively promote well-placed trust. Moreover, the identification of the trust components is fundamental to the assessment of risks that can emerge from trust relations.

From the perspective of an organization trustee, the modeling of trust in the context of enterprise architecture enables to bridge the gap between the stakeholders' trust concerns and the processes and other elements of the architecture that are needed to achieve the organization's goal of being trustworthy. The idea of modeling social and organizational concepts in the context of enterprise architecture has already been proposed in the literature in the context of value (Sales, Roelens, et al., 2019), risk (Mayer and Feltus, 2017; Sales, Almeida, et al., 2018), service contracts (Griffo, Almeida, Guizzardi, and Nardi, 2017), resources and capabilities (Azevedo, C.L.B. et al., 2015). However, the problem of linking the enterprise architecture to the stakeholders' trust concerns is still an open issue.

In this chapter, we address this subject by proposing a trust modeling approach for ArchiMate, which is based on a proper ontological theory that provides adequate real-world and formal semantics for the concept of trust. In particular, we leverage the concepts and relations defined in the Reference Ontology of Trust (see chapter 4) to propose a Trust Pattern Language (TPL) for ArchiMate — the most used modeling language in the EA field.

A pattern language (Buschmann et al., 2007) consists of a set of interrelated modeling patterns and its main advantage is that it offers a context in which related patterns can be combined, thus, reducing the space of design choices and design constraints (Falbo et al., 2016). We designed TPL following the Design Science Research methodology (Hevner and Chatterjee, 2010). In this chapter, we present the first iteration of the *design cycle* (building and evaluating), which includes the development of the pattern language and its demonstration by means of a real case study of trust in a COVID-19 data repository.

10.2 A Pattern Language for Trust Modeling in ArchiMate

10.2.1 ArchiMate

ArchiMate is a modeling standard that defines a layered structure by means of which the architecture of enterprises can be described (The Open Group, 2017). The language is organized in six layers, namely *Strategy*, *Business*, *Application*, *Technology*, *Physical*, and *Implementation & Migration* (The Open Group, 2017). In this work, we focus on the elements of the Strategy and Business layers.

A model in ArchiMate is a collection of elements and relationships. In ArchiMate, each element is classified according to its nature, referred to as "aspects": an *Active Structure Element* represents an entity that is capable of performing behavior, a *Passive Structure Element* represents a structural element that cannot perform behavior, a *Behavior Element* represents a unit of activity performed by one or more active structure elements, a *Motivation Element* is one that provides the context of or reason behind the architecture, and a *Composite Element* is simply one that aggregates other elements.

Table 10.1 lists the most relevant ArchiMate elements and relations for the TPL. The underlying logic for the relevance of each concept in TPL can be found in section 10.2.3. For a detailed definition of ArchiMate's modeling elements and relationships the reader should refer the ArchiMate specification (The Open Group, 2017).

Table 10.1: Overview of the relevant ArchiMate concepts for the TPL.

Type	Elements
Motivation	Stakeholder, Driver, Assessment, Goal, Value
Structure	Resource
Behavior	Capability, Business Event
Composite	Grouping
	Relations
Structure	Composition, Realization
Dependency	Influence
Dynamic	Triggering
Other	Association

10.2.2 Language Requirements

According to Buschmann et al. (2007), "a pattern describes a particular recurring design problem that arises in specific design contexts and presents a well-proven solution for the problem". Deutsch (2004) defines a pattern language as "a set of patterns and relationships among them that can be used to systematically solve coarse-grained problems". We have established two types of requirements in the design of the TPL: (i) *analysis requirements*, which refer to what the models produced with the language should help users to achieve, either by means of automated or manual analysis; and (ii) *ontological requirements*, which refer to the concepts and relations the language should have in order to accurately represent its domain of interest and thus support its intended uses.

Below we present the list of the analysis requirements for the TPL:

> **R1**. *Trustworthiness analysis*: an enterprise should be able to gain insight into why it trusts certain key resources, actors or partners (or event if they should do it in the first place!). In particular, for a given trust relation, the enterprise should be able to identify the capabilities and vulnerabilities of a particular trustee that are the focus of its beliefs, so that it can detect potential threats to the achievement of its goals. From the opposite perspective, the enterprise should be able to identify what makes them trustworthy (or not) from the point-of-view of their customers and partners, possibly identifying what it could change to increase trust levels, as well the key capabilities it needs to guarantee to promote well-placed trust.

> **R2**. *Risk analysis*: By modeling the elements that compose the trust complex mental state of a trustor regarding a trustee, an enterprise should be able to identify risks that can emerge as consequence of either the manifestation of a trustee's vulnerability or the unsatisfactory manifestation of a trustee's capability.

As for the ontological requirements, they consist of an isomorphic representation of the concepts and relations defined in the Reference Ontology of Trust (see chapter 4, in which it is based. In addition to the aforementioned requirements, we assume the following constraints for the TPL:

> **R3**. It should rely exclusively on constructs available in ArchiMate 3.0.1 (The Open Group, 2017), in an effort to retain its user base and tool support, as well as to prevent adding complexity to the language.

10.2. A Pattern Language for Trust Modeling in ArchiMate

R4. It should map trust-related concepts into ArchiMate constructs maintaining, as much as possible, their original meaning as described in the standard. Specialized semantics should be addressed via stereotypes, constituting thus a lightweight extension of the language.

10.2.3 Trust Modeling Patterns

Trust Assessment. This pattern allows modelers to represent a trust relation between a trustor and a trustee, in which the former trusts the latter with respect to an intention (whose propositional content is a goal, for the achievement of which the trustor counts upon the trustee). The trustor is always a cognitive agent, endowed with goals and beliefs. As for the trustee, it is an entity able to cause an impact (hopefully positive) on a trustor's goal by the outcome of its behavior. Note that the role of trustee can be played not just by agents, but also by objects, such as rules, procedures, conventions, infrastructures, tools, artifacts in general, as well as different types of social systems. For this reason, this pattern has two variants, depending on the type of the trustee.

The first variant, depicted in figure 10.1a, details the trust relation when the trustee is an object. It consists of a Structure Element, the trustee, connected to a «Trust» Assessment, which in turn is connected both to a Stakeholder, the trustor, and to the Goal she is counting on achieving. Attached to the «Trust» Assessment is the trust degree, an attribute that represents the extent to which the trustor trusts in the trustee, which can be described as an entry in a scale chosen by the modeler, such as a discrete scale like <Low,Medium,High> or a continuous scale like <0-100>. An example of this first variant is shown in figure 10.1b. In the second variant (figure 10.2), the trustee is a cognitive agent and thus is modeled as a «Trustee» Structure Element (or «Trustee» Stakeholder).

214   Chapter 10. Modeling Trust in Enterprise Architecture: A Pattern Language for ArchiMate

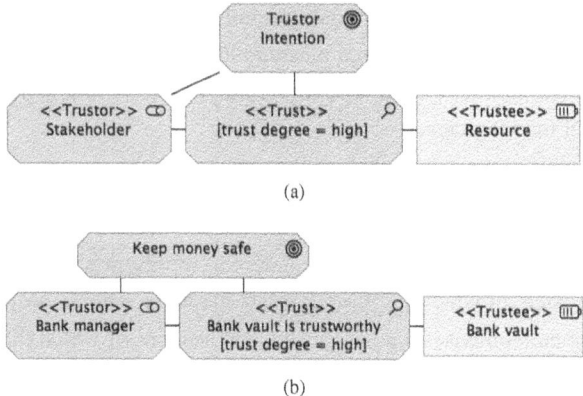

Figure 10.1: The Trust Assessment Pattern - Object Trustee.

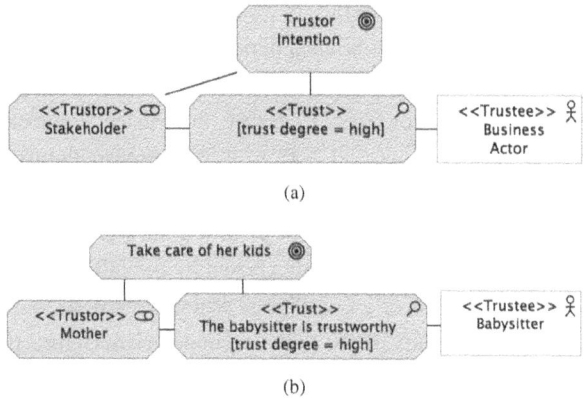

Figure 10.2: The Trust Assessment Pattern - Agent Trustee.

Capability Belief. This pattern allows modelers to express which capability of the trustee is the focus of a capability belief of the trustor. Capabilities are dispositions that inhere in agents and objects, which are manifested in particular situations, through the occurrence of events. They are usually understood as positive dispositions, in the sense that they enable the manifestation of events desired by an agent. The generic structure of the Capability Belief Pattern is depicted in figure 10.3a. It connects a Capability Belief Assessment of a «Trustor» Stakeholder to the corresponding Capability of a «Trustee».

Attached to the Capability Belief Assessment are the following attributes: (i) in-

10.2. A Pattern Language for Trust Modeling in ArchiMate

tensity: the strength of a trustor's belief; (ii) performance level: how well the trustor believes the trustee can perform the action; and (iii) manifestation likelihood: how strongly the trustor believes a disposition of the trustee may be manifested through the occurrence of certain events. All these attributes can be described as an entry in a scale chosen by the modeler, such as a discrete scale like <Low,Medium,High> or a continuous scale like <0-100>). An application of this pattern is presented in figure 10.3b.

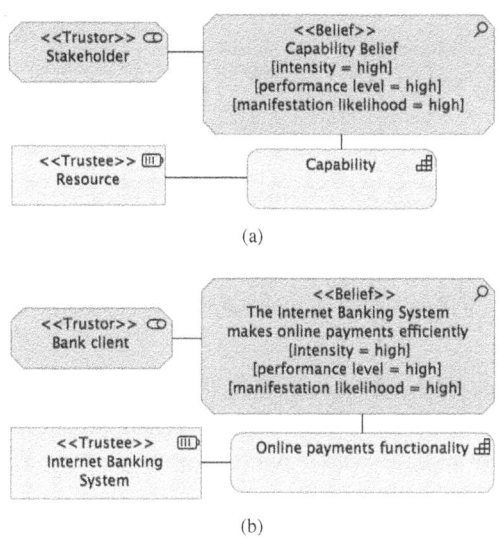

Figure 10.3: The Capability Belief Pattern.

Vulnerability Belief. This pattern allows modelers to express which vulnerability of the trustee is the focus of a vulnerability belief of the trustor. Vulnerabilities are a special type of disposition whose manifestation constitutes a loss or can potentially cause a loss from the perspective of a stakeholder. The generic structure of the Vulnerability Belief Pattern is depicted in figure 10.4a. It connects a Vulnerability Belief Assessment of a «Trustor» Stakeholder to the corresponding Vulnerability of a «Trustee». Similar to the Capability Belief Assessment, the Vulnerability Belief Assessment has following attributes: intensity, performance level and manifestation likelihood. Figure 10.4b presents an application example of this pattern.

216 Chapter 10. Modeling Trust in Enterprise Architecture: A Pattern Language for ArchiMate

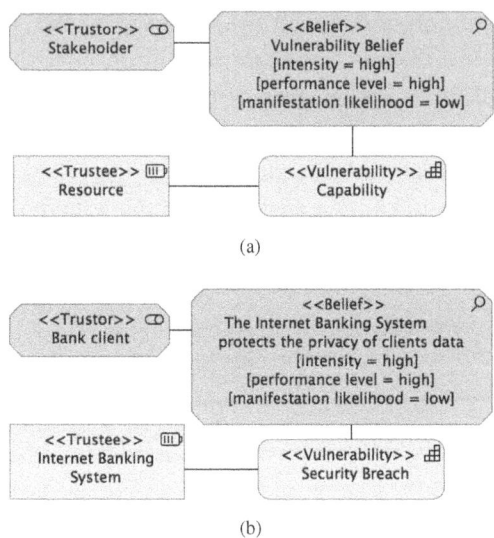

Figure 10.4: The Vulnerability Belief Pattern.

Intention Belief. This pattern allows modelers to express which intention of the trustee is the focus of an intention belief of the trustor. Its generic structure is depicted in figure 10.5a. It connects an Intention Belief Assessment of a «Trustor» Stakeholder to the corresponding Goal of a cognitive agent «Trustee». Attached to the Intention Belief Assessment is the intensity attribute. Figure 10.5b presents an application example for this pattern.

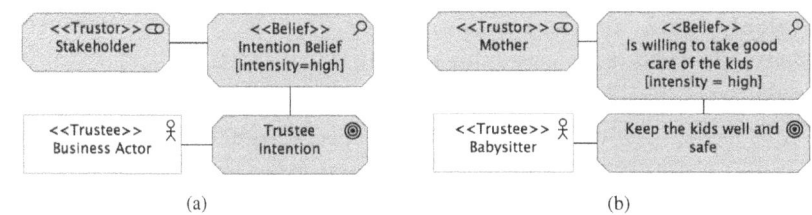

Figure 10.5: The Intention Belief Pattern.

Trust Composition. To account for what makes an agent trust a resource or another agent, we introduce the Trust Composition Pattern, which details the complex mental

10.2. A Pattern Language for Trust Modeling in ArchiMate

state of the trustor. The understanding of the elements that compose trust is important because they reveal the qualities and properties the trustee should have in order to be considered trustworthy and effectively promote well-placed trust. This pattern refines the Trust Assessment Pattern by detailing the decomposition of the «Trust» Assessment into the beliefs of the trustor about the trustee. It has two variants, as the beliefs of the trustor vary according to the trustee type.

The first variant, depicted in figure 10.6a, details trust when the trustee is not a cognitive agent. In this case, we make use of the Capability Pattern and the Vulnerability Pattern to represent that the «Trust» Assessment is composed of «Belief» Assessments of the trustor regarding the Capabilities and Vulnerabilities of the trustee (the trustor believes that the trustee has the capability to exhibit a desired behavior and that its vulnerabilities will not prevent it from exhibiting this behavior). Figure 10.6b shows an application example of this variant.

In the second variant, depicted in figure 10.7a, the trustee is a cognitive agent endowed with goals and, therefore, her intentions are also part of the set of beliefs that compose trust. Besides believing that the trustee is capable of exhibiting a desired behavior and that her vulnerabilities will not stop her from doing that, the trustor believes that trustee has the intention to exhibit the aforementioned behavior. Therefore, in this case, in addition to the Capability Belief and Vulnerability Belief Patterns, the Intention Belief Pattern is also used to represent the «Trust» Assessment. Figure 10.7b shows an application example of this variant.

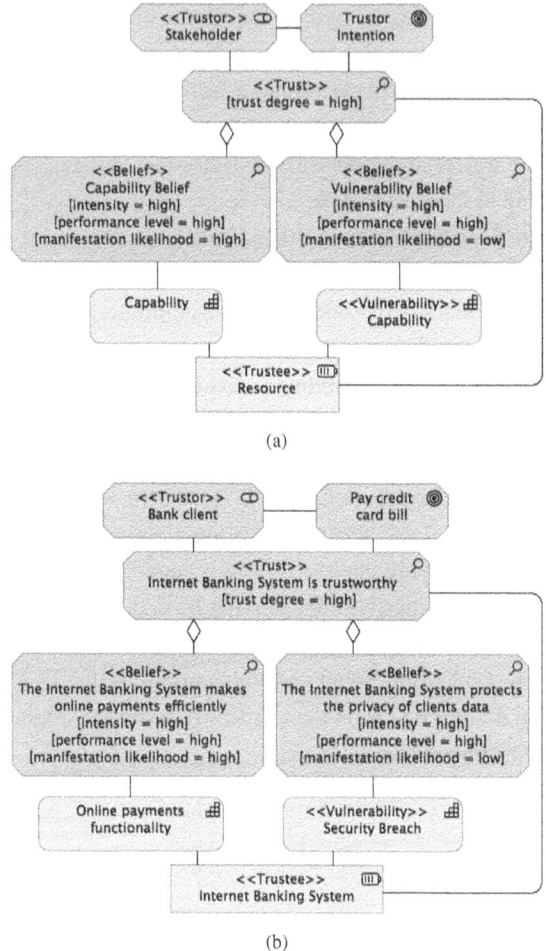

Figure 10.6: The Trust Composition Pattern - Object Trustee.

10.2. A Pattern Language for Trust Modeling in ArchiMate

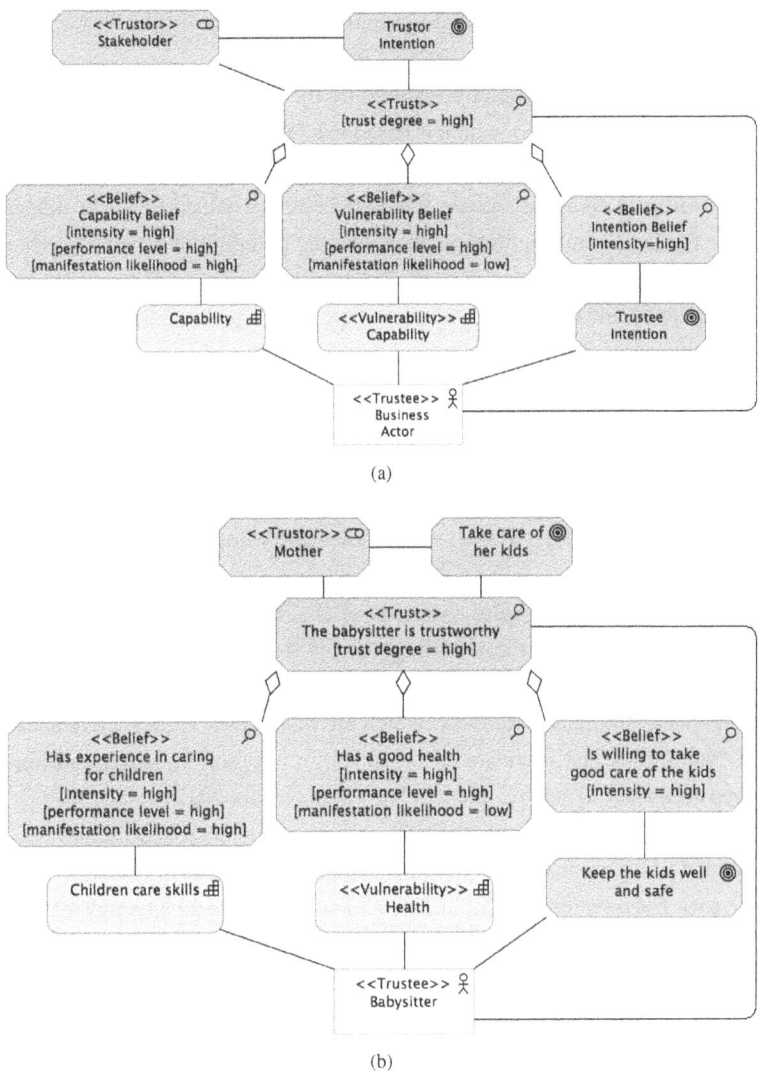

Figure 10.7: The Trust Composition Pattern - Agent Trustee.

Risk Experience. In order to account for how risk emerges from trust relations, we propose the Risk Experience Pattern, presented in figure 11.9. Once the components of trust are known (decomposed using the Trust Composition Pattern), it is possible to identify the risks related to the capabilities and vulnerabilities of the trustee, which are the focus of trustor's beliefs.

Our modeling strategy is directly inspired by the risk modeling approach proposed by Sales, Almeida, et al. (2018), which is based in COVER (see section 3.2 of chapter 3). Given the objectives of our pattern, we focus here on the perspective of risk as a chain of events that impact an agent's goals, which the authors named Risk Experience. Risk Experiences focus on unwanted events that have the potential of causing losses and are composed by events of two types, namely threat and loss events (Sales, Almeida, et al., 2018). A Threat Event is the one with the potential of causing a loss. As described in (Sales, Almeida, et al., 2018), it might be the manifestation of: (i) a Vulnerability; or (ii) Threat Capability (as aforementioned, capabilities are usually perceived as beneficial, as they enable the manifestation of events desired by an agent. However, when the manifestation of a capability enables undesired events that threaten agent's abilities to achieve a goal, it can be seen as a Threat Capability). The second mandatory component of a Risk Experience is a Loss Event, which necessarily impact intentions in a negative way.

Following the strategy of (Sales, Almeida, et al., 2018), we mapped Risk Experience as a Grouping decorated with the «RiskExperience» stereotype. Such a grouping should aggregate the elements and the relations in an experience. Then, we associated the «RiskExperience» Grouping with risks, which are mapped as «Risk» Drivers, as drivers represent "conditions that motivate an organization to define its goals and implement the changes necessary to achieve them" (The Open Group, 2017).

The first variant, depicted in figure 10.8a, allows modelers to represent the existence of risks related to Vulnerabilities of the trustee that are the focus of beliefs of the trustor. «ThreatEvent» Event might be the manifestation of a Vulnerability and may lead to a «LossEvent» Event, which impacts the Trustor Intention in a negative way, as it hurts her Intention of reaching a specific goal. «HazardAssessment» Assessment stands for situations that activate vulnerabilities and threat capabilities, which in turn will be manifested as «ThreatEvent» Events. Since ArchiMate does not provide a native construct for modeling situations in general, we followed the approach used in (Sales, Almeida, et al., 2018) and represent hazardous situations as assessments about them. Figure 10.8b shows an application example of this pattern.

The second variant is similar to the previous one, as it also represents the existence of risks related to a disposition of the trustee, though in this case the disposition is a Threat Capability. As previously mentioned, when the manifestation of a capability

10.2. A Pattern Language for Trust Modeling in ArchiMate

enables undesired events that threatens agent's abilities to achieve a goal, it can be seen as a Threat Capability. Analogous to the former variant, a «ThreatEvent» Event might be the manifestation of a Threat Capability of the trustee if the trustee fails to perform this specific Capability that was supposed to bring about an outcome desired by the trustor. Finally, the «ThreatEvent» Event can trigger a «LossEvent» Event, which has a negative impact on the Trustor Intention.

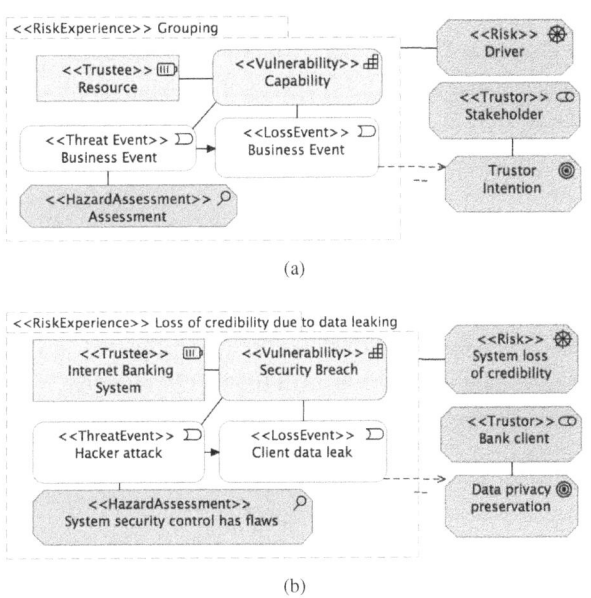

Figure 10.8: The Risk Experience Pattern (adapted from (Sales, Almeida, et al., 2018)).

Risk Assessment. This pattern, also extracted from (Sales, Almeida, et al., 2018), complements our approach on the modeling of risks that emerge from trust relations. It consists of a Risk Assessment made by a Stakeholder about a «Risk» Driver, which in turn is associated to a «RiskExperience» Grouping. In addition, the Risk Assessment is connected to a «ControlObjective» Goal, a sort of high level goal that defines what the organization intends to do about an identified risk. Control Goals are connected to «ControlMeasure» Requirements that represent desired properties of solutions – or means – to realize such goals. Using this pattern, depicted in figure 10.9, it is possible to model the realization of control measures by any set of core elements, such as business processes (e.g. a data quality management process), application services (e.g. a scanning service) or nodes (e.g. a document management system).

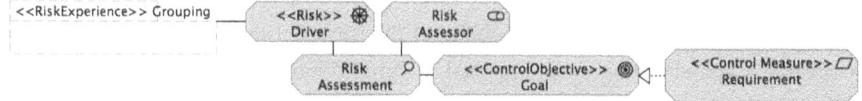

Figure 10.9: The Risk Assessment Pattern (adapted from (Sales, Almeida, et al., 2018)).

Trustworthiness Evidence Pattern. This pattern allows modelers to represent pieces of evidence that indicate that a trustee is capable of realizing its capabilities and shielding its vulnerabilities, thus suggesting that it is trustworthy. Examples of trustworthiness evidence are certifications, performance history, track record, recommendations, past successful experiences, risk mitigation measures, among others (Amaral, Sales, and Guizzardi, 2022). The generic structure of the Trustworthiness Evidence Pattern is depicted in figures 10.10a, 10.11a and 10.12a. It connects a «Trustee» and its Capability (or Vulnerability) to the «Trustworthiness Evidence». Trustworthiness evidence can be represented as Structure Elements, Principles, Requirements or Constraints, depending on their characteristics. Figures 10.10b, 10.11b, 10.12b represent applications of this pattern in which the «Trustworthiness Evidence» is respectivelly a Resource, Representation and a Requirement.

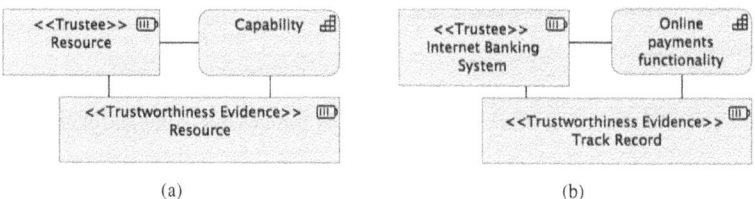

Figure 10.10: Trustworthiness Evidence Pattern - Resource.

10.2. A Pattern Language for Trust Modeling in ArchiMate

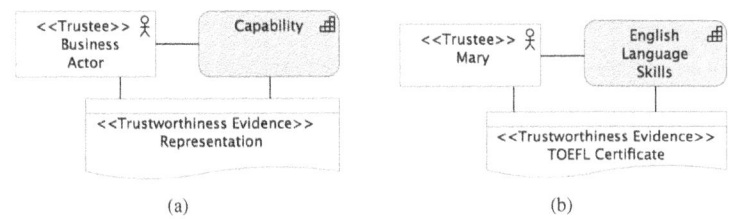

Figure 10.11: Trustworthiness Evidence Pattern - Representation.

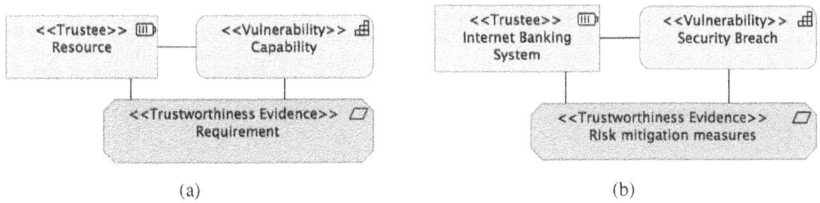

Figure 10.12: Trustworthiness Evidence Pattern - Requirement.

Trust Calibration Signal Pattern. This pattern allows modelers to represent signals emitted by the trustee to indicate trustworthy behavior. ROT (see chapter 4) distinguishes between two types of trust calibration signals: (i) trust-warranting signals, which indicate that the trustee can successfully realize its capabilities and prevent its vulnerabilities from being manifested (e.g. the establishment of a universal brand to create visual identity); and (ii) uncertainty signals, which communicate uncertainties regarding the realization of capabilities and the prevention of vulnerabilities (e.g. patient communication of uncertainties on the precision of medical diagnosis) (Amaral, Sales, and Guizzardi, 2022). Therefore, this pattern has two variants, depending on the type of signal.

The first variant, depicted in figure 10.13a, accounts for trust-warranting signals emitted by the trustee. It consists of a Structure Element, the trust-warranting signal, connected to the «Trustee» and to the Capability (or Vulnerability) to which the signal refers. An example of this first variant is shown in figure 10.13b.

The second variant (figure 10.14a), accounts for uncertainty signals emitted by the trustee. It consists of a Structure Element, the uncertainty signal, connected to the «Trustee» and to the Capability (or Vulnerability) to which the signal refers. An example of this second variant is shown in figure 10.14b.

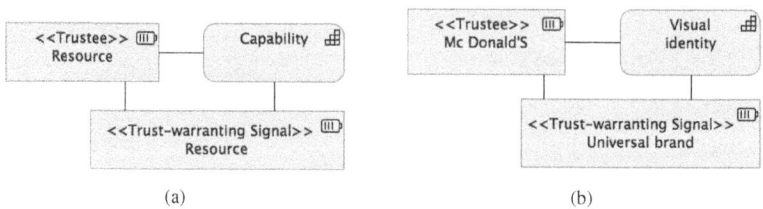

Figure 10.13: Trust-warranting Signal.

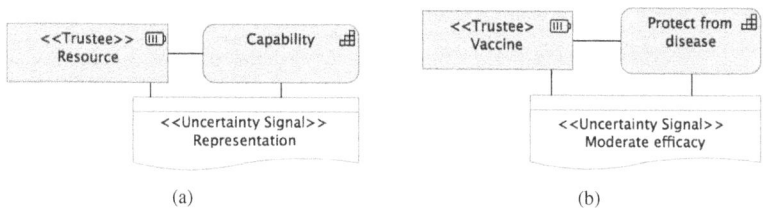

Figure 10.14: Uncertainty Signal.

Influence. To account for the many factors that can influence trust (either positively or negatively), we introduce the Influence Pattern, which details the different sources of influence that can affect the trustor's beliefs about the trustee's intentions and dispositions (capabilities and vulnerabilities) and, consequently, influence trust (see chapter 4). It connects a «Belief» Assessment of a «Trustor» Stakeholder to the source of influence, through an influence association. This pattern has four variants, according to the source of influence.

The first variant, depicted in figure 10.15a, details this relation when the source of influence is a trustworthiness evidence. It consists of a «Trustworthiness Evidence» connected (through an influence association) to the «Trustor» Stakeholder's «Belief» Assessment under its influence. An example of this first variant is shown in figure 10.15b.

The second variant details this relation when the source of influence is a trust calibration signal, that is, either a trust-warranting signal or an uncertainty signal. It consists of either a «Trust-warranting Signal» or an «Uncertainty Signal» connected (through

10.2. A Pattern Language for Trust Modeling in ArchiMate

an influence association) to the «Trustor» Stakeholder's «Belief» Assessment under its influence. Figure 10.16a shows the generic structure of this pattern and figure 10.16b presents an application example.

The third variant details this relation when the source of influence is a mental moment (concept from UFO) (Guizzardi, 2005). As explained in chapters 2 and 4, a Mental Moments can be a Perception, a Belief, a Desire or an Intention. Thus, this pattern consists of a «Trustor» Stakeholder's «Belief» Assessment connected (through an influence association) to either: (i) a «Perception» Assessment, or (ii) a «Belief» Assessment, or (iii) a «Desire» Assessment, or (iv) a Goal of «Trustor» (Intention). Figure 10.17a shows the generic structure of this pattern and figure 10.17b presents an application example.

Finally, the fourth variant details this relation when the source of influence is a trust relation. For example, one's trust in the local police officer may increase one's trust in the "judiciary system". The generic structure of this pattern, depicted in figure 10.18a, consists of a «Trust» Assessment connected (through an influence association) to the «Trustor» Stakeholder's «Belief» Assessment under its influence. Figure 10.18b presents an application of this pattern.

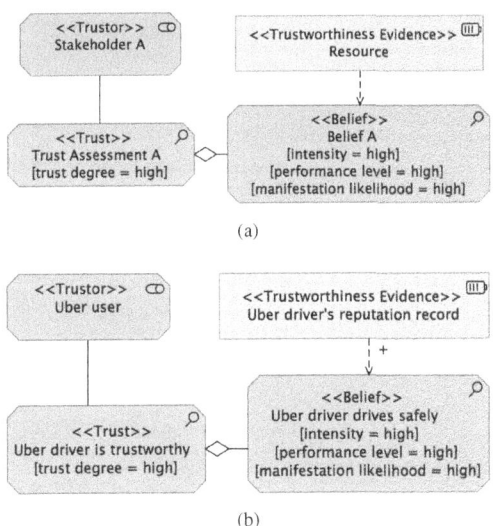

Figure 10.15: Trustworthiness Evidence Influence.

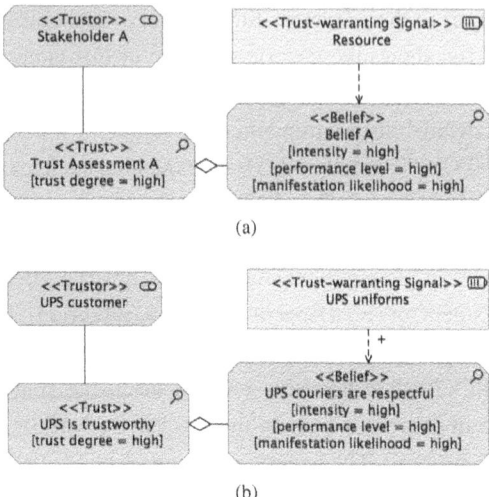

Figure 10.16: Trust Calibration Signal Influence.

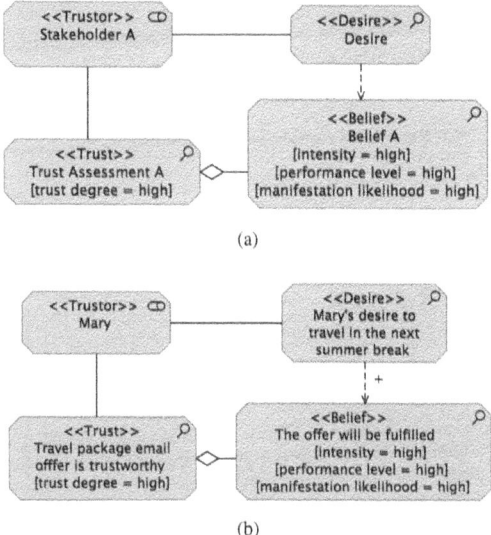

Figure 10.17: Mental Moment Influence.

10.2. A Pattern Language for Trust Modeling in ArchiMate

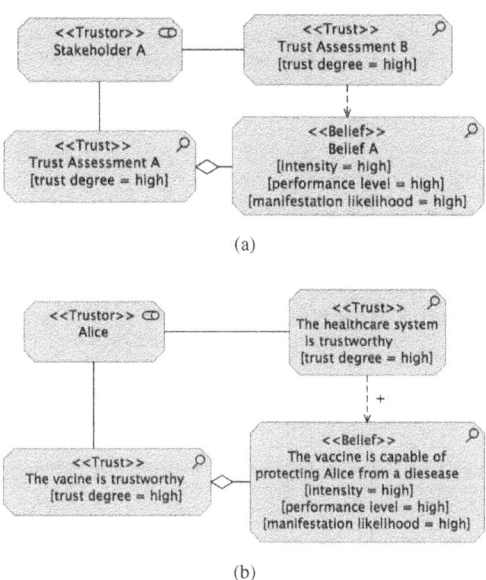

Figure 10.18: Trust Influencing Trust.

This pattern can be further used to characterize the existence of "trust by delegation". The idea behind "trust by delegation" is that when, for example, "Alice trusts her brother", and "her brother trusts a car mechanic", then Alice can derive a measure of "trust by delegation" in the car mechanic. In this case the «Trust» Assessments "Alice trusts her brother" and "Alice's brother trusts the car mechanic" positively influence one or more beliefs that compose the «Trust» Assessment "Alice trusts the car mechanic" (figure 10.19).

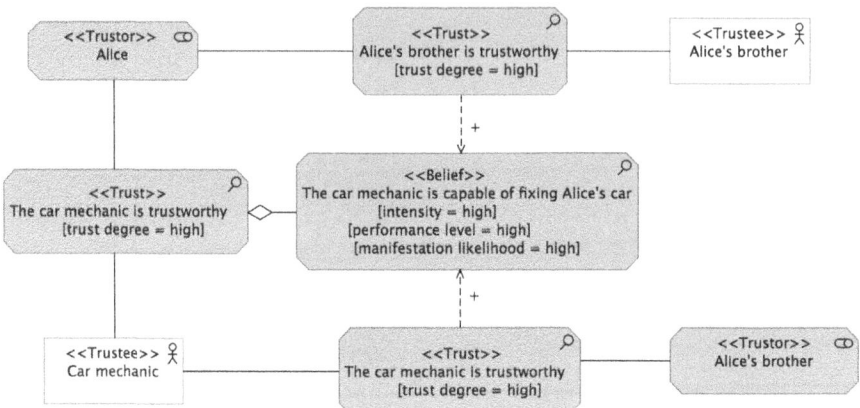

Figure 10.19: Trust Influencing Trust (trust by delegation).

The mapping between the ontological trust-related concepts and their representation in ArchiMate is listed in table 10.2.

10.2. A Pattern Language for Trust Modeling in ArchiMate   229

Table 10.2: Representation of trust and risk-related concepts in ArchiMate.

Concept	Representation in ArchiMate
Trust	«Trust» Assessment
Trustor	«Trustor» Stakeholder
Trustee	«Trustee» Stakeholder or «Trustee» Structure Element
Trust Degree	Attribute of a «Trust» Assessment
Capability	Capability
Vulnerability	«Vulnerability» Capability
Intention	Goal
Perception	«Perception» Assessment
Desire	«Desire» Assessment
Belief	«Belief» Assessment
Capability Belief	«Belief» Assessment connected to a Capability
Vulnerability Belief	«Belief» Assessment connected to a «Vulnerability» Capability
Intention Belief	«Belief» Assessment connected to a Goal
Intensity	Attribute of a «Belief» Assessment
Performance Level	Attribute of a «Belief» Assessment
Manifestation Likelihood	Attribute of a «Belief» Assessment
Trust-warranting Signal	«Trust-warranting Signal» Structure Element
Uncertainty Signal	«Uncertainty Signal» Structure Element
Trustworthiness Evidence	«Trustworthiness Evidence» Structure Element or
	«Trustworthiness Evidence» Principle or
	«Trustworthiness Evidence» Requirement or
	«Trustworthiness Evidence» Constraint
Risk	«Risk» Driver
Risk Assessment	Assessment connected to a «Risk» Driver
Risk Assessor	Stakeholder connected to a Risk Assessment
Risk Experience	«RiskExperience» Grouping
Threat Event	«ThreatEvent» Event
Loss Event	«LossEvent» Event
Hazard Assessment	«HazardAssessment» Assessment

10.2.4 Combining the Patterns

To use TPL, a modeler may start with the application of the Trust Assessment Pattern to identify both the trustor and the trustee, as well as the goal of the trustor, for the achievement of which she is counting on the trustee. Then, the user should use the Trust Composition Pattern by iteratively applying the Capability Belief Pattern, the Vulnerability Pattern, and the Intention Belief Pattern (this latter only if the trustee is an agent) in order to detail the components of trust: the capabilities, vulnerabilities, and intentions of the trustee, which are the focus of the trustor's beliefs.

For each vulnerability and capability, the modeler should apply the Risk Experience Pattern to identify the risks that can emerge when either the vulnerabilities are manifested or the capabilities are not manifested as expected (and in this case they play the role of threat capabilities). Then, for each risk driver identified, the user may apply the Risk Assessment Pattern to evaluate the impact of risks and establish procedures for effective risk control, treatment, and mitigation. As previously mentioned, from this pattern it is possible to model the realization of control measures by describing how the many pieces of an enterprise's application and technology infrastructure work together to properly manage risks that emerge from trust relations.

Similarly, for each capability and vulnerability, the modeler should apply both the Trustworthiness Evidence Pattern and Trust Calibration Signal Pattern to identify, respectively, pieces of evidence that suggest that the trustee should be trusted and the signals emitted by the trustee to indicate trustworthy behavior.

Additionally, the Influence Pattern variants can be applied to each belief in the Trust Composition Pattern to make explicit the factors that can influence trust. Figure 10.20 present the complete process of combining the patterns.

10.2. A Pattern Language for Trust Modeling in ArchiMate

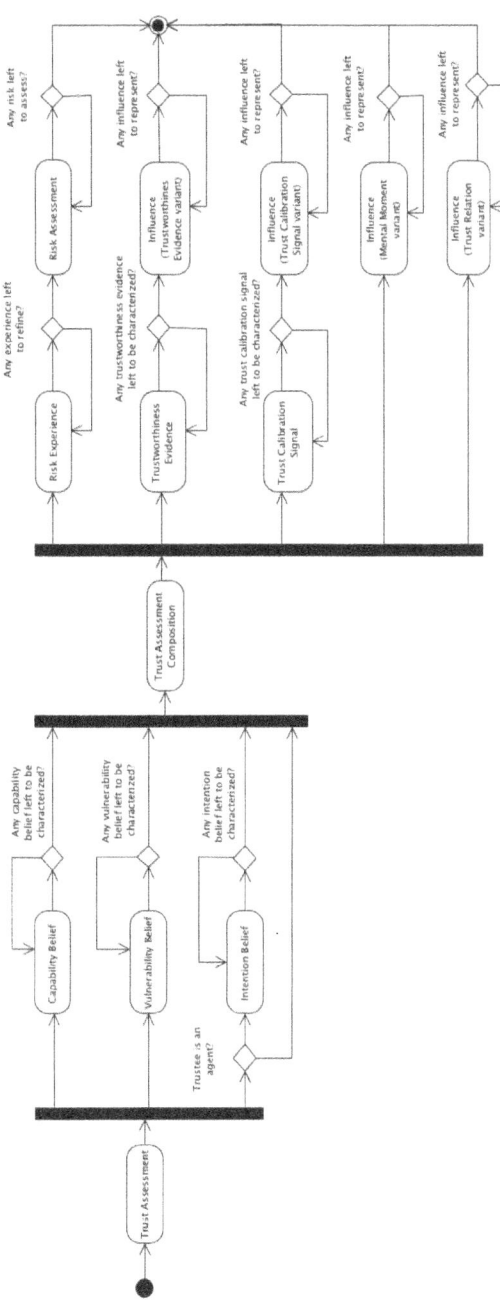

Figure 10.20: Combining the patterns.

10.3 Case Study

In this section, we present a realistic study in which we use the TPL to model a case of "misplaced trust" in a COVID-19 data repository, which resulted in the retraction of a publication from a highly influential and prestigious medical journal. In particular, we refer to the case of a recent study published in The Lancet journal (Mehra, Desai, et al., 2020), which relied on data gathered by a US healthcare analytics company called Surgisphere to report issues on the efficacy and safety of hydroxychloroquine (HCQ) for treating COVID-19. When the study was first published it prompted the World Health Organisation (WHO) along with several countries to pause trials on this drug. However, this very study was retracted (Mehra, Ruschitzka, et al., 2020) a few days later (and the clinical trials resumed), as concerns were raised with respect to the veracity of the data, leading the authors to recognize that they could no longer vouch for the veracity of the database at the heart of the study. Examples of problems encountered include errors in the Australian data and the fact that independent reviewers could not verify the validity of the data, as Surgisphere would not give access to the full dataset, citing confidentiality and client agreements (Mehra, Ruschitzka, et al., 2020).

In this thesis we present only the relevant fragments of the resulting model. The complete case study is available at `https : / / purl . org / krdb-core / trust-archimate`. An investigation of the characteristics a COVID-19 data repository should have, in order to be held in a position of trust by the communities they intend to serve, are presented in an accompanying technical report (Amaral, Sales, Guizzardi, and Porello, 2020b), available at the above-mentioned URL.

We start with the application of the Trust Assessment Pattern to identify the trustees, the trustors, and their goals. In our case study, different trust relations can be observed: (i) the Publication Authors trust the COVID-19 data repository to *evaluate the safety and effectiveness of hydroxychloroquine for treatment of COVID-19*; (ii) the Publication Authors trust the Surgisphere Staff about *creating and maintaining the COVID-19 data repository*; (iii) The Lancet trusts the Publication Authors to *accept publishing the study*; (iv) WHO trusts The Lancet to *have reliable information to make decisions w.r.t. recommendations on the treatment of diseases*; (v) WHO trusts (by delegation) the Publication Authors to *have reliable information to make decisions w.r.t. recommendations on the treatment of diseases*; and (vi) Countries trust WHO to *have reliable recommendations on the treatment of diseases*. Figure 10.21a and 10.21b depict the modeling of trust relations (i) and (ii), respectively.

10.3. Case Study

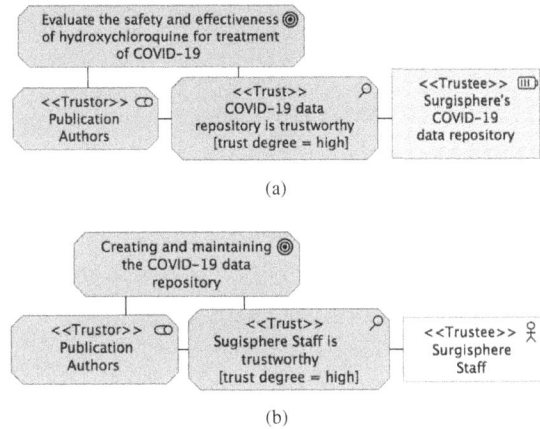

Figure 10.21: Application of the Trust Assessment Pattern.

We proceed by iteratively applying the Capability Belief Pattern (figure 10.22a) and the Vulnerability Belief Pattern (figure 10.22b) to detail the Publication Authors' beliefs with respect to the COVID-19 data repository (trust assessment depicted in figure 10.21a). For the sake of simplicity, the Beliefs' attributes were not represented in the diagrams. Finally, in figure 10.23 we use the Trust Composition Pattern to detail the trust complex mental state of the Publication Authors in their trust relation with the COVID-19 data repository. Note that the capabilities and vulnerabilities which are the focus of the Publication Authors' beliefs were identified based on the trust concerns for COVID-19 data presented in (Amaral, Sales, Guizzardi, and Porello, 2020b), such as *transparency*, *privacy of data*, *respect for human rights* and *data quality*.

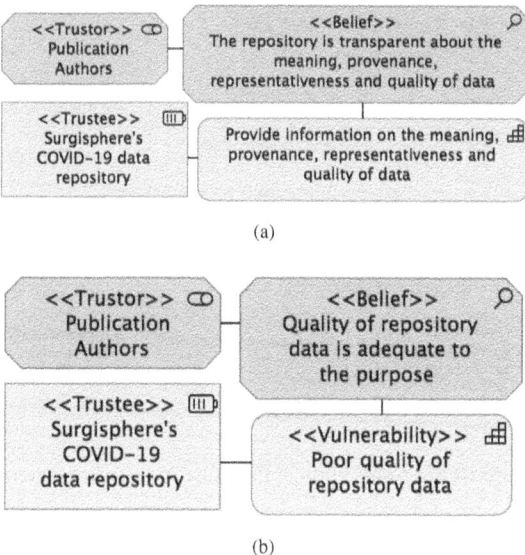

Figure 10.22: Capability and Vulnerability Beliefs.

10.3. Case Study

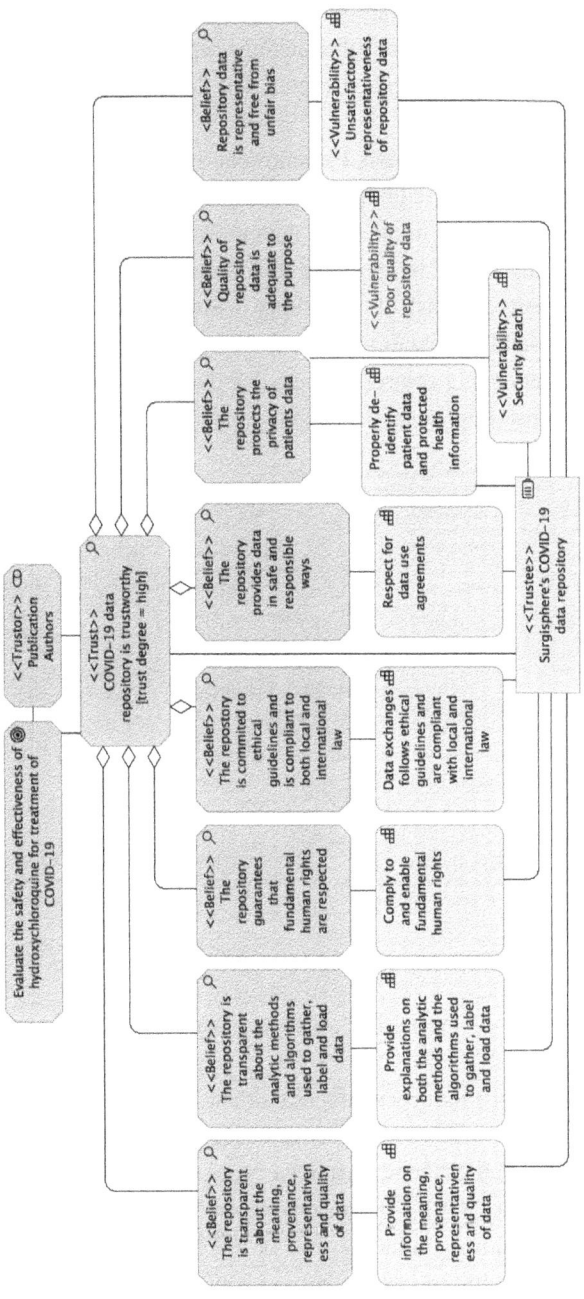

Figure 10.23: Composition.

Since the components of trust are known, it is possible to reason about possible manifestations of vulnerabilities and (threatening) capabilities of the COVID-19 data repository, which can enable undesired events that threaten the Publication Authors' abilities to achieve their goal.

Using the Risk Experience Pattern, we represent, in figure 10.24, the emergence of the risk of "repository loss of credibility" caused by the poor quality of data (a vulnerability), which revealed errors in the data, thus preventing the authors from attesting the validity of the study. Then we apply the Risk Assessment Pattern (figure 10.25) to represent the evaluation of the risk of "repository loss of credibility" by the Surgisphere Staff, as well as the establishment of procedures for effective risk control (improve data quality) and the definition of a control measure that describes how Surgisphere plans to realize these procedures (implement data quality management).

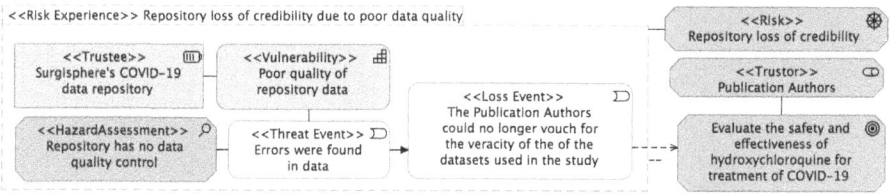

Figure 10.24: Risk Experience.

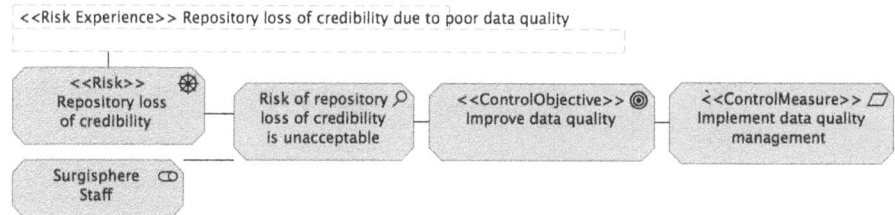

Figure 10.25: Risk Assessment.

Lastly, we use the Trust Influence Pattern (variant Trust Influencing Trust) to make explicit how some of these trust assessments influence each other. In figure 10.26 we can observe that the Publication Authors' trust in the Surgisphere's Staff expertise positively influences their trust in the COVID-19 data repository. Similarly, in figure 10.27, "WHO trusting The Lancet" positively influences one or more beliefs that are part of "WHO's trust in the Publication Authors". Note that as previously mentioned, this pattern can also be applied to characterize the existence of "trust by delegation". For example, considering that (1) "WHO trusts The Lancet" and (2) "The Lancet trusts the Publication Authors", there is a great chance that, (3) "WHO trusts the Publication Authors" by delegation, and in this case both (1) and (2) positively influences (3).

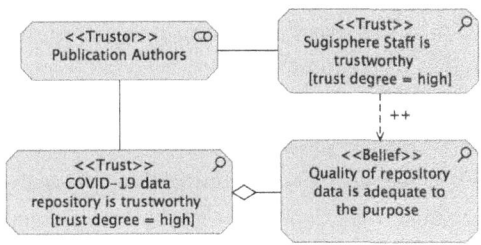

Figure 10.26: Trust Influencing Trust.

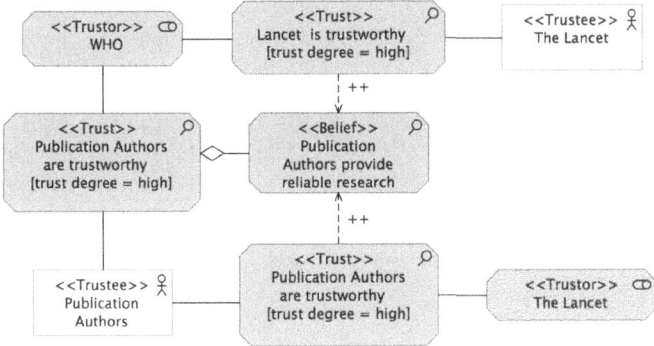

Figure 10.27: Trust Influencing Trust (trust delegation).

10.4 Final Considerations

In this chapter we presented TPL, a pattern language for modeling trust in ArchiMate that is based on ROT, a reference ontology that provides clear real-world semantics for the constituting elements of trust and describes the emergence of risk from trust relations. Although trust towards agents and resources is a known concern in the literature, little has been said about what constitutes the stakeholders' trust in a given organization or resource, as well as how these trust concerns permeate the enterprise architecture.

The TPL was designed aiming at addressing these issues.

By deriving the proposed patterns from ROT, we provided clear real-world semantics for its constituting elements, thus reducing ambiguity and conceptual complexity. In particular, we can represent: (i) the elements that constitute the trust of an agent with respect to a resource or another agent, including organizations; (ii) the capabilities and vulnerabilities of trustees that are the focus of the trustor's beliefs, in a trust assessment; (iii) the factors that can influence the trust assessments; (iv) the risks that can emerge from trust relations; and (v) risk assessments related to these risk drivers. Finally, the case study experience seems to indicate that both ROT and COVER, as a reference models, brought benefits for supporting ontological analysis and specification of the trust pattern language, for example, by minimizing ambiguities and increasing expressiveness.

Chapter 11

Modeling the Emergence of Value and Risk in Game Theoretical Approaches

In this chapter we apply the Common Ontology of Value and Risk (see section 3.2 of chapter 3) in the context of game theory (Amaral, Porello, et al., 2020). We conduct an ontological analysis on the emergence of value and risk from outcomes in game theoretical approaches. We make use of the concepts and relations defined in COVER to analyze the payoffs of a game in terms of value and risk, as well as how they emerge from outcomes in game theory. We formalize our analysis by means of an ontologically well-founded model, specified in OntoUML. In addition, we apply these results to represent the emergence of value and risk from game outcomes in enterprise architecture models in ArchiMate.

This chapter is organized as follows. Section 11.1 motivates the relevance of modeling the emergence of value and risk in game theoretical approaches. In Section 11.2, we provide an overview of some basic concepts of game theory and a discussion on the emergence of value and risk from outcomes. In section 11.3, we conduct our analysis based on the Common Ontology of Value and Risk and represent the results in a concise OntoUML model. In section 11.4, we instantiate the model using a Bank Run game example. To demonstrate the contribution of our proposal to the modeling practice, in section 11.5, we apply these results to represent the emergence of value and risk from game outcomes in enterprise architecture models in ArchiMate. We conclude with some final remarks in section 11.6.

11.1 Introduction

Game theory has become an important field of study and has been employed by practitioners of different disciplines, including economics, management, political science, biology, law, among others. In general, "game theory is concerned with situations in which decision-makers interact with one another, and in which the satisfaction of each participant with the outcome depends not just or her own decisions but on the decisions made by everyone" (Easley, Kleinberg, et al., 2012). Game-theoretic analysis include the modeling of the possible results of each strategy chosen by the players, taking into account uncertainties that neither player directly controls but that may influence outcomes, and assessing the expected utilities of these possible results. If we take the notion of risk presented in the ISO 3100:2018 standard (*ISO: Risk Management - Vocabulary* 2018; *ISO: Risk Management - Guidelines* 2009), which defines risk as the "effect of uncertainty on objective", we can conclude that an important part of choosing a strategy is understanding the risks involved in this decision.

Game outcomes may have either a positive or a negative effect on players' welfare, which are traditionally modeled in game theory by means of the Expected Utility Theory (Myerson, 1991).

As we shall see, in our account the positive and negative results shall be construed by means of the concepts of 'value' and 'risk', respectively; this move is motivated by the intent to provide a semantically transparent and interoperable qualitative account of the abstract quantitative theory of utilities. Thus, players must weight value and risks against each other when deciding whether to engage in a certain strategy. From this perspective, traditional risk analysis may help to advance the current state of the art of practical applications of game theory by modeling and assessing probable consequences for each outcome, thus allowing for understanding how value and risk emerge from combinations of actions of players.

Research into the foundations and the proper applications of game theory to real world scenarios has evolved at a vigorous pace throughout the past century (Myerson, 1991) and nowadays the theoretical analysis provided by game theory is nicely complemented by advanced sets of computational tools (McKelvey et al., 2006; Savani and Stengel, 2015). Over the past years "mathematicians and economists enriched the foundation, gradually building one of the most powerful and influential toolboxes of modern social science" (Watson, 2002).

Although the formalization of game components is quite well established, a detailed ontological understanding of the fundamental notions of game theory is missing. In particular, a clear ontological foundation of the objectives, or goals, of the interacting agents and of the emergence of value and risk from the outcomes of interaction is still to be developed. Without a precise conceptualization and rigorous definition of fundamental game theory notions, modeling and communication problems may arise. For example, when various modelers share a model without a clear semantics, different modelers come to different interpretations of the same model and are not aware of the conflict, running into a False Agreement problem (Guarino, 1998). As a result, practitioners have to make their own interpretations about the key concepts proposed in such models, which may lead to incorrect usage, and subsequently, them not obtaining the expected results (Jarzabkowski and Wilson, 2006). This problem can manifest itself, for example, in the modeling of enterprise architectures. A main challenge of incorporating the fundamental notions of game theory in enterprise architecture lies in identifying a precise conceptualization for these notions. Without such a precise conceptualization, different modelers may come to different interpretations of the same model, thus resulting in enterprise architecture models that cannot serve their purpose as tools for communication between stakeholders, decreasing the value of enterprise architecture models in the pursuit of informed decision-making.

In this chapter, we intend to contribute to filling these gaps by initiating the investigation of the ontological foundation of the emergence of value and risk in game theoretical approaches. We believe that a proper ontological understanding and modeling of the basic notions of game theory is mandatory to apply this rich body of knowledge and computational tools in designing information systems and supporting strategic decision making. This approach aligns with the growing interest in the area of philosophy of economics for qualitative models that ascribe ontological interpretations for the (otherwise, quantitative and abstract) phenomena in economics[1].

The contribution of this chapter is threefold. Firstly, we make use of the concepts and relations defined in the Common Ontology of Value and Risk (see chapter 3, section 3.2) to analyze the payoffs of a game in terms of value and risk, as well as how they emerge from outcomes in game theory. Secondly, we propose a precise representation of our analysis by means of an ontologically well-founded model, specified in OntoUML (Guizzardi, 2005) and thus, compliant with the meta-ontological commitments of the Unified Foundational Ontology (Guizzardi, 2005). Finally, we apply our ontological account for game theory concepts to model game outcomes in the context of enterprise

---

[1] See, for example, http://ceur-ws.org/Vol-2205/ and http://ceur-ws.org/Vol-2518/

architectures.

11.2 On Game Theory

11.2.1 Strategic Games

"Game Theory studies decisions in which the outcome depends partly on what other people do, and in which this is known to be the case by each decision maker" (Peterson, 2017). Shoam and Leyton-Brown (Shoham and Leyton-Brown, 2008) define game theory as "the mathematical study of interaction among independent, self-interested agents."

In game theory, a game is intended to refer to any social situation involving two or more agents, named players. A player may be interpreted as an individual or as a group of individuals making a decision. Two basic assumptions about players are that: (i) they are rational (Myerson, 1991), meaning that they make decisions consistently in pursuit of their own objectives and aiming at maximizing the expected value of their payoff; and (ii) they take into account their knowledge or expectations of other decision-makers' behavior (Shoham and Leyton-Brown, 2008). According to Shoham and Leyton-Brown (2008), each player "has his own description of which states of the world he likes" and "acts in an attempt to bring about these states of the world".

The dominant approach to modeling an agent's interests is Utility Theory, which aims at quantifying an agent's degree of preference across a set of available alternatives (Shoham and Leyton-Brown, 2008). Under a wide range of circumstances, the preference relation of a player in a strategic game can be represented by a utility function (also called a payoff function) (Osborne and Rubinstein, 1994). A utility function is a mapping from states of the world to real numbers. These numbers are interpreted as measures of an agent's level of happiness in the given states.

A strategic game is a model of interactive decision-making in which players (agents) simultaneously choose their plan of action to perform in the environment. The combination of each agent action (the *action profile*, in the game-theoretical jargon) brings about a possible outcome o in a set of outcomes O, that depends on the actions performed by the agents (Wooldridge, 2009). We can represent an agent utility function as a function from O to the real numbers $\mathbb{R}$ ($u : O \to \mathbb{R}$) that assigns to each outcome o in O a measure of how good o is for the considered agent. The greater the number, the better o is for that agent.

11.2. On Game Theory

Table 11.1: Payoff matrix example

		Player y	
		C	D
Player x	C	2,2	2,1
	D	1,3	3,2

Based on the above-mentioned definitions, a (strategic) game includes (cf. (Wooldridge, 2009)): a finite set N of n agents, indexed by i; for each agent $i \in N$, a nonempty set A_i of actions (or strategies) available to agent i; a set of outcomes O; the preferences or utilities u_i of the agents over the combinations of actions (outcomes). In Game Theory, to simplify the model, the set of outcomes is usually identified with the set of all possible combinations of agents' actions; however, we prefer to keep the two sets distinct, as in (Wooldridge, 2009), to facilitate our subsequent ontological analysis.

Let us take as example a set of agents $N = \{x, y\}$ and a set of actions $A = \{C, D\}$ available to both agents x and y. Assume that each combination of agents' actions brings about a distinct outcome, i.e. we have the following set $O = \{o_1, o_2, o_3, o_4\}$, where $o_1 = (C,C)$, $o_2 = (C,D)$, $o_3 = (D,C)$ and $o_4 = (D,D)$. In addition, for each agent, we can define the preferences or utilities directly on the combinations of actions (or outcomes). For instance:

$u_x(C,C) = 2$, $u_x(D,C) = 1$, $u_x(C,D) = 2$, $u_x(D,D) = 3$
$u_y(C,C) = 2$, $u_y(D,C) = 3$, $u_y(C,D) = 1$, $u_y(D,D) = 2$

A natural way to represent games is via an n-dimensional matrix, also known as *payoff matrix*. For example, in a two-dimensional matrix, in general, each row corresponds to a possible action for player x, each column corresponds to a possible action for player y, and each cell is a combination of actions that corresponds to one possible outcome. Each player's utility for an outcome is written in the cell corresponding to that outcome, with player x's utility listed first. Table 11.1 illustrates the payoff matrix for the example just mentioned.

A fundamental concept in game theory is that of Nash equilibrium. A Nash equilibrium is a set of actions (an action profile), one for each player (agent), such that no player could improve their payoff by unilaterally deviating from their assigned action. For example, considering two agents x and y, two actions a_1 and a_2 are in Nash equilibrium if: (i) assuming that agent x plays a_1, y can do no better than playing a_2; and (ii) assuming that agent y plays a_2, x can do no better than playing a_1. The game presented in table 11.1 has a unique Nash equilibrium, namely (C,C).

11.2.2 Example: Bank Run

The game theoretical literature on bank runs is largely built on the seminal paper by Diamond and Dybvig (1983).

A bank holds only a fraction of its deposits as cash reserves. It lends out as much of its deposits as it can (subject to a banking regulator's capital-adequacy requirements), making a profit from the interest it charges. A bank run occurs when a large number of customers of a bank or another financial institution withdraw their deposits simultaneously due to concerns about the bank's solvency, which is common in times of crisis. If the depositors do not withdraw and give bank enough time to tide over crisis, then payoff is highest and they can get their money with interest. However, if there is panic among depositors and all of them rush to withdraw their money, then due to insolvency each will end up getting a lesser amount. Finally, if few withdraws and the others do not, then the one who withdraws gets more than the one who do not withdraw.

To simplify, let us consider the example of a bank with just two depositors. Each depositor makes a deposit of 1000 euros in the bank. The bank invests these deposits in a long term project. If the bank is forced to liquidate its investments before the project matures, a total of 1600 euros can be recovered. However, if the bank allows the investment to reach maturity, the project will pay out a total of 2400 euros. Therefore, if both depositors make withdrawals before the project matures, each agent will receive 800 euros. If only one depositor withdrawal her money before the project matures, she receives 1000 euros and the other one, 600 euros. Finally, if both depositors retain the payment until the project matures, the bank returns 1200 euros for each one. Table 11.2 presents the payoff-matrix for this example, considering that the depositors may only choose between withdrawing their deposits before the project matures or retaining their deposits until it matures. Note that although in this example the payoffs are related to the value returned to depositors by the bank, payoffs are not necessarily the same as monetary worth. This is because payoffs or utilities identify the players' preferences, which are not necessarily measured in terms of profit or money (Peterson, 2017).

This game has two Nash equilibria: (i) both depositors withdraw; and (ii) both depositors retain. The first of these two outcomes (i) can be interpreted as a run on the bank. If depositor A believes that depositor B will withdraw before the project matures, then her best response is to withdraw as well, even though both depositors would be

11.2. On Game Theory

Table 11.2: Bank Run example

		Depositor B	
		Withdraw	Retain
Depositor A	Withdraw	800,800	1000,600
	Retain	600,1000	1200,1200

better off if they waited until the project matures.

Recently, some authors have compared the shortage of toilet paper, associated to the spread of coronavirus, to a bank run (Payolo, 2020). They state that "this panic buying is the result of the fear of missing out and is a phenomenon of consumer behaviour similar to what happens when there is a run on banks" (Payolo, 2020). According to Payolo (2020), "both banking and the toilet-paper market can be thought of as a coordination game with two players (one individual and everyone else) and two strategies (panic buy or act normally). Each strategy has an associated pay-off. If everyone acts normally, we have an equilibrium: there will be toilet paper on the shop shelves, and people can relax and buy it as they need it. But if others panic buy, the optimal strategy for the individual is to do the same, otherwise she'll be left without toilet paper. The result is another equilibrium, which is everyone panic buys".

11.2.3 Value, Risk and Outcomes

According to Sun and Sun (2018), "game theory is mainly about choosing the most advantageous plan of action given the effect the opponent has on us". Agents perform actions motivated by intentions, which are related to their goals. In game theory, an outcome corresponds to a combination of actions performed by agents. Payoffs are related to outcomes results, which can contribute to the achievement of agents' goals. Sun and Sun (2018) state that payoff "refers to the reward received after the player has chosen a certain strategy or action".

As extensively discussed in the literature (Kambil et al., 1996; Lanning and Michaels, 1988; Sales, Baião, et al., 2018), value is directly connected to the achievement of goals. Things and experiences have value to people because they allow them to achieve their goals. For example, an object has value to an agent because it has properties (e.g., capacities, "affordances", i.e., ultimately, *dispositions*) that can be leveraged to enact events that, in turn, bring about situations that contribute to satisfy that agent's goals

(Botti Benevides et al., 2019; Guizzardi, Wagner, Falbo, et al., 2013). In summary, the more an event makes progress towards achieving an agent's goals (i.e., the more the situation it brings about contributes to satisfying those goals), the more valuable it is to that agent. In other words, the results of outcomes, represented by payoffs, may create value for agents as they can positively impact their goals. But, as value is not an *intrinsic property*, the same object or experience may have different values to different agents, or even according to different goals adopted by the same agent. Thus, since the players have different goals and under different circumstances, they may feel differently w.r.t. the same reward. For example, a mask has a higher value during the COVID-19 pandemic because by wearing it, one is better protected from getting infected.

Interestingly, at the same time that outcome results can generate value, they also entail some risk, as they can negatively impact an agent's goal. The relation between value and risk is pointed out by several works in the literature. According to Sales et al. (Sales, Baião, et al., 2018), "the notion of risk is irreducibly intertwined with the notion of value" and one of the differences between them rely on "the expected impact on goals: negative for risks and positive for value".

Having a clear understanding of the influence of these forces over outcomes is fundamental to the agent's decision making. For example, "in an uncertain game, a rational agent would not always play the strategy that gives the highest expected payoff if the risk is too high. For a risk-averse agent, the strategy that takes the least risk has the highest dominance. For a risk-seeking agent, the strategy that may give the highest payoff has the highest dominance regardless of the risk and the expected payoff. For a risk-neutral agent, the dominant strategy is the one that gives the highest expected payoff" (GhavamiFar et al., 2007). Risk analysis, including probabilistic risk assessment of how events may unfold, can be very useful (perhaps even essential) for realistically complex problems, in populating the cells in payoff matrices. Therefore, as stated by (Cox, 2009), "risk analysis and game theory are also deeply complementary". Game-theoretic analyses require modeling the probable consequences of each choice of strategies by the players and assessing the expected utilities of these probable consequences. Decision and risk analysis methods are well suited to accomplish these tasks.

11.3 Modeling the Emergence of Value and Risk from Outcomes in UFO

In this section, we use the aforementioned theories to present a preliminary model of the emergence of value and risk from games outcomes. Our analysis relies on the concepts of value and risk defined in COVER, the Common Ontology of Value and Risk (see section 3.2 of chapter 3).

Note that, as argued in (Sales, Guarino, et al., 2017a), value can be ascribed to past, actual or envisioned experiences. Risk, however, is only ascribed to envisioned experiences that may (but are not certain to) happen (Sales, Baião, et al., 2018). Also agents' actions (or strategies) in a game may be about envisioned events (which may never occur). For instance, if a depositor decides to withdraw her money instead of retaining it in the bank, then the action of retaining the money will not happen. This means that we need to refer to future or envisioned events – whose expected temporal properties are not completely fixed – in our domain of discourse. Therefore, we shall talk of expected events as regular entities of our domain, not differently from, say, a planned air trip in a flight reservation system. In order to use this non-classical notion of events in our analysis while maintaining its ontological rigour, we employ the formulation of events as proposed in (Guarino, 2017), which was already successfully employed in (Sales, Baião, et al., 2018) and (Sales, Guarino, et al., 2017a).[2]

Our model is specified in OntoUML (Guizzardi, 2005) and thus, compliant with the meta-ontological commitments of the Unified Foundational Ontology (Guizzardi, 2005). In the diagram depicted in figures 11.1 and 11.2, we represent events in yellow, relators in green, objects in pink, qualities and modes in blue, situations in orange and datatypes in white.

We use the notion of *agent* defined in UFO-C (see section 2.3) to model a participant of a game as an Agent that plays the *role* of Game Player in a Game (figure 11.1). In UFO-C, agents are individuals that can perform actions, perceive events and bear mental aspects. A relevant type of mental aspect for our proposal is the *intention*. Intentions are desired state of affairs for which the agent commits to pursuing (e.g., the intention of going to a beach resort for the next summer break) (Castelfranchi, 1995). For this reason, intentions cause the agent to perform *actions*. In the ontology, Intentions are represented as modes that inhere in Agents.

---

[2] A different strategy that avoids introducing future or possible events is to rephrase the model using *types* of actions and events (Porello, Guizzardi, Sales, and Amaral, 2020).

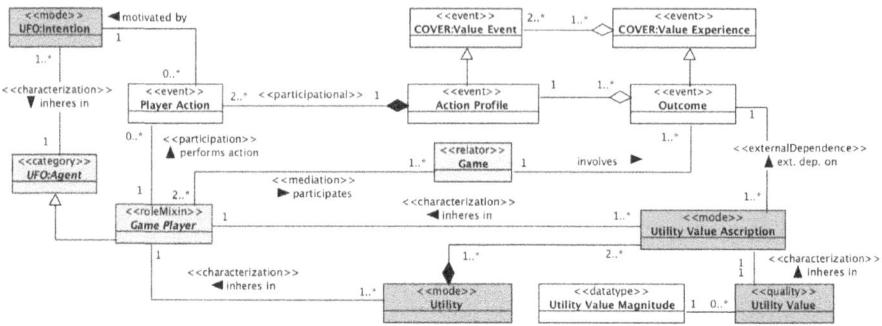

Figure 11.1: Modeling the emergence of value and risk from outcomes in OntoUML.

The Actions performed by Game Players are modeled as intentional events, in the sense that they have the specific purpose of satisfying some Intention. As events, actions can be atomic or complex. A complex action is composed of several actions. Action Profiles are complex events composed of Actions performed by the players in a Game.

In the ontology, the Action Profile is modeled as a type of Value Event (Sales, Baião, et al., 2018) (as defined in COVER (Sales, Baião, et al., 2018)) and can be classified into Impact and Trigger Event (figure 11.2). The former is the one that directly impact an Intention of reaching a goal. By contrast, a Trigger Event is simply the one that causes an Impact Event. Within the category of Impact Events we can further distinguish into Gain Event and Loss Event. The difference between them rely on the nature of the impact caused on goals (positive for Gain Events and negative for Loss Events).

A Game involves a set of Outcomes. Outcomes are modeled as a type of Value Experience (Sales, Baião, et al., 2018) (as defined in COVER (Sales, Baião, et al., 2018)) and thus are composed of Value Events. Among the Value Events that compose an Outcome there is exactly one Action Profile. Figure 11.2 presents a fragment of COVER depicting the different types of Value Events that can compose a Value Experience.

Outcomes have impact on Game Players' Intentions, which may affect her goals either positively or negatively. We analyze the emergence of risks from Outcomes, based on COVER (see section 3.2 of chapter 3). An Action Profile is a complex event that brings about a Resulting Situation (figure 11.2). The Resulting Situation may satisfy the Game Player's goals (and in this case it is considered a Successful Situation) or, in the worst case, it may not have the desired result and the Game Player will not be able to achieve her goal. In this case, the Resulting Situation stands for a Threatening

11.3. Modeling the Emergence of Value and Risk from Outcomes in UFO

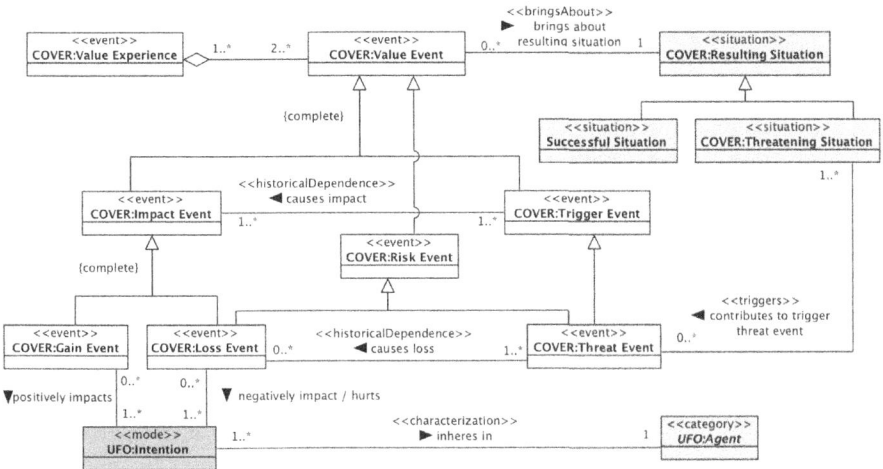

Figure 11.2: Value and risk events.

Situation that may trigger a Threat Event, which may cause a loss. The Loss Event is a Risk Event that impacts intentions in a negative way, as it hurts the Game Player's Intentions of reaching a specific goal.

As we have previously discussed, value emerges from achieving goals. Thus, the more an event contributes to the achievement of a goal, the more valuable it is. Outcomes that positively impact Game Players' Intentions can create value. However, whether or not value is produced in the realization of an Outcome is, in fact, a subjective notion, which depends on how the Game Players assess their participation, i.e., whether they ascribe to the experience a positive assessment (Sales, Baião, et al., 2018; Sales, Guarino, et al., 2017a).

The entity Utility Value Ascription represents this assessment. The Utility Value Ascription is an example of a mode that inheres in the Agent and is externally dependent on the Outcome. As aforementioned, a mode is an existentially dependent entity that, as such, can only exist by inhering in some other individual. In particular, the Utility Value Ascription is a relationally dependent mode (or an externally dependent mode), i.e., a mode that inheres in an individual but which is also externally dependent on a different individual. The Utility Value Ascription mode takes a value in at least one (but possibly several) Utility Value Magnitude Spaces, via the quality Utility Value. These spaces have, in OntoUML, the semantics of abstract conceptual spaces, delimiting the possible values an intrinsic property can be projected into (Guizzardi, 2005).

Finally, the Utility is composed of the Utility Value Ascriptions of the possible Outcomes, under the perspective of a particular Game Player. In the model, Utility is represented as a complex externally dependent mode that inheres in the Game Player and is composed of the mereological sum of Utility Value Ascription modes [3].

11.4 Use Case Illustration: Bank Run

In this section, we instantiate our model with two outcomes of the Bank Run example, described in section 11.2.2, which are Nash Equilibria.

Firstly, in figure 11.3, we illustrate the instantiation of the Outcome in which both Depositor A and Depositor B retain the invested amount until the project matures. In this case both Game Players have the Intention of 'making profit from the investment'. The Action Profile is composed of the Action of Depositor A, who decides to retain her money and the Action of Depositor B, who also decides to retain her deposit. Note that this is a case of Nash Equilibrium as once Depositor A has retained her deposit, Depositor B can do no better than retaining her deposit too. This Action Profile brings about a situation in which 'the bank does not need cash before the project completion', which stands for a Successful Situation. Consequently, the bank sells the project to another bank at price of 2400 euros, which is considered a Trigger Event that triggers two Gain Events, namely 'Bank pays out more than the amount invested by Depositor A' and 'Bank pays out more than the amount invested by Depositor B'. These two Gain Events positively impact the Intentions of Depositors A and B of 'making profit from their investments', as they will receive 1200 euros, which is more than the invested value (1000 euros).

Secondly, in figure 11.4, we illustrate the instantiation of the Outcome in which both Depositor A and Depositor B withdraw the invested amount before the project matures. Also in this case, both Game Players have the Intention of 'making profit from the investment'. The Action Profile is composed of the Action of Depositor A, who decides to withdraw her money and the Action of Depositor B, who also decides to withdraw her deposit. Note that here we also have a case of Nash Equilibrium. Although this outcome is not the one with the best payoff for both players, it can be seen as "a steady state, in which each player holds the correct expectation about the other players' behavior and acts rationally" (Osborne and Rubinstein, 1994): if Depositor A believes that Depositor

---

[3]This is compatible with the modeling of preferences according to UFO in (Porello and Guizzardi, 2018)

11.4. Use Case Illustration: Bank Run

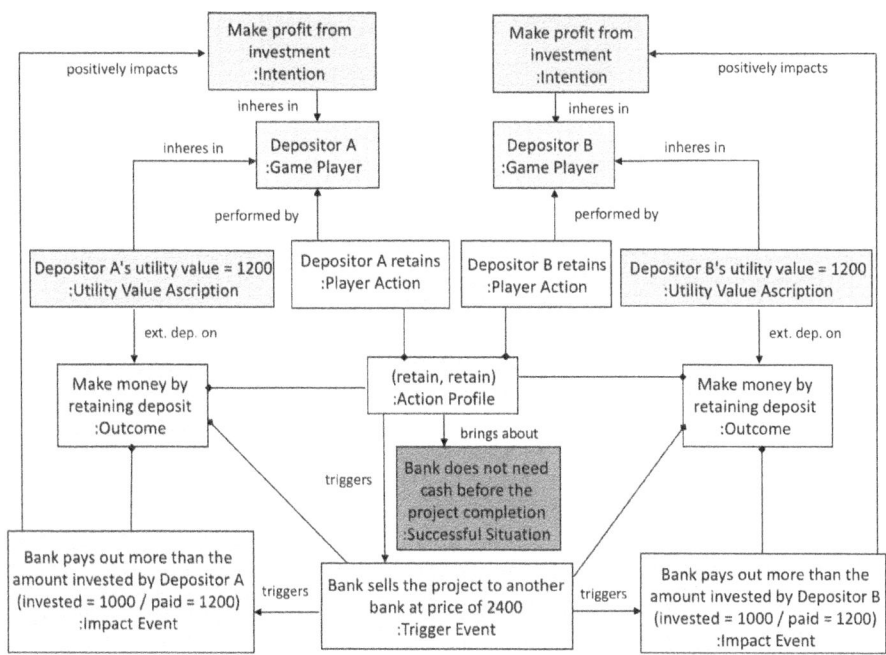

Figure 11.3: The emergence of value from outcomes.

B will withdraw before the project matures, then her best response is to withdraw as well.

In the sequel, this Action Profile brings about a situation in which 'the bank needs cash to repay the deposits before the project completion' that can be considered a Threatening Situation. This situation may trigger a Threat Event if, for example, 'the bank is forced to liquidate its investments before the project matures, and recovers only 1600 euros'. This Threat Event causes two Loss Events, which are 'the bank paying out less than the amount invested by Depositor A and Depositor B, respectively'. These Loss Events, in turn, hurt the Depositors' Intentions of 'making profit from their investments'.

We focused on the Nash Equilibria of the game; clearly our approach can be used also for modelling non-equilibrium states. It is interesting to notice that our models illustrate *why* in a Nash equilibrium players have no incentives to deviate from the current course of action. The chosen action (e.g. "retain" for both players *A* and *B* in figure 11.3) is the action that positively impacts the intention of each player more than any

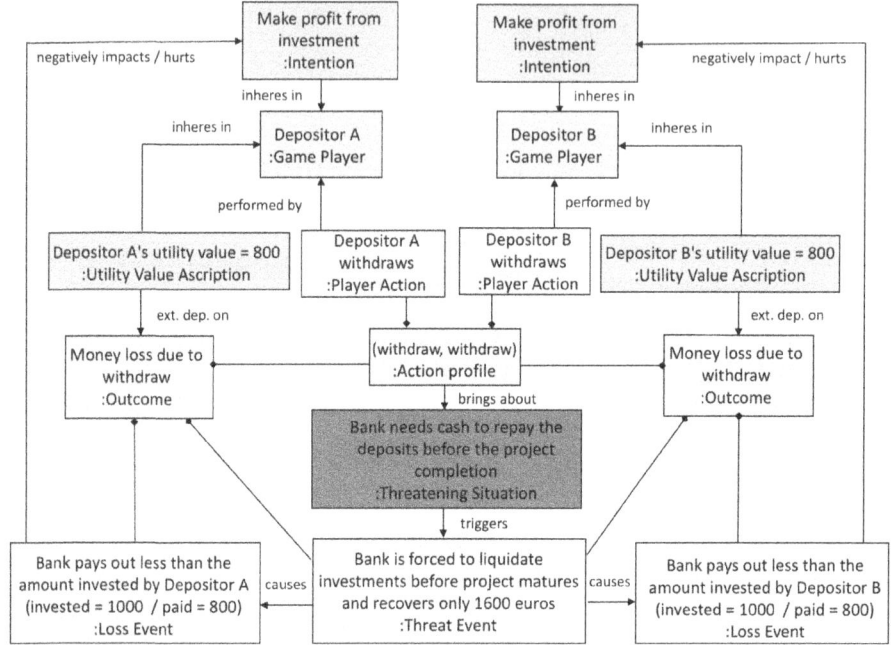

Figure 11.4: The emergence of risk from outcomes.

other action, given the other players' move (by definition). Thus, assuming that rational players are pursuing actions that better impact their intentions, players have indeed no reason to deviate from that choice in that context. By contrast, in a non-Nash Equilibrium outcome, players would have actions at their disposal that promote their intentions better, thus providing an incentive to deviate to the action that better impact their intention. Therefore, the ontological analysis provides a rich semantic understanding of equilibrium outcomes, associating the stability of the outcome with the satisfaction of the intentions of the players.

11.5 Modeling Game Outcomes in Enterprise Architecture

11.5.1 Value and Risk Experience Modeling in ArchiMate

ArchiMate is a modeling standard that defines a layered structure by means of which the architecture of enterprises can be described (The Open Group, 2017). Based on the

11.5. Modeling Game Outcomes in Enterprise Architecture

Common Ontology of Value and Risk (see section 3.2 of chapter 3), Sales, Roelens, et al. (2019) propose a pattern language for value modeling in ArchiMate that allows the representation of Value Experiences as well as Experience Valuations, among others. Similarly, in (Sales, Almeida, et al., 2018) Sales et al. conduct an ontological analysis of risk modeling in ArchiMate in the light of COVER, in which they propose a pattern to represent Risk Experiences. By deriving patterns from COVER, they provide clear real-world semantics for its constituting elements, thus reducing the ambiguity and conceptual complexity found in previous approaches to model value and risk in the literature.

In the sequel we briefly describe three patterns that are relevant in the context of our work, namely the Value Experience Pattern, the Experience Valuation Pattern and the Risk Experience Pattern. For a more detailed discussion on value and risk modeling patterns, one should refer to (Sales, Roelens, et al., 2019) and (Sales, Almeida, et al., 2018), respectively.

Value Experience. This pattern allows modelers to detail experiences that creates value for a given stakeholder. As shown in figure 11.5, it consists of a «ValueExperience» Grouping connected to a Stakeholder acting as the value subject (agent from whose perspective the experience creates value), and its decomposition into value events, which can be represented using Business Processes, Business Events and/or Business Interactions.

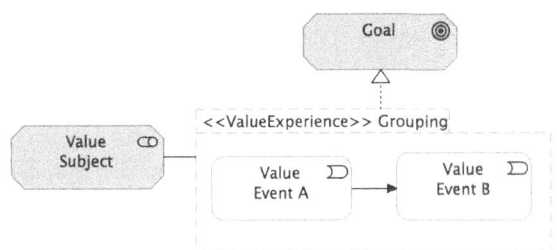

Figure 11.5: The Value Experience Pattern.

Experience Valuation. This pattern allows modelers to describe value judgments made towards experiences. As shown in figure 11.6, it consists of a «Valuation» Assessment made by a Stakeholder (Value Assessor) that a «ValueExperience» creates Value for another Stakeholder (Value Subject). The Value element corresponds to an entry in a scale chosen by the modeler.

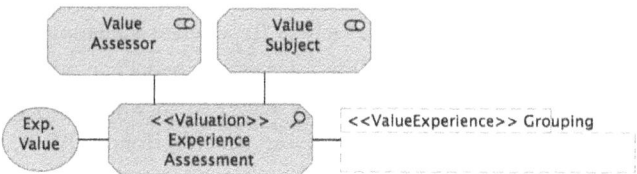

Figure 11.6: The Experience Valuation Pattern.

Risk Experience. According to Sales, Almeida, et al. (2018) risk experiences focus on unwanted events that have the potential of causing losses and are composed by events of two types, namely threat and loss events. A threat event is the one with the potential of causing a loss. As described in (Sales, Almeida, et al., 2018), it might be the manifestation of a vulnerability or a threatening capability. The second mandatory component of a risk experience is a loss event, which necessarily impact intentions in a negative way.

In (Sales, Almeida, et al., 2018) the authors map risk experience as a Grouping stereotyped as a «RiskExperience», which aggregates the elements and the relations in the experience. They associate the «RiskExperience» Grouping with risks, which are mapped as «Risk» Drivers, as drivers represent "conditions that motivate an organization to define its goals and implement the changes necessary to achieve them" (The Open Group, 2017). For the sake of simplicity, we represent here a simplified version of the Risk Experience pattern (figure 11.7), containing only the experience elements and relations that are relevant to our proposal.

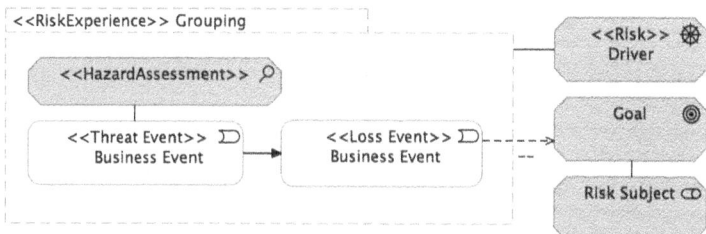

Figure 11.7: The Risk Experience Pattern.

11.5.2 The Bank Run Example in ArchiMate

In order to provide enterprise architects with a common ground to apply game theory notions in coherent enterprise architecture descriptions, we apply the results of the analysis conducted in the previous section to represent the emergence of value and risk from game outcomes in enterprise architecture.

In particular, we employ the ArchiMate modeling patterns based on COVER and presented in section 11.5.1. We use these patterns to represent the emergence of value and risk from outcomes in the context of the Bank Run example (section 11.2.2), under the perspective of Depositor A.

To illustrate the emergence of value, we represent the situation in which both Depositor A and Depositor B retain their deposits until the project matures. We start with the application of the Value Experience pattern. The value subject identifies the perspective from which the judgment is made and whose goals are considered, which in this case corresponds to Depositor A. We represent Depositor A's goal of "Making profit from investment" as the goal the experience realizes. The experience corresponds to the Outcome and is composed of the Action Profile retain-retain (a complex event composed of the actions Depositor A retains and Depositor B retains) that triggers the event "Bank sells the project to another bank after it matures", which in turn triggers the gain event "Bank pays out more than the amount invested". This gain event positively impacts Depositor A's goal of "Making profit from investment".

In order to represent how Depositor A ascribes value to the experience, we apply the Experience Valuation pattern. We connect a Valuation Assessment to the value experience named "Outcome Make profit by retaining deposit" (which corresponds to the Outcome) and to Depositor A, who plays the roles of value assessor and value subject simultaneously. The value ascribed corresponds to Depositor A's Utility Value for this Outcome. Figure 11.8 depicts the application of the patterns just described.

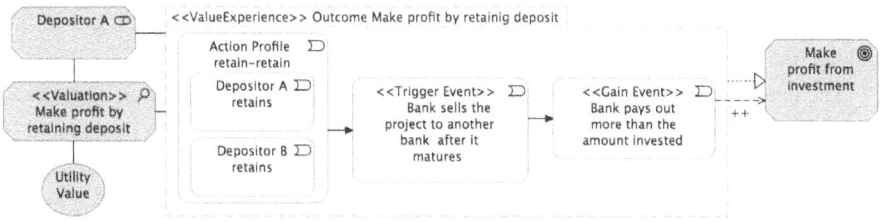

Figure 11.8: Application of the Value Experience and Experience Valuation Patterns.

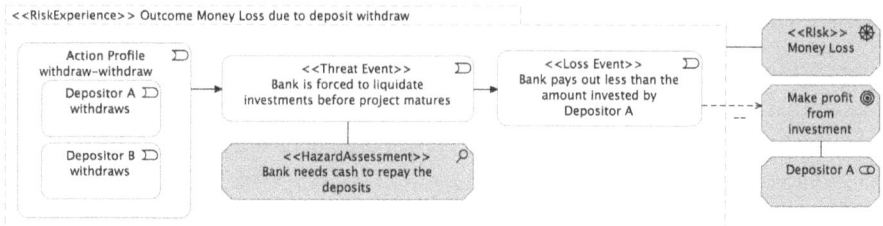

Figure 11.9: Application of the Risk Experience Pattern.

We illustrate the emergence of risk, by representing the situation in which both Depositor A and Depositor B withdraw their deposits before the project matures.

Using the Risk Experience pattern we represent, in figure 11.9, the emergence of the risk of "Money loss", under the perspective of Depositor A, who is the risk subject. The risk experience of "Outcome Money loss due to deposit withdraw" represents the Outcome and is composed of the Action Profile withdraw-withdraw (a complex event composed of the actions Depositor A withdraws and Depositor B withdraws) that brings about a situation in which the "Bank needs cash to repay the deposits". As a result, the "Bank is forced to liquidate investments before project matures", which stands for a threat event that triggers the loss event "Bank pays out less than the amount invested by Depositor A". This loss event hurts Depositor A's goal of "Making profit from investment".

11.6 Final Considerations

We presented an ontological analysis characterizing some basic concepts in game theory, which make clear the emergence of value and risks from game outcomes. We formalized it in OntoUML, aiming at providing an accessible and shareable conceptual model, which may be applied across domains to foster the interoperability and the mutual understanding among modelers.

The model proposed here illustrates a process of *conceptual clarification* that allows for unpacking the relevant domain notions that are frequently hidden in mathematical formulations of domain phenomena. Moreover, it allows for the *ontological grounding* of the variables constituting these mathematical formulations. These are in line with the requirements for conceptual models as discussed in (Guarino, Guizzardi, and Mylopoulos, 2020). In that paper, the authors discuss why a mathematical model (e.g., Newton's

11.6. Final Considerations

Second Law) is not a conceptual model. They argue that in a formula such as F = M * A *"the modeling constructs are operators and variables. The latter do not denote concepts, but rather actual values of physical quantities. Of course we need a mental model to make sense of such relationship, but such mental model is just presupposed, and not made explicit. In contrast, a conceptual model of the phenomenon described by Newton's second law would not represent the values of such physical quantities without representing the physical quantities themselves, which would be considered as qualities...But just having qualities in the conceptual model would not be enough: we cannot have a free-floating quality (say, a mass) without representing its bearer, which is a physical object...This is what we call the grounding requirement"*.

The relation between risk management and game theory has been broadly studied and different approaches have been proposed in the literature to explain how game theory approaches can be integrated into classical risk management (Cox, 2009; Ghavami-Far et al., 2007; Rajbhandari and Snekkenes, 2011; Rass, 2017). Differently from other approaches, our proposal explores the deep connections between the concepts of value and risk to analyse the impact (either positive or negative) of game outcomes on player's welfare.

Chapter 12
Capability Agreements and Risk

In this chapter we use the Common Ontology of Value and Risk (see section 3.2 of chapter 3, section 3.2) to conduct and ontological analysis about the emergence of value and risk in delegation relations, in capability agreements (Amaral, Guizzardi, Guarino, et al., 2019). We rely on the concepts on value and risk defined in COVER to investigate delegation relations, which emerge as a consequence of mismatches between agents' goals and their capabilities. The decision to delegate depends largely on the degree of trust. Interestingly, this decision may create value, as the trustor is endowed with new capabilities, but also implies some risk, as the trustor becomes dependent on the trustee, and consequently, more vulnerable.

This chapter is organized as follows. Section 12.1 motivates the relevance of analyzing the relation between delegation relations and risk, in capability agreements. Section 12.2 discusses what we mean by ontological analysis. In sections 12.3 and 12.4, we conduct an ontological analysis of capability agreements and risk, under the principles of the UFO, and based on COVER. We conclude and present final considerations in section 12.5.

12.1 Introduction

Since the early 1980s, the proliferation and increasing importance of interfirm alliances have received considerable attention in the strategic management literature (Lavie, 2006). As the study of alliance networks has gained popularity, theoretical analysis of the competitive advantage of organizations participating in alliances have been developed, focusing on resource-centric theories (Barney, 1991). Nevertheless, research has shown that it is the services that resources provide, not resources themselves, that generate value for the firm (Edith, 1959). Consequently, ownership or control of resources is not a necessary condition for competitive advantage. In this sense, capability-based theories, which focus on "adapting, integrating, and reconfiguring internal and external organizational skills, resources, and functional competences toward a changing environment" (Teece and Pisano, 1994), have taken shape.

Despite the relevance of capabilities to the success of enterprises, little attention has been given to the theoretical analysis of this concept in the context of interfirm alliances. In this chapter, we tackle this issue by conducting an ontological analysis on the nature of capability agreements, taking into account the broader implications of incorporating external capabilities embedded in the firm's alliance network.

Ontological analysis provides a foundation for our investigation as it enables a deep account of the meaning of a particular domain. Such analysis is based on a foundational ontology (UFO) to offer a domain-agnostic set of concepts drawing ideas from Philosophy and Cognitive Science. In our analysis, we rely on the Common Ontology of Value and Risk, which unifies and clarifies conceptualizations about value and risk, and was designed as an extension UFO.

In sections 12.3 and 12.4 we conduct an ontological analysis of capability agreements, under the principles of the Unified Foundational Ontology (Guizzardi, 2005). As we shall see, our analysis shows an important result: capability agreements expose external dependencies and reveal new vulnerabilities, which may enable the occurrence of risk events. Therefore, we can state that capability agreements imply a relation of duality between capabilities and vulnerabilities: at the same time that it creates a chain of dependencies on capabilities throughout the alliances network, it forms a chain of vulnerabilities, due to the possibility that one or more participant nodes fail to fulfill their commitments. We conclude and present final considerations in section 12.5.

12.2 Ontological Analysis

The notions of ontology and ontological analysis adopted here are akin to their interpretations in philosophy (Berto and Plebani, 2015). In this view, the goals of ontological analysis are: (i) characterize what kinds of entities are assumed to exist by a given conceptualization of a set of phenomena in reality; (ii) the metaphysical nature of these kinds of entities. An ontology, in turn, is a system of categories and their ties (here represented as an artifact) that makes justice to what is uncover by (i) and (ii). In this sense, an ontology is neither merely a logical specification nor it is mainly concerned with making terminological and taxonomic distinctions. For example, in addressing the domains of risk, one is less concerned with what specific subtypes of risk exist (e.g., physical, biological, financial, electronic), but instead with what exactly is risk? (What kind of entity is it? What is its nature?). Is it an object? an event? a relationship? a complex property? If the latter, is a categorical or dispositional property? what is the bearer of such a property?, and so on. Given the nature of this method of analysis, it must be supported by a domain-independent system comprising the most general categories, hence, crosscuting several domains (e.g., objects, events, relationships, dispositions, etc.), i.e., what is termed a foundational ontology (aka top-level or upper-level ontology). In this chapter, we adopt the Unified Foundational Ontology given its successful track record of supporting the ontological analysis of complex notions such as value, risk, service, trust, legal relations, money, decisions, economic preferences, among many others (Amaral, Sales, Guizzardi, and Porello, 2019; Amaral, Sales, Guizzardi, Porello, and Guarino, 2020; Guizzardi, Wagner, Almeida, et al., 2015; Nardi, J. et al., 2015; Porello, Guizzardi, Sales, and Amaral, 2020; Sales, Baião, et al., 2018).

12.3 Capability and Capability Agreement

The term capability is used in a variety of contexts with different meanings and interpretations. However, most views on capability agree that possessing a capability means to have competence and ability (and also the right resources in adequate amount) to do something. Sandkuhl and Stirna (2018) define capability as the ability and capacity that enables an enterprise to achieve a business goal in a certain context. In The Open Group Architecture Framework (TOGAF) (The Open Group, 2018) capability is defined as the ability that an organization, person, or system possesses. In this work we adopt the interpretation of capability proposed by Azevedo, C.L.B. et al. (2015), which defines capability as the power to bring about a desired outcome.

We use the UFO semantics of modes (more specifically, of dispositions) defined in Guizzardi (Guizzardi, Wagner, Falbo, et al., 2013) to represent capabilities. In UFO, a capability is a specific type of disposition that endows their bearers with the potential of exhibiting some behavior or bringing about a certain effect under certain conditions.

When an alliance is formed, a capability agreement is established, and the participants endow a subset of its capabilities to the alliance with the expectation of generating common benefits. Figure 12.1 shows an OntoUML (Guizzardi, 2005) model representing a capability agreement for a single dyadic alliance in which a Focal Agent is endowed with capabilities offered by a Partner Agent. Agent is a rolemixin (Guizzardi, 2005), since it represents roles played by entities of different kinds, e.g., persons and organizations. In our model, both the Focal Agent and the Partner Agent represent organizations.

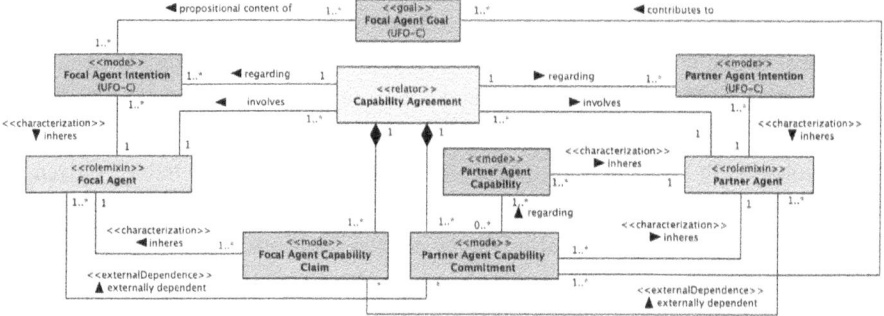

Figure 12.1: Capability Agreement.

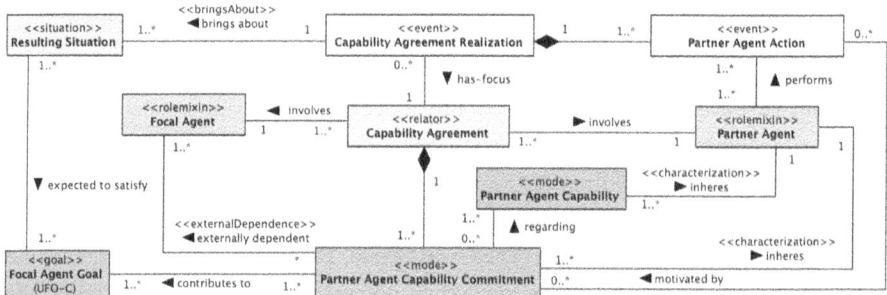

Figure 12.2: Capability Agreement execution.

The Capability Agreement mediates the relation between the Focal Agent and his partner by being a social relator (Guizzardi and Guizzardi, 2010) composed of the Partner Agent's commitments and the Focal Agent's claims with respect to the capabilities offered. Intentions are mental moments (Guizzardi and Guizzardi, 2010) that inhere both in the Focal Agent and in the Partner Agent and are tied to the motivation for establishing the agreement. The propositional contents of Agent's intentions are her goals. By virtue of the capability agreement, the Partner Agent commits to perform actions to achieve the results determined in the agreement. Figure 12.2 represents the execution of these actions.

12.4 Capability Incorporation and Risk

As a result of the capability agreement, the capabilities offered by the Partner Agent are aggregated to the set of capabilities of the Focal Agent, as well as some of the Partner Agent's non-offered capabilities, the latter being derived from opportunities that range beyond the capability agreement immediate scope (for example, an agent may benefit from the partner's reputation, which is not part of the agreement).

The UFO concept of disposition is also applicable for the external capabilities. When an agent delegates to another agent the performance of certain processes that realize a capability, he can still, in a sense, to be considered as having that capability, because he acquires that capability grounded in a relation of delegation (Guizzardi and Guizzardi, 2010). This is related to the idea of what an agent can "socially perform": If A has a commitment from B to execute S, then A (socially) can do S. An object can have dispositions which arise from its parts, or from the network of its delegation relations (Guizzardi and Guizzardi, 2010). In our example, if the Focal Agent has a commitment from the Partner Agent with respect to (w.r.t.) the offered capabilities, then the Focal Agent (socially) has these capabilities.

A further important aspect, related to the motivation behind the establishment of the capability agreement, is the Focal Agent's awareness of her dependence on external agents to satisfy the desire of achieving a certain goal G. With the (social) commitment of the Partner Agent, this desire becomes an intention to G inhering in the Focal Agent. Considering that intentions are self-commitments (Castelfranchi, 1995), the Focal Agent becomes more vulnerable and may be exposed to unanticipated risks. We may get until a much higher level of vulnerability if, believing he has the social capability w.r.t. G, the Focal Agent makes a commitment to someone else (e.g. a Third Agent) to employ this social capability to achieve G. In this case her vulnerability is bigger because, if the Partner Agent doesn't fulfill her commitment on G, not only the Focal Agent's self-commitment to G is frustrated but also her social-commitment to G is frustrated. Moreover, if it is true that a commitment without a corresponding capability entails liability then, if the Third Agent decides to exercise her claim towards the Focal Agent w.r.t. G, not only G but other goals of the Focal Agent may be dented (e.g., the Focal Agent might be subject to legal or social sanction from the Third Agent).

We analyze the relation between external capabilities and risk, based on the Common Ontology of Value and Risk (see section 3.2 of chapter 3). COVER proposes an ontological analysis of notions such as Risk, Risk Event (Threat Event, Loss Event) and Vulnerability, among others.

When a capability agreement is not successfully executed, because the Partner Agent fails to fulfill its commitments, the Resulting Situation (i.e., the one satisfying the Focal Agent's corresponding goal) may not be obtained, and consequently, the Focal Agent may not be able to achieve her goal. In the worst case, the Resulting Situation is a threatening situation that may trigger a Threat Event, which is the one with the potential of causing a loss. The Loss Event is a Risk Event that impacts intentions in a negative way, as it hurts the Focal Agent's intentions of reaching a specific goal. Figure 12.3 represents the relation between external capabilities, vulnerabilities and risk.

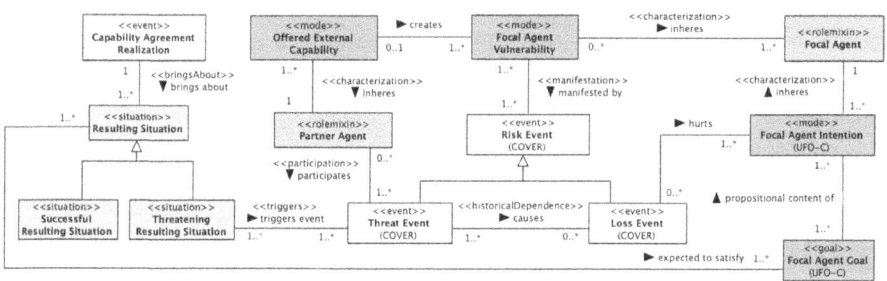

Figure 12.3: Shared capability and risk.

12.5 Final Considerations

In this chapter we conducted an investigation about delegation relations in capability agreements, which emerge as a consequence of mismatches between agents' goals and their capabilities. The ontological foundations on value and risk provided by COVER allowed us to identify some interesting relations between the emergence of value and risk from this kind of agreement. For example, we propose that capability agreements imply a relation of duality between capabilities and vulnerabilities: at the same time that it may create value, as the Focal Agent is endowed with new capabilities, it also implies some risk, as the this agent becomes dependent on the Partner Agent, and consequently, more vulnerable. Capability agreements involve delegation relations that create a chain of dependencies on capabilities throughout the alliances network, which, consequently, form a chain of vulnerabilities between the participant nodes, that may enable the occurrence of risk events. Having a clear understanding of the influence of these forces over delegation networks is fundamental both for the management of risks and for the awareness of the value created through the complex network of interdependencies.

Part V

CONCLUSIONS

Chapter 13
Conclusions

This chapter summarizes the main contributions made in this thesis and explains how they achieve the general and specific research objectives defined in chapter 1. We also discuss the main limitations involving our work and identify some areas for further research. The chapter is organized as follows. Section 13.1 outlines the most important contributions and discusses how they achieve the general and specific research objectives. Section 13.2 discusses the relevance of these outcomes to different stakeholders in the application domain. Section 13.3 explains the main limitations involving our work. Finally, section 13.4 provides recommendations for future work.

13.1 Research Contributions

This thesis presented OntoFINE: an Ontology Network in Finance and Economics. Its general purpose, as defined in the introduction of this work, is *"provide well-founded ontological accounts for the modeling of information in economics and finance, particularly that which is related to money, trust, value, risk and economic exchanges, in order to support economic and financial actors in reasoning with it and adapting to innovations in the financial industry"*. We refined it into more specific objectives, which guided the development of this thesis (see section 1.2). Now, we discuss how the ontologies and applications reported in this thesis achieve them.

The design of the Ontology Network in Finance and Economics (chapter 3). We designed OntoFINE as an integrated ontological framework, built incrementally and in an integrated way. The networked ontologies are developed as reference conceptual models to support humans in tasks such as conceptual clarifications, meaning negotiation and consensus establishment (Guizzardi, 2007). The ontologies are specified in OntoUML, which provides an ecosystem of tools and technologies that allow (among other functionalities) their representation as lightweight ontologies supported by computational algorithms, thus satisfying the need for computational tractability.

OntoFINE architecture is organized in three layers, according to the ontologies generality levels, namely, foundational, core and domain layers. The foundational layer holds the Unified Foundational Ontology, which provides the general ground knowledge for classifying concepts and relations in the ontology network. The core layer is composed of core ontologies, which represent the general domain knowledge, being the basis for the subdomain networked ontologies. At the core layer of OntoFINE are the core ontologies for the domains that are the focus of this thesis, namely, those of money, trust, value, risk and economic exchanges. Finally, at the domain layer, (sub) domain ontologies appear, describing the more specific knowledge. The reference ontology of trustworthiness requirements, developed within the scope of this thesis, is at the domain layer of OntoFINE. Being an ontology network, OntoFINE makes it possible to see the "whole" and at the same time understand each "part" separately. It is also easier to reuse and extend. Furthermore, it allows knowledge to be used as needed: whole or extracts of it.

By focusing on the notions of trust, money, and economic exchanges, OntoFINE provides conceptual clarity in domains that are central to distributed finances. As previously mentioned, with this new paradigm, new forms of trust and digital money, as well as new business models for digital exchanges emerged, giving rise to the need of a better understanding of (for example) the role of trust in this new environment, the emerging business models for decentralized exchanges, as well as the benefits and drawbacks of new forms of digital money. OntoFINE helps by providing a shared conceptualization to improve communication among the different participants in the financial industry, and support the definition of laws, regulations and proper governance models. Furthermore, its lightweight implementation using gUFO (see section 2.3.1 of chapter 2), contributes to dealing with semantic interoperability issues in heterogeneous scenarios, thereby improving information integration and increasing transparency of financial data exchange.

Overall, this contribution forms the backbone for the achievement of the specific objectives 1 to 5, which focus on *developing solid conceptual foundations on trust, money, economic exchanges, risk and value*, respectively (see section 1.2).

Development of a core reference ontology of trust (ROT) integrated to OntoFINE (see chapter 4). To achieve the objective of *developing solid conceptual foundations on trust* (specific objective 1, in section 1.2), we conducted an in-depth ontological analysis of the notion of trust, in which we explored the theoretical literature on trust and its relation to risk. This analysis allowed us to unpack the notion of trust and identify its core components. We identified that trust is always relative to an intention. An agent, the trustor, trusts an individual, the trustee, only relative to a certain intention, on which achievement she counts on the trustee. We argue that trust is a mental state of a trustor regarding a trustee and its behavior. This complex mental state is composed of: (i) an intention; (ii) beliefs that the trustee can perform a desired action or exhibit a desired behavior; (iii) beliefs that the trustee's vulnerabilities will not prevent it from performing the desired action or exhibiting the desired behavior; and (iv) if the trustee is an agent, beliefs that the trustee intends to exhibit that behavior. Understanding the core components of trust is important because if we know which capabilities and vulnerabilities are related to the trustor beliefs, we can reason about what can go wrong with the realization of the capabilities and the manifestation of the vulnerabilities, which will hurt the intentions of the trustor. These unwanted events correspond to risk events for which mitigation strategies may be defined in advance. Moreover, the understanding of the building blocks that compose the trust of agents in a given trustee (such as an organization) is of paramount importance, as they reveal the qualities and properties the trustee should have in order to be considered trustworthy and effectively promote well-placed trust.

Our analysis also identified that trust can be quantified. Our trust in a certain individual can increase or decrease in time, and we can trust certain individuals more than others. To account for these scenarios, our ontology of trust assumes that trust can be quantified, even if it does not commit to any particular scale or measurement strategy.

Lastly, we discussed the dynamic nature of trust. We identified that trust is context-dependent and highly dynamic. We extended our analysis to clarify and provide a deeper account of the different factors that can influence trust, such as mental biases, other trust relations, as well as pieces of evidence that suggest that a trustee should be trusted. We also discussed how trustees can properly communicate about their trustworthy behavior. Understanding the core components of trust and the factors that influence it is fundamental to to build sustainable trust that is not easily lost. Moreover, due to its dynamic nature, trust relations require constant monitoring, as trust changes with time.

Development of a core reference ontology of money and virtual currencies (ROME) integrated to OntoFINE (chapter 5). To accomplish the objective of *developing solid conceptual foundations on money* (specific objective 2, in section 1.2), we conducted an in-depth ontological analysis of the notions of money and currencies, based on the literature review of the most relevant theories on money in economics. In our analysis, we argue that money depends on the collective acceptance or recognition of its status as money. In contemporary society the status function of money is supported by law, which specifies both the currency and the objects that are considered money in a particular country or region. We also identified that money presupposes the existence of a credit/debt relation. Monetary objects establish this relation between the agent holding control of them and the central bank. As for central bank deposits and commercial bank deposits, they correspond to an electronic monetary credit denominated in a certain currency and represent a claim on the central bank or the issuing bank, respectively. From this, it followed that monetary objects and electronic monetary credits have an associated exchange value. Agents holding control of monetary objects or owing electronic monetary credits are endowed with the capacity of making economic transactions in the amount corresponding to their exchange value. The exchange power resulting from the total of electronic monetary credits and monetary objects controlled by an agent stands for an aggregated exchange power that corresponds to the total value in economic transactions the agent is capable to carry out. Furthermore, the aggregated exchange power of an agent has a correspondent purchasing power, which describes the quantity of goods an amount of money can buy.

The ontological unpacking of the notions of money and currency allowed us to properly analyse the ontologic nature of recent innovations in the financial industry, such as criptocurrencies, stablecoins and central bank digital currencies. We were able to characterize the notion of virtual currencies, and distinguish them from official currencies. For example, while central bank digital currencies is a new form of digital money, private cryptocurrencies, although similar to money within their user community, are still considered virtual currencies. An important observation is that things that are currently not considered money, may acquire this status in the future and be instantiated as such in the ontology. The ontological distinctions between money and virtual currencies provided by our ontology are important because, in the financial sector, different rules and controls may apply to official money and virtual currencies, in activities such as issuance, risk assessment, risk mitigation, tax calculations, the elaboration of regulatory responses and governance models, among others.

Development of a core reference ontology for economic exchanges (COEX) integrated to OntoFINE (chapter 6). To address the objective of *developing solid conceptual foundations on economic exchanges* (specific objective 3, in section 1.2), we conducted an ontological analysis on the notion of economic exchanges, based on the investigation of some theories and frameworks on this subject. As a result, we proposed a core ontology for economic exchanges, based on the Action Theory of Economic Exchanges (ATE) (Massin and Tieffenbach, 2016). In this theory, an economic exchange is based on an agreement in which agents commit to performing certain reciprocal actions. This allowed us it to accommodate exchanges involving both products and services. As in the ATE, our core assumption is that, in any economic transaction, the "object" of the transaction is a pair of actions to be performed by the relevant agents involved in it. By viewing the object of transactions as actions, our ontology is capable of accounting for economic transactions about goods as well as services. For this reason, our ontological account on economic exchanges, in addition to being applicable in the context of traditional finance, is ideally suited to applications in the decentralized finance paradigm, which includes decentralized digital exchanges of different types of objects and payments, such as tokenized assets, digital payments denominated in cryptocurrencies, stablecoins, and central bank digital currencies, among others.

In the following, we highlight the main contributions, which are the evidence about the achievement of the objective of *applying the theoretical foundation in practice* (specific objective 6, in section 1.2)

Development of a reference ontology of trustworthiness requirements (ROTwR) integrated to OntoFINE (chapter 7). We conducted an ontological analysis characterizing the concept of trustworthiness requirements of software systems, based on the trust-related concepts defined in our Reference Ontology of Trust and on the ontological interpretation of non-functional requirements presented in (Guizzardi, R. et al., 2014). We define trustworthiness requirements as non-functional requirements, where the desired states-of-affairs are stakeholder mental states that include an attitude of trust towards the system-to-be. Trustworthiness requirements are related to an intention that is part of a trust relation between a stakeholder (the trustor) and the system- to-be (the trustee). According to the Reference Ontology of Trustworthiness Requirements, the system can emit trust-warranting signals to ensure trustworthy behavior. Another important aspect is the role played by pieces of evidence that indicate that the system is is capable of successfully realizing the capabilities and prevent the manifestation of the vulnerabilities. The Reference Ontology of Trustworthiness Requirements ontology is intended to help by "semantically unpacking" the concept of trustworthiness, where the analysts may struggle in understanding, for example, which requirements can make the system under development trustworthy. Once we understand what trustworthiness means and how it relates to other important concepts, we can address trustworthiness since the system's inception thus enabling trustworthiness by design.

Development of an ontology-based requirements engineering method to support the elicitation of trustworthiness requirements (chapter 7). We proposed a novel methodology for ontology-based requirements engineering (ObRE), which applied ROTwR as ontological foundation for the modeling of trustworthiness requirements of software systems. ObRE aims at systematizing the elicitation and analysis of requirements, by using an ontology to conceptually clarify the meaning of challenging requirements such as trustworthiness. The ObRE method consists of three activities: 1) adopt or develop an ontology to conceptually clarify the meaning of a class of requirements; 2) instantiate the ontology for a system-to-be, resulting in a domain model; and 3) use the domain model to guide analysis, resulting in requirements models, such as goal models, requirements tables, user stories etc. ObRE is intended to help a requirements analyst cope with issues such as trustworthiness, where the analysts literally doesn't know where to begin in conducting elicitation and analysis. We demonstrate the working of ObRE by applying it to a real case study concerning trustworthiness requirements, which was conducted in collaboration with the Central Bank of Brazil (BCB). In this study, we made use of ObRE and ROTwR to help with the elicitation of trustworthiness requirements of Pix, the Brazilian Instant Payments Ecosystem created and managed by the BCB.

Modeling of citizens' trust in central bank digital currency ecosystems (chapter 8). As an initiative to demonstrate the applicability of OntoFINE in decentralized finance and its usability to solve real-world problems, we conducted a real case study concerning citizens' trust in central bank digital currency ecosystems, in close collaboration with a national central bank. The Reference Ontology of Trust served as guidance for our work from the beginning of the case study, helping us focus on the domain being investigated and supporting the creation of the questions that would guide the interviews with the stakeholders. As the proper understanding of citizen's trust in CBDCs is only possible if the notions of money, currency and CBDC are clear, we made use of ROME to provide conceptual clarification on these topics. The interviewees answers were used as input to instantiate elements of the ontology. Finally, we used the ontology instantiation as a domain model to create a goal model for this case using the i* framework (Dalpiaz et al., 2016).

Modeling of payments and linked obligation settlements (chapter 9). We proposed and ontology-based approach for the modeling of payments and linked obligation settlement mechanisms, aiming at providing conceptual clarification and supporting semantic interoperability in the context of decentralized finance. Firstly, we created two domain-related ontology patterns by reusing pieces of knowledge extracted from COEX and ROME. Then, we systematically applied these patterns to model payments and linked obligations in OntoUML. Finally, we exported the models to OWL using gUFO, a lightweight implementation of UFO suitable for Semantic Web OWL 2 DL applications.

Development of a trust pattern language for ArchiMate (chapter 10). As an application example of OntoFINE in the context of enterprise modeling, we developed a pattern language for trust modeling in ArchiMate, a standardized enterprise architecture modeling language that is adopted by many organizations. We made use of the concepts on trust and risk defined in ROT and COVER, respectively, to propose a pattern language that consists of a set of interrelated modeling patterns. We also defined a process to support users in combining these patterns. The advantage of a pattern language is that it offers a context in which related patterns can be combined, thus, reducing the space of design choices and design constraints (Falbo et al., 2016). We demonstrated the applicability of the pattern language by means of a realistic case study about trust in a COVID-19 data repository.

Modeling of the emergence of value and risk in game theoretical approaches (chapter 11). We conducted an ontological analysis characterizing some basic concepts in game theory, which made clear the emergence of value and risks from game outcomes. We made use of the concepts and relations defined in COVER to analyze the payoffs of a game in terms of value and risk, as well as how they emerge from outcomes in game theory. We also proposed a formalization of our analysis by means of an ontologically well-founded model, specified in OntoUML, and illustrate its working by instantiating a Bank Run game example. Lastly, apply these results to represent the emergence of value and risk from game outcomes in enterprise architecture models in ArchiMate.

Modeling of the emergence of value and risk from delegation relations in capability agreements (chapter 12). In this initiative, the ontological foundations provided by COVER were applied to analyze the relation between risk, vaule and delegation relations in capability agreements. We analyzed the ontological nature of capability agreements, taking into account the broader implications of incorporating external capabilities. This analysis shows an important result: capability agreements expose external dependencies and reveal new vulnerabilities, which may enable the occurrence of risk events. Moreover, capability agreements imply a relation of duality between value and risk: at the same time that it creates value for providing new capabilities, it creates a chain of dependencies throughout the alliances network. These dependencies makes the dependant entities more vulnerable and exposed to unanticipated risks, due to the possibility that one or more participant nodes fail to fulfill their commitments. This work can serve as inspiration to analyze the occurrence of systemic risks in finance (see subsection 13.4.2).

13.2 Relevance for the Application Domain

Monetary authorities. The conceptual clarity provided by the ontologies presented in this thesis (see chapters 3 to 6) can be used to assist monetary authorities in developing a comprehensive understanding of the potential and the implications of new technological developments for the financial system. This comprehension is fundamental for the definition and adjustment of monetary and financial stability policies before innovations. Our ontological investigation on trust (see chapter 4) can be used to support monetary authorities in their activities to ensure trust in currencies and in the monetary system, as it helps them to identify the building blocks that compose trust and what characteristic a particular institution or system should have to be considered trustworthy (see chapter 8). Furthermore, by improving information integration and semantic interoperability (see chapter 9), OntoFINE contributes to fulfill monetary authorities' needs of reliable analytical data for decision making.

Legislators and regulatory entities The ontologies put forth in this thesis (see chapters 3 to 6) contribute to create a shared understanding of the domains represented — namely, money, trust, value, risk and economic exhanges — among legislators, regulatory entities and other actors in the financial sector, thus avoiding conceptual confusion regarding key concepts. This conceptual clarification ensures unambiguous communication and facilitates consensus establishment in the definition of laws and regulatory frameworks, as well as in their adjustment to support innovations and the emergence of new business models in the financial industry.

Supervisory entities. Supervisory entities have the oversight of financial institutions and other participants of the financial system, by monitoring their capitalization, regulatory compliance and their conduct towards the financial consumers and users, aiming at evaluating and identifying vulnerabilities that may impact the financial system and preventing financial crimes. To exercise their supervisory functions, supervisory entities rely heavily on information obtained by integrating data from multiple and heterogeneous sources. In this context, OntoFINE's reference ontologies can be used as reference models to assign semantics during the integration analysis, thus providing semantic interoperability, as illustrated in chapter 9. Furthermore, these ontologies can play a key role in improving communication with the supervised entities.

Financial institutions. The conceptual clarification provided by OntoFINE (see chapters 3 to 6) is fundamental to help financial institutions to identify opportunities and risks created by technological developments, and consequently, provide better financial products and services to their clients. It also improves their communication with monetary authorities, supervisory entities, citizens and other participants of the financial system. Furthermore, by providing semantic interoperability, the reference ontologies can support financial institutions in regulatory reporting activities — the submission of information to supervisory entities to demonstrate compliance with policies, laws, rules and regulations. Finally, the ontological account on the nature of trust and trust dynamics (see chapter 4) can help financial institutions to identify the characteristics they should have to be considered trustworthy and promote well-placed trust.

Information technology practitioners in the financial sector. For *requirements engineers* and *business analysts* the Ontology-based Requirements Engineering method proposed in chapter 7 can help with the elicitation of challenging requirements, such as trustworthiness (see section 7.4), fairness, privacy and ethicality (Guizzardi, Amaral, et al., 2022). For *ontology engineers*, the reference ontologies proposed in this thesis can serve as ontological foundation and starting point for ontological analysis, as illustrated in chapter 12. They can also be used as ontological resources for building new ontologies (see section 1.3.2 of chapter 2) or creating ontological patterns (see section 9.3.1 of chapter 9). For *enterprise architects*, the Trust Pattern Language proposed in chapter 10 allows the modeling of trust in a meaningful manner. Using the pattern language, architects can model the elements that constitute the trust of an agent with respect to the organizations; the capabilities and vulnerabilities of the enterprise that are the focus of its customers and partner's beliefs, in a trust assessment; the factors that can influence trust assessments; and the risks that can emerge from the trust relations. For *business analysts*, *data scientists* and *data architects*, reference ontologies such as ROME and COEX can be employed in an effective manner to achieve semantic integration, for example, in the provision of solutions based on data analytics and artificial intelligence.

13.3 Limitations

The implementation of the ontologies reported in this thesis in OWL is developed using gUFO[1], a lightweight implementation of the Unified Foundational Ontology, suitable for Semantic Web OWL 2 DL applications, described in (see section 2.3.1 of chapter 2). Due to limitations imposed by the expressiveness of the OWL language, the OWL versions of the ontologies developed in this thesis are rather less expressive than their respective versions in OntoUML. As a lightweight language, gUFO employs little expressive means in an effort to retain computational properties for the resulting OWL ontology. Furthermore, it includes only a subset of UFO-A (Guizzardi, 2005; Guizzardi, Botti Benevides, et al., 2021) and UFO-B (Almeida, Falbo, et al., 2019; Guizzardi, Wagner, Falbo, et al., 2013). For example, the support for UFO-B is limited to the necessary to establish the participation of objects in events and to capture historical dependence between events. In chapter 2 we provide an overview of gUFO. For a detailed description and specification of gUFO, the reader is referred to (Almeida, Guizzardi, et al., 2020).

Another limitation concerns the validation of the ontologies in real-world decentralized production ecosystems. Although they have grown rapidly, decentralized ecosystems are still under design. The initiatives around the world are either at the stage of experimentation, proof-of-concept, or pilot arrangements. Therefore, the demonstrations presented in this thesis were conducted considering the current status of the ongoing initiatives.

A third limitation can be found in the ontology of trust, reported in chapter 4, as we did not model explicitly the decision-making process that creates the decision to trust. When modeling the behavioral perspective of trust we assumed that the *trustor* may take some *actions*, motivated by her *intention* to reach a goal and based on her *trust* in

---

[1] The lightweight versions of the ontologies implemented in gUFO/OWL can be reached through the OntoFINE website, available at purl.org/krdb-core/ontofine.

a particular *trustee*. However, we did not model explicitly the decision-making process that leads to the intention to trust, as it falls outside the scope of this thesis. This could be done, for instance, by reusing concepts and relations defined in the Core Ontology on Decision Making, proposed by Guizzardi, Carneiro, et al. (2020). According to this ontology, motivated by a certain *intention*, an *agent* performs a *deliberation* (an action), which in turn, creates a new *intention* termed a *decision*. As an *intention*, that *decision* can eventually manifest in the performing of an *action* termed a *decision resulting action*.

Another limitation we recognize is that the ontology of economic exchanges, reported in chapter 6, does not represent the unfolding of economic agreements and economic exchanges. For example, the different kinds of social commitments and claims established between *offeror* and *offeree* can ultimately drive the creation of contracts that may refer to resources and capabilities to be used in the fulfillment of a particular agreement. Despite their relevance, these developments fall outside the scope of this thesis and are not modeled in COEX. That is because COEX is a core ontology intended to provide just a general view that enables a unified treatment of economic exchanges, regardless the object of the transaction (e.g. goods and services). As the ontology network evolves, this development can be done by integrating OntoFINE to existing ontologies on this topic, such as the Core Ontology for Financial Reporting Information Systems (COFRIS) (Blums and Weigand, 2016; 2021) and the Financial Industry Business Ontology (FIBO) (Enterprise Data Management Council, 2015).

13.4 Future Work

This section is dedicated to the presentation of our future research agenda, which includes improvements in OntoFINE and its application in the solution of practical problems.

13.4.1 Improvements in OntoFINE

Being an ontology network, OntoFINE is like a living organism and is constantly evolving. Our long-term research objective is to enlarge its coverage by developing and integrating other well-founded ontologies in finance and economics to the ontology network. From this huge domain, we have only ontologically investigated and included some important concepts, namely, money, trust, value, risk and economic exchanges.

Plenty more are still left to be addressed. It requires a continuous and long-term effort with ontologies being added and integrated incrementally.

In order to realize this long-term plan, a possible direction is the integration of existing core and domain ontologies in finance and economics. As previously mentioned, one possibility is the integration of OntoFINE with FIBO, the Financial Industry Business Ontology, presented in section 3.4. FIBO's ontologies are specified in OWL and are not grounded on a foundational ontology, such as UFO (Guizzardi, 2005), GFO (Herre, 2010) or DOLCE (Borgo and Masolo, 2009). Therefore, a first step towards this integration would be the reengineering of FIBO's ontologies to ground them on UFO, which constitutes the foundational layer of OntoFINE.

Figure 13.1 presents an overview of an envisioned integration between OntoFINE and FIBO. This integration could be done by following one or more scenarios of the customized version of the NeOn methodology (Suárez-Figueroa et al., 2012) for building network ontologies, presented in section 1.3.2.

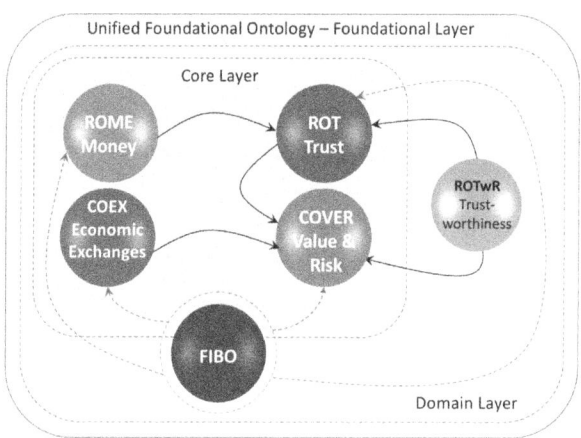

Figure 13.1: Envisioned integration between OntoFINE and FIBO

Another opportunity of improvement is it to broaden the scope of our analysis on trust, to consider the concept of *distrust*. Although the body of literature on trust is much larger than on distrust, conceptual clarification on the latter is important to the analysis of trust dynamics. Distrust is important not only because it allows one to avoid negative consequences, but also because, under some circumstances, it may displace trust as a social mechanism for dealing with risks (McKnight and Chervany, 2001).

13.4. Future Work

While trust, from the positive side, assumes the best of other people and of human institutions, distrust assumes that people are opportunistic and dishonest and must be controlled. According to McKnight and Chervany (2001) trustees may manifest both sides, and each of us is capable of viewing from either side. Analysis of both trust and distrust in a particular trustee is therefore important to balanced decision-making.

We also envision to deepen our analysis on economic exchanges to characterize the particularities of exchanges involving "fractional ownership". One of the benefits of asset tokenization is that it allows the creation of tokens that stand in for a specific fraction of the value of an asset. For example, rather than buying a real state of an artwork, the asset tokenization process allows investors to purchase fractional ownership of these assets. Asset tokenization is still in its infancy and some obstacles still need to be overcome, such as the lack of govern and industry regulation, cybersecurity threats and compliance with securities regulations like anti-money laundering. We believe the conceptual clarification on this subject is fundamental to deal with these challenges.

In this thesis, we follow a customized version of the NeOn methodology (Suárez-Figueroa et al., 2012) for building ontology networks, suited to our context and needs. NeOn provides a scenario-based methodological framework, which includes methods, techniques and tools for carrying out the processes and activities identified and defined in the ontology network development process, such as ontology requirements specification, ontological resources reuse and reengineering, ontology alignment, matching and modularization, as well as ontology evaluation. However, aspects related to the definition of policies, procedures, roles, responsibilities, and metrics that ensure the effective and efficient management of the network evolution are not covered by NeOn. The definition of a proper governance model for ontology networks is (to the best of our knowledge) currently an open issue, which shall be pursued in future investigations.

13.4.2 Applications of OntoFINE in the solution of practical problems

In addition to the improvements in the ontology network we have just discussed, we also envision some application-oriented research opportunities. One of them is to apply the Ontology-based Requirements Engineering (ObRE) method introduced in section 7.5.1 of chapter 7 in the elicitation of other classes of requirements. Besides the application for trustworthiness requirements presented in this thesis (see chapter 7), in (Guizzardi, Amaral, et al., 2022) we have applied it also to help with the elicitation of ethical requirements. We plan to apply it for other types of challenging requirements, such as fairness, privacy and sustainability.

Another opportunity is to leverage our investigation on capability agreements presented in chapter 12 to analyze systemic risk events in finance. We believe that our ontological analysis on the emergence of risks from delegation relations can serve as inspiration to analyze the potential for a threat to propagate disruptions or losses to multiple connected parts of a complex system, as is the case of systemic risks in finance. In the context of finance, systemic risk refers to the risk that the inability of one or more participants of the financial system to perform as expected will cause other participants to be unable to meet their obligations when due. These losses can propagate throughout the entire financial network and, in the worst case, lead to the breakdown of the whole system.

Finally, we plan to apply our results on the investigation on trust to develop a methodology to support trustworthiness by design, so that trust can be part of the design of systems (and ecosystems) since their inception and be prioritized in all aspects of the system (or ecosystem).

Bibliography

Agudo, I., Fernandez-Gago, C., and Lopez, J. (2008). "A Model for Trust Metrics Analysis". In: *Trust, Privacy and Security in Digital Business*. Ed. by S. Furnell, S. K. Katsikas, and A. Lioy. Springer, pp. 28–37.

Aguiar, C. Z. d., Almeida Falbo, R. d., and Souza, V. E. S. (2019). "OOC-O: A reference ontology on object-oriented code". In: *International Conference on Conceptual Modeling*. Springer, pp. 13–27.

Almeida, J., Guizzardi, G., Sales, T. P., and Falbo, R. (2020). *gUFO: A Lightweight Implementation of the Unified Foundational Ontology (UFO)*. Tech. rep. Ontology & Conceptual Modeling Research Group (NEMO) - Federal University of Espirito Santo.

Almeida, J. P. A., Falbo, R. A., and Guizzardi, G. (2019). "Events as entities in ontology-driven conceptual modeling". In: *38th International Conference on Conceptual Modeling*. Vol. 11788. Springer, pp. 469–483.

Almeida Falbo, R. (2014). "SABiO: Systematic Approach for Building Ontologies." In: *ONTO. COM/ODISE@FOIS*.

Almeida Falbo, R. de, Barcellos, M. P., Nardi, J. C., and Guizzardi, G. (2013). "Organizing ontology design patterns as ontology pattern languages". In: *Extended Semantic Web Conference*. Springer, pp. 61–75.

Amaral, G., Guizzardi, G., Guarino, N., Porello, D., and Sales, T. P. (2019). "Capability Agreements and Risk". In: *13th International Workshop on Value Modelling and Business Ontologies (VMBO)*. Vol. 2383. CEUR-WS.org.

Amaral, G., Guizzardi, R., Guizzardi, G., and Mylopoulos, J. (2020). "Ontology-based Modeling and Analysis of Trustworthiness Requirements: Preliminary Results". In: *39th International Conference on Conceptual Modeling (ER)*. Springer, pp. 342–352.

— (2021). "Trustworthiness Requirements: The Pix Case Study". In: *40th International Conference on Conceptual Modeling (ER)*. Springer, pp. 257–267.

Amaral, G., Porello, D., and Guizzardi, G. (2020). "Modeling the Emergence of Value and Risk in Game Theoretical Approaches". In: *10th Enterprise Engineering Working Conference (EEWC)*, pp. 70–91.

Amaral, G., Sales, T. P., and Guizzardi, G. (2021a). "Modeling Payments and Linked Obligation Settlements Mechanisms". In: *11th Enterprise Engineering Working Conference (EEWC)*. Springer.

— (2021b). "Ontological Foundations for Trust Management: Extending the Reference Ontology of Trust". In: *15th International Workshop on Value Modelling and Business Ontologies (VMBO)*. Vol. 2835. CEUR-WS.org, pp. 12–22.

— (2021c). "Towards an Ontology Network in Finance and Economics". In: *11th Enterprise Engineering Working Conference (EEWC)*. Springer.
— (2021d). "Towards Ontological Foundations for Central Bank Digital Currencies". In: *15th International Workshop on Value Modelling and Business Ontologies (VMBO)*. Vol. 2835. CEUR-WS.org, pp. 77–86.
— (2022). "Ontological Foundations for Trust Dynamics: The Case of Central Bank Digital Currency Ecosystems". In: *16th International Conference on Research Challenges in Information Science (RCIS)*. Springer.
Amaral, G., Sales, T. P., Guizzardi, G., Almeida, J. P. A., and Porello, D. (2020). "Modeling Trust in Enterprise Architecture: A Pattern Language for ArchiMate". In: *The Practice of Enterprise Modeling (PoEM)*. Springer, pp. 73–89.
Amaral, G., Sales, T. P., Guizzardi, G., and Porello, D. (2019). "Towards a Reference Ontology of Trust". In: *On the Move to Meaningful Internet Systems: OTM 2019 Conferences*. Springer, pp. 3–21.
— (2020a). "A Reference Ontology of Money and Virtual Currencies". In: *The Practice of Enterprise Modeling (PoEM)*. Springer, pp. 228–243.
— (2020b). *Trust Concerns for Digital Data Repositories: the COVID-19 Data Domain*. Tech. rep. Free University of Bozen-Bolzano.
Amaral, G., Sales, T. P., Guizzardi, G., Porello, D., and Guarino, N. (2020). "Towards a Reference Ontology of Money: Monetary Objects, Currencies and Related Concepts". In: *14th International Workshop on Value Modelling and Business Ontologies (VMBO)*. Vol. 2574. CEUR-WS.org, pp. 170–178.
Arner, D. W., Auer, R., and Frost, J. (2020). "Stablecoins: risks, potential and regulation". In: *Financial Stability Review. N° 39 (Autumm 2020), p. 95-123*.
Arner, D. W., Barberis, J., and Buckley, R. P. (2015). "The evolution of Fintech: A new post-crisis paradigm". In: *Georgetown Journal of International Law* 47, p. 1271.
Arp, R., Smith, B., and Spear, A. D. (2015). *Building ontologies with basic formal ontology*. Mit Press.
Azevedo, C.L.B. et al. (2015). "Modeling resources and capabilities in enterprise architecture: A well-founded ontology-based proposal for ArchiMate". In: *Information systems* 54, pp. 235–262.
Bank for International Settlements (2016). "A glossary of terms used in payments and settlement systems". In.
— (2020). "Enabling open finance through APIs". In.
Bank for International Settlements, Canada, B. of, Bank, E. C., Japan, B. of, Riksbank, S., Bank, S. N., England, B. of, and Governors of the Federal Reserve, B. of (2020). "Central Bank Digital Currencies: Foundational Principles and Core Features". In: *Bank for International Settlements*. Accessed: 2021-01-17. URL: https://www.bis.org/publ/othp33.pdf.
Bank for International Settlements / International Organization of Securities Commissions (2012). "Principles for financial market infrastructures". In.
Bank for International Settlements et al. (2021a). "Central bank digital currencies: system design and interoperability". In: *Bank for International Settlements*.
— (2021b). "Central bank digital currencies: users needs and adoption". In: *Bank for International Settlements*.

Bank of International Settlements (2021). *Ellipse: regulatory reporting and data analytics platform*. Available at https://www.bis.org/about/bisih/topics/suptech_regtech/ellipse.htm (2021/12/16).

Barber, B. (1983). *The logic and limits of trust*. 1st ed. Rutgers University Press.

Barcelos, P. P. F., Santos, V. A. dos, Silva, F. B., Monteiro, M. E., and Garcia, A. S. (2013). "An Automated Transformation from OntoUML to OWL and SWRL". In: *Ontobras* 1041, pp. 130–141.

Barney, J. (1991). "Firm resources and sustained competitive advantage". In: *Journal of management* 17.1, pp. 99–120.

Basel Committee (2013). *Principles for effective risk data aggregation and risk reporting*. URL: https://www.bis.org/publ/bcbs239.htm.

Batteux, E., Avri, B., Johnson, S. G., and Tuckett, D. (2021). "The negative consequences of failing to communicate uncertainties during a pandemic: The case of COVID-19 vaccines". In: *medRxiv*.

Battilossi, S., Cassis, Y., and Yago, K. (2020). *Handbook of the History of Money and Currency*. Springer.

Baxter, W. T. (1989). "Early accounting: The tally and checkerboard". In: *Accounting Historians Journal* 16.2, pp. 43–83.

Bech, M. L. and Garratt, R. (2017). "Central bank cryptocurrencies". In: *BIS Quarterly Review September*.

Bech, M. L., Hancock, J., Rice, T., and Wadsworth, A. (2020). "On the future of securities settlement". In: *BIS Quarterly Review*.

Benevides, A. B., Almeida, J. P. A., and Guizzardi, G. (2019). "Towards a Unified Theory of Endurants and Perdurants: UFO-AB". In: *Proceedings of the Joint Ontology Workshops 2019 Episode V: The Styrian Autumn of Ontology, Graz, Austria, September 23-25, 2019*. Vol. 2518. CEUR Workshop Proceedings. CEUR-WS.org.

Benevides, A. B., Guizzardi, G., Braga, B. F. B., and Almeida, J. P. A. (2010). "Validating Modal Aspects of OntoUML Conceptual Models Using Automatically Generated Visual World Structures". In: *J. Univers. Comput. Sci.* 16.20, pp. 2904–2933.

Bennett, M. (2013). "The financial industry business ontology: Best practice for big data". In: *Journal of Banking Regulation* 14.3, pp. 255–268.

Berentsen, A. and Schär, F. (2018). "A short introduction to the world of cryptocurrencies". In: *FRB of St. Louis Review*.

Berto, F. and Plebani, M. (2015). *Ontology and metaontology: A contemporary guide*. Bloomsbury Publishing.

Bijlsma, M., Cruijsen, C. van der, Jonker, N., and Reijerink, J. (2021). "What triggers consumer adoption of CBDC?" In: *De Nederlandsche Bank Working Paper* 709.

Blums, I. and Weigand, H. (2016). "Towards a reference ontology of complex economic exchanges for accounting information systems". In: *2016 IEEE 20th International Enterprise Distributed Object Computing Conference (EDOC)*. IEEE, pp. 1–10.

— (2017). "Financial Reporting by a Shared Ledger." In: *JOWO*.

— (2019). "A Financial Reporting Ontology for Market, Exchange, and Enterprise Shared Information Systems". In: *Proc. IFIP PoEM*. Springer.

— (2021). "Consolidating Economic Exchange Ontologies for Corporate Reporting Standard Setting". In: *International Conference on Conceptual Modeling*. Springer, pp. 315–329.

Boar, C., Holden, H., and Wadsworth, A. (2020). "Impending arrival - a sequel to the survey on central bank digital currency". In: *Bank for International Settlements* 107.

Boar, C. and Wehrli, A. (2021). "Ready, steady, go?-Results of the third BIS survey on central bank digital currency". In: *Bank for International Settlements*.

Borgo, S. and Masolo, C. (2009). "Foundational choices in DOLCE". In: *Handbook on ontologies*. Springer, pp. 361–381.

Botti Benevides, A., Bourguet, J.-R., Guizzardi, G., Peñaloza, R., and Almeida, J. P. A. (2019). "Representing a reference foundational ontology of events in SROIQ". In: *Applied Ontology* 14.3, pp. 293–334.

Brank, J., Grobelnik, M., and Mladenic, D. (2005). "A survey of ontology evaluation techniques". In: *Proceedings of the conference on data mining and data warehouses (SiKDD 2005)*. Citeseer Ljubljana Slovenia, pp. 166–170.

Bresciani, P., Perini, A., Giorgini, P., Giunchiglia, F., and Mylopoulos, J. (2004). "Tropos: An agent-oriented software development methodology". In: *Autonomous Agents and Multi-Agent Systems* 8.3, pp. 203–236.

Buschmann, F., Henney, K., and Schmidt, D. C. (2007). *Pattern-oriented software architecture, on patterns and pattern languages*. Vol. 5. John Wiley & Sons.

Casati, R. and Varzi, A. (2015). "Events". In: *The Stanford Encyclopedia of Philosophy*. Ed. by E. N. Zalta. Winter 2015. Metaphysics Research Lab, Stanford University.

Castelfranchi, C. and Falcone, R. (2010). *Trust theory: A socio-cognitive and computational model*. Vol. 18. John Wiley & Sons.

Castelfranchi, C. (1995). "Commitments: From Individual Intentions to Groups and Organizations". In: *1st International Conference on Multi-Agent Systems (ICMAS)*. Vol. 95, pp. 41–48.

Central Bank of Brazil (2007). *Synthesis of Brazilian Monetary Standards*. URL: `https://www.bcb.gov.br/ingles/museu-espacos/refmone-i.asp` (visited on 03/13/2020).

Charaf, M., Rosenkranz, C., and Holten, R. (2013). "The emergence of shared understanding: applying functional pragmatics to study the requirements development process". In: *Inf. Syst. J.* 23.2, pp. 115–135.

Chen, Y.-S. and Chang, C.-H. (2012). "Enhance green purchase intentions: The roles of green perceived value, green perceived risk, and green trust". In: *Management Decision*.

Chung, L., Nixon, B., Yu, E., and Mylopoulos, J. (2000). *Non-Functional Requirements in Software Engineering*. Vol. 5. Int. Series in Software Engineering. Springer.

Cohn, M. (2004). *User Stories Applied: For Agile Software Development*. USA: Addison Wesley Longman Publishing Co., Inc.

Committee on Payments and Market Infrastructures (2018). "Central bank digital currencies". In: *Bank for International Settlements*. Accessed: 2021-01-17. URL: `https://www.bis.org/cpmi/publ/d174.pdf`.

Cox Jr, L. A. (2009). "Game theory and risk analysis". In: *Risk Analysis: An International Journal* 29.8, pp. 1062–1068.

Cross, F. B. (2005). "Law and trust". In: *Georgetown Law Journal* 93, p. 1457.
d'Aquin, M. and Gangemi, A. (2011). "Is there beauty in ontologies?" In: *Applied Ontology* 6.3, pp. 165–175.
Dalpiaz, F., Franch, X., and Horkoff, J. (2016). "iStar 2.0 Language Guide". In: *CoRR* abs/1605.07767. URL: http://arxiv.org/abs/1605.07767.
De Bonis, R. and Vangelisti, M. I. (2019). *Moneta - Dai buoi di Omero ai Bitcoin*. Collana Universale Paperbacks il Mulino.
De Bruin, B., Herzog, L., O'Neill, M., and Sandberg, J. (2018). "Philosophy of Money and Finance". In: *Stanford Encyclopedia of Philosophy*.
European Central Bank (2013). "Decision of the European Central Bank of 19 April 2013 on the denominations, specifications, reproduction, exchange and withdrawal of euro banknotes (ECB/2013/10)". In: *Official Journal of the European Union* L118, pp. 37–42.
Derave, T., Prince Sales, T., Gailly, F., and Poels, G. (2021). "Comparing digital platform types in the platform economy". In: *International Conference on Advanced Information Systems Engineering*. Springer, pp. 417–431.
Deutsch, P. (2004). "Models and Patterns". In: *Software factories: Assembling applications with patterns, frameworks, models and tools*. John Wiley & Sons.
Diamond, D. W. and Dybvig, P. H. (1983). "Bank runs, deposit insurance, and liquidity". In: *Journal of political economy* 91.3, pp. 401–419.
Dokoohaki, N. and Matskin, M. (2008). "Effective design of trust ontologies for improvement in the structure of socio-semantic trust networks". In: *International Journal On Advances in Intelligent Systems* 1.1942-2679, pp. 23–42.
Duarte, B. B., Castro Leal, A. L. de, Almeida Falbo, R. de, Guizzardi, G., Guizzardi, R. S., and Souza, V. E. S. (2018). "Ontological foundations for software requirements with a focus on requirements at runtime". In: *Applied Ontology* 13.2, pp. 73–105.
Easley, D., Kleinberg, J., et al. (2012). "Networks, crowds, and markets: Reasoning about a highly connected world". In: *Significance* 9, pp. 43–44.
Edith, T. (1959). "Penrose, The theory of the growth of the firm". In: *New York and Oxford* 53.
Ennew, C. and Sekhon, H. (2007). "Measuring trust in financial services: The trust index". In: *Consumer Policy Review* 17.2, p. 62.
Enterprise Data Management Council (2015). *Financial Industry Business Ontology*. URL: https://spec.edmcouncil.org/fibo/.
Espinoza, A., Abi-Lahoud, E., and Butler, T. (2014). "Ontology-driven financial regulatory change management: an iterative development process". In: *2nd Semantic Web and Linked Open Data workshop (SW-LOD). Anais*.
European Central Bank (2010). *The payment system – payments, securities and derivatives, and the role of the Eurosystem*. Ed. by Tom Kokola. European Central Bank.
— (2012). *Virtual currency schemes*. Tech. rep. European Central Bank, Frankfurt am Main, Germany.
— (2020). "Report on a digital euro". In: *European Central Bank*.
— (2021). "Eurosystem report on the public consultation on a digital euro". In: *European Central Bank*.

European Central Bank, Bank of Japan (2018). "Securities settlement systems: delivery-versus-payment in a distributed ledger environment – Stella project report phase 2". In: *ECB*.

European CentralBank (2015). *Virtual currency schemes–a further analysis*. Tech. rep. European Central Bank, Frankfurt am Main, Germany.

Falbo, R., Barcellos, M., Ruy, F., Guizzardi, G., and Guizzardi, R. (2016). "Ontology pattern languages". In: *Ontology Engineering with Ontology Design Patterns: Foundations and Applications*. IOS Press.

Falcone, R. and Castelfranchi, C. (2004). "Trust dynamics: How trust is influenced by direct experiences and by trust itself". In: *Proceedings of the Third International Joint Conference on Autonomous Agents and Multiagent Systems, 2004. AAMAS 2004*. IEEE, pp. 740–747.

Ferrario, R., Masolo, C., and Porello, D. (2018). "Organisations and Variable Embodiments". In: *Proc. 10th FOIS*. IOS Press, pp. 127–140.

Fettke, P. and Loos, P. (2003). "Ontological evaluation of reference models using the Bunge-Wand-Weber model". In: *AMCIS 2003 Proceedings*, p. 384.

Firger, J. and Caldwell, T. (2020). *Third Alaskan health care worker has allergic reaction to Covid-19 vaccine*. Accessed: 2021-01-10. URL: https://edition.cnn.com/2020/12/18/health/alaska-third-allergic-reaction-vaccine/index.html.

Fischer, P., Lea, S. E., and Evans, K. M. (2013). "Why do individuals respond to fraudulent scam communications and lose money? The psychological determinants of scam compliance". In: *Journal of Applied Social Psychology* 43.10, pp. 2060–2072.

Fischer-Pauzenberger, C. and Schwaiger, W. S. (2017). "The OntoREA© Accounting and Finance model: ontological conceptualization of the accounting and finance domain". In: *International Conference on Conceptual Modeling*. Springer, pp. 506–519.

Fonseca, C. et al. (2019). "Relations in Ontology-Driven Conceptual Modeling". In: *38th International Conference on Conceptual Modeling (ER)*. Vol. 11788. Springer, pp. 28–42.

Fumagalli, M., Sales, T. P., and Guizzardi, G. (2020). "Towards automated support for conceptual model diagnosis and repair". In: *International Conference on Conceptual Modeling*. Springer, pp. 15–25.

Gambetta, D. et al. (2000). "Can we trust trust". In: *Trust: Making and breaking cooperative relations* 13, pp. 213–237.

Gärdenfors, P. (2004). *Conceptual spaces: The geometry of thought*. MIT press.

Gerstl, P. and Pribbenow, S. (1995). "Midwinters, end games, and body parts: a classification of part-whole relations". In: *International journal of human-computer studies* 43.5-6, pp. 865–889.

GhavamiFar, F., Taghiyareh, F., and Razavi, M. (2007). "Game Theory as a Tool for Converting Risk to Opportunity". In.

Giorgini, P., Massacci, F., Mylopoulos, J., and Zannone, N. (2005). "Modeling social and individual trust in requirements engineering methodologies". In: *International Conference on Trust Management*. Springer, pp. 161–176.

Glinz, M. and Fricker, S. (2015). "On shared understanding in software engineering: an essay". In: *Comput. Sci. Res. Dev.* 30.3-4, pp. 363–376.

Golbeck, J., Parsia, B., and Hendler, J. (2003). "Trust networks on the semantic web". In: *International workshop on cooperative information agents*. Springer.

Gonçalves, B., Guizzardi, G., and Pereira Filho, J. G. (2011). "Using an ECG reference ontology for semantic interoperability of ECG data". In: *Journal of biomedical informatics* 44.1, pp. 126–136.

Gordijn, J. and Akkermans, H. (2001). "Designing and evaluating e-business models". In: *IEEE intelligent Systems* 16.04, pp. 11–17.

Griffo, C., Almeida, J. P. A., and Guizzardi, G. (2018). "Conceptual modeling of legal relations". In: *International Conference on Conceptual Modeling*. Springer, pp. 169–183.

Griffo, C., Almeida, J. P. A., Guizzardi, G., and Nardi, J. C. (2017). "From an ontology of service contracts to contract modeling in enterprise architecture". In: *Proc. 21st IEEE EDOC*, pp. 40–49.

Guarino, N. (1998). *Formal ontology in information systems: Proceedings of the first international conference (FOIS'98), June 6-8, Trento, Italy*. Vol. 46. IOS press, pp. 3–15.

— (2017). "On the semantics of ongoing and future occurrence identifiers". In: *International Conference on Conceptual Modeling*. Springer, pp. 477–490.

Guarino, N. and Guizzardi, G. (2015). ""We need to discuss the Relationship": Revisiting Relationships as Modeling Constructs". In: *Proc. 27th CAiSE*. Springer.

— (2016). "Relationships and events: towards a general theory of reification and truthmaking". In: *Conference of the Italian Association for Artificial Intelligence*. Springer, pp. 237–249.

Guarino, N., Guizzardi, G., and Mylopoulos, J. (2020). "On the Philosophical Foundations of Conceptual Models". In: *Information Modelling and Knowledge Bases XXXI* 321, p. 1.

Guarino, N., Guizzardi, G., and Sales, T. P. (2018a). "On the Ontological Nature of REA Core Relations". In: *Value Modeling and Business Ontologies (VMBO)*, pp. 89–98.

— (2018b). "On the Ontological Nature of REA Core Relations." In: *VMBO*, pp. 89–98.

Guidoni, G. L., Almeida, J. P. A., and Guizzardi, G. (2021). "Forward Engineering Relational Schemas and High-Level Data Access from Conceptual Models". In: *International Conference on Conceptual Modeling*. Springer, pp. 133–148.

Guizzardi, G. (2005). *Ontological foundations for structural conceptual models*. Telematica Instituut / CTIT.

— (2006a). "The role of foundational ontologies for conceptual modeling and domain ontology representation". In: *2006 7th International Baltic conference on databases and information systems*. IEEE, pp. 17–25.

— (2007). "On ontology, ontologies, conceptualizations, modeling languages, and (meta) models". In: *Frontiers in artificial intelligence and applications* 155, p. 18.

Guizzardi, G., Baião, F., Lopes, M., and Falbo, R. (2010). "The role of foundational ontologies for domain ontology engineering: An industrial case study in the domain of oil and gas exploration and production". In: *International Journal of Information System Modeling and Design (IJISMD)* 1.2, pp. 1–22.

Guizzardi, G., Botti Benevides, A., Fonseca, C. M., Porello, D., Almeida, J. P. A., and Prince Sales, T. (2021). "UFO: Unified Foundational Ontology". In: *Applied Ontology* Preprint, pp. 1–44.

Guizzardi, G., Falbo, R. A., and Guizzardi, R. S. (2008a). "The role of Foundational Ontologies for Domain Ontology Engineering: a case study in the Software Process Domain". In: *IEEE Latin America Transactions* 6.3, pp. 244–251.

Guizzardi, G., Falbo, R. A., and Guizzardi, R. S. S. (2008b). "Grounding software domain ontologies in the Unified Foundational Ontology (UFO)". In: *11th Ibero-American Conference on Software Engineering (CIbSE)*, pp. 127–140.

Guizzardi, G., Fonseca, C. M., Almeida, J. P. A., Sales, T. P., Benevides, A. B., and Porello, D. (2021). "Types and taxonomic structures in conceptual modeling: A novel ontological theory and engineering support". In: *Data & Knowledge Engineering* 134.

Guizzardi, G., Fonseca, C. M., Benevides, A. B., Almeida, J. P. A., Porello, D., and Sales, T. P. (2018). "Endurant Types in Ontology-Driven Conceptual Modeling: Towards OntoUML 2.0". In: *37th International Conference on Conceptual Modeling*. Springer, pp. 136–150.

Guizzardi, G., Graças, A. P. das, and Guizzardi, R. S. (2011). "Design patterns and inductive modeling rules to support the construction of ontologically well-founded conceptual models in OntoUML". In: *CAISE Workshops*. Springer, pp. 402–413.

Guizzardi, G., Wagner, G., Almeida, J. P. A., and Guizzardi, R. S. S. (2015). "Towards ontological foundations for conceptual modeling: the Unified Foundational Ontology (UFO) story". In: *Applied ontology* 10.3-4, pp. 259–271.

Guizzardi, G., Wagner, G., Falbo, R. A., Guizzardi, R. S. S., and Almeida, J. P. A. (2013). "Towards ontological foundations for the conceptual modeling of events". In: *32nd International Conference on Conceptual Modeling (ER)*. Springer, pp. 327–341.

Guizzardi, R. (2006b). "Agent-oriented Constructivist Knowledge Management". PhD thesis. Netherlands: University of Twente.

Guizzardi, R., Amaral, G., Guizzardi, G., and Mylopoulos, J. (2022). "Eliciting Ethicality Requirements Using the Ontology-Based Requirements Engineering Method". In: *27th International Conference on Evaluation and Modeling Methods for Systems Analysis and Development (EMMSAD)*. Springer, pp. 221–236.

Guizzardi, R. S. S. and Guizzardi, G. (2010). "Ontology-based transformation framework from TROPOS to AORML". In: *Social modeling for requirements engineering*. The MIT Press, pp. 547–570.

Guizzardi, R. S., Carneiro, B. G., Porello, D., and Guizzardi, G. (2020). "A Core Ontology on Decision Making." In: *ONTOBRAS*, pp. 9–21.

Guizzardi, R. et al. (2014). "An Ontological Interpretation of Non-Functional Requirements." In: *8th International Conference on Formal Ontology in Information Systems*. Vol. 14, pp. 344–357.

Gunning, D. and Aha, D. W. (2019). "DARPA's Explainable Artificial Intelligence Program". In: *AI Magazine* 40.2, pp. 44–58.

Herre, H. (2010). "General Formal Ontology (GFO): A foundational ontology for conceptual modelling". In: *Theory and applications of ontology: computer applications*. Springer, pp. 297–345.

Herzog, L. (2017). "Markets". In: *The Stanford Encyclopedia of Philosophy*. Ed. by E. N. Zalta. Fall 2017. Metaphysics Research Lab, Stanford University.

Hevner, A. and Chatterjee, S. (2010). "Design science research in information systems". In: *Design research in information systems*. Springer, pp. 9–22.

Hleg, A.I. (2019). "Ethics Guidelines for Trustworthy AI". In: *B-1049 Brussels*.

Hoekstra, R., Breuker, J., Di Bello, M., Boer, A., et al. (2007). "The LKIF Core Ontology of Basic Legal Concepts." In: *LOAIT* 321, pp. 43–63.

Huang, J. and Fox, M. S. (2006). "An ontology of trust: formal semantics and transitivity". In: *Proceedings of the 8th international conference on Electronic commerce: The new e-commerce: innovations for conquering current barriers, obstacles and limitations to conducting successful business on the internet*. ACM, pp. 259–270.

Hussain, A., Mkpojiogu, E., and Kamal, F. (Oct. 2016). "The Role of Requirements in the Success or Failure of Software Projects". In: *EJ Econjournals* 6, pp. 6–7.

Innes, A. M. (1913). "What is Money?" In: *The Banking Law Journal. maio*.

ISO (2013). *Financial services - Universal financial industry message scheme - ISO 20022:2013*.

— (2015). *Codes for the representation of currencies - ISO 4217:2015*.

ISO: Risk Management - Vocabulary (2018). Standard. International Organization for Standardization.

ISO: Risk Management - Guidelines (2009). Standard. International Organization for Standardization.

Jacobsen, A. et al. (2020). "FAIR Principles: Interpretations and Implementation Considerations". In: *Data Intelligence* 2.1-2, pp. 10–29.

Jacquette, D. (2013). "Belief state intensity". In: *New Essays on Belief*. Springer, pp. 209–229.

Jarzabkowski, P. and Wilson, D. C. (2006). "Actionable Strategy Knowledge: A Practice Perspective". In: *European Management Journal* 24.5, pp. 348–367.

Jureta, I. J., Mylopoulos, J., and Faulkner, S. (2009). "A core ontology for requirements". In: *Applied Ontology* 4.3-4, pp. 169–244.

Kambil, A., Ginsberg, A., and Bloch, M. (1996). "Re-inventing value propositions". In: *Information Systems Working Papers Series, Vol*.

Keet, C. M. (2011). "The use of foundational ontologies in ontology development: an empirical assessment". In: *Extended Semantic Web Conference*. Springer, pp. 321–335.

Keynes, J. M. (1971). *A Treatise on Money: V. 1: The Pure Theory of Money*. Macmillan, St. Martin's for the Royal Economic Society.

Khadjimamedov, A. and Kizi, K. M. (2021). "THE ESSENCE OF SWIFT NETWORK IN INTERNATIONAL TRANSACTIONS". In: *ResearchJet Journal of Analysis and Inventions* 2.07, pp. 51–57.

Knapp, G. F. (1924). *The state theory of money*. Tech. rep. McMaster University Archive for the History of Economic Thought.

Kochergina, D. and Yangirovab, A. (2019). "Central Bank Digital Currencies: Key Characteristics and Directions of Influence on Monetary and Credit and Payment Systems". In: *Finance: Theory and Practice* 23.4, pp. 80–98.

Kud, A. (2019). "Substantiation of the Term "Digital Asset": Economic and Legal Aspects ". In: *International Journal of Education and Science* 2.1, pp. 41–52.

Lanning, M. J. and Michaels, E. G. (1988). "A business is a value delivery system". In: *McKinsey staff paper* 41.July.

Laurent, P., Chollet, T., Burke, M., and Seers, T. (2018). "The tokenization of assets is disrupting the financial industry. Are you ready?" In: *Inside Magazine* 19, pp. 62–67.

Laurier, W., Kiehn, J., and Polovina, S. (2018). "REA 2: A unified formalisation of the Resource-Event-Agent ontology". In: *Applied Ontology* 13.3, pp. 201–224.

Lavie, D. (2006). "The competitive advantage of interconnected firms: An extension of the resource-based view". In: *Academy of management review* 31.3, pp. 638–658.

Leite, L. and Cappelli, C. (2010). "Software transparency". In: *Bus Inf Syst Eng* 2.3.
Lemieux, V. L. and Feng, C. (2021). *Building Decentralized Trust*. Springer.
Letier, E. and Van Lamsweerde, A. (2004). "Reasoning about partial goal satisfaction for requirements and design engineering". In: *Proc. 12th ACM SIGSOFT on Foundations of software engineering*, pp. 53–62.
Lewis, J. D. and Weigert, A. (1985). "Trust as a social reality". In: *Social forces* 63.4.
Luhmann, N. (2018). *Trust and power*. John Wiley & Sons.
Macleod, H. (1890). *The Theory of Credit*. Vol. 2. Longmans, Green, and Company.
Mancini-Griffoli, T., Peria, M. S. M., Agur, I., Ari, A., Kiff, J., Popescu, A., and Rochon, C. (2018). "Casting light on central bank digital currency". In: *IMF Staff Discussion Notes* 18-08.
Mann, F. A. (1938). *The Legal Aspect of Money*. Milford.
Marsh, S. P. (1994). "Formalising trust as a computational concept. Ph.D. thesis". In: *University of Stirling, Department of Computer Science and Mathematics*.
Masolo, C., Borgo, S., Gangemi, A., Guarino, N., and Oltramari, A. (2003). "Ontology library (wonderweb deliverable d18)". In: *URL: http://www. loa-cnr. it/Papers D* 18, p. 36.
Massin, O. and Tieffenbach, E. (2016). "The metaphysics of economic exchanges". In: *Journal of Social Ontology* 3.2, pp. 167–205.
Mayer, N. and Feltus, C. (2017). "Evaluation of the risk and security overlay of ArchiMate to model information system security risks". In: *2017 IEEE 21st International Enterprise Distributed Object Computing Workshop*. IEEE, pp. 106–116.
Mayer, R. C., Davis, J. H., and Schoorman, F. D. (1995). "An integrative model of organizational trust". In: *Academy of management review* 20.3, pp. 709–734.
McCarthy, W. (June 2007). *ISO 15944-4 - REA Ontology*. ISO.
McGuinness, D. L., Ding, L., Da Silva, P. P., and Chang, C. (2007). "PML 2: A Modular Explanation Interlingua." In: *ExaCt*, pp. 49–55.
McKelvey, R. D., McLennan, A. M., and Turocy, T. L. (2006). "Gambit: Software tools for game theory". In.
McKnight, D. H. and Chervany, N. L. (2001). "Trust and distrust definitions: One bite at a time". In: *Trust in Cyber-societies*. Springer, pp. 27–54.
McKnight, D. H., Liu, P., and Pentland, B. T. (2012). "How events affect trust: A baseline information processing model with three extensions". In: *IFIP International Conference on Trust Management*. Springer, pp. 217–224.
Mehra, M. R., Desai, S. S., Ruschitzka, F., and Patel, A. N. (May 2020). "RETRACTED: Hydroxychloroquine or chloroquine with or without a macrolide for treatment of COVID-19: a multinational registry analysis". In: *The Lancet*.
Mehra, M. R., Ruschitzka, F., and Patel, A. N. (2020). "Retraction—Hydroxychloroquine or chloroquine with or without a macrolide for treatment of COVID-19: a multinational registry analysis". In: *The Lancet* 395.10240, p. 1820.
Menger, C. (2009). "On the Origins of Money". In: *CA Foley, Auburn, AL: Ludwig von Mises Institute*.
Mohammadi, G. (2019). *Trustworthy Cyber-Physical Systems*. Springer.

Moltmann, F. (2020). "Variable Objects and Truthmaking Friederike Moltmann". In: *Metaphysics, Meaning, and Modality*, pp. 368–394.

Moreira, J. L. R., Sales, T. P., Guerson, J., Braga, B. F. B., Brasileiro, F., and Sobral, V. (2016). "Menthor Editor: An Ontology-Driven Conceptual Modeling Platform." In: *JOWO@ FOIS*.

Moyano, F., Fernandez-Gago, C., and Lopez, J. (2012). "A conceptual framework for trust models". In: *International Conference on Trust, Privacy and Security in Digital Business*. Springer, pp. 93–104.

Mukhopadhyay, U., Skjellum, A., Hambolu, O., Oakley, J., Yu, L., and Brooks, R. (2016). "A brief survey of cryptocurrency systems". In: *14th annual conference on privacy, security and trust*. IEEE, pp. 745–752.

Myerson, R. (1991). "Game Theory: Analysis of Conflict". In: *Press, Cambridge*.

Nardi, J. C., Almeida Falbo, R. de, Almeida, J. P. A., Guizzardi, G., Pires, L. F., Sinderen, M. J. van, and Guarino, N. (2013). "Towards a commitment-based reference ontology for services". In: *2013 17th IEEE International Enterprise Distributed Object Computing Conference*. IEEE, pp. 175–184.

Nardi, J. et al. (2015). "A commitment-based ref. ontology for services". In: *Inf.Syst.* 54.

— (2019). "An Ontology-based Diagnosis of Mainstream Service Modeling Languages". In: *Proc. IEEE 23rd EDOC*. IEEE, pp. 112–121.

Nassar, M., Salah, K., Rehman, M. H. ur, and Svetinovic, D. (2020). "Blockchain for explainable and trustworthy artificial intelligence". In: *Wiley Interdisciplinary Reviews: Data Mining and Knowledge Discovery* 10.1, e1340.

Niles, I. and Pease, A. (2001). "Towards a standard upper ontology". In: *Proceedings of the international conference on Formal Ontology in Information Systems-Volume 2001*, pp. 2–9.

O'Leary, D. E. (1998). "Using AI in knowledge management: Knowledge bases and ontologies". In: *IEEE Intelligent Systems and Their Applications* 13.3, pp. 34–39.

Oberle, D., Grimm, S., and Staab, S. (2009). "An ontology for software". In: *Handbook on ontologies*. Springer, pp. 383–402.

Oliveira Bringuente, A. C. de, Almeida Falbo, R. de, and Guizzardi, G. (2011). "Using a foundational ontology for reengineering a software process ontology". In: *Journal of Information and Data Management* 2.3, pp. 511–511.

Osborne, M. J. and Rubinstein, A. (1994). *A course in game theory*. MIT press.

"Oxford English Dictionary" (1989). In: *Simpson, JA & Weiner, ESC*.

Paja, E., Chopra, A. K., and Giorgini, P. (2013). "Trust-based specification of sociotechnical systems". In: *Data & Knowledge Engineering* 87, pp. 339–353.

Papadopoulos, G. (2015). *The ontology of money: institutions, power and collective intentionality*. Erasmus University Rotterdam.

Payolo, A. R. (2020). "A toilet paper run is like a bank run. The economic fixes are about the same". In: *The Conversation*. URL: %7Bhttps://theconversation.com/a-toilet-paper-run-is-like-a-bank-run-the-economic-fixes-are-about-the-same-133065%7D.

Peffers, K., Tuunanen, T., Rothenberger, M. A., and Chatterjee, S. (2007). "A design science research methodology for information systems research". In: *Journal of management information systems* 24.3, pp. 45–77.

Peterson, M. (2017). *An introduction to decision theory*. Cambridge University Press.

Polack, F. P., Thomas, S. J., Kitchin, N., Absalon, J., Gurtman, A., Lockhart, S., Perez, J. L., Pérez Marc, G., Moreira, E. D., Zerbini, C., et al. (2020). "Safety and efficacy of the BNT162b2 mRNA Covid-19 vaccine". In: *New England Journal of Medicine*.

Porello, D., Bottazzi, E., and Ferrario, R. (2014). "The Ontology of Group Agency". In: *Proc. 8th FOIS, Rio de Janeiro, IOS Press*, pp. 183–196. DOI: 10.3233/978-1-61499-438-1-183.

Porello, D. and Guizzardi, G. (2018). "Towards an Ontological Modelling of Preference Relations". In: *International Conference of the Italian Association for Artificial Intelligence*, pp. 152–165.

Porello, D., Guizzardi, G., Sales, T. P., and Amaral, G. (2020). "A Core Ontology for Economic Exchanges". In: *39th International Conference on Conceptual Modeling (ER)*. Springer, pp. 364–374.

Porello, D., Guizzardi, G., Sales, T. P., Amaral, G., and Guarino, N. (2020). "An ontological account of the action theory of economic exchanges". In: *14th International Workshop on Value Modelling and Business Ontologies (VMBO)*. Vol. 2574. CEUR-WS.org, pp. 157–169.

Pribbenow, S. (2002). "Meronymic relationships: From classical mereology to complex part-whole relations". In: *The semantics of relationships*. Springer, pp. 35–50.

Rajbhandari, L. and Snekkenes, E. A. (2011). "Mapping between classical risk management and game theoretical approaches". In: *IFIP International Conference on Communications and Multimedia Security*. Springer, pp. 147–154.

Rass, S. (2017). "On game-theoretic risk management (part three)-modeling and applications". In: *arXiv preprint arXiv:1711.00708*.

Riegelsberger, J., Sasse, M. A., and McCarthy, J. D. (2005). "The mechanics of trust: A framework for research and design". In: *International Journal of Human-Computer Studies* 62.3, pp. 381–422.

Rosemann, M. (2019). "Trust-Aware Process Design". In: *International Conference on Business Process Management*. Springer, pp. 305–321.

Rosemann, M., Green, P., and Indulska, M. (2004). "A reference methodology for conducting ontological analyses". In: *International Conference on Conceptual Modeling*. Springer, pp. 110–121.

Ross, D. T. and Schoman, K. E. (1977). "Structured analysis for requirements definition". In: *IEEE transactions on Software Engineering* 1, pp. 6–15.

Rotter, J. B. (1967). "A new scale for the measurement of interpersonal trust". In: *Journal of personality* 35.4, pp. 651–665.

Rousseau, D. M., Sitkin, S. B., Burt, R. S., and Camerer, C. (1998). "Not so different after all: A cross-discipline view of trust". In: *Academy of management review* 23.3.

Rybola, Z. and Pergl, R. (2016). "Towards OntoUML for software engineering: transformation of anti-rigid sortal types into relational databases". In: *International Conference on Model and Data Engineering*. Springer, pp. 1–15.

Sadhya, V., Sadhya, H., Hirschheim, R., and Watson, E. (2018). "Exploring technology trust in Bitcoin: The blockchain exemplar". In: *European Conference in Information Systems*. Research Papers 5.

Saleme, E. B., Santos, C. A., Almeida Falbo, R. de, Ghinea, G., and Andres, F. (2019). "MulseOnto: a Reference Ontology to Support the Design of Mulsemedia Systems." In: *J. Univers. Comput. Sci.* 25.13, pp. 1761–1786.

Sales, T. P. (2019). "Ontological Foundations for Strategic Business Modeling: The Case of Value, Risk and Competition". PhD thesis. University of Trento.

Sales, T. P., Almeida, J. P. A., Santini, S., Baião, F., and Guizzardi, G. (2018). "Ontological Analysis and Redesign of Risk Modeling in ArchiMate". In: *2018 IEEE 22nd International Enterprise Distributed Object Computing Conference*. IEEE, pp. 154–163.

Sales, T. P., Baião, F., Guizzardi, G., Guarino, N., and Mylopoulos, J. (2018). "The Common Ontology of Value and Risk". In: *37th International Conference on Conceptual Modeling (ER)*. Vol. 11157. Springer, pp. 121–135.

Sales, T. P., Guarino, N., Guizzardi, G., and Mylopoulos, J. (2017a). "An Ontological Analysis of Value Propositions". In: *21st IEEE International Enterprise Distributed Object Computing Conference (EDOC)*. IEEE, pp. 184–193.

— (2017b). "An ontological analysis of value propositions". In: *Proc. IEEE 21st EDOC*. IEEE, pp. 184–193.

Sales, T. P. and Guizzardi, G. (2015). "Ontological anti-patterns: Empirically uncovered error-prone structures in ontology-driven conceptual models". In: *Data & Knowledge Eng.* 99, pp. 72–104.

— (2017). ""Is It a Fleet or a Collection of Ships?": Ontological Anti-patterns in the Modeling of Part-Whole Relations". In: *European Conference on Advances in Databases and Information Systems*. Springer, pp. 28–41.

Sales, T. P., Porello, D., Guarino, N., Guizzardi, G., and Mylopoulos, J. (2018). "Ontological Foundations of Competition." In: *FOIS*, pp. 96–109.

Sales, T. P., Roelens, B., Poels, G., Guizzardi, G., Guarino, N., and Mylopoulos, J. (2019). "A pattern language for value modeling in ArchiMate". In: *International Conference on Advanced Information Systems Engineering*. Springer, pp. 230–245.

Sandkuhl, K. and Stirna, J. (2018). *Capability Management in Digital Enterprises*. 1. Springer.

Santos Jr, P. S., Almeida, J. P. A., and Guizzardi, G. (2010). "An ontology-based semantic foundation for organizational structure modeling in the aris method". In: *2010 14th IEEE International Enterprise Distributed Object Computing Conference Workshops*. IEEE, pp. 272–282.

Savani, R. and Stengel, B. von (2015). "Game Theory Explorer: software for the applied game theorist". In: *Computational Management Science* 12.1, pp. 5–33.

Sazandrishvili, G. (2020). "Asset tokenization in plain English". In: *Journal of Corporate Accounting & Finance* 31.2, pp. 68–73.

Schär, F. (2021). "Decentralized finance: On blockchain-and smart contract-based financial markets". In: *FRB of St. Louis Review*.

Scherp, A., Saathoff, C., Franz, T., and Staab, S. (2011). "Designing core ontologies". In: *Applied Ontology* 6.3, pp. 177–221.

Scholes, M. et al. (2010). *Regulating Wall Street: The Dodd-Frank Act and the new architecture of global finance*. Vol. 608. John Wiley & Sons.

Schulz, S. (2018). "The Role of Foundational Ontologies for Preventing Bad Ontology Design." In: *JOWO*.

Searle, J. (1995). *The Construction of Social Reality*. Free Press.

Searle, J. R. (2017). "Money: ontology and deception". In: *Cambridge Journal of Economics* 41.5, pp. 1453–1470.

Shanks, G., Tansley, E., and Weber, R. (2003). "Using ontology to validate conceptual models". In: *Communications of the ACM* 46.10, pp. 85–89.

Sharifi, S., Parvizimosaed, A., Amyot, D., Logrippo, L., and Mylopoulos, J. (2020). "Symboleo: Towards a specification language for legal contracts". In: *2020 IEEE 28th International Requirements Engineering Conference (RE)*. IEEE, pp. 364–369.

Shoham, Y. and Leyton-Brown, K. (2008). *Multiagent systems: Algorithmic, game-theoretic, and logical foundations*. Cambridge University Press.

Simmel, G. (2004). *The philosophy of money*. Psychology Press.

Söilen, K. S. and Benhayoun, L. (2021). "Household acceptance of central bank digital currency: the role of institutional trust". In: *International Journal of Bank Marketing*.

Stanley-Smith, J. and Schwanke, A. (2016). "Pokemon GO Could Get Caught in a Tax Bubble". In: *Int'l Tax Rev.* 27, p. 22.

Suarez-Figueroa, M. C., Gomez-Perez, A., Motta, E., and Gangemi, A. (2012). "Introduction: Ontology engineering in a networked world". In: *Ontology engineering in a networked world*. Springer, pp. 1–6.

Suárez-Figueroa, M. C., Gómez-Pérez, A., Motta, E., and Gangemi, A., eds. (2012). *Ontology Engineering in a Networked World*. Springer Berlin Heidelberg.

Sullivan, K. (2020). *Biden receives first dose of Covid-19 vaccine on live television*. Accessed: 2021-01-10. URL: https://edition.cnn.com/2020/12/21/politics/bidens-coronavirus-vaccination/index.html.

Sun, S. and Sun, N. (2018). "The Fundamentals of Non-cooperative Games". In: *Management Game Theory*. Singapore: Springer Singapore, pp. 1–21.

Teece, D. and Pisano, G. (1994). "The dynamic capabilities of firms: an introduction". In: *Industrial and corporate change* 3.3, pp. 537–556.

"Treaty on the Functioning of the European Union" (2012). In: *Official Journal of the European Union* C326, pp. 47–390.

The Open Group (2017). *ArchiMate 3.0.1 Specification. Standard C179*.

— (2018). *TOGAF Standard, Version 9.2*.

Tomsett, Richard et al. (2020). "Rapid trust calibration through interpretable and uncertainty-aware AI". In: *Patterns* 1.4, p. 100049.

Tyler, T. R. (2006). *Why people obey the law*. Princeton University Press.

Vajda, J., Merrell, E., and Smith, B. (2019). "Toward an Ontology of Commercial Exchange". In: *Proc. 5th JOWO*. Vol. 2518. CEUR-WS.org.

Van Lamsweerde, A. (2009). *Requirements Engineering - From System Goals to UML Models to Software Specifications*. Chichester, UK: John Wiley & Sons.

Varzi, A. C. (2007). "Omissions and causal explanations". In: *Agency and Causation in the Human Sciences*. Paderborn, Germany: Mentis Verlag, pp. 155–67.

Verdonck, M. and Gailly, F. (2016). "Insights on the Use and Application of Ontology and Conceptual Modeling Languages in Ontology-Driven Conceptual Modeling". In: *Proc.35th ER*.

Viljanen, L. (2005). "Towards an ontology of trust". In: *International Conference on Trust, Privacy and Security in Digital Business*. Springer, pp. 175–184.

Von Mises, L. (2013). *The theory of money and credit*. Skyhorse Publishing, Inc.

Vrandečić, D. (2009). "Ontology evaluation". In: *Handbook on ontologies*. Springer, pp. 293–313.

Walterbusch, M., Gräuler, M., and Teuteberg, F. (2020). "How trust is defined: A qualitative and quantitative analysis of scientific literature". In: *Twentieth Americas Conference on Information Systems*.

Watson, J. (2002). *Strategy: an introduction to game theory*. Vol. 139. WW Norton New York.

Weber, I. and Staples, M. (2022). "Programmable money: next-generation blockchain-based conditional payments". In: *Digital Finance*, pp. 1–17.

Weigand, H., Blums, I., and Kruijff, J. de (2020). "Shared Ledger Accounting—Implementing the Economic Exchange pattern". In: *Information Systems* 90, p. 101437.

Werner, C., Li, Z., Ernst, N., and Damian, D. (2020). "The Lack of Shared Understanding of Non-Functional Requirements in Continuous Software Engineering: Accidental or Essential?" In: *28th IEEE International Requirements Engineering Conference, RE 2020, Zurich, Switzerland, August 31 - September 4, 2020*. IEEE, pp. 90–101.

Williamson, O. E. (1993). "Calculativeness, trust, and economic organization". In: *The journal of law and economics* 36.1, Part 2, pp. 453–486.

Wolla, S. A. (2013). "Money and inflation: a functional relationship". In: *Page One Economics*.

Wooldridge, M. (2009). *An introduction to multiagent systems*. John Wiley & Sons.

World Health Organization (2020). *COVID-19 vaccines*. Accessed: 2021-01-10. URL: https://www.who.int/emergencies/diseases/novel-coronavirus-2019/covid-19-vaccines.

Yin, R. K. (2008). *Case Study Research: Design and Methods (Applied Social Research Methods)*. Sage Publications.

Zelmanovitz, L. (2015). *The ontology and function of money: the philosophical fundamentals of monetary institutions*. Lexington Books.

Zetzsche, D. A., Arner, D. W., and Buckley, R. P. (2020). "Decentralized finance (DeFi)". In: *IIEL Issue Brief* 2.

Zheng, Z., Xie, S., Dai, H., Chen, X., and Wang, H. (2017). "An overview of blockchain technology: Architecture, consensus, and future trends". In: *2017 IEEE international congress on big data (BigData congress)*. Ieee, pp. 557–564.

Ziemer, J. (n.d.). *Financial Regulation Ontology*. URL: http://finregont.com/fro/html_widoco/index-en.html.

Zou, W., Lo, D., Kochhar, P. S., Le, X.-B. D., Xia, X., Feng, Y., Chen, Z., and Xu, B. (2019). "Smart contract development: Challenges and opportunities". In: *IEEE Transactions on Software Engineering* 47.10, pp. 2084–2106.

SPRINGER NATURE

GPSR Compliance

The European Union's (EU) General Product Safety Regulation (GPSR) is a set of rules that requires consumer products to be safe and our obligations to ensure this.

If you have any concerns about our products, you can contact us on ProductSafety@springernature.com

In case Publisher is established outside the EU, the EU authorized representative is:

Springer Nature Customer Service Center GmbH
Europaplatz 3
69115 Heidelberg, Germany

The manufacturer's authorised representative in the EU is Springer Nature Customer Service Centre GmbH, Europaplatz 3, 69115 Heidelberg, Germany. If you have any concerns regarding our products, please contact ProductSafety@springernature.com

Printed and bound by CPI Group (UK) Ltd, Croydon, CR0 4YY

25/03/2026

02078191-0015